T0250118

Getting Started in Zbrush

Getting Started in ZBrush is a gentle introduction to ZBrush, today's premier digital sculpting program. Beginning with the fundamentals of digital sculpting as well as a thorough introduction to the user interface, *Getting Started in ZBrush* will have you creating a variety of professional-level 3D models in no time. More than just another button-pushing manual, this comprehensive guide is packed with start-to-finish projects that ease you into the workflow of the program, while at the same time providing tips and tricks that will allow you to achieve certain tasks much more quickly. After progressing through the tutorials, you will be shown how to customize brushes, materials, scripts, and the interface so that you can utilize these tools to their full advantage.

Special consideration is given to ZBrush's integration plug-ins with Maya and 3ds Max, allowing you to properly import and export your models in all programs. Texturing, painting, mapping, decimation, baking, and topology are also fully covered, so your Zbrush creations can come to life without sacrificing that high-resolution look.

- Ease your way into this complex subject with this straight-forward approach to Zbrush.
- Perfect your technique with step-by-step tutorials that allow you to create high-resolution models from start to finish.
- Expand your knowledge by visiting the companion website, which features video demonstrations, project files, texture and model files, scripts, customized menus, brushes, and additional resources.

Written with the digital beginner in mind, this book will teach you all of the necessary information to begin working in ZBrush to create magnificent works of digital artwork! Through this book, ZBrush will empower you to be the digital artist you always wanted to be.

Getting Started in Zbrush

An Introduction to Digital Sculpting
and Illustration

Second Edition

Gregory S. Johnson

CRC Press
Taylor & Francis Group
Boca Raton London New York

CRC Press is an imprint of the
Taylor & Francis Group, an **informa** business

Second edition published 2024
by CRC Press
2385 NW Executive Center Drive, Suite 320, Boca Raton FL 33431

and by CRC Press
4 Park Square, Milton Park, Abingdon, Oxon, OX14 4RN

CRC Press is an imprint of Taylor & Francis Group, LLC

First edition published by Focal Press 2014

Library of Congress Cataloging-in-Publication Data
Names: Johnson, Greg, 1969-author.
Title: Getting started in Zbrush : an introduction to digital sculpting and
illustration / Gregory S. Johnson.
Description: Second edition. | Boca Raton, FL : CRC Press, 2024. |
Includes bibliographical references and index.
Identifiers: LCCN 2023057733 (print) | LCCN 2023057734 (ebook) | ISBN 9781032104256 (pbk) |
ISBN 9781032104300 (hbk) | ISBN 9781003215288 (ebk)
Subjects: LCSH: ZBrush. | Computer graphics–Computer programs. |
Computer art–Computer programs. | BISAC: ART / Techniques / Cartooning. | ART / Digital.
Classification: LCC T386.Z33 J65 2024 (print) | LCC T386.Z33 (ebook) |
DDC 006.6/93–dc23/eng/20240325
LC record available at https://lccn.loc.gov/2023057733
LC ebook record available at https://lccn.loc.gov/2023057734

ISBN: 978-1-032-10430-0 (hbk)
ISBN: 978-1-032-10425-6 (pbk)
ISBN: 978-1-003-21528-8 (ebk)

DOI: 10.1201/9781003215288

Typeset in Myriad Pro
by codeMantra

Access the Support Materials: www.routledge.com/9781032104256

To my wife Penny — for her inexhaustible patience.

Contents

Contents

Contents

Contents

Contents

Acknowledgements

I would like to thank the various people who helped to get this project to publication: Professor Charles Shami for his editing and Professor Michael Betancourt for all of his advice.

Author

Gregory S. Johnson has had the privilege of teaching thousands of students a wide array of courses, including digital sculpture, 3D modeling, texturing, animation, rigging, visual effects, digital painting, programming, game design, and development, as a professor for almost 30 years. This book is a compilation of material developed from his introduction to digital sculpting lectures and all of the excellent advice he has managed to cultivate over the years. He is a member of the International Game Developers Association (igda.org), the Guild of Natural Science Illustrators (www.gnsi.org), and the Association of Science Fiction Illustrators (asfa-art.ning.com) and has worked for years as a 3D artist. You can find examples of his work, additional ZBrush resources, and other educational material on his website (GregTheArtist.com). If you enjoy this book, you can check out his other published work by going to www.Toonzy.com and downloading a free PDF of *Toonzy! the Cartoon Role Playing Game* or purchasing a copy of his game design book, *Developing Creative Content for Games*. Ensure you visit the publisher's website for the video recordings of each chapter of this book.

Introduction

Overview

This book is an easy-to-use introduction to digital sculpting and painting with ZBrush. Contained within this book is everything you need to get started working in ZBrush. This book will guide you through the process of sculpting and illustrating your own fantastic digital creations. Topics covered include a thorough introduction to the software's user interface, professional workflow, sculpting, and illustration techniques, and how to customize the tools and interface to suit your personal work habits. Written with the digital beginner in mind, this book will teach you the necessary information to begin working in ZBrush to create magnificent works of digital artwork! Through this book, ZBrush will empower you to be the digital artist you have always wanted to be.

ZBrush is a wondrously powerful program capable of doing things previously thought impossible. Still, like other three-dimensional (3D)

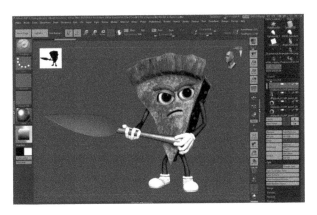

FIGURE 1.1 ZBrush character.

DOI: 10.1201/9781003215288-1

programs, it is a very complex and deep program with thousands of different buttons and options that can easily confuse and overwhelm someone new to 3D modeling. This book introduces you to the workflows and techniques that will make you a productive artist with this program. It is not a guide to every button in the program; the official ZBrush documentation (docs.pixologic.com) already exists for that, and including all of that material here would be redundant. Instead, this book will show you how to work with the program to produce the artwork you want to create and will serve as an entry point into the larger world of 3D. While you will not need any other resources aside from this book to become a better artist using ZBrush, I would still suggest that you take advantage of the wealth of existing free material found on Pixologic's main website (pixologic.com), the official ZBrush forum (www.zbrushcentral.com), and the parent company Maxon's website (www.maxon.net/en/zbrush). You will quickly discover that the vast majority of artists working in 3D are an amiable and helpful bunch, provided that you treat them with respect.

Why ZBrush? ZBrush is an artist-oriented digital 3D sculpting and painting package. Since its inception over a decade ago, ZBrush has become a critical component of many industries, such as film, video games, and illustration. The reason for this is that, unlike any other 3D program on the market today, ZBrush is the only one capable of displaying millions of polygons on screen simultaneously. This capability is due to how ZBrush handles its internal memory and camera, since it treats everything as a 2.5D object instead of an actual 3D object. While this approach imposes additional work when translating ZBrush objects into other 3D packages, it allows the creation of complex 3D objects within ZBrush that no other package can replicate. ZBrush is frequently required knowledge for 3D artists working in the movie and game production fields. ZBrush has also become a very influential player in illustration, as many artists incorporate 3D into their workflow. To become a professional 3D artist for games, movies, or illustrations, you need to know ZBrush. The program is particularly beneficial for character artists and is now used extensively for detail-oriented work, whether in character, environment, or object modeling. Simply visiting the gallery on ZBrushCentral (www.zbrush-central.com) will show just how many projects ZBrush is currently used for.

Simply put, knowing ZBrush has become critical for many artists. Indeed, Ofer Alon, the founder of Pixologic, won the 2014 Scientific and Engineering Academy Award for creating ZBrush. Having some great ZBrush models in your portfolio is now an essential requirement for anyone trying to get a job in the digital arts in film or video games, and it is becoming ever more important to artists in other fields.

Let's begin learning with some basic universal advice and suggestions, then we will move on to the more technical material.

Professional practices

Here's a brief set of suggestions that should be helpful to anyone in the field of digital art. If you intend to pursue a career in the 3D visual arts, consider these suggestions.

Sketchbook: The ability to draw is integral to working in this field. Constantly practicing and improving your drawing skills is crucial. You should purchase a small, easily portable sketchbook and always keep it with you. Anytime you have a minute, when waiting for food, standing in line, or just hanging out, get out the sketchbook and draw whatever you see nearby. It is important to draw what you see, not what is in your head (that goes into your idea book)! You are training your eye to see and effortlessly coordinate with your hand. After a few months, you will notice a significant improvement in your skill level. After two years, you'll be pretty good.

Idea book: You need inspiration. Keep a small sketchbook with you and write down or sketch out any ideas that you have. Cut out exciting photos or articles from magazines and paste them into the sketchbook. You can include photographs and photocopies as well. Keep a file folder on your computer and fill it with images that you find intriguing.

FIGURE 1.2 Sketch and idea books.

Later, whenever you are stuck for an idea, open up your idea book or file folder and browse through it. Soon, inspiration will strike!

Technique library: Keep a file folder and populate it with any interesting tutorials or techniques you find. If you see an interesting image that has, let's say, a neat-looking approach to doing hair, save it and put it in your techniques folder. Afterwards, when you need to do hair yourself, you can look at that approach and some other techniques you've found and use one of those techniques or combine them and come up with your own unique approach.

Job research: You must learn what you need in your portfolio to get your desired job. To acquire this information, select five companies you'd like to work for one day. Go to their website and search the job postings for your desired position. Most companies provide a very detailed breakdown of the skill sets and requirements for each job. You need to identify the common elements each job description shares between the different companies. If there is a skill set that every one of the jobs lists, then you must be sure that you have that skill demonstrated in your portfolio. Conversely, if there are skills that only one of the jobs talks about, then that is a skill that you should focus on only if you want to work for that specific company (since no one else will care that you have that skill set). Remember to only compare jobs with the same (or almost the same) titles.

File naming conventions and organization: It is critical to name your files in a consistent and organized fashion. Doing so will allow you to keep track of the different variations and permutations of file types and iterations that you will use in a complicated scene or model. In addition to being organizationally beneficial, being able to follow a set of naming conventions is critical once you begin professional work. You will not be employable if you cannot follow the naming conventions that your employer uses! While the details of the exact naming convention used will vary depending upon the precise production pipeline that the company follows, here is a set of guidelines that I use myself.

Use only letters, numbers, and _ or -. Do not use any unusual characters such as (!@#$%^&^&*). Keep your files organized into descriptively named file folders and files. When naming a file, include a version number and a current iteration number.

For example;

> woollyMammoth_v2_205.ztl (the 3d file)
> woollyMammoth_v2_20_textureMapsMasterFile.psd (the master texture maps file)
> woollyMammoth_v2_03_diffuseMap.jpg (color texture map file for the 3d model)

woollyMammoth_v1_04_normalMap.jpg (normal map file for the 3d model)

woollyMammoth_v1_06_specularMap.jpg (specular level texture map file for the 3d model)

All of these files would be stored in the *woollyMammoth* project folder.

Broken down, each name consists of a description of the subject (a woolly mammoth, a prehistoric elephant), a version number (_v2), and an iteration number (_205). If more clarity is needed about what the file is used for, then an additional descriptor is added, i.e. *textureMaps*, *diffuseMap*, and so forth.

Each time you save the file (3D, photoshop, or otherwise), increment the iteration number by one. So from *vulcanBomber_v6_048.ztl* to *vulcanBomber_v6_049.ztl* and so on. If you make a serious change, you can increment the version number. This way, if a problem develops in the file (it gets corrupted or you make a mistake), you can always go back and find an earlier file that isn't messed up. Following a good set of naming conventions will save you hours and maybe even days' worth of work.

Don't stress out about any of this! The book will have plenty of examples as you read through it. It is important to cover the philosophy and approach we will use when naming files. A good set of naming conventions can be found here (docs.unrealengine.com/5.1/en-US/recommended-asset-naming-conventions-in-unreal-engine-projects/). The *"Recommended Asset Naming Conventions"* used in the Unreal Game Engine makes for a valuable standard for anyone entering the video game industry.

Backups: Remember to back up your work! External drives and cloud backup services are cheap, so there is no excuse for failing to back up your work. I use around four external drives and back my work up to a different one each week. I also have copies of my files at an online backup site and a copy of my working files on my portable drive. Using one of the vast arrays of online backup services available offers an excellent way to store your most critical pieces of work remotely. Over the many years I have been a professor, I cannot even begin to count the number of times students have lost all of their work due to a hard drive crash or other unfortunate circumstances. A simple enough problem to fix if they have backed up their work to an external hard drive or a cloud storage service! Another common mistake is to keep saving work in the same file. You could lose hours, if not weeks or months, of work if something happens to that one file. Using a file naming convention and iterating their file names would have saved you! I speak from personal experience. Several of my earliest animations are now lost. Even though I backed up the files, the storage device I used became inoperable and outdated, making the files unrecoverable. Losing your work after spending many hours, days, and weeks working on a project is awful – especially when the solution is so easy.

Anatomy: There is simply no substitute for knowing proper anatomy. It is the difference between getting a job as a character modeler or not. Ignore studying this material at your own risk! You must show competency in drawing, physical sculpture, general anatomy, musculature, and bone structure. The best approach is to take a class in constructive anatomy. This class should not be about memorizing the muscle groups and bone names – the class you take should involve making an écorché sculpture. In this process, you first create the model's bones, then painstakingly apply each muscle to the model to build up the form until you eventually add the soft organs, fat, and skin to finish the model. It is a laborious and time-consuming approach, but it is the best way for an artist to learn proper anatomy.

Skills: There's a lot to digital art that you can teach yourself – and then there's some stuff you probably need help doing. Almost all of the technical stuff can be self-taught. The technical side of things is well-documented and easily accessible. A good book (like this one!) is enough to get you started. Then, you can pick up most of the remaining techniques from quality websites (ZBrushCentral, CGSociety, Polycount, etc.) and read the help files included with every reputable software package. Taking an entry-level programming class is an excellent idea to get a good foundation for computer work's crunchy technical aspects. If you have a real knack for it, as some people do, you can teach yourself programming from a site like the Python for Beginners web page (www.python.org/about/gettingstarted/). The problem begins when you start talking about learning art. It is challenging to teach yourself the proper techniques in drawing, anatomy, color, and design. While there are countless books on each subject, nothing beats having a good instructor. Please pay close attention to the fundamental art courses such as color theory, 2D design, and drawing. These are the classes that make you an artist. Learning this material well will make you an artist. Otherwise, you aren't and probably never will be (though there are many jobs for purely technical people in the entertainment industry). As I get older and more experienced, the material I keep going back to and working on is color, design, and my drawing skills.

Education: You don't have to go to college to get a job in the entertainment industry working on digital art. All these companies care about is the art skills that you can bring to the table. They don't care about your grades, just the quality of your portfolio. You also have to be capable of working well with others in a group. If you cannot work well in a group, then you will be unemployed in the film and video game industries. Having said all of this, college is still a good idea. Why do you ask? Because it will open up opportunities that would be denied to someone who doesn't have that educational background. While the entertainment industry might not care about your educational background to start with, they care a lot about it when it comes to promoting people. Many employers consider a college degree a basic requirement for employment and that is a very important thing to consider. The entertainment industry is not for the faint of heart. The hours are long, and the employment contracts can be short – sometimes no more than a couple of months before you are looking for new work. Reputation is everything. If you have the reputation of someone who is easy to work with, takes direction well, and has a lot of artistic capability, then you will find it pretty straightforward to keep getting employment. If you are at the point in life where you are thinking marriage and kids, then you might want to look at other opportunities that will provide regular working hours and good benefits, and for that, college is essential. One good approach is to work in the industry until the job market crumbles (which happens about once every ten years or so in sync with the overall economy) and you can't get a job. If that happens, then go back to school for a few years and earn the next degree in the sequence. Get your Bachelor of Fine Arts degree if you don't have one or your Master of Fine Arts if you already do. By the time you finish the degree program, the job market will have heated back up, and you will be employed again with a sparkling new set of qualifications. It doesn't hurt that advanced degrees like a Masters of Fine Arts (MFA) or a Doctorate (PhD) help in getting promotions.

Pay attention to your interpersonal skills! Connections can make or break your career. While this can be the most uncomfortable aspect of career development for many digital artists, it is still essential. Eventually, you will have to go out and get a job. If you have good interpersonal skills, then this poses no real problem. You will be able to present yourself and your work with confidence during the required job interviews and presentations. But if you are a shy and introverted person (like myself), the interview process can become a stressful or even overwhelming proposition. Reading a book like *How to Win Friends and Influence People* by Dale Carnegie can be a good starting point, as can talking to a few successful salespeople about how they establish rapport with their customers. That said, the best solution to address this issue is simply practice. Go out and meet new people. Get used to saying hello and introducing yourself to people you don't know. After you are comfortable with that, try engaging them in meaningful dialogue. Start with pleasantries and eventually get to the point where you can comfortably establish a connection with someone. If you are currently cringing at this prospect, you need to work on this skill. Getting a job will require you to approach a person or group of people you don't know, connect with them, and persuade them that their company needs you! Like any skill, practice will make this task more accessible and less intimidating when using it.

You don't need to spend a fortune to get a good education. Many outstanding colleges only require a small amount of monetary investment, but you have to do your research. Look into who is teaching at the college and what they've accomplished – do they know their stuff? Tour the campus and see if you are impressed after talking to them face to face. Be careful with the 'rate my teacher' sites – frequently, the people complaining are the ones who did the worst in class. Find students whose work you admire and ask their opinion about a teacher or class. It is best to ignore the views of people who aren't striving to succeed. The most critical element of success is your determination. If you are willing to put in the hard work, you can succeed no matter where you go to school, or you can spend a jaw-dropping amount of money at the world's best art academy and still be unemployable if you don't put in the personal time and effort it takes. Play it smart. Take your language, math, and other core requirement classes at a cheaper college and transfer the credits later. You might be able to take almost half your credits somewhere other than where you graduate, but it is best to check ahead and find out what will eventually transfer over and what will not – so that you don't waste any of your time or money. If you're going somewhere with an excellent reputation, getting a good education is easier, but make sure you can eventually pay off those student loans. There's little point in getting a $500,000 education in a

FIGURE 1.3 Dragonfly.

field where the starting salary is $35,000 a year. The point is to do your research. Find out what it will cost, how best to work the system, and who to take classes with to get the most out of your education. Make the system work for you!

Creativity

Creativity does not occur in a vacuum. You must continually feed your brain with fresh ideas and stimuli if you want to develop content that is original and unique. You need to be doing more than just playing popular video games or watching current movies. If you only do that, you will regurgitate the same sort of material backup that you've seen. There's plenty of repetition in the industry as it is, and there's no need to add another space marine, robot, or monster that looks like everything else already out there. So, how does one break out of the rut? By finding fresh material to serve as input, reading, and being inspired by original work.

Go out and research as broad a variety of topics as possible. Almost anything can inspire, but some areas of study are especially beneficial for a digital sculptor. One of the most helpful areas of study is zoology and anatomy. Studying the shapes and forms of the myriad creatures that make up our beautiful biosphere is rewarding on several levels.

FIGURE 1.4 Spiders.

FIGURE 1.5 Fungus.

It will help teach you more about anatomy. Learning how muscles and bones work on other creatures will help inform your decisions when designing your creatures and make the ones you create all the more believable. So much so that I suggest you take animal anatomy classes if you can. Knowing the visual elements that define a predator versus a prey creature will allow you to create creatures with the correct traits for their role. Let's take a few examples. A rabbit is a prey animal. As such, it has large ears that swivel to enable it to detect the stealthy approach of a predator early on and pinpoint the direction from which it is attacking. The rabbit possesses powerful legs so it can flee from danger and a sensitive nose for additional detection abilities. One of the most telling attributes of a prey animal is how its eyes are poisitioned upon its head. Most prey animals, such as the rabbit, have their eyes set far apart on the side of the head. Their eyes provide the creature with a wide field of vision through which it can easily detect the movement of a potential predator. Prey animals can also possess various defenses, such as armor, camouflage, mimicry, poison, a foul smell, or even ink. Teeth are another vital clue to a creature's habits. Blunt teeth are found in herbivores; a mixed set of teeth is found in omnivores; and predators have many sharp, pointy teeth. A predator's teeth will tell you what prey it eats. Many small, sharp teeth are for eating small, slippery prey, while big, cutting teeth are for ripping chunks out of their victim, or a pair of saber teeth for delivering a killing bite to the throat. Predators typically have their eyes set in front, providing stereoscopic vision and good depth perception for judging how far it is to the prey animal for the final pounce. Combine this with additional senses such as a capable nose, sensitive ears, or something more exotic like a bat's radar or a dolphin's sonar for locating their prey. Add powerful claws for grabbing and holding onto their prey, and you have an efficient predator. Predators usually fall into either pursuit or ambush types. Ambush predators need good camouflage and blinding reflexes. Pursuit predators require powerful legs and high endurance. Some of my favorites for inspiration include the strange creatures from the deep sea and the insect world.

Searching for a scientific term relating to oceanic studies, such as "bathypelagic" or "abyssopelagic," will turn up many wonderful and exotic animals. Searching zoological terms such as isopod, nauplius, or arthropod is a good start, as is searching for paleontology phrases such as "Cambrian Explosion," Arthrodires, or "Terror Birds." Studying zoology, biology, paleontology, and related fields can provide valuable insight into your creature designs.

The best work from the science fiction and fantasy genres is also worth reading. Knowing the work of luminaries such as Arthur C. Clark, Isaac

FIGURE 1.6 Shield-back Katydid. Note the ruler used to determine scale.

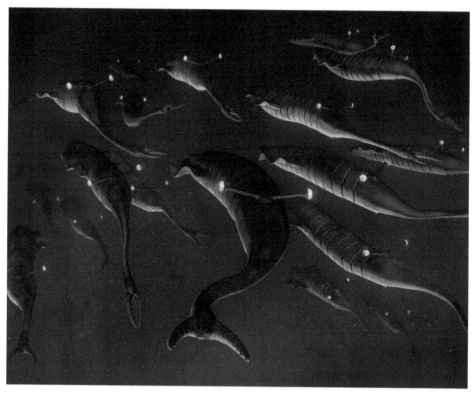

FIGURE 1.7 Tullimonstrum as an invertebrate, illustration using ZBrush and photoshop.

Asimov, and Robert Heinlein will provide endless amounts of inspiration and educate you on where most of the current themes in science fiction come from. Authors such as Edgar Rice Burroughs, H.G. Wells, Jules Verne, and others have helped define the genre and are well worth reading. Fantasy authors such as J.R.R. Tolkien, Robert E. Howard, Tanith Lee, Michael Moorcock, Andre Norton, Fritz Leiber, Patricia A. McKillip, and Jack Vance are the origin points for many themes in modern fantasy games and movies. Similarly, Edgar Allan Poe, Mary Shelley, and H.P. Lovecraft helped define the horror genre. Reading the books written by these authors will help you understand where most of the ideas in modern video games and entertainment come from and inspire you to create your unique creative visions. You can find many of these works for free at Project Gutenberg (www.gutenberg.org).

History is replete with colorful examples from which to draw inspiration, from the ancient warriors of Assyria to the Polish Winged Hussars or perhaps the F-94C Starfire fighter airplane, SR-71 Blackbird spy plane, or M-4 Sherman tank. History provides a plethora of inspiration. A good starting point for discovering odd tidbits about ancient cultures is "The Golden Bough" by Sir James George Frazer. A broad survey of mythology

FIGURE 1.8 F-94C Starfire fighter airplane.

and religion, the book introduces the diverse subjects of cultures and beliefs that humanity has manifested at one time or another. Best of all, it is freely available on Project Gutenberg (www.gutenberg.org/ebooks/author/1241). Searching for "Arms and Armour" in Google Books will also turn up numerous historical books on weapons and armor. Familiarize yourself with how weapons and armor are worn and used, so you can make your creations more believable.

Reference material

One common element I have noted in student work over many years is the constant need for proper reference materials before starting a project. Every professional artist I know keeps a well-stocked library of reference images and objects related to their subject material. For example, an artist working on a dragon will do thorough studies of snakes, alligators, lizards, and such to make their creatures as realistic and believable as possible.

A team working on a sports racing game will schedule visits to actual race car shops. The game studio usually has a licensing agreement with specific teams to use the appropriate logos, insignia, drivers, and vehicles. A professional studio creating a modern military first-person shooter game will have real machine guns (non-functioning, though), clips, backpacks, and uniforms available to their artists so they can have the item they are modeling on the desk in front of them as they create the 3D model. I guarantee you that a studio that focuses on a particular subject or on a specific period will know EVERYTHING there is to know about the subject. If you submit a portfolio piece to them as part of a job interview, they will know whether or not you have done your research and if you get any details wrong. I have had clients look up the serial number on the airplanes I have made paintings of!

FIGURE 1.9 Rattlesnake reference photo.

If you are sculpting a medieval knight, you better ensure you get the armor and clothing right. Your warrior will need a long-sleeved undershirt, a gambeson (quilted under armor padding), proper chain mail, and a surcoat to go on top, plus his sword belt, knight's spurs, cloak, and other accoutrement as befits their station. The type and look will vary depending on exactly when and where the knight is from and their rank. You must do the proper research to get the details right – it is all about the details. You will have to gather as much reference material on your subject as possible before you start. Having good reference material to work from is the difference between making a good model and a great one that will get you a job. For example, suppose I wanted to model the historic M42 Duster anti-aircraft armored vehicle. In that case, I'd make it a point of visiting every museum I could that had one and photo documenting every aspect of the vehicle, from top to bottom, taking thousands of digital pictures. It is only through this process that you will learn what the object really looks like. There is no substitute for firsthand experience of something. I'd also read as many books as I could about the vehicle and thoroughly research the tank's various unit markings during its decades-long career. Doing this

FIGURE 1.10 Alligator reference photo.

research results in a thorough knowledge of the different variations of the vehicle and enables the creation of an accurate 3D model.

The current standard for making a professional model is more than just making a perfect 3D version of the object. It is creating a perfect object that has a personality and conveys a mood. It isn't just any generic object – it is a specific object with a unique history, a distinctive look, and an emotional feel. It is not just modeling a tank; it is making a tank with the correct unit markings, the dirt and mud from where it has seen service, the long scrapes on the side armor skirts where it has rubbed against buildings or obstacles, the shiny spot on the lip of the barrel where repeated firings of the gun have blasted the paint off, the boxes, crates, and gear that the crew has accumulated, the exhaust grime, the oil leaks, and so forth. You must create a rich visual description full of detailed information describing the object's history. It is not enough to describe the object; you must show where it has been, who it has been with, and what it has been doing. Every character, monster, environment, or object that you create must convey a history and evoke an emotion. Everything should tell a story. Do that, and you will be a successful modeler.

FIGURE 1.11 M42 Duster armored vehicle. Note that vehicles put on display in museums usually do not look like they did when in service. Wear and tear, bad paint jobs, and missing equipment are the norm in a lot of museums.

Copyright

There are a few things that everyone working in the digital arts field should know about copyright. The first is that you automatically have ownership and copyright to your work. It is a good idea to put the copyright symbol (©), the year of the first publication of the work, and the name of the copyright holder somewhere on the work (example: © 2013 Greg Johnson) to make it evident that the work is under copyright. The flip side of that equation is: don't infringe on anyone else's copyright. It simply isn't worth it. If a company even suspects you have violated their copyright, they will sue you. The operative idea is that they bankrupt you – whether or not the case against you has any real merit. Most companies that engage in these types of lawsuits have far deeper pockets than the people they sue and can afford the money, time, and effort required, while you simply cannot. If your employer thinks you have infringed on someone's copyright, they will fire you immediately. In addition, word of your infringement will spread and make you unemployable in the entertainment industry. I have seen it happen. The entertainment industry is a small one where your reputation is priceless. Everyone knows everyone else or knows someone

FIGURE 1.12 Siemens Schuckert D.III from World War I at Old Rhinebeck Aerodrome, New York.

who does, and your reputation will precede you. It is critical to make sure that your reputation regarding copyright is spotless. Always remember that the entertainment industry has a zero-tolerance policy for copyright infringement.

The easiest way to ensure your work doesn't infringe on anyone's copyright is to always use your own photographs whenever possible. Take a camera with you wherever you go. If you see something interesting – an old sewer cover, a rusty steel wall, an old brick wall, a section of sidewalk, or whatever – simply take a snapshot of it for later use. A few general guidelines exist for taking images for reference or texture use. It is best to take the pictures in diffuse light (a light that has no obvious source). The best time of day for this is the hour immediately after sunrise or before sunset, often called the "golden hour" in photography. Otherwise, any cloudy, overcast day will suffice, or take the picture with the subject in the shade. The worst times are at noon or in strong light that creates dark shadows. It is more trouble than it is worth trying to paint out or fix bad lighting later on when you need the image for a texture or reference.

The rules regarding copyright are different for students. Students get a small amount of legal leeway regarding copyrights, but it is best not to cultivate bad habits. While you can use copyrighted works for educational purposes, anything you create with someone else's images will be something you can never enter into shows or even put into your portfolio. If you include the image in your portfolio and someone recognizes the other work, then that raises questions about your integrity and ends your job chances immediately. As such, even though it is technically allowed, it isn't worth doing. Putting in the extra effort and creating and using your own images is far better. It is safer and promotes proper professional work habits, which you will need to develop anyway.

If you are desperate or simply cannot get the correct references you need, then you can buy reference images and textures from certain websites. Always check their terms of use to make sure that these resources are legal to use in the application you want them for. You can obtain good imagery for money from 3D.SK (www.3d.sk) and GameTextures (gametextures.com).

You can get legitimate texture references for free in a few places. One such site is Textures (textures.com), which has both free and paid versions. But again, always check the terms of usage on the website before you use the image. You can also use Google's advanced image search with the usage rights search restrictions turned on, but I would be EXTREMELY careful about doing so and verify that the image you want to use is indeed free to use for that purpose. The penalties for being wrong are severe, and you don't want to take any chances with this. Another source of usable images is the United States government. Pictures made by U.S. government workers pursuing their official jobs have no copyright restrictions on the reproduction, distribution, display, or creation of derivative works from their images. These make excellent reference or texture sources. However, you always need to thoroughly check and ensure there aren't any other copyright holders on the work before you use it. These are some of the best and safest places to get high-quality images. Here are a few good sources for government images:

- NASA's image gallery (www.nasa.gov/multimedia/imagegallery/index.html).
- The U.S. Department of Defense photo gallery (www.defense.gov/Multimedia/Photos/).
- The National Oceanographic and Atmospheric Administration's photo library (www.photolib.noaa.gov).

Publicizing your work

Once you get started making artwork, make a point of posting your work online in professional forums. The best forum for posting ZBrush artwork is ZBrush Central (www.zbrushcentral.com). Once you post your work, pay close attention to any constructive criticism offered and quickly fix any problems that people point out. Doing this will help you develop a reputation for working fast and taking criticism well. These are two qualities that any company treasures in their employees, and if you can display those principles on this and other forums, people will take notice. It may take a while, and you must be persistent and consistent in your work and online habits. Many human resource people peruse this site looking for artistic talent, and having a good reputation on this forum will help you get a job.

Make sure that you have a good portfolio website. You can use a free hosting service like ArtStation (www.artstation.com) to place your portfolio online. Put only your best work on display. Include only your strongest work. A mere handful of pieces will suffice. Place an Adobe PDF of your current resume and a valid email address on your website. Do not post your telephone number unless you want everyone on the World Wide Web to have it! It also helps to have a business card. Even something as simple as your name, website gallery address, contact information, and job position or artistic title printed on a plain white card will suffice. A few good places to get your cards printed cheaply are VistaPrint (www.vistaprint.com) or Moo (www.moo.com). The website and business card don't have to be fancy – you're not trying to be a graphic designer or web designer. You just need to get people to your website, where you can show off your work and let people know who you are and how to contact you.

The last thing to do is to get yourself out there. Go and talk to the companies and professionals in the entertainment industry. An excellent place to do this is at some of the various conferences held every year. A few that I can wholeheartedly recommend are the Game Developer's Conference (GDC) (www.gdconf.com) for video game artists, the South by Southwest conference (www.sxsw.com), the annual ZBrush Summit (zbrushsummit.com) specifically for ZBrush artists, and ACM SIGGRAPH (www.siggraph.org) for everything else computer art related. Thousands of people from the entertainment industry attend these conferences, and they are great places to meet people and make connections.

Resources

Many great ZBrush resources are available for anyone interested in the program. The best place to start is Maxon's ZBrush Central forum (www.zbrushcentral.com). Before posting any questions, search through the forum's existing posts for an answer beforehand. Nothing irritates the experienced posters like being asked a question for the hundredth time, so make sure the question has not already been answered previously. Check out the ZBrush documentation website (docs.pixologic.com). It is a great place to learn what each button in the program does. Another great Pixologic resource is the ZClassroom site (pixologic.com/zclassroom/) for more learning resources, including official ZBrush video courses. For general 3D resources, the Polycount wiki is an excellent place to go (wiki.polycount.com), as is the Autodesk Forums (forums.autodesk.com). Once you have come to grips with ZBrush by completing this book, these websites are the places to go to further your knowledge of ZBrush and expand your repertoire of techniques.

You should also have a good book on human anatomy. There are plenty out there to choose from, so browse around and find one that suits your taste. I've discovered *"Dynamic Anatomy"* by Hogarth to be immensely valuable, but there are a lot of good anatomy books out there. Pick up a book or two on animal anatomy for your creature designs. *"The Human Figure in Motion"* and *"Animals in Motion"* by Eadweard Muybridge are great resources for animation studies. Of particular use are the Citadel guides to painting miniatures, especially the older versions of the books, and a lot of old plastic model and diorama magazines such as *"Fine Scale Modeler,"* *"Scale Aviation Modeller,"* *"Airfix Magazine,"* and the like have great tips for texturing characters, objects, and environments, plus you can find digital copies of old editions online. The techniques they include are easily adapted to the digital realm and will undoubtedly improve your texturing skills significantly.

Conclusion

The learning process is a messy one. You will learn from your mistakes, so don't be afraid or upset when you make them. It happens. Reflect on what happened and figure out a better way to do it next time you try. That is how learning works. If you find yourself getting frustrated or upset, take a break. Get up, walk around, do something else for a while, and then come back fresh and reinvigorated, ready to learn more. There is a lot to learn in this program. It is incredibly complex and deep, and it will take you a couple of weeks to become comfortable with it. When working on a piece of artwork, I find it very beneficial to reach a stopping point and walk away from it for a while so I can come back after a day or two and look at the piece with a fresh eye and spot several flaws I had earlier missed and fix them. The same is true when learning new software. It is like the old trick of looking at your artwork in a mirror to see it anew. It forces you to re-evaluate your work and gain insight into it. Don't let the mammoth amount of material to absorb make you miserable. Take it at your own pace and enjoy the process of learning. Ensuring you enjoy the process will guarantee you learn more from it. Now, let's get started!

Further reading

"2022 ZBrush Summit." Maxon Computer GMBH. https://zbrushsummit. com. Accessed 15 Dec. 2022.

"Airfix Model World | Key Model World." Key Publishing Ltd. https://www. keymodelworld.com/airfix-model-world. Accessed 15 Dec. 2022.

"ArtStation - All Channels." Epic Games, Inc. https://www.artstation.com. Accessed 15 Dec. 2022.

"ASFA Community Network." Association of Science Fiction & Fantasy Artists, https://asfa-art.ning.com. Accessed 15 Dec. 2022.

"Autodesk Community, Autodesk Forums, Autodesk Forum." Autodesk Inc. https://forums.autodesk.com. Accessed 15 Dec. 2022.

Carnegie, Dale. *How to Win Friends [And] Influence People.* Kingswood, The World's Work, 1913.

Priestley, Rick. How to Paint Citadel Miniatures. Nottingham, England, Games Workshop, 2008. Guide. 1993.

"Fine Scale Modeler." Kalmbach Media. https://finescale.com/. Accessed 15 Dec. 2022.

Frazer, James George. "The Golden Bough (Vol. 1 of 2)." https://www.gutenberg.org/Files/41082, 16 Oct. 2012, www.gutenberg.org/cache/epub/41082/pg41082-images.html. Accessed 15 Dec. 2022.

"Free eBooks | Project Gutenberg." Project Gutenberg Literary Archive Foundation. https://www.gutenberg.org. Accessed 15 Dec. 2022.

"Game Developer's Conference (GDC)." Informa PLC. https://www.gdconf.com. Accessed 15 Dec. 2022.

"GameTextures.com | The Largest Substance Library." Gametextures. https://gametextures.com. Accessed 15 Dec. 2022.

"Guild of Natural Science Illustrators - Home." GNSI. https://www.gnsi.org/. Accessed 15 Dec. 2022.

Hogarth, Burne. *Dynamic Anatomy.* Broadway, New York, Watson-Guptill, 2003.

"Home - ACM SIGGRAPH." ACM SIGGRAPH. https://www.siggraph.org. Accessed 15 Dec. 2022.

"Human Photo References and Textures for Artists - 3D.SK - Site." 3Dsk. https://www.3d.sk. Accessed 15 Dec. 2022.

"IGDA - International Game Developers Association." IGDA. https://igda.org/. Accessed 15 Dec. 2022.

Johnson, Greg. "Greg the Artist." https://www.gregtheartist.com. Accessed 15 Dec. 2022.

"MOO Print Official Website Country Selector | MOO (United States)." MOO Inc. https://www.moo.com. Accessed 15 Dec. 2022.

Muybridge, Eadweard. *Animals in Motion.* New York, Dover Publ, 1957.

Muybridge, Eadweard. *The Human Figure in Motion, an Electro-Photographic Investigation of Consecutive Phases of Muscular Actions.* London, Chapman & Hall, 1931.

"NASA Images | NASA." National Aeronautics and Space Administration. https://www.nasa.gov/multimedia/imagegallery/index.html. Accessed 15 Dec. 2022.

"NOAA Photo Library > Home". The National Oceanographic and Atmospheric Administration. https://www.photolib.noaa.gov. Accessed 15 Dec. 2022.

"Photos." United States Department of Defense. https://www.defense.gov/Multimedia/Photos/. Accessed 15 Dec. 2022.

"polycount." Polycount. http://wiki.polycount.com/wiki/Polycount. Accessed 15 Dec. 2022.

Priestly, Rick, et al. *How to Paint Citadel Miniatures.* Nottingham, Games Workshop, 2003.

"Python for Beginners | Python.org." Python Software Foundation. https://www.python.org/about/gettingstarted/. Accessed 15 Dec. 2022.

"Recommended Asset Naming Conventions in Unreal Engine Projects | Unreal Engine 5.1 Documentation." Epic Games, Inc. https://docs.unrealengine.com/5.1/en-US/recommended-asset-naming-conventions-in-unreal-engine-projects/. Accessed 15 Dec. 2022.

"SAMMI Latest Issue." Scale Aviation & Military Modeller. iHobby. https://www.i-hobby.co.uk/webshop/scale-aviation-military-modeller-international/sammi-latest-issue/. Accessed 15 Dec. 2022.

"SXSW Conference & Festivals | March 10-19, 2023." SXSW, LLC. https://www.sxsw.com. Accessed 15 Dec. 2022.

"Textures for 3D, Graphic Design and Photoshop!" Textures.com. https://textures.com. Accessed 15 Dec. 2022.

"Vistaprint US Online Printing: Business Cards, Signage & More." Cimpress plc. https://www.vistaprint.com. Accessed 15 Dec. 2022.

"ZBrush - The All-in-One-Digital Sculpting Solution." Maxon Computer GMBH. https://pixologic.com/. Accessed 15 Dec. 2022.

"ZBrush Docs | Pixologic ZBrush Documentation." Maxon Computer GMBH. https://docs.pixologic.com/. Accessed 15 Dec. 2022.

"ZBrush." Maxon Computer GMBH. https://www.maxon.net/en/zbrush. Accessed 15 Dec. 2022.

"ZBrushCentral - Your Home for ZBrush." Maxon Computer GMBH. https://www.zbrushcentral.com/. Accessed 15 Dec. 2022.

"ZClassroom - ZBrush Training from the Source." Maxon Computer GMBH. https://pixologic.com/zclassroom/. Accessed 15 Dec. 2022.

2

The Fundamentals

Getting and installing ZBrush

The first thing you will need to do is create a Maxon account at my.maxon.net. To install ZBrush, download the Maxon App from www. maxon.net/en/try. After the download finishes, you should quit any other open programs and install the Maxon App on your computer. Next, open the Maxon App and sign in using your Maxon account. You can now use the Maxon App to install ZBrush. If you need any help with the process, you can go to Maxon's Knowledge Base (support. maxon.net) to get some support from the company. To run ZBrush, you will need a software license. At the top of Maxon's home page, you will see links to either "Try" or "Buy" the software. If you use the "Try" link, you can get a temporary license that is usable for two weeks. If you decide to buy the software, click the "Buy" link and check out the options available at monthly and yearly subscription rates. Note that cheaper student licenses are available for anyone in college or school. ZBrush works on either Windows or Macintosh machines and requires at least 8 GB of RAM, 100 GB of free space on the hard drive, and a monitor resolution of 1,920 × 1,080 pixels minimum.

When using ZBrush for illustration purposes, it helps to have a separate image editing software package installed, such as Adobe Photoshop (www.adobe.com) or the free GNU Image Manipulation Program (www.gimp.org), or GIMP for short. A standard 3D modeling package such as Maya or 3dsMax, both available from www.autodesk.com, Cinema 4D from Maxon, or a free copy of Blender (www.blender.org) is handy for anyone interested in using ZBrush for video games, film, or television production. Take your time trying to learn all these different software packages. Generally speaking, you only need to be good at one illustration package and one general-purpose 3D package. If you

DOI: 10.1201/9781003215288-2

need professional-grade software, a copy of Autodesk Maya and a subscription to the Adobe Creative Cloud will give you a fully functional studio. If you would rather keep things cheap, then a free copy of Blender and GIMP will suffice quite nicely.

Interface layout
Menus

The interface in ZBrush is very complex. There are hundreds of different buttons, sliders, options, and features for you to learn about. The good news is that most of these buttons are optional for using the program. Many of the buttons are rarely used. You don't have to memorize a list of a thousand buttons to get the program to work. That said, ZBrush has a rather complex and unusual interface, and it will take around 2 weeks of solid practice before you get comfortable with it. ZBrush is very sensitive to your workflow – the order in which commands occur – so pay close attention to the process workflow of each chapter.

This chapter is relatively dry and technical. After all, we're just going through the program's various interface items and menus! You can jump ahead to the next chapter and try working with the program as you go through this chapter. You can refer to this chapter to clarify any interface elements or features as needed.

The ZBrush window contains every element within ZBrush. While you cannot move things outside this main window, you have a great deal of freedom moving the interface elements around it. If you somehow mess up the interface and want to reset it back to default, go to the *Preferences* button on the top shelf, click it with the left mouse button (LMB), in the pull-down menu that opens, click the *Config* button, then click *Restore Standard UI*.

Conventions and mouse buttons

I will use an abbreviated format for this sort of instruction in the future: *Preferences > Config > Restore Standard UI* or *Preferences.Config.Restore Standard UI*, rather than go through the whole click on this, then this, then this procedure. Similarly, when I say click, I mean left mouse click (LMB for short). If you need to right- or middle mouse click on something, I will specify that exactly using the abbreviations RMB or MMB, respectively. When I refer to a key on the keyboard that you need to press, I will place it in italics, like this *P*. Similarly, any element that refers to a ZBrush function or command will also be in *italics*.

Note that your copy of ZBrush may look slightly different from the one in the book or the videos. This is perfectly okay. Customizing ZBrush's interface colors is straightforward, and I frequently work with a lighter color interface to make it easier for students to see my screen. ZBrush also gets updated with some frequency, but the commands and

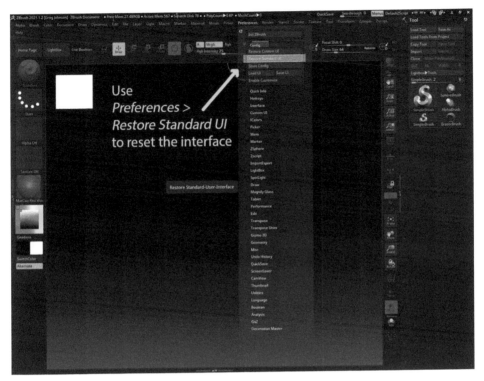

Use
Preferences >
Restore Standard UI
to reset the interface

FIGURE 2.1 *Preferences > Restore Standard UI* button location.

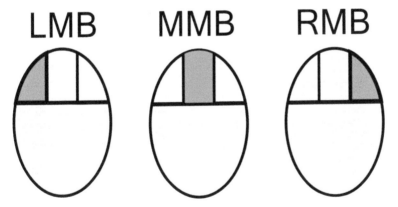

FIGURE 2.2 Mouse buttons and abbreviations.

processes in this book are basic enough to stay the same between the updates to the package.

Controls

The interface controls are composed of many different types of elements for adjusting ZBrush, but almost all of them fall into one of the following categories:

FIGURE 2.3 ZBrush controls.

Buttons

Whether text or an icon, buttons comprise the vast majority of interface elements in ZBrush. Buttons often provide access to drop-down or expandable menus, which in turn opens up more menus with additional buttons and controls. The buttons in the palette menu near the top of the screen, such as *Alpha* or *Document*, are examples of this sort of button.

Graphs and curves

Sometimes, you will come across a box that gives you access to a graph or curve. To use one of these, click and drag a point to move it around, click on the curve to place a new point, or drag a point on the side of the graph to delete it. You will only see these graphs infrequently.

Pop-up menus

There are a few tools that will present you with a pop-up menu or interface item. A simple example of this is the *spacebar* shortcut. Pressing and holding down the *spacebar* while it is in the painting area will bring up an interface centered on the current location of the mouse that includes the most useful tools and controls for painting and sculpting. You can then click on any of these buttons or swatches to access these items quickly.

Sliders

Sliders allow you to change a numeric value by clicking and dragging a bar along a line or by clicking on the slider and entering a number on the keyboard, then pressing *Enter*. If you change your mind while typing the new number, simply left mouse click (LMB) outside of the highlit slider to ignore the new value.

Swatches

There are a few areas, such as the color menu, where ZBrush uses a swatch for the interface. To pick a color, simply click the outside ring to select the hue and then click in the inside box to set the saturation and value you want.

Switches

Some buttons don't bring up additional menus but serve as simple on/off buttons. These will be highlighted in orange when they are active and become a dark gray when turned off.

Interface

The interface is composed of several different groups or areas, each with its own distinct flavor of function.

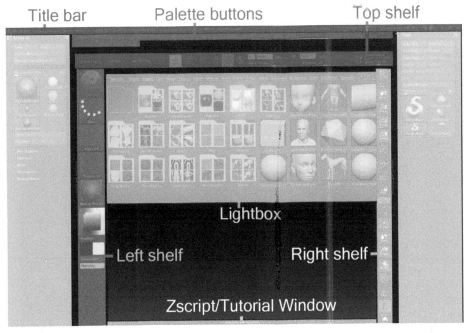

FIGURE 2.4 ZBrush interface.

27

Title bar

At the very topmost portion of the screen is a thin display and menu bar called the title bar. It contains information about ZBrush and your memory usage. On the right side of the title bar, you can find a set of handy buttons for creating a "quicksave," adjusting the overall transparency of the ZBrush window, a "Menu" visibility menu, a button to run a default script, and a suite of buttons for quickly changing the look and layout of the interface.

Palette buttons

The palette buttons at the top of the screen, just underneath the title bar, are where you can access the main menu items for ZBrush. The palette items are arranged alphabetically across the screen from left to right. Left mouse click (LMB) a palette item to access that pull-down menu list.

Palettes are often divided into various sub-palettes to place similar features together. Sub-palettes are sometimes divided into groups called "UI groups." Simply clicking on the name of the sub-palette or UI group will open it up. ZBrush typically only allows one sub-palette or UI group to be open at a time. Still, you can open another one by *SHIFT* + clicking the name of the other sub-palette/UI group or by changing the preference for how this feature works by toggling off the *Preferences > Interface > Palettes > Open One Subpalette* and *Preferences > Interface > UI Groups > AutoClose UI Groups* buttons. ZBrush will only remember your changes to preferences for next time if you save out the preference

FIGURE 2.5 Store Config, One Open Subpalette, and AutoClose UI Groups button locations.

settings by clicking *Preferences* > *Config* > *Store Config* or pressing the shortcut for this command *SHIFT + CTRL + i*.

Top shelf

The top shelf holds some of the most commonly used and important buttons in the program. Buttons and sliders for moving, rotating, and scaling items are located here, as are painting and sculpting controls, plus a few other important tools. You can press the TAB button to toggle the visibility of the shelves.

Left shelf

This shelf holds important menu items for controlling your paint-brushes and colors.

Right shelf

The right shelf has menu items for controlling your painting canvas. Tools for zooming in and moving about the canvas, as well as some uniquely 3D modes such as *Persp*, *Solo*, and *Floor*, are located here.

LightBox

The LightBox provides a simple interface for accessing your files, although it has the annoying habit of taking up a large section of the interface on start-up. Click the *LightBox* button in the top left corner of the ZBrush interface or tap the comma key on the keyboard to toggle this menu on or off.

Canvas or document area

The document area is where you paint and sculpt and occupies most of the center screen. You can adjust the color and gradient of the background. Click the *Document* button in the Palette menu strip at the top of the page. Look through the pull-down menu until you see the *Back* swatch and the *Range*, *Center*, and *Rate* sliders. You can adjust the sliders to change the gradient, and if you click and hold down the LMB while on the *Back* swatch, the cursor will change to a *Pick* function and let you move around the interface and choose a new background color by selecting it. If you ever mess something up in ZBrush and need to reset everything, remember that you can always go to the *Preferences* pull-down menu and select the *Init ZBrush* button. It should reset everything to ZBrush's startup setup.

Left and right trays

The left and right trays hold places for palette menu drop-down menus. By default, the right tray has the *Tool* palette open, and the left tray is closed. The trays can be opened and closed by clicking on the divider icons for each tray.

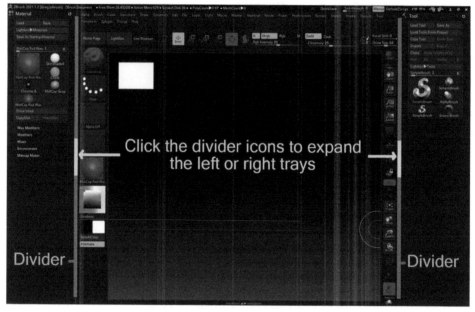

Click the divider icons to expand the left or right trays

Divider

Divider

FIGURE 2.6 Divider locations.

ZScript/tutorial window

This tray is used for ZScripts (programming for ZBrush) and tutorial purposes. You can scroll up and down within a tray by clicking and dragging any blank space within the tray. To place a palette menu on a tray, first open the palette menu you want. Once the palette is open, find the circular palette icon (it should be the icon in the upper left corner of the menu), click on it, and drag it to the tray you want the menu to be in, or click the icon once to move it into a tray automatically. Clicking the palette icon for a palette inside one of the trays will send it back to the palette menu bar and remove it from that tray.

Help

Getting help in ZBrush is very easy. Place your mouse cursor on top of a button without clicking it. A dialogue box will pop up with the full name of that button and the shortcut for quickly accessing it. If you press and hold down the *CTRL* key while doing this, ZBrush will give you a complete description of what that button does. The help function should work on every button in ZBrush and is a fast way of figuring out what everything is.

Shortcuts

ZBrush has shortcuts available for many of the most commonly used tools. Examples include the *SPACEBAR* shortcut to bring up the painting and sculpting tools and the comma button to toggle the LightBox

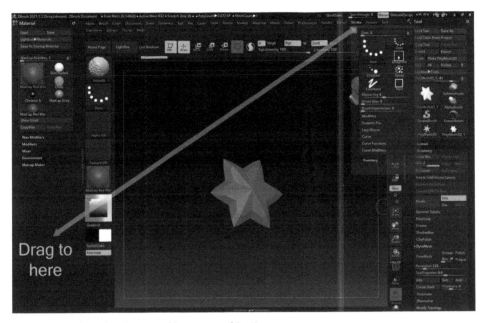

FIGURE 2.7 Click the circular palette icon and drag it into one of the side trays.

on and off. You can look at the ZBrush documentation to see a list of the various shortcuts available in the program here (docs.pixologic. com/user-guide/keyboard-shortcuts/). The keyboard shortcuts will be written in all capitals to make them easier to read in the book. Note that you do not need to capitalize the shortcut when you use it. For instance, you can press the *B* key on your keyboard to access the Brush Palette – you do not need to hold down the *SHIFT* key or activate the *Caps Lock* key to use the shortcut.

Critical concepts

What follows are a handful of critical concepts that you must familiarize yourself with before starting to use ZBrush productively.

2D, 3D, and 2.5D and bit depth

ZBrush is quite an odd duck in the software world since it is one of the few programs capable of working in 2D and 3D at the same time. A 2D image is a flat image composed of just the width (X) and height (Y) dimensions. A 3D image adds the dimension of depth (Z) to the mix.

Pixel

A regular 2D program works around a basal unit called the pixel. A pixel is simply one of the square dots that make up a digital image on your screen. If you zoom in far enough to a digital image, you can see

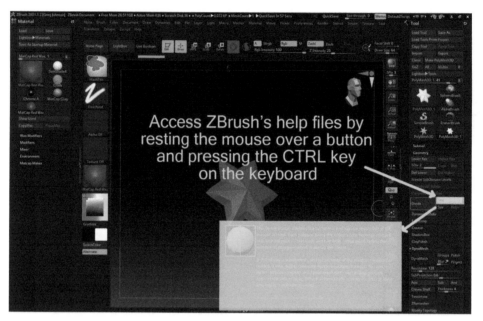

FIGURE 2.8 Access ZBrush's help files by resting the mouse over a button and pressing the *CTRL* key on the keyboard.

the pixels individually or look hard enough at your monitor (especially along diagonal edges). A computer image's resolution consists of the number of horizontal and vertical pixels it has. Digital images made up of pixels are also known as raster images. Another digital image element is the "bit depth" of the image file. Bit depth controls the number of possible colors each pixel in the image can represent (but remember that one pixel can only be one color at any given time). For example, a 1-bit image consists of strictly black-and-white pixels. In an 8-bit image, each pixel can be one of up to 256 levels of gray, from 0 (black) to 255 (white). A 24-bit image is often called a true color image. The 24 bits are divided into three 8-bit channels in a true color image. One channel each for red, green, and blue. Each channel holds 256 levels of that specific color, ranging from 0 to 255. These channels combine to provide a color range of some 16.7 million possible colors. Most digital images are of this type. However, you will occasionally see references to RGBA images, which add a separate 8-bit Alpha (A) channel or mask to the standard RGB color channels. There are many other variations, from 48-bit deep color images with billions of colors to additional alpha channels and different color spaces. These alternate color models fall more into the realm of image editing software and are largely outside the scope of this book. Just make sure you are familiar with full-color 24-bit RGB image files and know what an alpha channel/mask is, and you should be just fine working in ZBrush.

FIGURE 2.9 *Document > Save*, *Save As*, and *Export* buttons.

Pixol

ZBrush's big trick is that it adds the elements of depth, orientation, and material to the standard pixel. ZBrush calls this a Pixol. This feature enables the use of lighting, materials, and a host of other features not found in most image-editing software packages. The pixol is what ZBrush means when it talks about a 2.5D image. Pixols are a unique feature of the ZBrush canvas and are stored only in special ZBrush files called ZBR files. To save your ZBrush canvas with its pixol information, go to *Document > Save* and save a ZBR file of the document you are working on. You can use *Document > Save As* to save the ZBR file with a new name. Note that this DOES NOT save any 3D models you have been working on! It just saves the image document on the canvas with its pixol information intact. You can save just the pixel information using *Document > Export* to create a lossless Photoshop PSD, BMP, or TIF-type image file or a compressed JPG or PNG image file. I suggest always using uncompressed file types to save your artwork. Using an image compression algorithm on your artwork can lead to data loss and the images derezzing or losing quality.

Working with the canvas and documents

Now that you've got a few of the basic ideas down, let's dive right in and draw something. On the right side of the screen, you should see the *Tool* menu. If not, then you can open up the *Tool* menu under the

Preferences
> Init ZBrush

FIGURE 2.10 Preferences > Init ZBrush.

Palette bar at the top and drag it using the *Palette icon* to the *Right Tray*, or you could just reinitialize ZBrush by going to *Preferences > Init ZBrush*.

Under the tool menu, you will see a golden "S"-shaped icon for the *SimpleBrush*. If you click on that, it will open up a pop-up menu that will let you select from a variety of brushes. I'm going to choose the *Ring* under the *3D Meshes* section.

ZBrush will remember the most commonly chosen brushes and keep them in the *Quick Pick* section of the brushes menu as you continue to work.

Click and drag on the canvas. That should create a nice reddish-colored ring. Go around the canvas and make as many rings as you like. It's fun, but clicking and dragging all the time gets tedious fast. In the left tray, find the hollow square white icon labeled *DragRect*, which is the current stroke for the ring brush. Click on it and choose one of the other strokes – I'm choosing *Color Spray*. Now, try drawing on the canvas. You get a completely different result!

Try out a few of the other strokes and see what happens. Next, look in the left tray and find the red sphere icon labeled *MatCap Red Wax*. Click on this and choose a different material, such as *SketchShaded*, under the *MatCap* section. Try painting some more.

FIGURE 2.11 *SimpleBrush* and *Ring3D*.

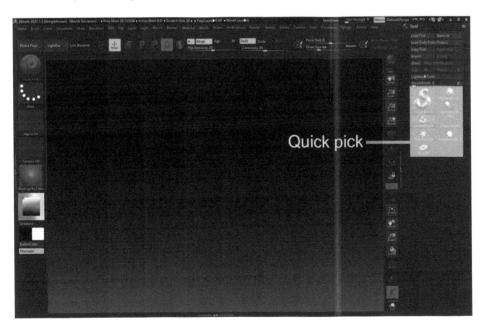

FIGURE 2.12 Quick pick brushes.

Now look underneath the material chooser and find the *Current Color* swatch. Use it to pick a new color. You can even select a color from the canvas by clicking and holding the LMB mouse button down on the

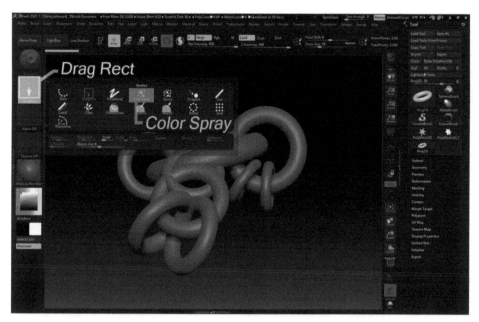

FIGURE 2.13 *DragRect* and *Color Spray* strokes.

FIGURE 2.14 MatCap Red Wax and SketchShaded.

color swatch and dragging to sample a new color from anywhere on the screen. Sampling this way also works for selecting materials from the canvas if you click and drag from the materials icon instead.

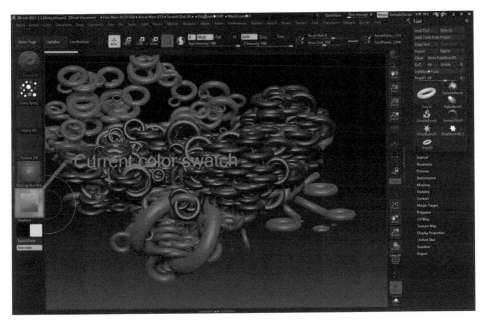

FIGURE 2.15 Current color swatch.

Save your document under *Document > Save*. Make sure you remember where on your computer system you are saving your files! Let's switch our brush back to the *SimpleBrush* by clicking on the *Ring3D* icon under the *Tool* menu in the right tray and selecting *SimpleBrush* from the *Brush* pop-up menu, or you can just click on the *SimpleBrush* icon in the *Quick Pick* area.

Now choose a stroke from the left-hand tray (I'm using *FreeHand*), a new material, and a new color.

Under the stroke selector, you will find the *Alpha* pop-up menu, which is a way to control the shape of the brush, so click on it and choose an alpha (I chose *Alpha 10*, the star-shaped one). Try painting with it. You should get a completely new result as the brush affects the previous work you did on the canvas – replacing the color, material, and sculpting the surface.

Select a texture from the texture selector, which is just above the material selector. Click on the blank gray square that says *Texture Off* and choose a new texture from the pop-up menu (I'm using *Texture 25*, for instance). When you use it, notice how the texture overrides your color selection. You can set texture back to *Texture Off* by selecting that option in the texture menu.

Under the color swatch, you will find two separate square color patches. These are the main color and alternate color swatches. You can set each one by clicking the color square and then choosing a color in

FIGURE 2.16 *Ring3D*, *SimpleBrush*, and *QuickPick*.

FIGURE 2.17 Stroke (set to FreeHand), Material (set to MatCap Red Wax), and Color.

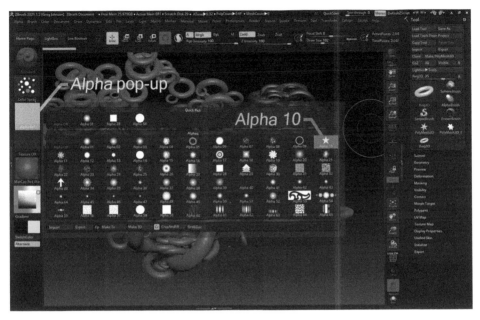

FIGURE 2.18 Alpha palette.

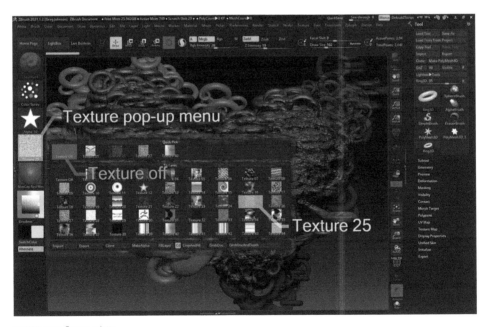

FIGURE 2.19 Texture palette.

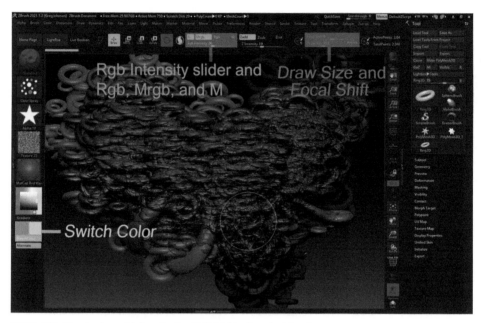

FIGURE 2.20 *Alternate* color swatch, *Draw Size*, *Focal Shift*, *Rgb Intensity*, and paint modes.

the main color selector. If you tap the *V* key on the keyboard or press the *SwitchColor* button under the color swatches, you can switch back and forth between the two color swatches.

There are a few other controls for painting that you need to know about. If you look at the top shelf, you can find the *Draw Size* slider. Use this to control the size of your paintbrush. You can also use the *[and]* keyboard shortcuts to decrease or increase your brush size quickly while you work. Atop the *Draw Size* slider, you can find the *Focal Shift* control. *Focal Shift* controls the amount of falloff the brush tip has. Try it out while you paint to fully understand what it is doing with the different 2D paint brushes. You can find the *Rgb Intensity* slider to the left of these controls, which controls the amount of color the brush deposits. Above the *Rgb Intensity* slider are buttons for selecting the mode to paint in. Select either *Mrgb* to paint with material and color, *Rgb* to paint with color only, or *M* to change just the material used. Be aware that *M* does NOT have ANY falloff between materials. Materials are an all-or-nothing affair. Materials don't blend in ZBrush. Pressing the *spacebar* key will bring up a pop-up menu for accessing these and other essential controls quickly while you are working.

The last bit of information you need to work in 2D within ZBrush is how to use the *Move*, *Scale*, and *Rotate* transform tools to affect your brush strokes. Draw a stroke on the canvas. I will use the *Ring3D* brush and the *DragRect* stroke that we used in our earlier example. Now,

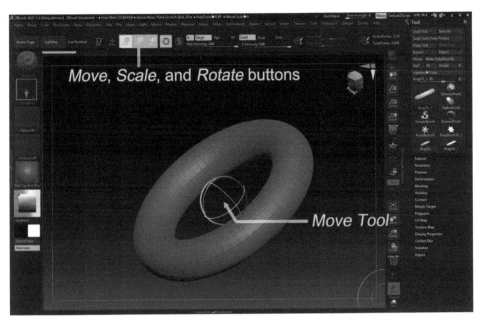

FIGURE 2.21 *Move, Scale*, and *Rotate* buttons and tool.

locate and press the *Move* button on the top shelf, or press the *W* shortcut key to switch to Move mode automatically. A colorful icon of three intersecting circles will appear over your last brush stroke. Clicking the different parts of the move tool will move your stroke around the canvas in various ways. The different colors on the tool indicate which axis clicking and dragging on that spot will move the stroke – red for the X plane, green for the Y plane, and blue for the Z plane. Clicking and dragging on the yellow intersection of the green and red circles will move the last brush stroke along the Z axis, the cyan intersection along the X axis, and the magenta section along the Y. If you click and drag using the empty center space, you will move the stroke along the surface defined by your painting. Once you get used to the move tool, try out the scale (*E* shortcut) and rotate (*R* shortcut) tools. They use the same tool interface as Move but have dramatically different effects. You can quickly switch back to the standard painting mode by clicking the *Draw* icon on the top shelf or pressing the *Q* key.

If you mess up while working, you can quickly fix things by going to *Edit > Undo* in the palette bar or using the keyboard shortcut of *CTRL + Z*. You will find the "Redo" button immediately next to the undo button. The redo shortcut is *CTRL + SHIFT + Z*. If the back part of your ring disappears, it has moved too far back along the Z-axis and disappeared underneath the document canvas. You can use the undo button or draw another ring to replace the old one.

FIGURE 2.22 Thumbnail or Silhouette view.

The Silhouette view in the corner

The little white rectangle in the upper left corner of the document window is called the *Thumbnail or Silhouette View*. The window shows you a silhouette of the object you are working on, or it can offer you a thumbnail version of that object. If you go to the *Preferences > Thumbnail* sub-palette, you can access all the settings for this preview window. In this menu, you can turn off the *Silhouette* button if you want a rendered thumbnail of your object. If you toggle off the *Thumbnail* button, the little preview window will disappear.

Saving your work

Now is an excellent time to save your work again using *Document > Save*. Be aware that ZBrush is the only program that can open the resulting ZBR file. If you want to edit this image further using a different software package, you will have to export it as an image file using *Document > Export* to save out a standard raster file type such as BMP (BitMap). If you'd rather not save this particular image, then go to *Document > New Document*.

Organizing files and paths

One last little note to add: Ensure you have a specific place in which you are saving your files. You probably don't want the files you create cluttering your ZBrush install folder! Being well organized will help you immensely further down the line, so go ahead and create a folder to

FIGURE 2.23 Document > new document.

save things into. Call the new folder "ZBrush_Files" or something else that labels it as a file folder for your ZBrush files. When you create the folder, you will need to be able to find it later, so you will need to have an understanding of how paths work on computer systems. A path is simply a guide to a specific location on a computer. There are two flavors of paths used – global and local paths. A global path starts from one of the lettered drives on your computer, like the *C*: drive. After that, you have the names of the folders on the C drive and the sub-folders inside them, each separated by a backslash \ (at least on a Windows machine). Linux and Apple computers use a forward slash / instead. A typical example might look something like this: "C:\ZBrush_Files\Tools." This path tells you that the Tools folder is inside the ZBrush_Files folder on the C drive on your computer. Another way to get around on a computer is to use a local path, which tells the computer the path from one place to another, but it doesn't use the drive name, just the relative locations of the different folders. Local paths can get complicated. Since this isn't a book about using Microsoft Windows or any other operating system, I will not go into a lot of details, other than to advise you to look up "path computing" for more information.

Additional help

It is always helpful to have more resources available. Make sure you look through the official ZBrush documentation (docs.pixologic.com) and read through the "Getting Started" section (docs.pixologic.com/getting-started/). Support is available online through the ZBrush forum (www.zbrushcentral.com), and the Pixologic ZBrush Classroom is extremely useful (pixologic.com/zclassroom/). There are also a lot of helpful tutorials on YouTube and from other internet sources, but you should always ensure the tutorial you are watching is for the current version of the software. Avail yourself of these additional resources, but don't let the volume of information overwhelm you. Everything you need is in this book – but it is nice to have extra resources available.

Conclusion

We can now wrap up our discussion of the basic elements of ZBrush's interface. Make sure that you familiarize yourself with what you have learned so far. Remember that it is okay to make mistakes. Making mistakes and figuring out how to fix them are how we learn. Once you have mastered the contents of this chapter, you can move on to the next chapter.

Further reading

"Adobe: Creative, Marketing and Document Management Solutions". Adobe Inc. https://www.adobe.com/. Accessed 15 Dec. 2022.

"Application Manager - Maxon." Maxon Computer GMBH. https://www.maxon.net/en/try/. Accessed 15 Dec. 2022.

"Autodesk | 3D Design, Engineering & Construction Software". Autodesk, Inc. https://www.autodesk.com/. Accessed 15 Dec. 2022.

"blender.org - Home of the Blender Project - Free and Open 3D Creation Software". Blender Foundation, Community. https://www.blender.org/. Accessed 15 Dec. 2022.

"GIMP - GNU Image Manipulation Program". GIMP Development Team. https://www.gimp.org/. Accessed 15 Dec. 2022.

"Knowledge Base." Maxon Computer GMBH. https://support.maxon.net/. Accessed 15 Dec. 2022.

Maxon Computer GMBH. https://docs.pixologic.com/getting-started/. Accessed 15 Dec. 2022.

"Sign in." Maxon Computer GMBH. https://my.maxon.net/. Accessed 15 Dec. 2022.

"ZBrushCentral - Your Home for ZBrush." Maxon Computer GMBH. https://www.zbrushcentral.com/. Accessed 15 Dec. 2022.

"ZBrush Docs | Pixologic ZBrush Documentation." Maxon Computer GMBH. https://docs.pixologic.com/. Accessed 15 Dec. 2022.

"ZClassroom - ZBrush Training from the Source." Maxon Computer GMBH. https://pixologic.com/zclassroom/. Accessed 15 Dec. 2022.

3

The Basics, Part 1

Working with 3-D ZTools

Up until now, we've been using ZBrush as sort of a painting package. It's time to switch gears and start working with 3D. First, we need to reinitialize ZBrush so we can start fresh. Click *Preferences > Init ZBrush* from the top menu bar, or if you are just now starting ZBrush, press the comma key on the keyboard or the *Lightbox* button in the upper left-hand corner of the interface to turn off the large Lightbox interface that pops up on startup.

In the right tray under the *Tool* menu, click the *SimpleBrush* icon, the largest icon in the top left corner of the icon list, and pick *Cube3D* from the pop-up menu.

Click and drag on the center of the canvas to create a large cube. The very next thing you must do is press the *T* key or click the *Edit* button on the top shelf.

This activates ZBrush's 3D mode, with the cube as the current 3D object. Now if your right mouse button (RMB) clicks and drags on the canvas area, you will rotate the view of the cube around on the canvas! If instead you get a new cube drawn on the canvas, it's because you didn't press the *T* key or *Edit* button immediately after drawing the cube. That's OK. Just reinitialize ZBrush by clicking *Preferences > Init ZBrush* from the top menu bar and try again – and this time don't forget to press the *T* key immediately after you draw the cube on the screen. When you rotate your view of the cube around, if you also press the *SHIFT* key, it will lock the rotation to 90-degree angles. If you want to move the object within the canvas view, press the *ALT* button and right mouse click (RMB) and drag the mouse on the canvas (*ALT + drag*). If you instead press the *CTRL* button and RMB click and drag, you will

DOI: 10.1201/9781003215288-3

45

FIGURE 3.1 *Lightbox and Preferences > Init ZBrush.*

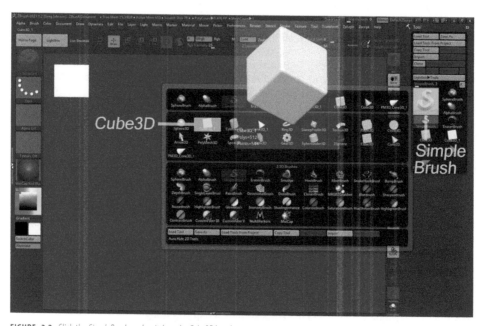

FIGURE 3.2 Click the *SimpleBrush and switch to the Cube3D* brush.

adjust the size of the object on the screen. What these three commands are doing is moving your viewpoint around – they do not move
the object around at all.

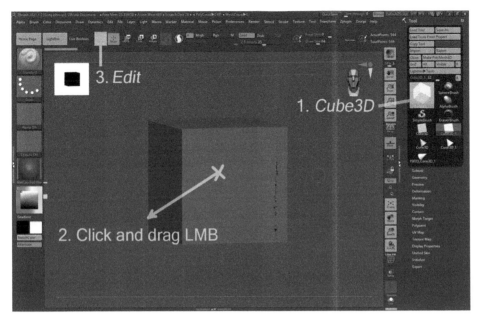

FIGURE 3.3 How to draw a cube on the screen.

An alternate way of doing the same view transformations is to use the
LMB (left mouse button) and click and drag on any blank area of the
canvas to rotate around as well. If you want to move the object within
the canvas, you can also press the *ALT* button and left mouse click and
drag the mouse on the canvas (*ALT + drag*). You can also press *ALT*, then
the right mouse button (RMB), let go of the *ALT* button, and now drag
the mouse while still holding down the RMB to zoom, which sounds
more complicated written out than it is to perform!

Of course, mouse shortcuts aren't the only way to access these transformations. You can also rotate the object by clicking and dragging on
the *Rotate* icon located on the bottom half of the right shelf. You will
find buttons for *Zoom3D* and *Move* immediately above the *Rotate* button, which works the same way.

These view transformations (*Move View*, *Zoom3D*, and *Rotate View*)
are centered on the last point clicked on the object. To try this out,
just click the left mouse button with the mouse pointer on the cube,
then rotate it. If ZBrush pops up a warning about enabling sculpting, just ignore it – we will get to sculpting soon. See how the object
rotates around the point where you last clicked on it. Now press the
Frame button on the right shelf, which is right above where the move
button is located, or simply press the *F* key to frame and center the
object on your canvas. The object now rotates around the object's
center. As you can see, ZBrush usually provides several ways to do
anything you might want. It is all about finding a workflow that is
comfortable for you.

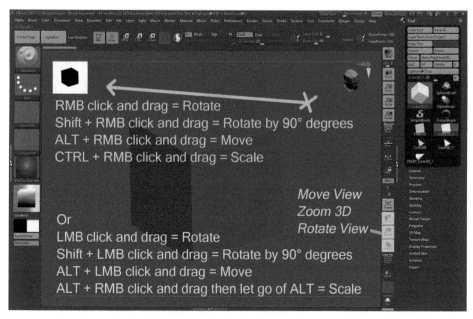

FIGURE 3.4 *Rotate View, Move View,* and *Zoom3D.*

If you need to delete an object from the canvas, turn off the *Edit* button, then click on the *Layer* button on the top menu bar and then the *Clear* button in the resulting pull-down menu to get rid of whatever objects are currently drawn on the canvas. Deleting an object from the canvas does NOT remove that object from the Tool menu or erase it from the program. You can always draw the same object onto the canvas again if you desire. It merely wipes the canvas clean.

Let's take a moment and finish going up the right shelf button list while we are there. Above the frame button, you can find the icons for locking the object's rotation to a specific axis or allowing it to rotate freely around all three axes. The currently active button will be high-lighted in orange. Atop that, we find the *Lock Camera* button. When pressed, this button prevents camera transformations. This is useful when you are detailing parts of a model and don't want the model to get accidentally moved by mistake. Right above the *Lock Camera* button is the *L.Sym* button or *Local Symmetry* button. The *L.Sym* toggle button is useful to turn on once you have multiple objects in the scene to preserve each object's unique symmetry when sculpting (we'll talk about this more later).

The next button requires some technical explanation. ZBrush, like every other 3D program, uses a Cartesian coordinate system to define 3D space. If you've ever had a geometry class and worked with a grid system, then you have seen this system before and might recognize it. The basic idea is that the X axis defines the right and left directions, Y up and down, and Z backward and forward.

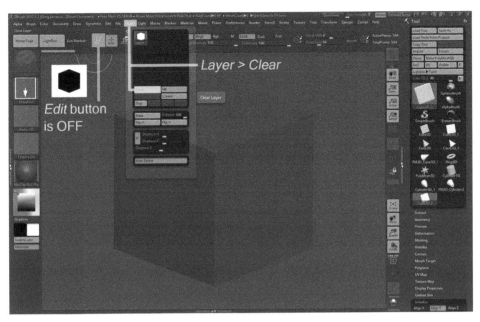

Layer > Clear

Edit button is OFF

FIGURE 3.5 With the *Edit* button OFF, use *Layer* > *Clear* to clean the Canvas.

The *Floor* button (*Shift* + *P* shortcut) activates a transparent plane that lets you see the XZ coordinate plane that exists within ZBrush. The Y axis is perpendicular to this plane and defines the up direction within ZBrush. With the Floor button turned on, you can faintly see the axis lines showing the X axis in red, Y in green, and Z in blue at the origin or center point of the floor grid. This is very important information, especially if you are working with another 3D package like Maya, 3dsMax, or Blender. In almost all modern 3D programs, these axes are color-coded for easy identification. The X-axis is in red, the Y-axis is in green, and the Z-axis is in blue. To see a visual representation of these axes in ZBrush, you can turn the Floor button on. Click on the *X*, *Y*, and *Z* characters inside the *Floor* button to display the coordinate grids. The colored grid is perpendicular to the axis it represents – in other words, the axis goes straight up and out of the grid. If you turn all three characters on (X, Y, and Z), you will have all three coordinate grids displayed, like in the example image below. It is a very good idea to make sure that your object always has its up direction aligned to the Y axis and its front aligned along the Z axis. This is so if you ever take the model into another program, it won't be facing the wrong direction, and it is a good work habit to get into. Another important idea is to always try and place your models in the center of the world, i.e. right on top of the little XYZ axis that shows up in the middle of the green grid when the Floor button is turned on. This will help ZBrush maintain symmetry in your model and make your life a lot easier if you ever export your ZBrush model to another 3D program.

To make all of this a bit easier, ZBrush provides both a simple head model and an XYZ viewing axis placed in the upper right-hand corner of the canvas. Known as *CamView*, this little model head is very useful for determining the orientation of your model. If the head is facing you, then you are looking at the front of the model. Other viewing angles are matched by the corresponding position of the little head in the corner. This makes it very easy for you to tell from what position you are looking at the model. It is a very good idea to make sure that your object is always aligned with the little head in the corner. This ensures that the model always has its up direction aligned to the Y axis and its front aligned along the Z axis. If you click on one of the color-coded axis arms on the uppermost right-hand corner icon, then you will move the view to that corresponding axis. If you click on one of the CamView axes a second time, the view will go to the opposite side of the axis you selected.

It is a quick way to go to a top, front, or side view of your object.

Just above the *Floor* button is the *Persp* button, which activates perspective camera mode in ZBrush (*P* shortcut). By default, ZBrush uses an orthographic camera, which is why when you turned on the floor, the grid lines didn't converge. If you look at the floor grid with the *Persp* button on, you will notice the grid lines converging toward the horizon line. While it is usually easier to work in orthographic mode, you will want to turn on perspective when it comes time to render images of your final product. The *AAHalf* button shrinks the canvas view to half size, while the *Actual* button restores it to full size. The *AAHalf* button

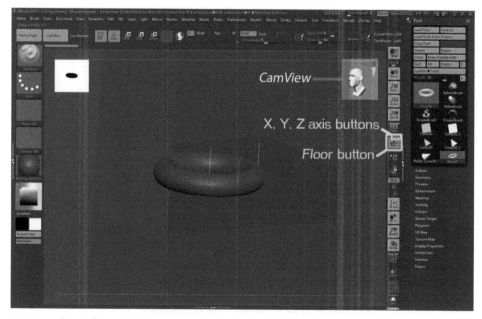

FIGURE 3.6 *CamView, Floor,* and the Cartesian coordinate system.

is there so an artist can check the image at something more like print size without having to go through the imprecise process of zooming. The *Zoom* button does exactly that, but it doesn't affect the size of the object; it is zooming into the canvas instead. Zoom in enough, and you will see the individual pixels that make up the image document.

Inside the *Document* menu found on the top shelf, you will find the *Width* and *Height* sliders, which control the dimensions of the image document you are working on. If you are working on an image that will eventually get printed, then you will have to work on a much bigger document size than if you are going to video, for example. It is always important to know where your artwork will end up. If you are going to print, then you need an image resolution of somewhere between 150 and 300 dpi (dots per inch), so if you want an 8 × 10 inch picture, you will need an image resolution of 2,400 pixels by 3,000 pixels. Whereas video has a much lower resolution of 1,920 × 1,080 pixels for HDTV, for instance.

The *Scroll* button moves the canvas around. The *SPix* slider lets you adjust the quality of the anti-aliasing for your images. Just be aware that higher values mean it will take longer to render you high-quality images. Set the *Spix* value to 0 to turn off anti-aliasing. Anti-aliasing in digital images is the process of adding a slight blurring effect to diagonal lines to make them appear smoother and less jagged.

Press the *BPR* button to create a *Best-Preview Render* of what you are working on. It is a quick and simple way of creating a nice render. Once the render is done, if you want to save it, just go to *Document > Export*

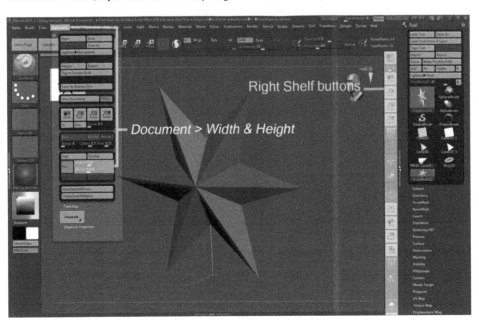

FIGURE 3.7 Right shelf buttons location, and *Document > Width & Height.*

FIGURE 3.8 Aliased and Anti-aliased letters.

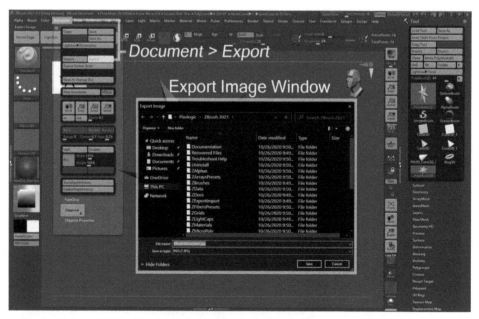

FIGURE 3.9 *Document > Export and the Export Image window.*

and save an image file. *Document > Export* will bring up an export image window to let you choose where to save the file and pick what file format you'd like to use. Make sure you save your files somewhere you can find them again on your computer! Use the *Save as type* pull-down menu to choose your file format. The default Photoshop PSD format is a good choice if you have an image editor on your system. BMP and TIF are good choices for archival images or images you want to work on later since they're widely supported formats, whereas JPG and PNG are web formats that will compress your image, and I don't suggest using them unless you want to post the image directly to the internet.

At the bottom of the right shelf, you will find a set of buttons that control object transparency and isolation for working with multiple objects. We will save talking about these for later, when we start working with multiple objects.

Let's start a new document, *Document > New Document*. Go to the *Tool* menu, click the top-left tool icon, and select from the pop-up menu *Cylinder3D*. Now draw the cylinder onto the canvas, then press *T* on the keyboard to enter edit mode. Look down the *Tool* menu until you find the *Initialize* menu, and click on it. In this menu, you adjust the shape of the cylinder. Play with the slider values and watch what happens to the cylinder on the screen. I'm leaving the X, Y, and Z sizes at 100 and giving my own an *Inner Radius* of 50, *HDivide* of 10, *VDivide* of 4, and setting the *Taper* to 50. To sculpt this object, we need to convert it to an editable 3D object by pressing the *Make PolyMesh 3D* button in the *Tool* menu. If you have trouble using the sliders to set specific numbers, remember that you can click on the numbers themselves and set them using the keyboard. You can even use the *TAB* key on the keyboard to cycle between the numeric slider values.

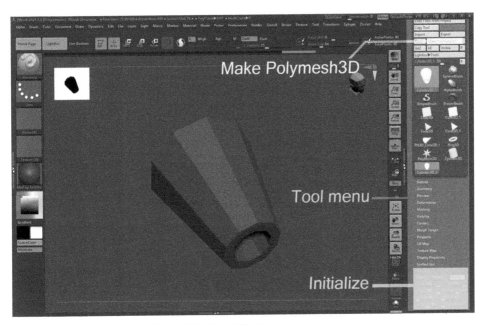

FIGURE 3.10 The Tool menu, *Tool > Initialize*, and *Make Polymesh3D* buttons.

Now that we have a usable polymesh object, we can start to work on it. Perhaps the most elementary thing to do with an object is to transform it, that is, to move, scale, and rotate the object in our 3D virtual world. To do this, we use ZBrush's Gizmo 3D manipulator. To turn on the Gizmo 3D, simply press the *Move* button at the top of the ZBrush interface or press the *W* key on your keyboard to access the shortcut.

When you hover your mouse over the Gizmo, the part of the Gizmo that is currently active will be highlighted for your convenience so that you know which part would be activated by your mouse click at that point. If you click with the left mouse button and drag on one of the colored cones at the tip of each of the Gizmo's arms, then you can move your object on that axis. Just remember that Red = X axis, Green = Y axis, and Blue = Z axis.

If instead you drag and click on one of the four gray corner marks, you will move the object around the viewing screen. If you click and drag on one of the colored circles, you will rotate the object around the axis determined by the RGB color of that circle. If you click and drag on the gray circle at the border of the tool, you will rotate the object perpendicular to your current viewing plane. It is like driving an invisible spike from your current camera angle through the object and then rotating the object around it.

If you click and drag on one of the colored boxes on the Gizmo, you can scale the object on that axis. If you click and drag on the yellow square at the center of the Gizmo, you will scale the object on all three axes simultaneously.

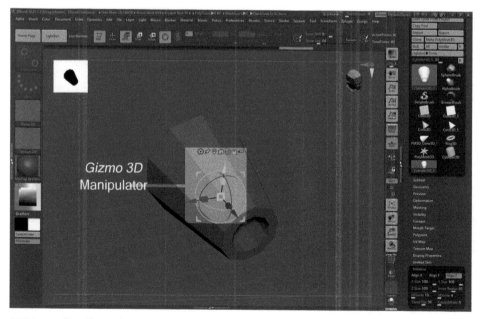

FIGURE 3.11 *Gizmo 3D* manipulator.

Oddly enough, it does not seem to matter which button you push to access the Gizmo 3D manipulator. The *Move* (*W* shortcut key), *Scale* (*E* shortcut key), and *Rotate* (*R* shortcut key) buttons and their shortcuts will all simply bring up the Gizmo 3D Manipulator. While doing any of these transformations using the Gizmo, if you hold down the *Shift* button on your keyboard, you will cause any of these transformations to occur in fixed increments and either rotate in 5° increments, scale in 0.5 increments, or move in 0.1 unit increments. If you hold down the *Ctrl* button while you click on one of the move arrows, you will make a copy of the object while leaving behind the masked original. If you hold down *Ctrl* and use the RGB scale boxes, you will squash the extremities of the object on that axis. *Ctrl* and using the central yellow square will inflate or deflate the object. *Ctrl* and using rotation will mask off portions of your object, but this option is a bit finicky to where you click on the Gizmo to activate this option.

At this point, if you are probably thinking that's a lot of details to remember, just keep in mind that you just have to get to know the basics right now. Most of these extended options can be safely ignored for the time being until you get used to the program and begin picking up the details on how to use it. I mention most of this stuff now just to let you know that these extended options exist. Being aware of these options also helps when you accidentally click on something or press a button while trying to do a specific task and the program does something completely unexpected. If you are aware of all of these different options, then it is easier to track back and figure out what you did wrong. Otherwise, you would have no idea what you did! This program is very complicated and sensitive to how you do each operation. The order in which you do each operation matters, and you can get radically different results from very small changes in how you go about things. While this sensitivity can be very frustrating to a beginner, it also makes ZBrush a very powerful program for an expert – but it does make the learning curve on this program quite steep. Speaking of which, the Gizmo does a lot more than just basic transformations. When you have activated the Gizmo, you should see a row of small icons a little bit above the Gizmo interface. These buttons allow you to customize the Gizmo and how it operates. There is a lot of information and power packed into this row of buttons, so much so that I will explain these Gizmo options as we use them later on. Instead of writing a whole dreary chapter about them here at the beginning of the book, we will just look at one option as a taster.

An alternative to the more traditional Gizmo 3D interface that ZBrush provides is the *Transpose brush*. To access the transpose brush, simply turn the *Gizmo 3D* button located at the top of your screen off. The *Y* key on your keyboard is the shortcut to toggle the Gizmo 3D button on and off. Once that is done, we can start using *Move*, *Scale*, and *Rotate* with the *Transpose* line interface. On the top shelf, click on the *Move* button (*W* shortcut). You should see a small, complicated icon appear

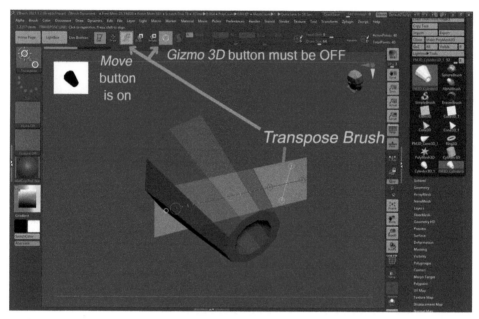

FIGURE 3.12 *The Transpose brush.*

over your object. The icon consists of a series of three orange circles connected by a straight line with a small white circle at the tip and an array of red, green, and blue lines tipped with tiny circles radiating from the origin point. The small red, green, and blue lines represent the coordinate axes. Red for the X axis, green for the Y axis, and blue for the Z axis. If you click inside any of the tiny red or green circles, the orange circles will align themselves with the corresponding axis. If you click inside the tiny white circle at the tip of the transpose line, it will move the transpose line to start at the center of the object. You can adjust the position of the transpose tool by clicking and dragging ON the rings of the different orange circles. Clicking and dragging on the orange rings at either end of the transpose line will change the shape and orientation of the transpose line. Clicking on the middle circle or the orange line connecting the orange circles will move the transpose tool around. If you click inside the orange circles, you affect the object in different ways depending on which of the orange circles you click and drag.

Clicking and dragging inside the orange circle that does not have the red and green axis lines around it will distort the object around a center defined by the other end of the transpose tool. Doing the same to the middle circle will move the whole object around, while clicking and dragging the inside of the circle with the red and green lines surrounding it will cause the object to collapse down along the transpose line as you drag it. Play around with this tool until you are comfortable with it. It has a very strange interface and is difficult to master. The trick is remembering that clicking on the transpose line itself or its orange rings will adjust the transpose line, whereas clicking inside the orange rings will affect the object you are working on.

The scale button (*E* shortcut) works very similarly to the move tool, but clicking inside either of the end circles scales the whole object proportionately centered on the other end of the tool. Clicking inside the middle circle scales the object along an axis perpendicular to the transpose line.

The rotate button (*R* shortcut) makes more sense. It acts as a lever and pivots around whichever end isn't being clicked on. In other words, when using the rotate tool, clicking and dragging either end of the circle will rotate the object around a pivot point defined by the other end of the transpose tool. Using the middle circle will rotate the object around the axis defined by the transpose tool.

The ZBrush transpose brushes are some of the most unusual 3D transformation tools to be found in any software package. They are rather strange and take a lot of getting used to, so don't be upset if you find them difficult to use. That said the transpose line interface is quite powerful and has some unique features that are unavailable using the Gizmo 3D interface.

As an alternative to using the transpose tools, you can always resort to using the *Offset*, *Rotate*, and *Size* sliders found in the *Tool.Deformation* menu (*Tool > Deformation > Offset, Rotate*, or *Size*). These sliders are fairly straightforward to use, though the *Rotate* slider always revolves around the global origin, i.e. the center of the ZBrush Cartesian coordinate system, and can thus be a bit tricky to predict. If you look carefully at each of these sliders, you will see tiny *X*, *Y*, and *Z* letters on each button's right side. You can carefully press these letters to activate the indicated axis and constrain the operation to that specific axis or combination of axes.

Saving your work

Now let's save the work that we have done. In ZBrush, 3D objects are considered tools, and the *Tool* interface has most of the commands related to them. When you are working on a 3D object, what you are doing is affecting an instance or copy of the actual tool which lives in the tool menu. What this means is that if you accidentally drop the 3D object onto the canvas by turning off *Edit* mode, you haven't lost your 3D object. In fact, you can place as many copies of your object on your canvas as you want – it doesn't affect the tool itself at all until you go into edit mode and make changes to the object itself. One EXTREMELY important aspect of this is that when you save a document or export an image, you ARE NOT saving the 3D object you've been working on! To save your 3D object for later, you need to go to the *Tool* menu and click on *Save As* (*Tool > Save As*) and save out a ZTL file. This is a

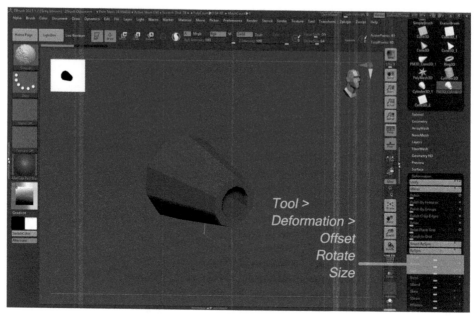

FIGURE 3.13 *Tool > Deformation > Offset, Rotate, or Size.*

ZTool file format that contains your 3D object. The current file format you are working with is visible as the file extension. The file extension is a three-letter code at the end of the file name after a period, for example: *"My_ZBrush_Tool_File_01.ZTL"* where .ZTL is the file extension. If you are working inside the *Windows* operating system to see the file extensions, you may have to open *Windows Explorer* and go to *View > Options*, then choose the *View* tab, and make sure that the *Hide extensions for known file types* option is turned OFF.

If you want to save everything – all of your loaded tools, the canvas, animation, and everything else about your current ZBrush session, then go to *File > Save As* or press *CTRL + S* on the keyboard and save out a ZBrush ZPR project file. Because you are saving everything, these files are much larger than either the ZBR canvas files or the ZTL tool files. Be aware that when you load a project file using *File > Open* it will replace everything that was previously loaded in ZBrush, so be careful with it!

To save the ZBrush canvas as an image file, use the *Document > Save* or *Document > Save As* buttons. These two buttons will save a ZBR file that captures what you are currently looking at on the ZBrush canvas. Unfortunately, there aren't any other programs out there that will read a ZBrush ZBR file type, which means that you are usually better off using the *Document > Export* button to create a more useful image type, such as a JPG, PSD, PNG, BMP, or TIF file. A JPG or PNG image type is useful if you want to distribute the image online. BMP and TIF files are good for archiving your image. PSD files are Adobe Photoshop's

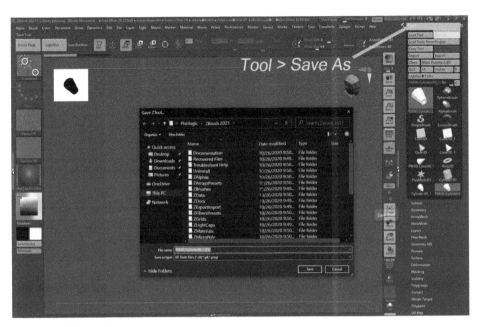

FIGURE 3.14 *Tool > Save As.*

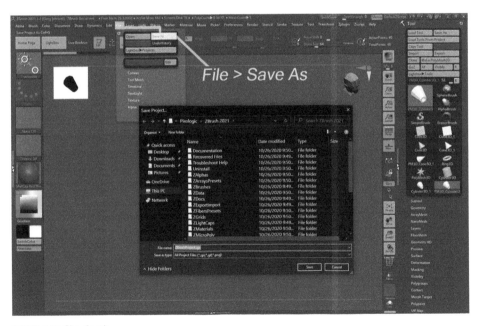

FIGURE 3.15 *File > Save As.*

native file type and an excellent choice if you want to paint on the image you have exported from ZBrush.

If you choose to export the image as a JPG, a special interface will pop up during the process that lets you crop your image and set the quality

FIGURE 3.16 *Document > Export.*

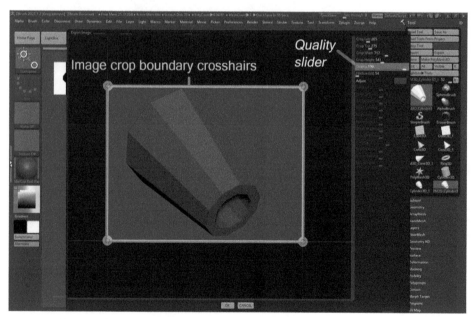

FIGURE 3.17 *Document > Export* as JPG interface.

of the file. Use the red crosshair icons to set the image crop boundaries and the *Quality* slider to control the amount of image compression. A *Quality* value of 100 will give you a large, high-quality image, while a lower-quality setting will give you a smaller, lower quality, and more compressed JPG image.

Take some time and play around with all of the material that you have learned so far. Become familiar with where buttons are located and how the interface is laid out, because things are going to start getting more complicated from now on.

Conclusion

Practice what you have learned in this chapter until you are completely comfortable with what has been discussed so far. It is important to master the basics before you move on to more formidable topics. Doing so will provide you with a strong foundation upon which to build your ZBrush skills. Try out the various shortcuts that have been described. These shortcuts will speed up your process immensely going forward.

4

The Basics, Part 2

Getting started

This chapter will introduce you to the proper project workflow and the basic toolset you will use throughout the book. First, make sure that you have gone through ZBrush and familiarized yourself with the program's interface. Then, if you still need to do so, read the preceding chapters before starting the project contained herein. Now that has been sorted, let's dive into ZBrush and start!

The first thing you must do is close the browser pop-up that appears when you first launch ZBrush. Simply clicking on the close button, i.e., the [X] in the upper right-hand corner of the pop-up window, will accomplish this.

The next thing we need to close before we start working is the ZBrush *LightBox* interface. *LightBox* is a quick and visual way of accessing the various ZBrush projects stored on your machine. It has an easy-to-use graphical interface in the top half of the ZBrush document canvas (the big blank gray space in the center of ZBrush). While *LightBox* can be a quick way to access your files, it has the annoying tendency to pop up by default at the start of every ZBrush session (though you can change this behavior later on in your *Preferences* menu). Move the mouse over the *LightBox* button band and tap the left mouse button (hereafter called the LMB for brevity). Press the comma key on your keyboard to toggle the LightBox off.

So, you'll first notice that, by default, ZBrush has a gradient in the background of its *Canvas Document* window. While this default gradient is perfectly fine, I prefer a flat middle gray background instead, so let me show you how to change the document background. First, go up and

DOI: 10.1201/9781003215288-4

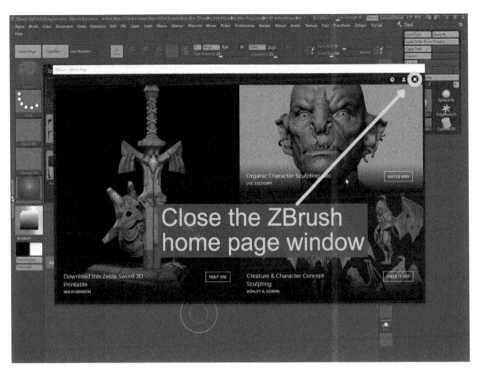

FIGURE 4.1 Close the ZBrush home page window.

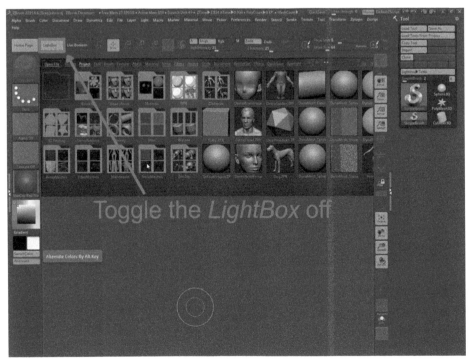

FIGURE 4.2 Toggle the *LightBox* off.

LMB (hereafter just called a click) on the *Document* menu item in the top menu bar within ZBrush. Doing this opens the *Document* menu. Now, go down and find the *Range* slider. You can simply hold down your LMB on the slider and drag it to change the value. Alternatively, you can click on the slider and type in the number you want, in this case, a 0. That will get rid of the gradient.

You can set the background color by going to the Document menu and finding the Back button (*Document > Back*). Next, click and hold down the LMB on top of this button. Now, slide your mouse around while still holding down the LMB. You will see how ZBrush samples whatever color the mouse icon sits on top of. Use this to set the background color to something you like. For example, I always prefer a mid-tone gray for my canvas documents.

If you go to the *Canvas Document* and use the mouse to start drawing, you will get a strange boxy pattern on the canvas. This result is because ZBrush defaults to a peculiar two-dimensional painting package. While playing with the default paint features can be fun, it isn't a regular use for ZBrush. To remove the digital scribble created so far, go to the *Layer* menu item on the top bar, find the *Clear* button, and press it. In the future, I will put *Layer > Clear* in this book as a shorthand form of saying all of that.

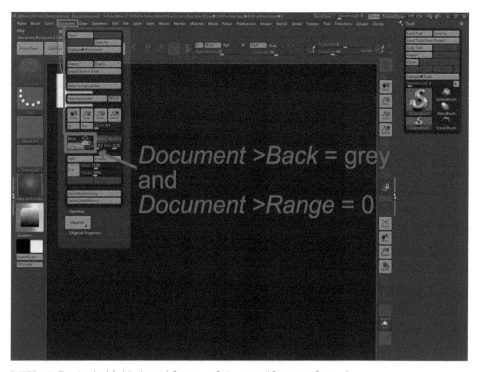

FIGURE 4.3 Changing the default background. *Document > Back = gray* and *Document > Range = 0.*

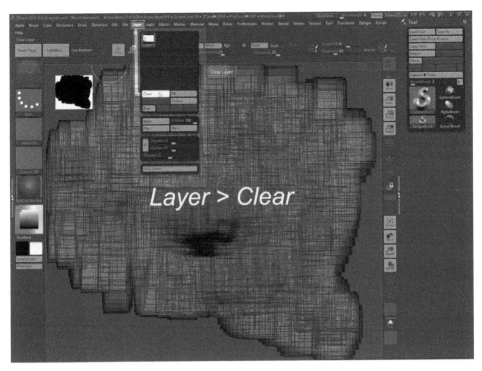

Layer > Clear

FIGURE 4.4 Use *Layer > Clear* to empty to canvas document.

To work in 3D in ZBrush, we must visit the *Tool* menu. In ZBrush parlance, all 3D objects are known as Tools within the program. One of the things you will quickly learn about ZBrush is just how non-standard it is. ZBrush has its own unusual terminology and processes compared to 3D programs such as Autodesk Maya or Blender. Think of ZBrush as more of a 2½D program rather than a full-fledged 3D program. The math ZBrush uses is not quite the same as most other 3D programs. This alternate approach comes with a lot of consequences. While ZBrush does not have all the functionality of a standard 3D program like Maya, 3dsMax, or Blender, it offers a unique set of capabilities that no other program possesses. On the plus side, ZBrush's approach to 3D allows it to sculpt and work with extremely high-resolution models, typically in the several million polygon range, that other 3D programs cannot handle at all. The problem is that the way something looks inside ZBrush cannot be matched using another 3D program. ZBrush isn't a WYSIWYG (what you see is what you get) program. You cannot just export a high-resolution 3D model from ZBrush into a video game engine and have it work and look correct. Going from ZBrush into another 3D package usually involves a lot of effort to massage the data into the proper format and make the process work correctly. That is the downside to ZBrush's approach to 3D.

FIGURE 4.5 *Tool > SimpleBrush*, then select the *Sphere3D*.

To experience ZBrush's strengths, we should set about sculpting something. First, go to the *Tool* menu and click on the large golden "S" shape – the *SimpleBrush*. Doing so opens up a selection menu from which you should click the *Sphere3D* icon.

Placing a Sphere3D on the canvas

The large icon in the *Tool* menu should now say *Sphere3D*. This large icon shows you which 3D Tool is currently active. Now, go to the center of the *Canvas Document*. Press the LMB and hold it down while dragging out a new *Sphere3D* on the *Canvas*. As long as you keep the LMB pressed, you can adjust the size of the sphere on the canvas. If you now press and hold down the *Shift* key on your keyboard while still creating the sphere, the model will lock to a 90° or 45° angle.

To turn the sphere into an object you can sculpt, the next thing you must do is click the *Edit* button at the top of the ZBrush menu bar, directly over the *Canvas*. Alternatively, you can press the *T* key on your keyboard, which is the shortcut to the *Edit* button. Doing so tells ZBrush to stop thinking of your sphere as a painting and start thinking of it as a three-dimensional object. As a result, you should see a small 3D head model and a colorful gadget appear in the upper

FIGURE 4.6 Click and hold down the left mouse button while dragging the mouse to draw a sphere.

FIGURE 4.7 Press the *Edit* button to work in 3D mode.

right-hand corner of the *Canvas*, as well as a white line along the outside edge of the *Document*.

Once you start placing things on the canvas, you will see a small white rectangle in the upper left-hand corner of the canvas. This rectangle shows you the current document's alpha channel, or silhouette, of whatever you have placed on the canvas. If you forget to activate the *Edit* button, you will end up drawing multiple spheres on the canvas instead. If you accidentally make a bunch of spheres on the canvas, you can use the *Document > New Document* command to start over on a fresh canvas or use the *Layer > Clear* button to get rid of your work, as we did earlier. Then, you can draw another sphere on the blank canvas and press *Edit* to activate the 3D mode.

You must adhere to this strict workflow to get ZBrush to do anything productive. Getting anything useful from the program will be immensely challenging if you deviate from this basic 3D workflow. However, once you have mastered the basics, the program opens up a wondrous assortment of possibilities.

If you haven't already done so, go ahead and draw a single *Sphere3D* on the Canvas and press *Edit* to get into 3D mode. Now, look at the upper right-hand corner of the interface within the *Tool* menu, find the *Sphere3D* icon, and click on it. The tool we most recently worked on

FIGURE 4.8 Click on the large sphere icon and then select the *Spiral3D* icon.

should be the biggest icon in the group of tool icons. Clicking on this icon will open up a menu that allows you to select a different 3D mesh quickly. Go ahead and pick one of these other meshes, say the *Spiral3D* mesh, and watch what happens. A spiral immediately replaces the sphere model. Don't panic! You can swap right back to your previous model by simply clicking on its icon in the same menu. All of the icons in the *Tool* location are the tools currently loaded into active memory, and you can swap between them effortlessly. It is easy to have several different models (or tools, as ZBrush calls them) open simultaneously and be able to switch back and forth between them all.

Parametric meshes

Click on the *Sphere3D* icon again and load the sphere back onto the screen. If you click on the sphere on the canvas, ZBrush will give you a warning. That is because the sphere is still a parametric mesh. A parametric mesh is a polygonal primitive object. A parametric model allows you to use the *Initialize* menu to adjust its settings and topology (i.e., shape). Go to *Tool > Initialize* and take a look at all of the settings therein. You can use the Initialize menu to adjust the size, coverage, and resolution by using the *X Size, Y Size, Z Size, HDivide,* and *VDivide* sliders. Play around with these settings and observe the results on the screen.

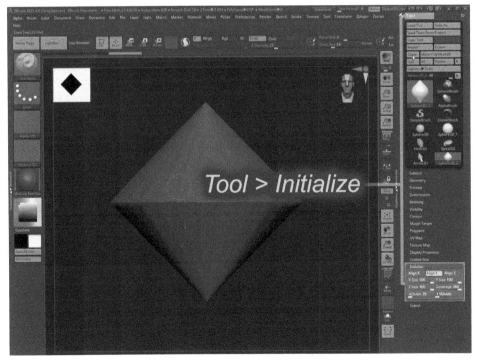

FIGURE 4.9 Use *Tool > Initialize* to adjust parametric objects.

Now select a *Helix3D* parametric object within the *Tool* palette. Go to *Tool* > *Initialize* menu and click on *Thickness*. The *Thickness Curve* graph that opens up can be adjusted to change the spiral. First, try moving the small white point in the upper left corner of the graph around and watch what this does to the shape of the object. Now, try clicking in the middle of the graph. Doing so should place a new control point on the curve and give you more control over the *Helix3D*'s shape. To delete this new point, grab it by holding the *LMB* while on top of that point, dragging it off the graph to one side, and then letting go of the mouse button. Now add the point back in, grab it again, and this time, when you drag off one side, keep pressing the *LMB* down and drag the point back onto the graph. Doing so will convert the control point from a smooth curve to a sharp linear control point and give you a different effect on the *Thickness* value for the helix. Finally, press the *Reset* button just underneath the *Thickness Curve* graph to restore the default settings.

If you press and hold down the LMB or right mouse button (RMB) on the background of the canvas behind the object, you can rotate your view around the object on the screen. If ZBrush does something else, such as drawing a new sphere, that means that you aren't in *Edit* mode. If this is the case, you need to clear the *Layer* and start over by drawing a new *Sphere3D* on the document canvas and then pressing the *Edit* button immediately after doing so. Remember from the last chapter

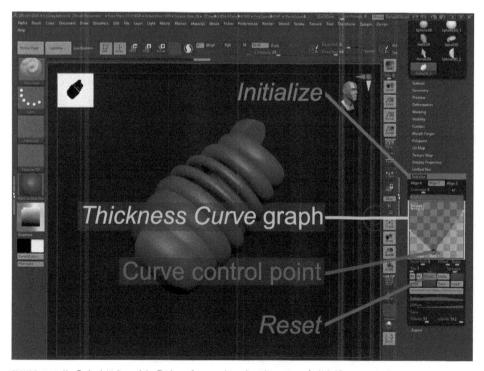

FIGURE 4.10 Use *Tool* > *Initialize* and the *Thickness Curve* graph to adjust the settings of a *Helix3D* parametric object.

FIGURE 4.11 The canvas border plus the *Frame, Move, Zoom3D,* and *Rotate* buttons.

that combining the ALT key while holding down either the LMB or RMB on the background will let you pan (i.e., move) the camera around. Holding down the CTR + ALT keys while pressing the RMB will let you dolly the camera (i.e., move closer or further away). Alternatively, you can use the ALT key + LMB to start moving about, then let go of the ALT key to dolly the camera – practice orbiting, panning, and dollying your view around for a bit. If you zoom in really close to your model, there may not be any background for you to click on to do these operations. If that is the case, you can click anywhere between the outer edge of the canvas document and the thin white border line that frames it. ZBrush treats this area as part of the canvas background. You can also use the *Move, Zoom3D,* and *Rotate* buttons near the bottom on the right side of the canvas document by simply holding down the LMB and dragging while on the button. If you get lost, press the *Frame* button or use the *F* shortcut key to center and zoom your object to the middle of the canvas document. These are the most common actions in ZBrush. It helps to be comfortable doing them.

Sculpting a mesh

To sculpt your sphere, go to the *Tool* menu and press the *Make PolyMesh3D* button near the top of the menu. As soon as you do that, ZBrush converts the *Sphere3D* primitive into a *PM3D_Sphere3D* object.

71

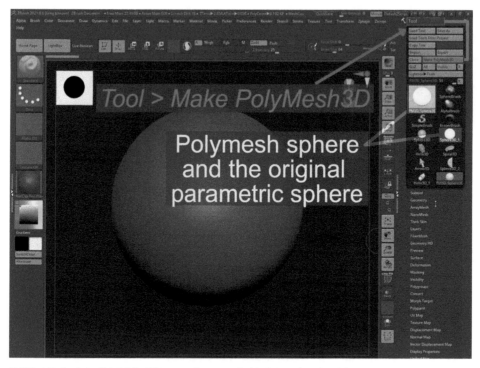

FIGURE 4.12 Use *Tool* > *Make PolyMesh3D* to convert the parametric object into a polymesh model.

You will now see an icon for your PM3D_Sphere3D object as well as the Sphere3D icon nearby at the icons at the top of the Tool menu. ZBrush doesn't simply convert the parametric object. Instead, it makes a new copy, converts it, and leaves the original model intact and available in the Tool menu.

ZBrush will often quietly place the results of an operation into the stack of active tools. Unfortunately, this approach can be a severe source of confusion for new users who don't think to look in the Tool menu for the results of a command that they just used. So, if you ever perform an operation in ZBrush and don't see any results, make sure that you check your active tools to see if ZBrush sneaked the results into the tool stack without telling you about it.

Now that we have an editable polymesh, let's take a look around the interface some more. Notice that after you click anywhere on your model, the camera will now orbit around that spot. Now, look along the right edge of the canvas, find the *Floor* button, and activate it (or press SHIFT+P to use the shortcut). The button will turn orange to indicate that it is active. If you rotate your view around, you will see that your model now sits on a grid. At the center of this grid, you should see a very faint set of axes. Red indicates the X-axis, green the Y-axis, and blue the Z-axis. This color coding for the axis is standard among 3D packages. The colored axis represents the center of ZBrush's mathematical universe – the 0, 0, 0 coordinate position in space. It is an excellent idea to keep your polymeshes centered above this point while you model them. It will make quite a lot of operations in ZBrush much more predictable if you can keep your model centered in ZBrush's world space by doing so.

Look at the upper right corner of the canvas. You should see a small RGB-colored icon. This colorful widget allows you to quickly align your camera to a specific axis by simply clicking on the color of the axis you want to look down along. Just remember that RGB=XYZ while you navigate these XYZ controllers, and you will do just fine. If you click on the same axis a second time, it will flip your view to the opposite side.

Immediately to the left of the RGB navigation widget, you should find a small head model. This head is the *CamView* figure. It can help orient you and your model in space. One look at the small head should let you know the face of your object. You can even click and drag on the head to orbit your viewpoint around.

If the object suddenly disappears while you are working, don't worry; it is just a glitch. Just click anywhere in the ZBrush interface, and the model should pop right back. Unfortunately, ZBrush sometimes has trouble communicating with certain graphics cards and drivers. When it does, your object on the screen can vanish until you force ZBrush to refresh the view screen.

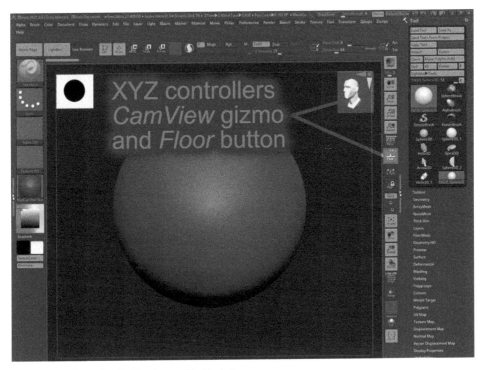

FIGURE 4.13 XYZ controllers, *CamView* gizmo, and the *Floor* button.

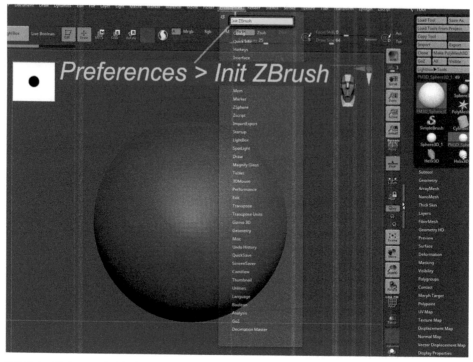

FIGURE 4.14 Preferences > Init ZBrush.

Let's stop exploring the interface now and get to work. If you want to start completely fresh in ZBrush, go to the *Preferences* menu bar and click the *Initialize* button (*Preferences > Initialize*). Doing so essentially restarts ZBrush without exiting the program and clears everything done earlier.

Select your Sphere3D model, draw it on the screen, and press the *Edit* button to go into 3D mode. Now press the *Make PolyMesh3D* button to convert your sphere into an editable polymesh. This process is the starting sequence for most models built inside of ZBrush.

Now press and hold down your LMB on the sphere and drag your mouse across it. Now you are sculpting! Try drawing a few more lines on your sphere to get the hang of it.

If you look immediately above the canvas, you will find the *Undo History* selector bar. You can use this to undo and redo your actions in ZBrush. You can find the actual edit and redo buttons inside the *Edit* menu, or you can use the CTRL+Z shortcut to undo and the CTRL+SHIFT+Z shortcut to redo an action in ZBrush. If you mess up, then just go back to *Preferences > Init ZBrush* to start over.

Remember that if you rest your mouse pointer over any button, ZBrush will provide a pop-up window that will let you know the name of that function and tell you the shortcut for that command as well. If you

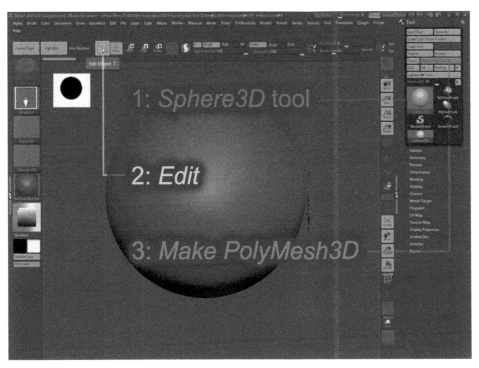

FIGURE 4.15 1: Draw the *Sphere3D* on the canvas. 2: Press the *Edit* button. 3: Click the *Make PolyMesh3D* button.

FIGURE 4.16 The *Undo History* selector and the *Edit > Undo* and *Redo* buttons.

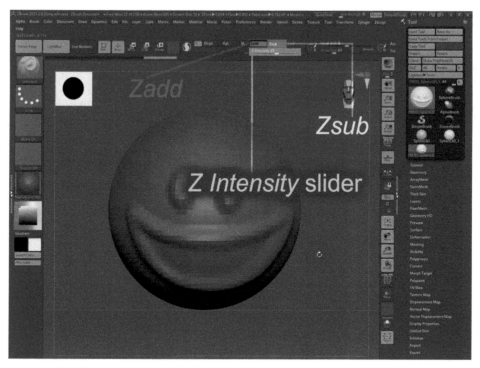

FIGURE 4.17 *Zadd*, *Zsub*, and the *Z Intensity* slider.

press down the CTRL button while doing this, ZBrush will give you helpful information about that function. It is a straightforward and elegant means of providing access to the ZBrush help files.

Try sculpting a simple face on your sphere. By default, ZBrush is pulling the surface towards the camera. This *Zadd* is the default behavior for many brushes in ZBrush. You can find the *Zadd* button just on top of the canvas. Next to *Zadd* is the *Zsub* button. Pressing this inverts the behavior of the brush. With *Zsub* active, your brush strokes now push the model away from the camera. You can press the ALT button while sculpting to switch to the other behavior. Just underneath the *Zadd* and *Zsub* buttons is the *Z Intensity* slider, which adjusts the strength of the brush. When you are sculpting, if you make a brushstroke that you like, you can press the number "1" key on your keyboard to repeat the stroke. Go ahead and try it!

Using DynaMesh

Turn on the *Draw Polyframe* button, located underneath the *Rotate* button just to the right side of the canvas, or use the SHIFT+F shortcut to turn it on. ZBrush will now outline the edges of all of your model's polygons. Doing so will give us a graphic view of the object's geometry that we're working on right now. You can now see that this is a rather low-resolution object for ZBrush. If you rest your mouse over the icon of your current object in the Tool menu, you can see the current polygon count of your model. A ZBrush sphere, our starting object, defaults to around 8,192 polygons unless you play with its Initialize settings before converting it to a Polymesh object. As we sculpt our model, the polygons get more and more stretched out and begin to look quite funky. To solve this problem, we need to give our model some more polygons. The method we will focus on, pretty much throughout this book, can be found in the *Tool* menu. Click on the *Geometry* label to open that sub-menu. Now, find the *DynaMesh* label and open its sub-menu. When you press the big *DynaMesh* button, ZBrush will resurface and rebuild the entire model. If you have the *Draw Polyframe* button active, you can watch the geometry change. You can get different numbers of polygons in the resulting mesh by altering the value of the *Resolution* slider below the big *DynaMesh* button. You can undo the operation, change the *Dynamesh Resolution* slider value, and press *DynaMesh* again to see the difference. Be careful! Setting the *Resolution* slider too high can result in a mesh with tens of millions of polygons and can crash ZBrush if set too high. After you dynamesh your object, you can check the poly count of your model by resting the mouse on top of the object's icon and then turning off *Draw Polyframe* (SHIFT + F) if you still have it on.

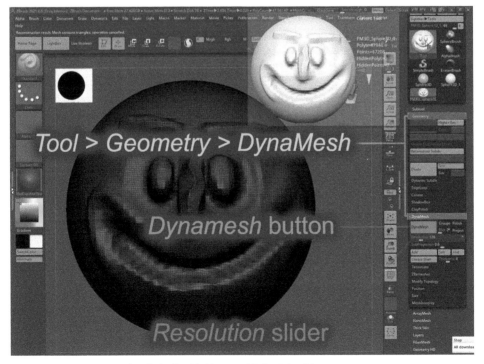

FIGURE 4.18 Tool > Geometry > DynaMesh > DynaMesh button and the Resolution slider.

FIGURE 4.19 CTRL + LMB click and drag on the canvas background while the *DynaMesh* button is active to DynaMesh your object.

Whenever you make a bunch of significant changes to your model and begin to see your polygons stretch out or otherwise deform, you can use DynaMesh to rebuild your model and then continue sculpting. If the *DynaMesh* button is turned on (active buttons are orange), you can dynamesh your object by holding down CTRL, then LMB click and drag a small dark gray rectangle out on the canvas background. Doing so will invoke the DynaMesh function, just as if you had turned off the big DynaMesh button and then turned it back on again. You have to be careful with this since holding down the CTRL button is the shortcut to access the Masking brushes, and ZBrush will not let you use DynaMesh if any part of your mesh is masked. If you accidentally mask part of your object (part of the object will turn gray), you can clear the mask by pressing the *Tool > Masking > Clear* button.

Sculptris pPro mMode

Another way of adding geometry to your model is to do so while you sculpt with your brush. To do this, turn on the *Activate Sculptris Pro Mode* button located in the middle of the *Top Shelf* row of icons or press the \ shortcut. With the *Activate Sculptris Pro Mode* button active, ZBrush will add new polygons to the model as you sculpt. Typically, this results in a very dense mesh, and you will need to carefully keep track of your polygon count if you use this feature. *Sculptris Pro Mode* can

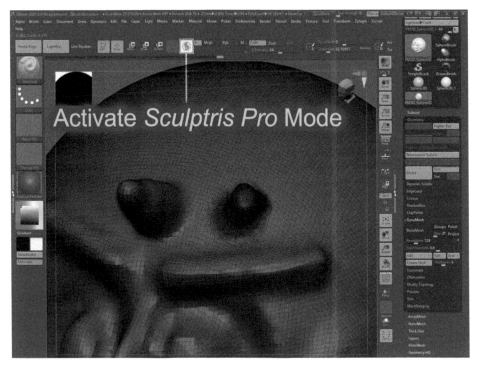

FIGURE 4.20 The *Activate Sculptris Pro Mode* button.

be useful for adding in areas of high resolution only where needed on your model. Once finished, remember to turn *Sculptris Pro Mode* off by clicking on the *Activate Sculptris Pro Mode* button again.

Subdivision

The other way of increasing the resolution of your model is using subdivision. When you subdivide your model, you take every polygon and insert new edges in the middle of each existing edge in all of your model's polygons.

This subdivision process happens across the entire model, effectively multiplying the total number of polygons in your model by four. To subdivide your model, go to *Tool > Geometry* and press the large *Divide* button there. Subdividing your model can quickly build up extremely high polygon counts that will overwhelm your system if you abuse the *Divide* button too much. After you subdivide your model, you can use the *SDiv* (Subdivision Level) slider to control which subdivision level you are currently working on.

Interestingly, ZBrush keeps track of the detail on each level of subdivision separately, a fact we will return to later on when we start detailing our final model.

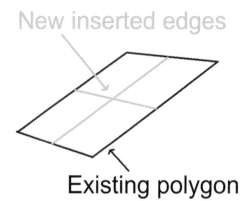

New inserted edges

Existing polygon

FIGURE 4.21 Subdividing a polygon.

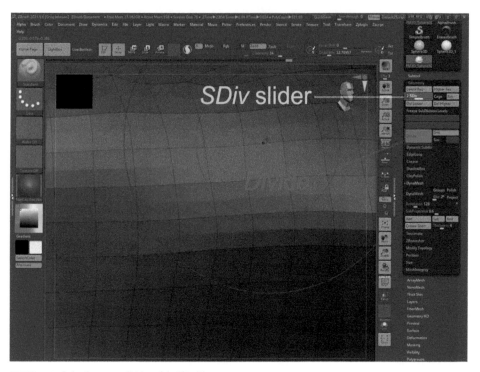

SD*iv* slider

FIGURE 4.22 *Tool > Geometry > Divide*, and the *SDiv* slider.

Symmetry

Let's start a completely new model now. Use *Preferences > Initialize* to refresh ZBrush. Initialize blasts any unsaved information, like the model we were working on, out of existence. Go ahead and draw a new sphere on the screen, turn on *Edit* mode, and press the *Make PolyMesh3D* button again to make an editable sphere that you can sculpt. Before we go any further, I should teach you a simple trick to

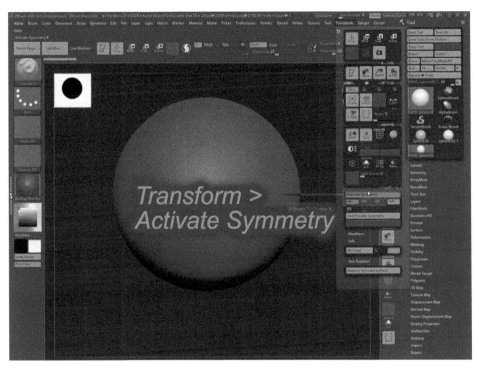

FIGURE 4.23 *Transform > Activate Symmetry*, and the >*X*<, >*Y*<, and >*Z*< axis options.

make you more productive in ZBrush. Open the *Transform* menu on the main menu bar, find the *Activate Symmetry* button, and turn it on. You can also use the X shortcut key to toggle symmetry on and off. With symmetry turned on, try sculpting your model. By default, symmetry uses the X-axis as its center. However, you can use the symmetry menu to activate the Y or Z axis either singly or in combination as well. After turning the Symmetry button on, when you look at the front of your object, you should see an additional red dot mirroring your brush's movements.

The smooth brush

Right now, we are working with our *Standard* brush, whose icon you can see at the upper left side of the menu just under the large *Home Page* button. If you hold down the SHIFT button on your keyboard, you will see the currently selected *Standard* brush change to the *Smooth* brush for as long as you keep the button pressed down. You can use the Smooth brush to smooth out details and blend your forms. The brush settings for the Smooth brush are independent from those used for the *Standard* brush. Keep in mind while working that the Smooth brush has a more substantial effect on low polygon objects. A good workflow within ZBrush is to sculpt in a form, smooth it down a bit,

FIGURE 4.24 *Smooth* brush.

then build it back, smooth it down again, and keep repeating this
process until you have the shape you want. Slowly building up your
model's features like this will give you a more subtle and sophisticated
sculpt than just hammering in your details directly. Take some time,
have some fun, and familiarize yourself with the program until you are
comfortable with it. ZBrush is a large and complex program, so we're
just covering the essential elements in this session's workflow. You will
need to be comfortable with the program before you can move on to
more complicated tasks.

Saving your work – 3D tools

There are several different ways to save what you have been working
on inside ZBrush. You have to be very aware of which method you
are using to save your file. To save the 3D model you are working
on, use the *Tool > Save As* button to save the model as a ZBrush tool.
To do so, click on the *Tool > Save As* button, give your file a name,
and make sure that you are saving your file in a location on your
computer that you will be able to remember later on. This process
saves a ZTL, or ZTool, file. Unfortunately, ZBrush is pretty much
the only program in the world that reads the ZTL file format. Usually, this is a manageable hurdle since ZBrush works on files with

FIGURE 4.25 *Tool > Save As* and the *Tool > Export* option.

millions of polygons. Taking a model with several million polygons into another 3D program other than ZBrush will probably crash that program since most programs cannot handle the kind of polygon counts that ZBrush typically uses. If you do need to get your file into another 3D package, then you can use the *Tool > Export* button to export the model from ZBrush using a different file format, such as OBJ (a generic object file), MA (Maya ASCII), or STL (for 3D printing). Please make sure you always give your files meaningful names to quickly identify them later on.

To load your model back into ZBrush, go to *Tool > Load Tool* and then find your file using the standard file explorer interface that then pops up. Doing so will load your file into the list of active tools. You can then select that tool, draw it onto your canvas document, turn on the *Edit* button, and start modifying your sculpture from there.

Saving your work – canvas document

If you want to save just the canvas document, then use the *Document > Save* button. Be very careful with this one. This command saves the canvas document (the picture on the screen), not the model, and nothing else – just the image. Users were confused

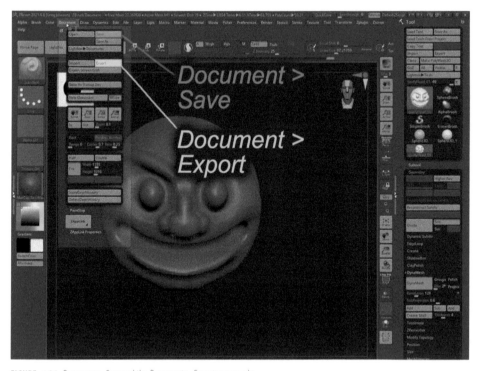

FIGURE 4.26 *Document > Save* and the *Document > Export* commands.

enough by this command that ZBrush added a warning popup that appears when using the *Document > Save* button to warn users that their 3D model is not getting saved. The *Save Document* button creates a ZBR file type. Unfortunately, the only program that reads a ZBR file is ZBrush itself. Using the *Document > Export* button is frequently more helpful. *Document > Export* saves more widely used file formats. Use the TIFF (archival format), BMP (Windows), or PSD (Photoshop) file formats to save a large but uncompressed file, or you can create a compressed web-compatible file format such as PNG or JPG.

If you choose *Document > Export* and select the JPG file format, ZBrush will open the *Export Image* options interface. Use this interface to set the *Quality* of the JPG image (choose 100 if you want a high-quality picture). You can also adjust the four *Crop* marks to set the boundaries of your new JPG image. After selecting the options you want, press *OK* to create the file. Remember that the *Document > Save, Save As,* and *Export* buttons make a simple image of what you are working on and nothing else. To load a ZBR ZDoc back into the program, use *Document > Open*. Alternatively, you can use the *Document > Import* command to bring in a wide variety of different image formats onto the canvas.

FIGURE 4.27 Setting the *Document* > *Export* - JPG options.

Saving your work – files

The last save option that we will discuss in this session is found at
File > *Save As*. Using this option saves the entire ZBrush project. This file
includes your current model and any other loaded tools, lights, canvas
document information, and everything else about your current ZBrush
session. It essentially saves everything in your current ZBrush session.
While this is a safe method to keep your work, it does have the draw-
back of creating huge files. You can use the *File* > *Open* command to
load your saved session file back into ZBrush when you need it again.

Occasionally, you will encounter a problem where a duplicate of your
model appears on the canvas. If this happens, don't panic. You have
merely bumped the Shift + S shortcut or turned off *Edit* mode by
accident. To get rid of the extra copies, use the *Layer* > *Clear* command.
If you turned off edit mode completely, create a new document using
Document > *New Document* or do a *Layer* > *Clear* and draw your tool
back onto the canvas, then activate *Edit* mode again.

Conclusion

After reading this chapter and watching the accompanying video, spend some time playing around inside ZBrush and getting used to this interface. Familiarize yourself with the basic commands you've learned so far until you're comfortable with orbiting, zooming, and panning around a 3D model. Next, try your hand at sculpting six different little funny faces or heads. Creating a cartoon head or face out of a sphere is good practice and provides an excellent opportunity for you to be creative. If you want a challenge, then give each face a different emotion and expression. Create each face quickly. These are just for practice, so keep each one quick and low-resolution. Use this exercise to ensure that you know how to do all of the procedures discussed in this chapter. Make sure that you watch the video associated with this chapter to help you understand all of the methods we have gone over. Finally, make sure that you know how to save and load your work back into ZBrush. Without a doubt, ZBrush has the most challenging learning curve of any popular 3D modeling package in the world today. It is very non-standard and has many unique commands, weird workflows, and unusual processes that no other 3D package has. This odd workflow makes the first week or two of learning this package extremely difficult. With that in mind, take your time and be patient. ZBrush rewards practice.

5

The Fish, Part 1 – The Primary Form

Introduction

In this chapter, we are going to put our newfound knowledge to use and build a proper 3D model. Since we are still in the early stages of our ZBrush experience, it is best to keep our goals reasonable. With that in mind, we are going to make a fish! A fish is a great place to start since it is easy to find reference material and because a fish does not require a lot of complicated details to create. We will make the sculpture a bit cartoony since hyper-realistic models are more difficult than artsy or abstract ones. That approach will also let us have some fun with the model. If you have a difficult time getting your model to look like you want it to, don't stress out. It usually takes a handful of tries before your models begin to look the way you want them to. With our goal now set, let's get started!

First off, we can decide what kind of fish we want to make. Since I am partial to local fish, I think that the Yellow Perch (Perca flavescens) would make an excellent choice for a starting 3D sculpt. A little digging on the internet provides a usable, out-of-copy image for us to use as a reference picture.

Launch ZBrush if it isn't already open on your computer. Close the ZBrush home page pop-up, then turn off the LightBox interface (press the, on your keyboard). If ZBrush is already open and you need to start fresh, then you can get ZBrush into working order by initializing it (Preferences > Init ZBrush, then say Yes to the little warning pop-up that appears). Afterward, finish setting up your document by changing the range to zero (Document > Range = 0) and picking a background color (Document > Back, click and drag to choose a neutral gray color).

DOI: 10.1201/9781003215288-5

FIGURE 5.1 Yellow Perch, illustration by Waterhouse Hawkins, 1836.

Once you have gotten ZBrush set up, go to the Tool menu, find the large golden "S" icon, and click on it. Choose the Sphere3D object from the list of 3D meshes. Next, go to the center of the Document Canvas, and click and drag using the left mouse button to draw a sphere. Try holding down the Shift key while you make the sphere to lock it to a 45° or 90° angle. Make the sphere nice and big, and then let go of your mouse. The very next thing you must do is press the Edit button at the top of the canvas or press "T" on your keyboard for the shortcut to the Edit command. Once you have a sphere drawn on the screen and are in Edit mode, go up into the Transform menu at the top of the page and turn on Activate Symmetry, or you can simply press the "X" key on your keyboard to use the shortcut. These initial steps are the same ones we took in the last chapter. Take a moment to review the process in that chapter if you need to reference the picture guides or video.

There are many various approaches to sculpting 3D models in ZBrush. It is important to pick the right approach for the project you are working on because each approach entails a different specific workflow. One of the most versatile approaches to modeling in ZBrush is that of concept sculpting, and it is this method that I will focus on in this book. To begin building a concept sculpture, you start by creating the primary form of the model. During this step, you block out the basic shapes of the model you are building. The goal of the first step is to get your model's overall shape and silhouette established. Once you have sculpted the primary forms, you can construct your secondary features such as the muscle structures, folds, and other elements that uniquely define the look of your model. Only after the secondary features are finished do you go back in and add tertiary details such as wrinkles, scales, pores, eyelashes, and other fine details. Afterward, you can proceed with painting, posing, lighting, and rendering your model. The first steps are the most critical. If you mess up the primary form, no amount of work on the secondary shapes or details will salvage the model. It is important to be finished with a given stage before you move on to the next one. Otherwise, you will end up having to redo your work and make time-consuming fixes while the overall quality of your final model deteriorates. To sum up:

- Establish your primary form.
- Create your secondary features.
- Add the tertiary details and polish.

You want to work on each step as a whole. In other words, do not go in and bring one piece of the model up to the detailing phase when other parts are still getting their primary or secondary forms established. If you do this, then your final model will look uneven, and the pieces will not match each other. Work in unified steps, making the primary shapes of the whole model, then the secondary shapes of the entire model, and then the tertiary details for the whole model. Build up your sculpture by working in layers on the overall thing, not in a piecemeal fashion. Don't skip back and forth. Work progressively from the largest structures in the model down to the smallest and most granular details. The result will be a much more consistent-looking and unified sculpture.

Unlike other 3D modeling packages, ZBrush really cares about your drawing skills. If you decide that you are serious about developing your ZBrush skills, then improving your drawing skills will have to be part of the process. Make sure that you always have a sketchbook with you. Anytime you have a moment, take out your sketchbook and draw whatever you see. Sketching will train your hands and eyes to work together and improve your drawing and observation skills. Take some drawing classes, and set aside some time every day to practice your drawing skills. You will also want to work on your anatomy skills. You will need to take what's called a constructive human anatomy course at some point in which you construct a person from the inside out to learn all of the skeletal and muscle structures. Known as an écorché figure – this is a drawing or sculpture of a human body done without the skin. In this process, you first build the skeleton, then lay on all the muscles, add in all of the viscera and fat, and finally add on the skin and hair. You literally build up a person from the inside out in clay or on paper. Doing this process is the best way for an artist to learn anatomy. It isn't so much about what each muscle or bone is called as it is about

FIGURE 5.2 Écorché arm.

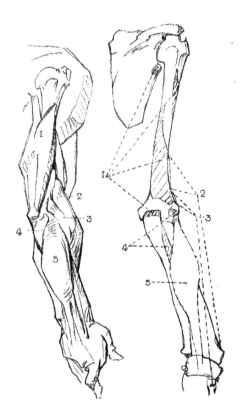

what they look like and how they function and move. There isn't any substitute for learning how to do this. I cannot stress this enough: if you are serious about ZBrush, then you must master drawing and anatomy! While this stuff falls beyond the scope of this book (after all, this is just an introductory text), you can take a look at the books written by Madeline Scott Spencer once you have finished this book. Her ZBrush books are really good for learning intermediate and advanced ZBrush skills and form a very good next step in your ZBrush evolution once you've mastered the basics through this book.

If you decide that you really like ZBrush and want to make a good investment in honing your digital art skills, then I can wholeheartedly suggest buying a good Wacom tablet (www.wacom.com). Some off-brand digital drawing tablets can also work, but Wacom is the industry standard, being very reliable and technically well-supported. Wacom tablets come in a wide variety of shapes and sizes, but you don't need one of the really big, expensive tablets. One of the small, six-by-nine or even five-by-four-inch tablets will do – but the smaller tablets do take a week or two to get used to since you have to train your eye to look at the screen while you draw with your hand on the tablet. The large tablets, where you draw on the screen itself, are more intuitive to use, but they are also ten times more expensive than the small tablets. I have used all of the various types of Wacom tablets available, and the choice really just comes down to budget.

Brushes and brush controls

Let's get to making our model. Begin by going over to the top left side of the interface and finding a large icon that should look like a gray sphere with a squiggle drawn on it. That icon is for the *Standard Brush*. Click on it to open up the *Brush Palette*. Inside is a wall of icons. These are all of the brushes loaded into ZBrush by default. To select a brush, simply click on its icon.

The palette is a bit overwhelming until you realize that the vast majority of these brushes are specialty brushes; in other words, they're only there for one very narrow use and aren't commonly utilized. In fact, there are only a handful that we're actually going to be using to do basic sculpting. Here is a brief list of brushes that you should try out:

- *Clay*
- *ClayBuildup*
- *ClayTubes*

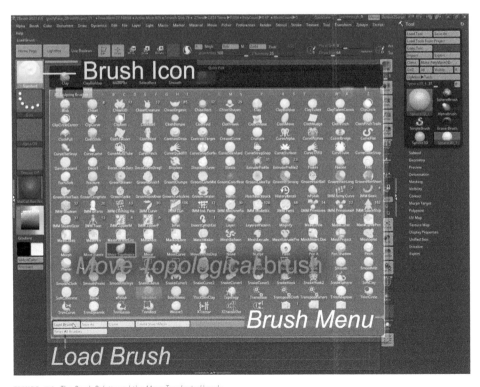

FIGURE 5.3 The *Brush Palette* and the *Move Topological* brush.

- *ClayTubesConstant*
- *DamStandard*
- *hPolish*
- *Inflate*
- *Layer*
- *LayeredPattern*
- *Move Topological*
- *Move*
- *Pinch*
- *Planar*
- *Polish*
- *Rake*
- *sPolish*

Go ahead and try these brushes out and see what they do. Take your time. There is no rush. If you don't like what the brush does, then simply undo it.

Some of the brushes in this palette should be left alone for the time being. The *Chisel* brushes, *Clip*, *Cloth*, *Curve*, *Extrude*, *Groom*, *IMM*, *Mask*, *Mesh*, *Slice*, *StitchBasic*, *Topology*, *Transpose*, *Trim*, *XTractor*, *ZModeler*, *ZProject*, and *ZRemersherGuide* brushes are all either too narrow in function or difficult to use, and we are going to avoid those for the time being. There are a few others, like the Snake brushes, which have some options that you will need to know before using them. We will get to these brushes a bit later. If these brushes weren't enough, at the bottom left-hand corner of the *Brush Palette* is the *Load Brush* command. There are a couple of hundred extra brushes sitting on the hard drive, which you can load up to access.

What we are looking for right now is a brush to move our shape around. We could use either the *Move* or *Move Topological* brush for this. There's a subtle difference between how these two brushes work. The *Move* brush does just that. Any part, or parts, of the model under the brush moves in the direction you drag the brush, so long as you keep the LMB held down. The *Draw Size* setting of the *Move* brush determines what part(s) of the model are affected. The *Move Topological* brush, on the other hand, also uses the distance along the surface of our object in conjunction with the *Draw Size* setting to determine what parts of our object are affected. What this means is that if you're working on, say, a hand and you want to move just one digit out of the five on the hand. If you use the *Move* brush, it's going to move that finger and anything else the brush touches. If you use the *Move Topological* brush, you can adjust each finger individually without messing up the other fingers because the brush includes the distance along the surface of your model in the brush calculations. Typically, I default to using the *Move Topological* brush when working. I find that brush a little easier to work with, but this is just a personal preference. You can use either the *Move* or *Move Topological* brush or the next step. Go ahead and try both brushes and see which one you like better.

Take a look up at the top row of buttons and find the *Draw Size* slider on the right side. The *Draw Size* setting controls how big the current brush is. You can change the size of the current brush by either sliding the little gray knob on the slider around or by clicking on the button and typing in a specific value. If you press the "S" key shortcut on your keyboard, the *Draw Size* slider will pop up underneath your current mouse position. You can also use the "[" key to shrink the *Draw Size* or the "]" key on your keyboard to increase it. You can also simply press the "Spacebar" or right-mouse click on the canvas to bring up a quick interface that includes *Draw Size* at the top. For right now, make sure that you have the *Move Topological* brush selected and set your *Draw Size* to a very large value. In the demo video that goes along with this book, the *Draw Size* value is set to around 500, but what constitutes a "large" value in ZBrush can vary depending on the size of the object you are working on.

Just above the *Draw Size* slider, you should see the *Focal Shift* slider. *Focal Shift* controls how hard the edges of your current brush are. Moving the *Focal Shift* slider to the right or typing in a positive number

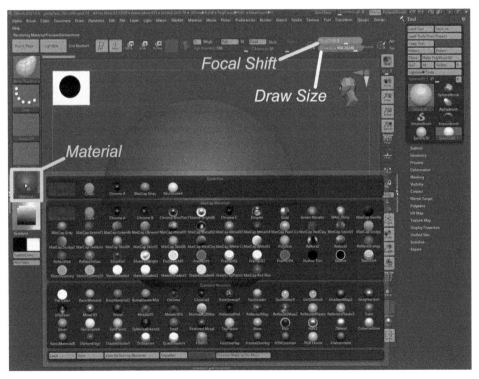

FIGURE 5.4 Draw size, focal shift, and material.

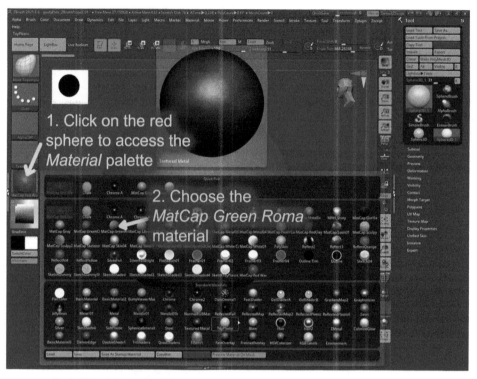

FIGURE 5.5 Use the *Material* palette to change the object's current material.

between 01 and 100 softens the brush. Moving the *Focal Shift* slider to the left or typing in a negative number between −01 and −100 hardens the edges of the brush. The shortcut to the *Focal Shift* slider is the "o" key. Your brush on the screen provides you with a graphic representation of the *Focal Shift* setting. You should see an inner circle and an outer circle on your mouse cursor while hovering over the ZBrush canvas. Everything within your brush's inner circle has 100% of the effect. The outer circle denotes the limit of the brush's effect. The area between the inner and outer circles marks the fall-off between the maximum and minimum levels of effect.

Picking a material

To help you see the brush, it helps to change the material of our object to something other than the default *MatCap Red Wax* material. After all, it is difficult to see the red outline for our brush icon against the red of the default material. To change materials, simply click on the large red sphere icon on the left-hand side of the screen that should say "*MatCap Red Wax*" underneath it. Doing so opens up the *Material* palette, which is much like the *Brush* palette menu. At the top is the *Quick Pick* list of materials that you have recently used. The middle section consists of the various *MatCap Materials*. *MatCap Materials* have lighting baked into the material as well as color and material information. At the bottom are the *Standard Materials*, which will respond to any lights that you may add to your scene file later on. For the moment, don't worry about the specific details of the various materials. Simply choose the *MatCap GreenRoma* material. You should see the appearance of your model change to match the material that you have just chosen. Whenever you select a new material in ZBrush, your model will automatically update to it, unless you have deliberately assigned a material to the model. This quick change method for swapping materials is a handy feature that allows you to quickly see what a given material will look like on your sculpture before you permanently assign a material to the model. Go ahead and try out a few other materials and see what they look like. Once you are finished trying out various materials, choose the *MatCap GreenRoma* material and proceed.

Making and moving a PolyMesh3D object

Now go to the *Tool* menu and click the *Make PolyMesh3D* button to convert the sphere into an editable model. Make sure that you have turned on *Symmetry* by checking that the *Transform > Activate Symmetry* button and the *X* icon are turned on. Both buttons should be bright orange. You should have the *Move Topological* brush selected and the material set to *MatCap GreenRoma*. Use the *Move Topological* brush to push in one side of the sphere to create a large indentation and form a sideways bowl shape. Next, pull the upper lip of this bowl out and over to form the upper jaw and face of our fish. Now, go pull the lower lip of the bowl out and up to create the lower jaw. Push and pull the face around until you are happy with the shape. Go to the reverse side opposite the face, the bottom of the bowl, and just pull this side straight out away from the rest of the object to form the rear of the fish's body.

Take a moment and rotate all around your model to check and make sure that it looks okay from various angles of view. It is a good habit to perform this sort of check periodically. Otherwise, you might inadvertently make a mistake that you cannot see from the viewpoint you are working from. After doing this check, I noticed that the fish was a bit too thick in the cross-section. To fix this, simply make the brush size as large as possible (use the *Draw Size* slider or the S button), and then gently nudge the sides closer together from a top-down view of my model.

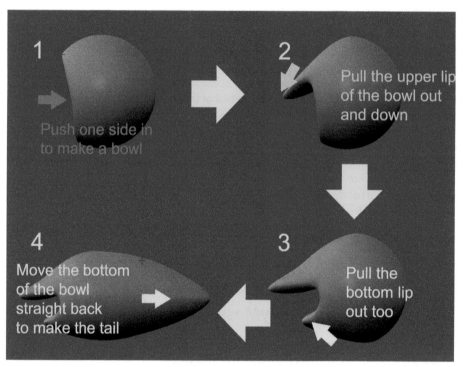

FIGURE 5.6 Use the *Move Topological* brush to rough out a fish shape.

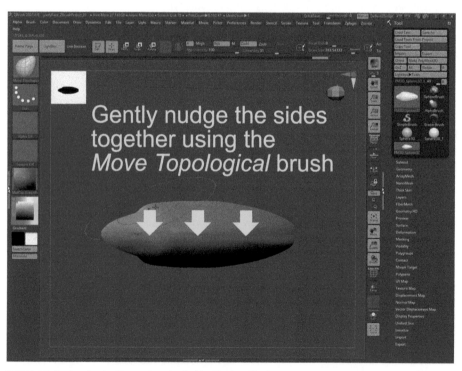

FIGURE 5.7 Gently nudge the sides together using the *Move Topological* brush.

Introducing DynaMesh

If you turn on the *PolyF* button (PolyFrame) on the right side of the canvas and look closely at the model, you will be able to see the polygons of our fish starting to distort. To fix this distortion, we should now retopologize our model, which will rebuild the polygons comprising it. Go to *Tool > Geometry > DynaMesh* and press the large *DynaMesh* button. *DynaMesh* will reconstruct the polygons of our model, creating a much denser polygonal mesh. You can adjust the number of polygons in the resulting mesh by changing the value of the *Resolution* slider immediately underneath the *DynaMesh* button. Right now, the default value of 128 will probably suffice. If you choose to change the *Resolution* slider before you use *DynaMesh*, just keep in mind that really high-resolution values can result in models so dense that they are difficult to work with or can even cause ZBrush to run out of memory and crash.

It is always a good idea to save the model you are working on using the *Tool > Save As* command before you perform any major operations on your model. I try to save my model at least once every 15 minutes or so just in case ZBrush crashes – that way, I never lose more than a little work when the system dies. ZBrush is very good about saving your current progress when it crashes and providing a recovery file in the

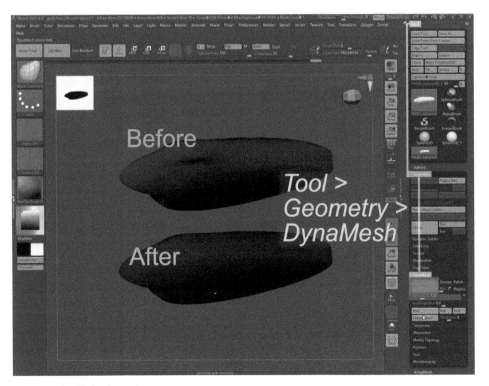

FIGURE 5.8 *DynaMesh* and its results.

LightBox when you restart the program. Even so, it is a good idea not to rely on ZBrush to back up your work since it will occasionally fail to automatically back up your files when you need them the most.

For your convenience, here is a step-by-step overview of the basic sculpting process in ZBrush.

Summary of 3D sculpting steps

1. Open ZBrush.
2. Close the ZBrush Home Page window.
3. Turn off the *LightBox* by pressing the *LightBox* button or "," on the keyboard.
4. In the *Document* menu, set the *Range = 0*, and set the *Back* color to a neutral gray.
5. Go to the *Tool* menu, click on the *SimpleBrush* icon and choose the *Sphere3D* mesh from the pop-up menu.
6. Press and hold down the left mouse button in the middle of the canvas and drag out a sphere model on screen. Hold down the Shift key while doing so to straighten up the model.
7. The very next thing you do after you release the mouse button is to click the *Edit* button or press "T" on your keyboard.
8. Click on *Tool > Make PolyMesh3D* to convert the parametric sphere into an editable mesh.
9. Turn on *Symmetry* on the *X* axis in the Transform menu.
10. Pick a suitable material, such as the *MatCap GreenRoma*, for your model.
11. Select a brush, such as the *Move Topological* brush, and start shaping your model.
12. Once you are finished, don't forget to go to *Tool > Save As* and save out the 3d model you have been working on.

Hold down the Shift key on your keyboard to switch to the *Smooth* brush and blend out any roughness in your model. When you are sculpting your model, it is a good idea to build up your features slowly, smooth those features down, and then build them up again. This building-up and smoothing process creates a level of detail and subtlety in your sculpture.

Transforming the model

You can also make more drastic changes to the whole model by transforming it using the *Move, Scale,* and *Rotate* buttons. These three buttons are located along the top of the *Canvas.* You can activate them by clicking on the transformation you are interested in or by using their keyboard shortcuts: *Move* [W], *Scale* [E], and *Rotate* [R]. When you click on any of these buttons, the *Gizmo 3D* transformation mechanism will appear on the screen. This interface gives you access to a number of different transformations. Clicking and dragging on one of the colored arrows allows you to move the object along that axis. Remember that red is the X-axis, green is the Y-axis, and blue is the Z-axis. Clicking and dragging on one of the colored circles performs a rotation along that axis, while using one of the colored boxes will scale along the chosen axis. Utilizing the central yellow cube will scale your model on all three axes simultaneously. If you use the gray circle around the gizmo, you can rotate your object perpendicular to your current camera view. Similarly, if you click and drag on one of the four gray corners just outside of the gray circle, you can move the object along your current viewing plane. Oddly enough, it doesn't really matter which of the transformation buttons or shortcuts you use. They all simply pop up with the same transformation gizmo. A very useful trick is that if you hold down the Shift key while you use one of these transformations, ZBrush will perform the transform operation in a regular numeric increment.

If you look carefully at the top of the *Gizmo 3D*, you can see a row of operators. From left to right, these are *Customize, Sticky Mode, Unmasked Center Mesh, Mesh To Axis, Reset Mesh Orientation, Lock/ Unlock,* and *Multiple Subtools.* The gear icon is *Customize,* which lets you access the settings and options for the *Gizmo 3D.* There are quite a large number of these options, and you can find a full description

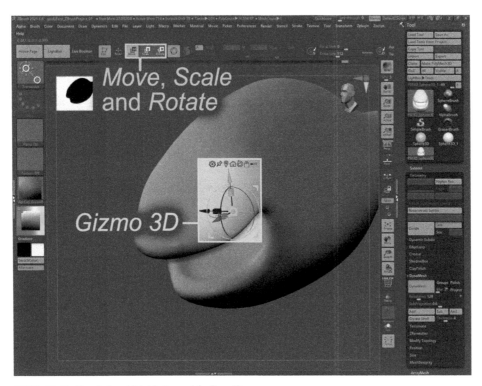

FIGURE 5.9 The *Move, Scale,* and *Rotate* buttons and the *Gizmo 3D.*

of all of them at the ZBrush Documentation website (docs.pixologic. com). Clicking the pin icon activates the sticky mode, which pins the Gizmo to the canvas as you move your model around. Clicking the inverted teardrop with a circle inside the icon, *Unmasked Center Mesh*, will move the gizmo to the center of the unmasked portion of your currently selected mesh. The *Mesh to Axis* home icon will move your object to the center of the global axis; that's the $x=0$, $y=0$, and $z=0$ position. The *Reset Mesh Orientation* icon, the small gray circle with an arrow, will reset the *Gizmo 3D* to its default orientation. If the *Lock* icon is unlocked, it will just reset the gizmo. If the lock is active, it will rotate the entire model along with the gizmo. If opened, the *Lock/Unlock* icon affects only the gizmo. If locked, the *Lock/Unlock* icon operates on the entire model. The final option, *Multiple Subtools*, allows you to transform multiple subtools at the same time.

If you want to transform your object precisely, just go to T*ool > Deformation* and find the *Offset*, *Rotate*, and *Size* sliders. You can click on any of these and input a specific number, or you can simply adjust the slider. If you look at the right-hand side of each slider, you will see a

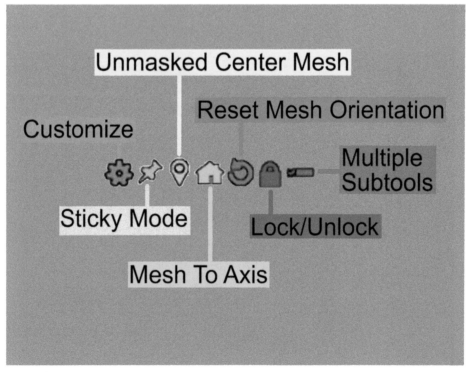

FIGURE 5.10 *Gizmo 3D* operators.

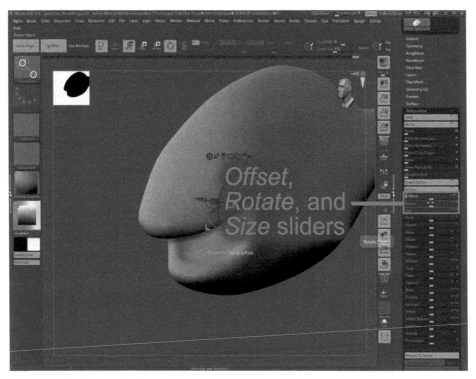

FIGURE 5.11 *Offset*, *Rotate*, and *Size* sliders.

tiny *X, Y,* and *Z.* You can click on any combination of these to control
what axis that slider will affect. Use the *Offset* slider to precisely move
your object around, *Size* to scale your object, and the *Rotate* slider for
rotations. One thing to keep in mind as you use these sliders is that
each slider resets to 0 after you use it. If you set the *Size* slider to 10 and
then take a look at the slider's value, it will be 0, not 10. If you type in 10
again, your object will just get even bigger. Immediately underneath
Size is a whole list of other *Deformation* tools. If you have some time, go
through each one and try it to see what it does.

The *hPolish* brush

After you have played a bit with the deformation tools, go back in with
your *Move* or *Move Topological* brush and finish roughing out the body
of your fish. If you need something a bit more subtle than the *Move*
brush, then you can try out the *hPolish* brush. To access this brush, you
can click on the large brush icon and then select the brush you want,
but it is a lot faster to learn how to use the proper shortcut to access

each brush. Simply press the *B* key on your keyboard to access the brush list. Now press the first letter of the name of the brush you are trying to use, in this case, *H*, on your keyboard. Pressing *H* isolates all of the brushes whose names begin with that letter. You should see a bright orange letter just to the left of each brush icon now. Press the letter next to the brush you'd like to select. For the *hPolish* brush, that would be *P*. To do the whole process quickly, simply press *B*, then *H*, then *P* in that order to shortcut to the *hPolish* brush. This key sequence should load the *hPolish* up as your current brush. The polish brush is a very useful general-purpose brush that gently flattens your model out wherever you use it. Like a lot of brushes in ZBrush, it takes a little bit of getting used to, but once you are comfortable with the brush, it will allow you to really clean up your model and add some structure to your sculpture. This brush is great for preventing your model from becoming a blobby mess and will let you add some planar definitions to the forms that compose your sculpture. Go ahead and try it out. I am using it here to clean up and subtly shape the head of the fish. You may have noticed that we are going through a bunch of different brushes to familiarize you with the most useful ones!

FIGURE 5.12 Using the *hPolish* brush.

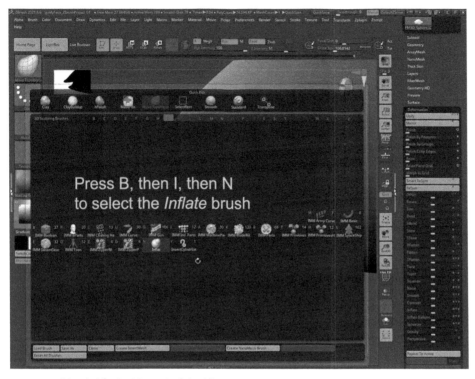

FIGURE 5.13 Select the *Inflate* brush by pressing *B*, *I*, and *N*.

The *Inflate* brush

Next, let's try out the *Inflate* brush. That's *B*, *I*, then *N* on your keyboard. The *Inflate* brush does just what you would expect it to: it inflates the geometry under the brush stroke, much like you would blow up a balloon. Use the *Inflate* brush to thicken up any part of your fish that needs a bit more meat on its bones. If you hold down the *Alt* key on your keyboard while using the *Inflate* brush, it will invert the effect of the brush and turn it into a deflate brush. Using this one brush, you can easily inflate or deflate part of your model, then switch to *Smooth* by holding down the *Shift* key to blend everything together.

After you have tried out the *Inflate* brush, take a moment and save what you have been working on using the *Tool > Save As* command. Make sure that you give your model a descriptive file name and save it to an easy-to-remember place on your hard drive so you can find it again later on as we continue to work on this model.

FIGURE 5.14 Use the *Tool* > *Save As* button to save your 3d model.

Later on, if you need to open a saved file, simply use the Tool > Load Tool command which will bring up a file explorer. Navigate to where the file you wish to open is located and choose the file by clicking on it. Press the Open command to finish the operation. This will place your saved tool into the list of active tools and you can now draw the tool on screen and press the Edit command to begin sculpting the model once more.

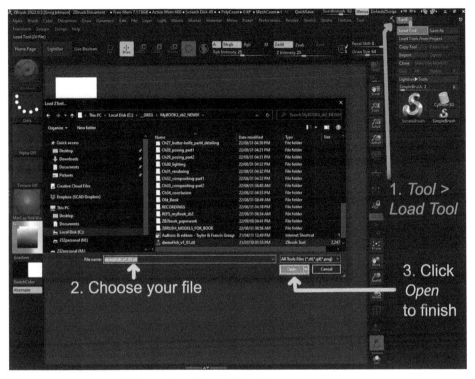

FIGURE 5.15 Use the *Tool > Load Tool* command to reload a saved 3d model.

Conclusion

After you have saved your progress, it is a good time to go back and review the contents of this chapter. Make sure that you have tried all of the basic brushes that we have talked about so far and know how to save your 3D model files. While it may not look like much yet, we are well on our way towards completing our model. Make sure that you watch the video associated with this chapter to help you understand all of the things we have done. Now, take a little break!

Further reading

Bridgeman, George Brant. *Constructive Anatomy*. Belchertown, MA, E. C. Bridgeman, 1920.

Hawkins, Waterhouse. Illustration of a Yellow Perch. Fauna Boreali-Americana; or the Zoology of the Northern Parts of British America: Containing descriptions of the objects of natural history collected on the late northern land expeditions under command of Captain Sir John Franklin, R.N. Part Third. The Fish., by Richardson, John, Richard Bentley, 1836, plate 74.

6

The Fish, Part 2 – Fins and Secondary Shapes

Getting started

In this chapter, we are going to finish creating the primary form of our fish by building the fins. Once that is completed, we can begin to tackle the secondary shapes, such as the gill covers. Now, let's get started on our fish again. There is a process that you must follow to begin working on your model once more. The first thing to do is to open your file. Simply go to the *Tool > Load Tool* button (it is just to the left of the *Save As* button on the tool menu), click it, and use the little Windows interface that pops up to find your 3D model ".ZTL" file that you saved at the end of the last session. Select your file and click the *Open* button on the file explorer interface, which will load your model into the Tool menu. The model should now appear as the largest icon, i.e. the active *Tool*, in the *Tool Palette*.

The model will be editable once you LMB click and drag from the middle of the screen. This action will place a copy of your model in the center of the screen. The very next thing that you must do is to press the *Edit* button just above the top of the *Canvas Document* about a third of the way across from the left side. This process is how you load a saved model back into ZBrush and make it editable once again. While it may seem quite a strange and convoluted process at first, it is a procedure that you will soon get quite used to.

An alternate approach is to use the *LightBox* interface that pops up when you first start ZBrush. Simply click on the file you want to load. You can always access the *Lightbox* interface by merely pressing the comma key on the keyboard or clicking the large *LightBox* button at

DOI: 10.1201/9781003215288-6

FIGURE 6.1 Use the *Tool > Load Tool* button to load your model into ZBrush.

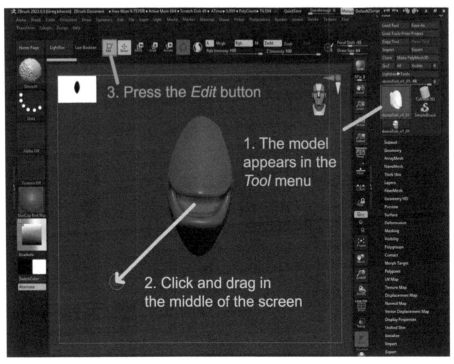

FIGURE 6.2 Draw your model on the screen and press the *Edit* button to resume working on your model.

the top left of the *Canvas Document*. The *LightBox* is where you can easily access all of the *QuickSave* files that ZBrush makes as backups while you work if your machine ever crashes while you are in the middle of working on a project.

Determining the polygon count of your model

Once you have the model loaded up and ready for editing, we can take a look at the polygon count of the model. It is important to keep track of your model's polygon count as you work. If the polygon count starts getting too high, then your ZBrush can begin to slow down or even crash if the count gets high enough. That said, ZBrush is amazingly robust when it comes to this, and it is common to have properly organized models that can run into the 35–40 million polygon range. I have even gotten ZBrush up to the 100 million polygon mark – but ZBrush was not happy about it! On the other end of the spectrum, you need to have at least a million or so polygons in your model if you are trying to sculpt any sort of detail and do a nice job of painting it. Usually, for a simple project like this, it is enough to have anywhere from 1 to 20 million or so polygons. A good rule of thumb is that if the model looks a bit rough or if you cannot add

FIGURE 6.3 Set the *DynaMesh Resolution* slider and then *DynaMesh* the model. Now, check your model's polygon count.

the detail you want, then add more polygons. Conversely, if ZBrush starts slowing down, then you probably need to lower your polygon count a bit. Keep in mind that ZBrush is a memory hog. If you have a bunch of other programs open or background processes running, then ZBrush can start acting up. It is a good idea to check and make sure that you don't have a lot of other programs eating up your computer's memory before working in ZBrush. To actually measure the model's polygon count, simply rest your mouse pointer over the model's icon in the *Tool* menu. A small pop-up window should appear with your model's file name, polygon count, and point count. This pop-up window will also let you know how many points and polygons, if any, are currently hidden. You can set the *DynaMesh Resolution* slider and then use *DynaMesh* to change the total polygon count of the sculpture.

As we continue to work with *DynaMesh* and start increasing our model's polygon count to add detail, the brushes that we use will have to change. One of the things you will notice early on is that the default *Smooth* brush will begin to lose potency the higher our polygon count climbs. The strength of the *Smooth* brush is tied directly to the number of polygons in our model. *Smooth* is very strong on low polygon models and still quite effective on medium-resolution ones. However, the *Smooth* brush's strength declines once you have lots of polygons in your model. Luckily, there is an easy fix for this issue – you can simply load up a stronger Smooth brush. ZBrush comes with over 200 extra brushes sitting inside the ZBrush install folder that you can load into the program. To access a brush from the hard drive, click the large icon for your currently selected brush in the upper left-hand side of ZBrush. A large brush selection menu will appear. Scroll your mouse over the brush icons and pause for a second. Now look down to the bottom left-hand side of the pop-up brushes interface, find the *Load Brush* button, and click on it. A small file explorer window will pop up. Now you have to go to ZBrush's install folder, go into the ZBrushes folder, and then double-click the sub-folder whose name matches the type of brush you are looking for (in this case, the Smooth folder). Usually, the path to this location is this: "C:\Program Files\Pixologic\ZBrush 2022\ZBrushes" (or something very similar). Inside the Smooth folder, you will find a diverse array of different smooth brushes. Double-click on the "Smooth Stronger.ZBP" file. A small note will now appear, letting you know that you have now changed the default smoothing brush. Now, you can simply press SHIFT while working and access the Smooth Stronger brush. You can also use this method to load new brushes off of the hard drive and into the Brush Menu, where you can now try them out. There are quite a lot of brushes on the hard drive by default, and you can also download a number of them from the ZBrush Central forum as well. Remember that you can adjust the *ZIntensity* of your *Smooth Stronger* brush to tone down its effect if it is too powerful.

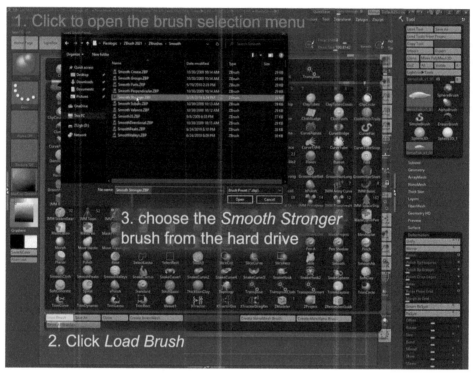

1. Click to open the brush selection menu

3. choose the *Smooth Stronger* brush from the hard drive

2. Click *Load Brush*

FIGURE 6.4 How to load a brush from the hard disk.

Masking

Now, we can talk about masking. When you mask off part of your model, you are making that part of the model immune to any brush-work or command that you then use in ZBrush. The masked-off parts simply will not be affected by what you do. To access the *Masking Brush*, hold down the CONTROL button on your keyboard. You should see your current brush swapped to the *MaskPen* brush. While the *Mask-Pen* brush is active, you can paint a mask onto your model. Go ahead and try it.

One thing to be aware of is that the *DynaMesh* command that we use to re-mesh our model will not work if part of the model is masked. If you hold down control and drag a small square in the background behind your model, it will get rid of the mask. You can also use that little CTRL+dragging on the background action as a shortcut to *DynaMesh* provided that the large *DynaMesh* button is active (if a button is orange, then it is turned on).

If you hold down the CTRL key and switch back to the *MaskPen* brush, you can add it to an existing mask. If you look really closely at the cursor, it has a little "+MASK" sign to let you know that you're adding to the mask. If you hold down the CTRL and the ALT keys at the

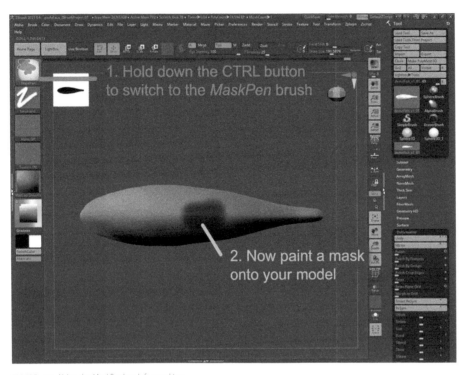

FIGURE 6.5 Using the *MaskPen* brush for masking.

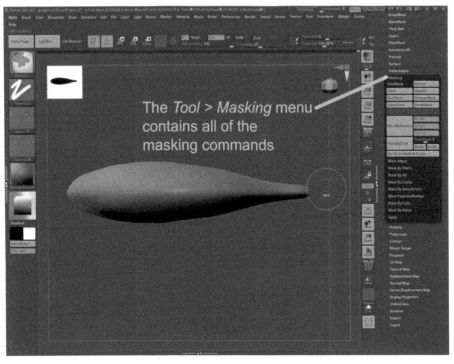

FIGURE 6.6 The *Tool > Masking* menu contains all of the masking commands.

same time, you will see that change to a "–MASK" sign. With both CTRL + ALT held down, you can erase parts of an existing mask. If you hold down the CTRL key and simply click on the background of the *Document Canvas*, you can invert the current mask. To blur the mask, hold down CTRL and tap the masked-off area. To sharpen the mask, hold down CTRL + ALT and tap the masked-off area. If you are thinking, geez, that is a lot of shortcuts that you are throwing out there, and then you can go to the *Tool > Masking* sub-palette and find all of the relevant masking commands there. Remember that if you simply rest the cursor over a button, it will show you the shortcut for that button. Take a bit of time and play around with ZBrush's masking features to get comfortable with them.

Creating the fins

We now need to create some fins for our fish, and we can do this very quickly using masking. First, move your camera so that you are looking straight down. Simply hold down the left mouse button while the pointer is over the background behind the model to orbit towards the top of the model and then hold down the SHIFT button. That should snap your viewpoint so that you are now looking straight down at the model. Now hold down the CTRL key on the keyboard to switch the

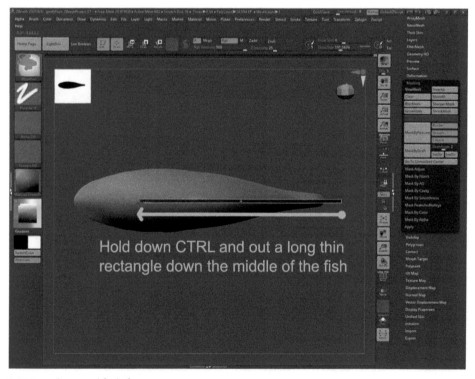

FIGURE 6.7 Create a mask for the fins.

current brush out for your *MaskPen* brush, and then click and drag on the background from just next to the tail to create a long, thin masking rectangle down the middle of the fish.

You can now rotate your viewpoint so you are looking at the side of the fish by pressing down the LMB and orbiting your camera. Remember to press the SHIFT key to snap the camera to the exact view you want. We now need to clean up the mask we have created. Press CTRL + ALT while clicking on the background near the front end of the fish to drag out a new unmasking rectangle. You will notice that by adding the ALT key while we drag out the mask, the rectangle turns white. This rectangle will subtract from what we currently have masked off. If you press the SPACEBAR while drawing the rectangle, you can move its position around. Note that as long as you don't let go of the mouse button, you can press and release various keys on the keyboard without changing the location of the rectangle.

You can also simply hold down CTRL + ALT and paint out the parts of the mask that you do not want. Remember to check the inside of the fish's mouth for any stray bits of masking that might be lurking there. Masking (or unmasking) off an area using the selection rectangle goes all the way through the object, and it is easy not to notice some little

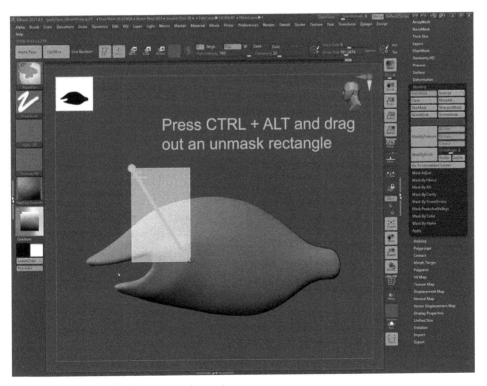

FIGURE 6.8 Press CTRL + ALT to drag out an unmask rectangle.

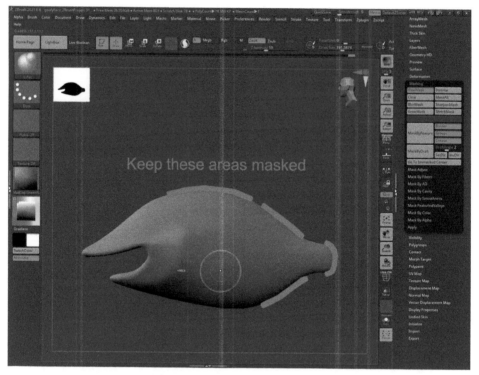

FIGURE 6.9 Keep these areas masked to create the fins later on.

bit of masking created this way. Use either method to unmask any portion of the fish model that you do not want to turn into a fin later on. Refer to the following image as a guide. If your fish looks different from the demo model, that is perfectly fine. You don't need to copy what I am doing exactly to learn ZBrush. Your very first model probably won't look like much. That is okay. Keep going. It is all part of the learning process. It usually takes creating a dozen models before a person really starts getting good at ZBrush.

To actually create the fins, we are going to use the *Move Topological* brush (that is, B-M-T on your keyboard) to pull the fins out of the model. To do this, we need to invert the mask. Hold down the CTRL key and simply click on the background behind the model. That should invert the mask. If you have any trouble, you can always use the *Tool > Masking > Inverse* button to invert the current mask, or simply use the CTRL + I shortcut. Now, make sure that you have your *Move Topological* brush selected, and press the *S* key to access the *Draw Size* for the brush. Make your brush nice and large. Click on one of the unmasked edges of your model and drag out a fin, then just keep going around and dragging the fins out from the unmasked areas.

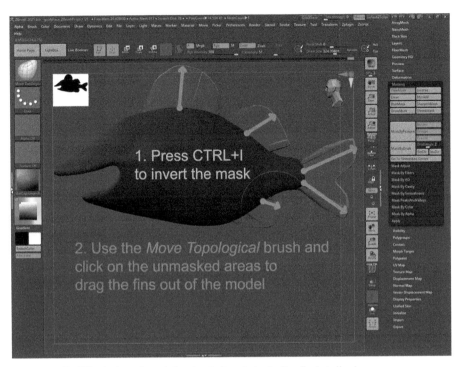

FIGURE 6.10 Use CTRL + I to invert the mask, then drag the fins out using the *Move Topological* brush.

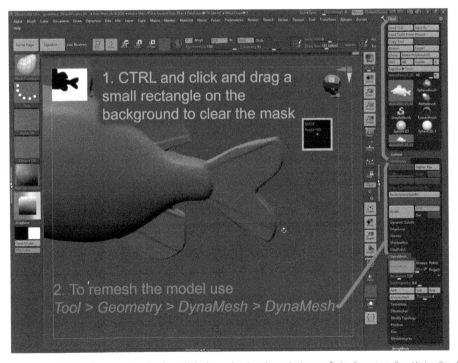

FIGURE 6.11 CTRL and drag a mask rectangle on the background to clear the mask, then use *Tool > Geometry > DynaMesh > DynaMesh* to re-mesh the model.

When you adjust the fins, try to click on the outermost rim of the fin. Because we are stretching these polygons out quite a bit, clicking on the outer edges will let you adjust the silhouette and shape of the fins a bit easier than clicking inside the main portion of the fin itself. Notice how the masked areas are completely unaffected by the brush. If you turn on *Polyframe* (SHIFT+F), you will be able to see the polygons of the fins all stretched out and deformed. Tap SHIFT+F again to turn off *Polyframe*, and then clear the mask by either holding down CTRL and dragging out a small masking rectangle on the background or using the *Tool > Masking > Clear* button. Now that the mask has been cleared, you can go to *Tool > Geometry > DynaMesh* and press the big *DynaMesh* button to re-mesh the model and fix those stretched-out polygons on the fins.

After you have re-meshed the model, you can go into the fins using the *Smooth Stronger* brush that we loaded up earlier to smooth out any roughness in the model. Remember that to access the *Smooth* brush, all you have to do is hold down the SHIFT key. You can adjust the strength of the *Smooth* brush by changing the *ZIntensity* slider while the *Smooth Stronger* brush is activated. To access the *ZIntensity* slider using a shortcut, simply press the U key on the keyboard.

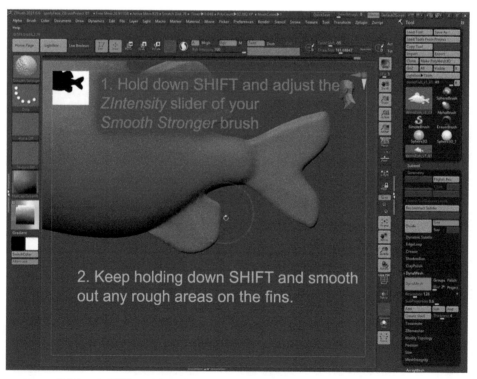

FIGURE 6.12 Hold down the SHIFT key and change the *ZIntensity* slider, then smooth out the fins.

Add more fins

We still have some more fins to do. There are some paired (on both sides) fins on the front end of the fish we need to create. Make sure that you still have *Transform > Activate Symmetry* turned on with the *X* option active. We will use the same masking technique as before, but this time, we will simply draw the mask directly onto the fish model. Use the [and] keys to change the size of your brush. You want to reduce the size of your brush until it is the width of the fin you wish to create. Hold down CTRL and draw the fins where you want them on the fish using the *MaskPen* brush.

Now, use the CTRL+I shortcut to invert the mask. Switch to the *Move Topological* brush using the B-M-T shortcut and use the] key to make that brush nice and large. Alternatively, you could CTRL and click on the background to invert the mask, click on the brush icon, choose the *Move Topological* brush from the *Brush Palette*, and then adjust the *Draw Size* slider at the top of the screen. Either way, it works just fine, but the shortcut method is much faster. Next, change your camera view so that you have a good angle to draw the fins out from. What this means is that you need to be aware of the fact that even though the model is 3D, you are working on it through the 2D

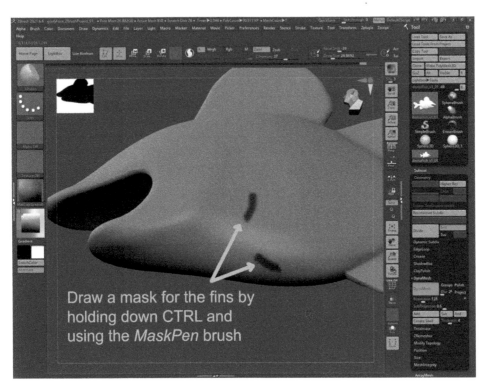

FIGURE 6.13 Hold down the CTRL key and use the *MaskPen* brush to mask out some new fins.

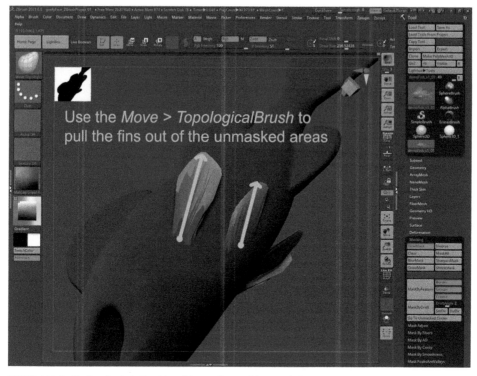

Use the *Move > TopologicalBrush* to pull the fins out of the unmasked areas

FIGURE 6.14 Use the *Move Topological* brush to pull the new fins out of the unmasked areas.

plane that is on your screen. The camera defines the plane that you will be moving on. The result of this is that your camera view affects how certain brushes and operations work in the program. Regarding the *Move Topological* brush, you want the camera to be more or less perpendicular to the direction in which you want to move things around. Basically, you have to make sure that your camera is looking at your model in a way that facilitates using your brush. You can use CTRL + Z to undo any mistakes that you make.

Notice that I made the fins fairly thick. The reason for that is that if you make a 3D surface too thin in ZBrush when you *DynaMesh* that object, you can end up with small holes appearing. If this happens, use the *Inflate* brush (B-I-N shortcut) to close the holes, and then *DynaMesh* the model. That should fix any holes that have appeared. If it doesn't, then hopefully you have a backup of your model that you can go back to. Once we get a little deeper into the program, I will go over how to cut out problem areas from your model and patch it, but for now, just remember to save frequent backups.

Finally, use the *Smooth Stronger* and *hPolish* brushes to smooth and flatten any fins that are still a bit lumpy. Continue smoothing, moving, and occasionally dynameshing your object until it looks the way you want it.

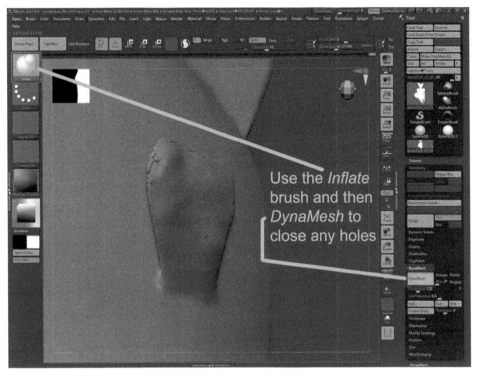

Use the *Inflate* brush and then *DynaMesh* to close any holes

FIGURE 6.15 Use the *Inflate* brush to close up any holes and then *DynaMesh* the mode.

Introducing selection brushes and object visibility

The inside face of the fin is going to require a bit more clean-up effort. You would be really hard-pressed to get a good angle on that side of the fin because the rest of the fish is in the way. In ZBrush, there is always a way! Rotate your camera around until you get a good top view of that troublesome fin. Hold down CTRL+SHIFT. If you look at the brush currently selected, you will see that it now reads *SelectRect*, which is one of ZBrush's selection brushes. Drag the green rectangle over the fin to isolate that part of the model and hide anything not selected.

To unhide the rest of the fish, simply hold down CTRL+SHIFT and click on the background. If you hold down CTRL+SHIFT+ALT, the selection box will turn red and hide whatever you select instead, or you can use it to refine your selection. Once part of the model is hidden, if you hold down CTRL+SHIFT and click on the model, it will inverse what is currently visible. While holding down the CTRL+SHIFT buttons, go to your brush icon, which should now read *SelectRect*. Click on that brush and choose the *SelectLasso* brush instead. Now, when you hold down the CTRL+SHIFT buttons, you get the *SelectLasso* brush, which

119

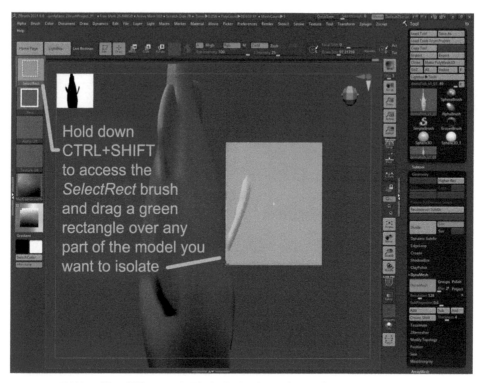

FIGURE 6.16 Hold down CTRL + SHIFT to access the *SelectRect* brush and isolate elements of your model.

Hold down CTRL+SHIFT and change the brush from the *SelectRect* to the *SelectLasso* brush.

FIGURE 6.17 Hold down CTRL + SHIFT and change the current brush to the *SelectLasso* brush.

offers a bit more precision when you are trying to hide parts of your model. Once you start drawing a selection area, you can let go of CTRL + SHIFT and keep going. The selection brushes only need those buttons to get started. While drawing your selection area, you can press the SPACEBAR and move the whole selection area around, just like we did with the masking brushes earlier. Play around a bit with the selection brushes, and then use either the *SelectLasso* brush or the *SelectRect* brush to isolate any irksome fins and refine their inside

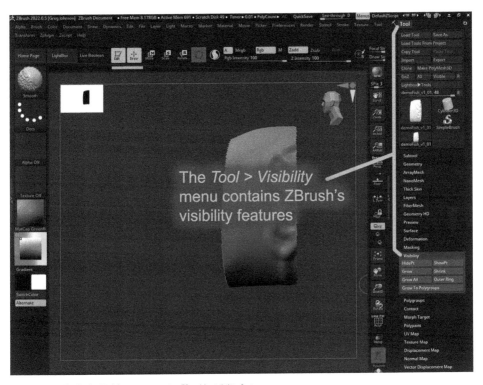

FIGURE 6.18 The *Tool* > *Visibility* menu contains ZBrush's visibility features.

surface using the *Smooth Stronger* and *hPolish* brushes. One last thing to keep in mind regarding hidden selections is that if you sculpt along the hidden edge, it can create some funky geometry when you unhide the model.

The *Tool* > *Visibility* menu contains ZBrush's visibility features. Hide a portion of your model and try out the various buttons in the *Visibility* menu to become more familiar with them. Practice using these procedures until you are completely comfortable using them.

The *Lazy Mouse* feature

If you look closely at the cursor when you are sculpting (or using the *SelectLasso* brush, for instance), you will see a tiny little red line extending away from the crosshairs. This line tells you that ZBrush's *LazyMouse* feature is turned on. *LazyMouse* smooths out your stroke by averaging together your mouse movements over a short distance and then actually applying the brush at the end of the little red line. *LazyMouse* does a great job of making each stroke more even and natural-looking. You can find all of the settings for *LazyMouse* under the *Stroke* > *LazyMouse* menu at the top of the ZBrush interface. When the *LazyMouse* button is bright orange, it is turned on. While the

121

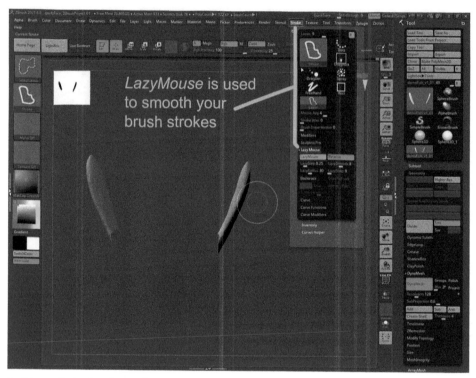

FIGURE 6.19 The *LazyMouse* feature will make your brush strokes smoother and more natural.

smoothing effect can be quite nice, it comes at the cost of responsiveness and memory. I often turn *LazyMouse* off since I am working on an older machine, and *LazyMouse* can eat up memory. To toggle *LazyMouse* on and off, simply press the *Stroke > LazyMouse > LazyMouse* button. If you look around the *LazyMouse* button, you can find all of the different options for the *LazyMouse* feature. You can turn up the *LazySmooth* and *LazyRadius* values to increase the smoothing effect on your brush strokes. If you really want to dive in and examine the details of any of these options, remember that you can always simply hold down the CTRL key and rest your cursor over that command to see the help file on that topic. Alternatively, you can always explore the ZBrush reference guide at (docs.pixologic.com/reference-guide/) to examine each feature in some depth. Remember that each brush remembers its settings by default, so even if you turn this feature off for one brush, the feature may still be turned on for a different brush.

Using DynaMesh's *Resolution* feature

As you work on the model, you may start to find that the model is looking a bit rough in spots, the curves are not particularly smooth, or you cannot seem to get the detail you would like sculpted into the model. These are all signs that your model needs more polygons to work with. To increase the resolution of the model, you will have to increase its polygon count. While there are different ways of doing this, the method we will use right now is to increase the *Resolution* of our *DynaMesh* command. First, check your polycount by resting your cursor over the model's icon in the *Tool* menu, as we learned how to do a little bit earlier. Second, go down to *Tool > Geometry > DynaMesh*, and right under the big *DynaMesh* button, you should see the *Resolution* slider. Try doubling the *Resolution* value to, say, 256. Now, turn on the *DynaMesh* button. If the button is already turned on, you can simply turn it off and then on again. Check your polycount again. The number of polygons should have gone up significantly.

If it has not, then try adding a brush stroke or doing some smoothing on the model and the *DynaMesh* the model again. Sometimes, ZBrush will only apply *DynaMesh* to a model if there has been no change to the model's geometry since the last time the model got dynameshed. The exact polygon count that results from a *DynaMesh* can be difficult to predict as the results vary depending on the size of the model. Be very careful when setting the *Resolution* slider for *DynaMesh*. Large *DynaMesh Resolution* values can create models that will crash the program. If a calculation is taking too long, you can hold down the ESC

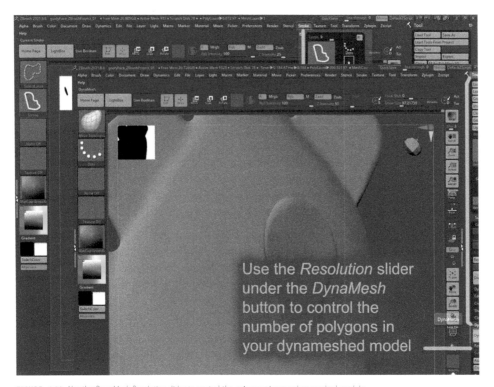

FIGURE 6.20 Use the *DynaMesh Resolution* slider to control the **polycount** in your dynameshed models.

key on the keyboard to cancel the operation. Canceling an operation can make the program unresponsive, but a modicum of patience will usually allow the program to recover.

Once you have increased the model's polycount, you should notice that your brush strokes produce more detailed results. Now, one thing you've got to be aware of when working with *DynaMesh* is that if you put two surfaces close together when you apply *DynaMesh*, it will merge those two surfaces, which can become a real problem when you are working with fine details. The easiest solution is to simply keep surfaces as far apart from each other as possible and then move parts of the object in place once you are sure that you are finished with *DynaMesh*. If *DynaMesh* refuses to work, check the upper left-hand side of the program to see if a "NOTE: Mask must be cleared in order to *DynaMesh*." error message appears. If you get this error message, use the *Tool > Masking > Clear* button to get rid of the problematic mask, and then try to *DynaMesh* the model again.

Fixing common problems

Since we are on the topic of fixing problems, I may as well go ahead and tell you how to fix a few common issues that crop up. One problem that pops up when using *DynaMesh* is the issue of spikes in the model. Sometimes, a portion of the model can become a sharp spike. If you try to smooth this away, the spike can get, if anything, even spikier. If this happens, undo a few steps to see if that helps. If not, then change your brush to either the *Move* or *Move Topological* brush and shove the tip of the spike back into the model. It doesn't have to look pretty. Just cram the spike back down into the model. After you do this, *DynaMesh* your model, and it should get rid of the spike.

In fact, *DynaMesh* can be a great way to fix many common problems with a model. Simply thrust the problem area deeper into the model, then use either the Inflate brush or the *ClayTubes* brush to make sure that the polygons overlap each other (don't worry if it looks messy). Now *DynaMesh* the model and then *Smooth* away any remaining blemishes. Repeat as necessary until the problem is fixed.

While not strictly a problem, a great trick if you need to work on low polygon objects is to use the Move or *Move Topological* brush to make fine-scale adjustments to your model. Simply lower the brush *Draw Size* to a very small value, which will allow you to work on just a few polygons, or even only one point, at a time.

Going back to our fish model, just keep moving, smoothing, and refining the sculpture until you are happy with the result. Use the *MaskPen* brush to draw in another masked line for some extra side fins, invert the mask using *Tool > Masking > Inverse*, then use the *Move Topological* brush to pull the additional fins out and shape them.

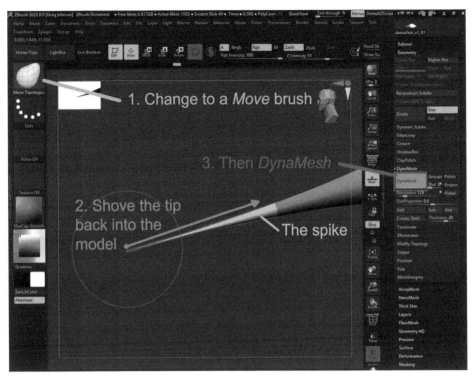

FIGURE 6.21 How to fix a spike.

Saving and backing up your model file

Once you have added all of the fins that you need and have got your fish looking quite nice, it is time to save the model. Click on *Tool > Save As*. Take careful note of what folder you are in. If you loaded up the *SmoothStronger* brush earlier on, ZBrush will try to save your file into the brushes folder! You will need to navigate using the small window explorer that has popped up to where you want to keep your model file. Remember to iterate the name of your file, i.e., save the file as "demoFish_02.ZTL" instead of "demoFish_01.ZTL". This way, you are creating a new file and not saving over an existing one. The reason for doing this is that when you're working in a professional environment or even when you're working at home, it helps to have multiple backups of an important file that you are working on. If something goes wrong with one of your files, this way, you have multiple backups that you can resort to. Files can go wrong in any number of ways. A file can simply become corrupted and unusable. Worse, you may make a critical error in your process and need to go back many steps, or even days, to fix the problem. If you have a bunch of iteratively saved model files backed up, then this becomes a straightforward process of just loading up the correct file. If you have these backup files, though, you can save hours, days, or even weeks' worth of work. If you lose a week's worth of work at a professional job, then you are likely to get fired. It is far easier just to get into the habit of backing up your files in an organized fashion with descriptive names, version numbers, and iteration numbers like, say, "happyFish_v1_001.ZTL" (descriptiveName_versionNumber_iterationNumber.fileExtension). Hard drive space is cheap. Adding an external hard drive is as simple as just plugging in the drive. This principle applies to all of your projects. For some big projects, I may end up with a couple of 100 files with different versions of them. But if there's ever a problem that I can't fix, I just go back through the different versions and recover the last working version of the file. In this manner, I never lose more than a smidgeon of work if something goes wrong.

Making the gills

Let's create our fish's gills, and then we can do the eyes in a very different manner so that I can show you some new techniques. Alright, so to create the guild structure, we're going to explore a new brush. Press the B key, then D, then S on the keyboard, which will load up the interestingly named *DamStandard* brush, named after its creator and character artist, Damien Canderle. Look him up on ArtStation.com. So this is Damien's Standard Brush, and it is one of the better brushes available in ZBrush. Use the *DamStandard* brush to carve a line for the gills of

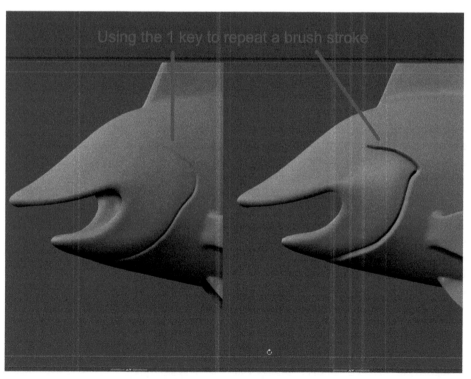

FIGURE 6.22 Using the 1 key to repeat a brush stroke.

your fish. Once you have done that, the very next thing you must do is press the 1 key on your keyboard (the 1 on the row of number keys, not the 1 on the number pad). Pressing the 1 key repeats the command in ZBrush and can be a very useful way to strengthen a brush stroke when you need it. As long as you do not do anything else, like move the camera or whatnot, you can keep pressing 1 and strengthen the effect as much as you like.

Now, go in and smooth your gill crevasse a bit. Next, set the *Z Intensity* of your *Smooth Stronger* brush all the way up to 100. Shrink the *Draw Size* of your brush down a bit so you can see what you are doing. Then, smooth out the posterior portion of the gill valley that you made. Make sure that you don't accidentally smooth out the bottom of the gills. You want to keep that part of the gills sharply defined.

To refine the gill area further, go to *Tool > Masking > Mask By Cavity* and press the *Mask By Cavity* button, which will automatically mask out the lower portions of your model and should mask off the bottom of the gill crevasse automatically. *Mask By Cavity* and other procedural masking techniques can be extremely useful when creating models.

Now, we can use the *MaskLasso* and *MaskPen* to refine our mask by masking off all of the parts of the fish that we don't want to work with. You want to leave the area immediately forward of the gill crevasse

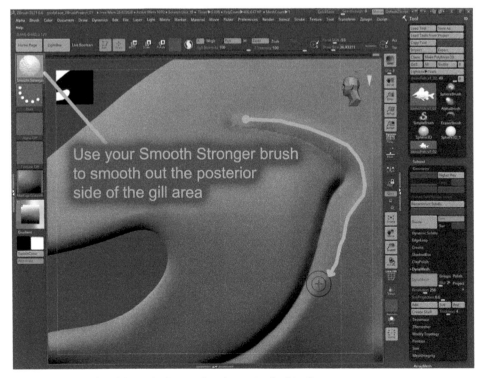

FIGURE 6.23 Use your *Smooth Stronger* brush to smooth out the posterior side of the gill area.

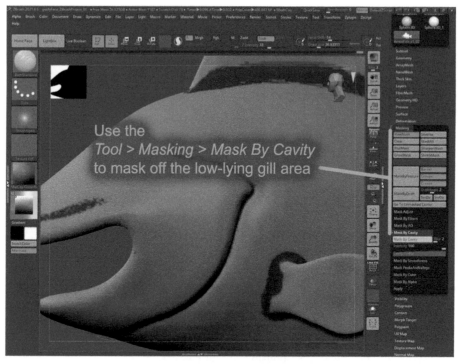

FIGURE 6.24 Use the *Tool* > *Masking* > *Mask By Cavity* to mask off the low-lying gill area.

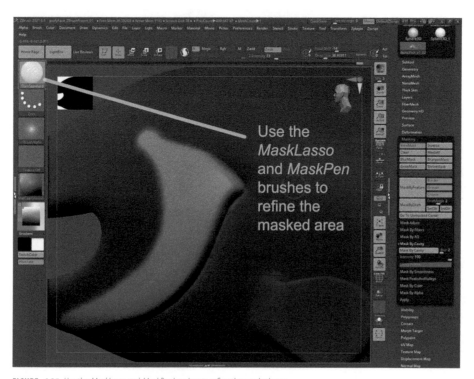

FIGURE 6.25 Use the *MaskLasso* and *MaskPen* brushes to refine the masked area.

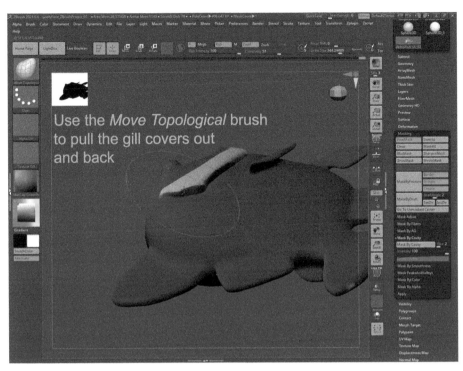

FIGURE 6.26 Use the *Move Topological* brush to pull the gill covers out and back.

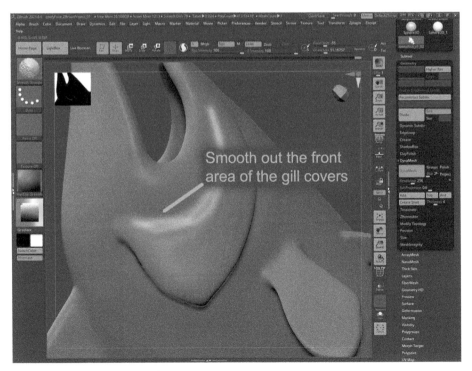

FIGURE 6.27 Smooth out the front area of the gill covers.

unmasked. The rest of the fish should be completely masked off. Press CTRL and tap the mask to blur it once for a smoother border.

Now, use the *Move Topological* brush to pull the front of the gills out and back to make the fish's gill covers.

Hold down CTRL and click and drag on the background, or use *Tool* > *Masking* > *Clear* to clear the mask. *DynaMesh* the fish by clicking on *Tool* > *Geometry* > *DynaMesh* > *DynaMesh*, or, if the *DynaMesh* button is already active, simply hold down CTRL and click and drag a small selection box on the background. Now, you can smooth out the rough area at the front of the gill covers and do some clean-up work. The *hPolish* brush can be very useful for flattening out rough areas here.

Conclusion

By now, your fish should be looking very fishy! Go ahead and save your model file using *Tool* > *Save As*, and remember to iterate the number on the file name and pay attention to where you save the file. In the next chapter, we will add some eyes to our fish. Make sure that you watch the video associated with this chapter to help you understand all of the methods we have used so far. Take a well-earned break!

Further reading

"Reference Guide | ZBrush Docs." Maxon Computer GMBH. https://docs. pixologic.com/reference-guide/. Accessed 15 Dec. 2022.

7

The Fish, Part 3 – Making Eyes

Getting started

Welcome back! We are going to get started with the next part of our fish, creating the eyeballs. Rather than sculpt the eyes directly into our fish, we're going to make the eyes a bit differently and introduce some new concepts to you. Go to the *Tool* menu, select the *Sphere3D* tool from the *Tool Palette*, and draw a sphere on the screen. Immediately afterward, turn on the *Edit* button.

Using parametric objects

Right now, this sphere on our screen is still a parametric primitive, which is to say that we can control the settings for the sphere. Scroll down the *Tool* menu by clicking and dragging on any blank space within the *Tool* menu, and at the bottom, you should see the *Initialize* menu header. Go ahead and click on the word *Initialize*. The menu should open up, and you can now increase the *HDivide* and *VDivide* sliders until the sphere looks nice and smooth. What these sliders do is increase the subdivisions along the horizontal or vertical axis of the sphere.

Adjusting the *HDivide* and *VDivide* sliders will significantly increase the number of polygons in the sphere, which you can check by simply resting your mouse pointer on top of the *Sphere3D* icon in the *Tool* palette. The resulting pop-up window will let you know the details of the tool. It is a good idea to check this value and make sure that your sphere is not exceeding, say, roughly a couple of million polygons. Let's go ahead and convert our sphere from a parametric object into an editable polygonal mesh by clicking on the *Tool > Make PolyMesh3D* button

DOI: 10.1201/9781003215288-7

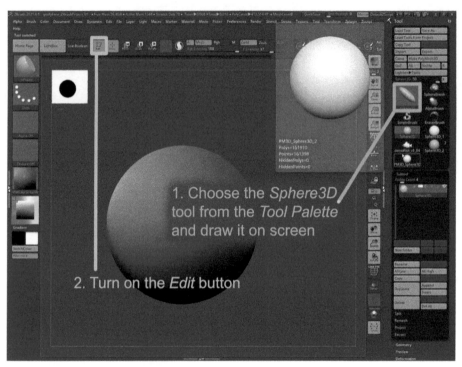

FIGURE 7.1 Choose the *Sphere3D* tool from the *Tool Palette* and draw it on screen. Next, turn on the *Edit* button.

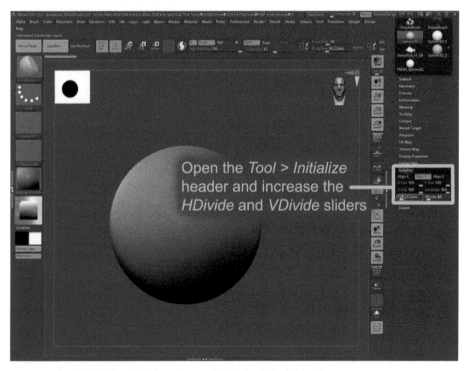

FIGURE 7.2 Open the *Tool > Initialize* header and increase the *HDivide* and *VDivide* sliders therein.

now. The resulting *PM3D_Sphere3D* tool will form the core component of our fish eyeball. ZBrush will let you work on multiple objects at the same time using its *Tool > Subtool* menu. The *Subtool* menu enables you to combine multiple models into one tool file while retaining the ability to model each one individually. There is a lot of power to be found in the *Subtool* menu, and we are going to leverage its capabilities during this demo to make our fish's eyeballs. Each component we use can be many millions of polygons in size, just so long as we don't end up with so many polygons that ZBrush starts slowing down. When working in ZBrush, it is perfectly fine to create objects in the several million polygon range. Just make sure that the total polygon count of all of the objects on screen doesn't exceed more than about 25–45 million polygons split up between all of the subtools being used. The exact number of polygons ZBrush will tolerate before it starts slowing down is going to vary depending on your computer, so this number is just a very general guideline.

Introducing colors and materials

Before we delve into the *Subtool* menu, we have a glaring problem to fix. Eyeballs shouldn't be gray. To fix that, let's take a look at how to set an object's color and material in ZBrush. Click on the *Material* icon, which is the large sphere icon in the middle of the left side of the interface. At the top of the resulting large pop-up menu, you'll see that we have a *Quick Pick* row of materials at the top. These are your recently used materials. Next, we have what are called the *MatCap* materials. The *MatCap* materials are really good for previewing objects, but because they have lighting baked into them, *MatCap* materials can create problems later if you're trying to add your own lights to your ZBrush scene. Down at the bottom, we have the *Standard Materials*. The standard materials respond to lights normally within ZBrush, which gives you more control over the final look of your ZBrush scene. If you are interested, you can download a lot of extra materials and much, much more from the ZBrush Resource Center (pixologic.com/zbrush/downloadcenter/library/). For eyeballs, we want something shiny and pale, so I think the *Toy Plastic* material should work pretty well. Go ahead and select the *Toy Plastic* material from the Materials pop-up window.

Next, we need to choose a color using the ZBrush *Color Picker*. The *Color Picker* is a colorful square interface that lets you select a hue on the outside rim and then set your intensity and shading options in the center square. Alternatively, if you want to be more precise, you can go up to the top shelf, click on the *Color* menu, and set the exact color values using the *R* (red), *G* (green), and *B* (blue) sliders. I don't like using pure white for eyeballs and usually pick something along the lines of kind of a dingy yellow color for the sclera.

FIGURE 7.3 Click on the *Materials* icon and select the *ToyPlastic* material from the list of *Standard Materials*.

FIGURE 7.4 Use the *Color Picker* or the *Color Palette* menu to set the color you want.

One of the odd things about ZBrush is that even after you have selected your material and color, you still aren't done. By default, ZBrush will automatically update any object to the currently selected material and color unless that object has had a material and color specifically assigned to it. To make this color and material stick to your object, you need to go up to the top shelf, find the *Mrgb* button, and make sure that it is turned on. Having the *Mrgb* button active means that ZBrush will affect both the material and the RGB (red, green, and blue) values of your current tool. Next to the *Mrgb* button, you will see the *Rgb* button, which is, you guessed it, just for working with the RGB color of an object. Next to that, you can find the *M* button, which only affects the material of the current tool on the screen. Since we are going to be assigning both the RGB value and the material, we want to make sure the *Mrgb* button is active. Under the *Mrgb* button is the *Rgb Intensity* slider. Make sure that this slider is set to 100 (that should be the default value). Finally, go to the *Color* menu and press the *FillObject* button (*Color > FillObject*) to embed your chosen color and material into your object. This sphere will form the sclera, or white, of the eye.

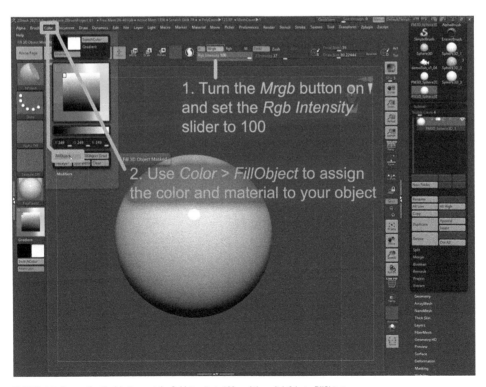

FIGURE 7.5 Turn on the *Mrgb* button, set the *RgbIntensity* to 100, and then *click Color > FillObject.*

Creating the eye

To make the other parts of the eye, first, use the *Tool > Subtool > Duplicate* button to create a copy of our existing sphere. You should see a second sphere show up in the *Subtool* menu. Next, select the *Move* button from the top *Shelf* or simply press W on the keyboard to turn on the *Gizmo 3D* manipulator. Click and drag on the green up arrow to move the new subtool sphere up a bit. Use the color picker to select the color you want the cornea, the colored part of the front of the eye, to be. Now, use *Color > FillObject* to change the color of the second sphere to the eye color that you have chosen. Next, make sure that you have the *Move* tool active, and click and drag on the center yellow box to scale this colored sphere down to form the cornea.

To make the pupil, we follow the same process again. Use *Tool > Subtool > Duplicate* to copy the sphere we are using as a cornea, then move and scale it into place to make a pupil. Next, we need to make the pupil black, but this is one of the things you have to be careful with. ZBrush has a kind of weirdness occasionally, and this is one such case. When you are assigning a color to an object, you want to avoid what's called a super-black or pure black. A super-black is a color that has an RGB

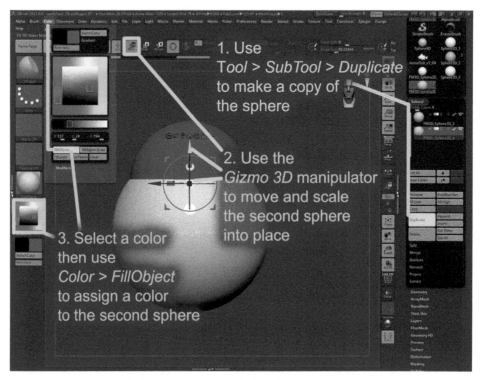

FIGURE 7.6 Copy, move, scale, and color a second sphere to make the cornea of the eye.

value of 0, i.e., $R=0$, $G=0$, and $B=0$. If you use a pure black like this, ZBrush will occasionally try to make this color transparent, which can be a real problem when you are working with an object. I think it was an early attempt by the maker of ZBRush to add a sort of transparency to ZBrush. Unfortunately, this super black transparency feature doesn't work quite right and isn't reliable. Now, it is just a bug that crops up every so often, but it can be confusing if you don't know how to avoid it. Speaking of which, preventing the problem is really easy – just don't use an absolutely pure black! Instead, set the color to $R=1$, $G=0$, and $B=0$ or something similar. Your eye won't be able to tell the difference, and ZBrush won't try to do weird, transparent things to your object.

At this point, we now have three different spheres, and each of these objects has a different color assigned to it. If you look at the stack of objects in your *Subtool* menu, you should see that each sphere has a dissimilar colored icon. In your *Tool > Subtool* menu, select the topmost sphere. Now, click on the *Tool > Subtool > Merge* header, find the *Merge-Down* button, and click on it. A pop-up window will appear warning you that "This is not an undoable operation" and asking if you want to proceed; tell it OK. Now merge the resulting sphere down again, which should combine all three spheres into one subtool.

FIGURE 7.7 Do not use a pure black color while making the pupil to avoid transparency issues.

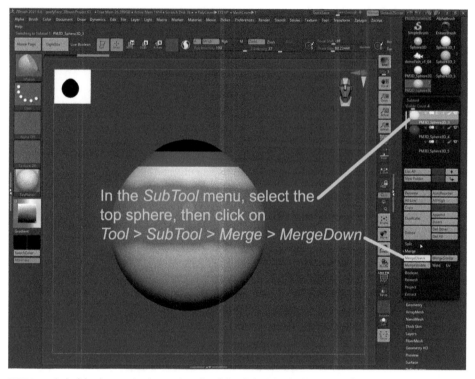

In the *SubTool* menu, select the top sphere, then click on *Tool > SubTool > Merge > MergeDown*.

FIGURE 7.8 In the *Subtool* menu, select the top sphere, then click on *Tool > Subtool > Merge > MergeDown*.

Making the eyelids

To make the eyelids, go to the *Tool* palette and select the *Sphere3D* icon, which will switch out the current eye model for a new Sphere tool. Click on the *Tool > Make PolyMesh3D* button to convert this new sphere into a polymesh object. You will also notice that the color and material of the new sphere have changed. Any object that has not had a material and color specifically assigned to it will automatically update to the currently selected color and material. Try changing the current color and watching the new sphere update. Change the color to white and the material to *MatCap GreenRoma* to go back to the default color and material we were working on before we started creating the eyeball. We don't really need to assign a specific color or material to this sphere just yet. Instead, press the W key to activate the *Gizmo 3D*, hold down the CTRL key, and drag a selection rectangle over the top half of the sphere to mask that part off. The *Gizmo 3D* makes a good reference point for where the middle of the sphere is. Click and drag on the green rectangle in the *Gizmo 3D* to scale down half of the sphere. Scale the sphere down until the bottom of the sphere is flat. Hold down CTRL and drag a tiny selection window in the background to get rid of your mask to finish.

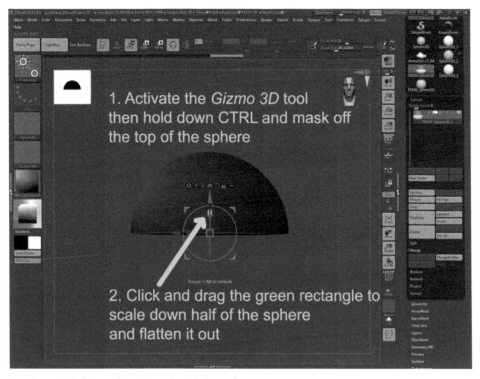

1. Activate the *Gizmo 3D* tool then hold down CTRL and mask off the top of the sphere

2. Click and drag the green rectangle to scale down half of the sphere and flatten it out

FIGURE 7.9 Mask off the top of the sphere and scale the bottom flat.

Go to your *Tool* menu and select the icon there for the eyeball that you have created, which should automatically switch your current model to the eyeball. Now, click on *Tool > Subtool > Append*. A pop-up menu containing all of your currently loaded tools will appear. In the *Quick Pick* section at the top of this pop-up menu, you should see the half-sphere model that you just made. Click on that half-sphere model to select it, which will add your half-sphere model as a subtool to your eyeball model.

After you have appended your eyelid tool to your eyeball tool, you will probably see a weird interference pattern or moiré pattern appear on your model. When you see this kind of strange look, that means that you have two co-planar surfaces. In other words, two models (or portions of models) that are right on top of each other and are in the same space. You want to avoid co-planar surfaces when you are modeling, since this will create all sorts of problems for you if you let the situation persist. To fix it in this case, select the eyelid subtool (the half-sphere), turn on the *Gizmo 3D* by pressing W, and use the small yellow cube at the center of the gizmo to scale our half-sphere up until it hides the cornea and pupil.

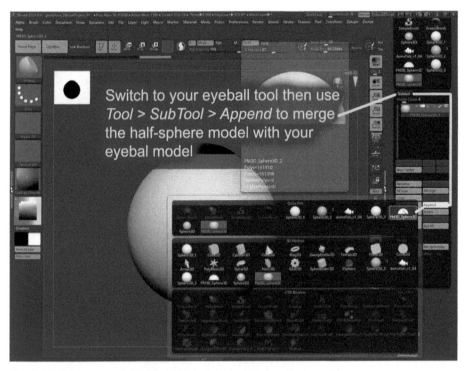

FIGURE 7.10 Switch to your eyeball tool, then use *Tool* > *Subtool* > *Append* to merge your models.

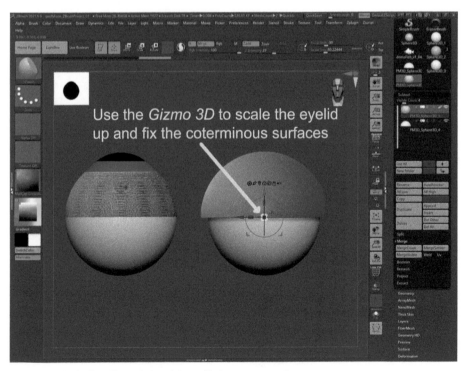

FIGURE 7.11 Use the *Gizmo 3D* to scale the eyelid up and fix the coterminous surfaces.

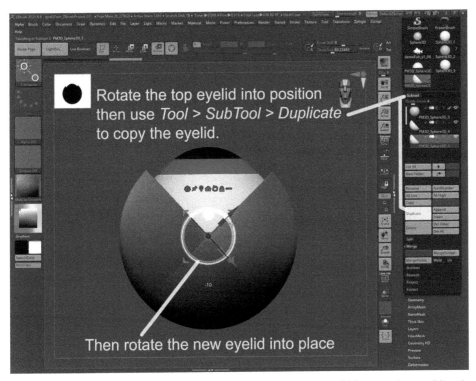

Rotate the top eyelid into position then use *Tool > SubTool > Duplicate* to copy the eyelid.

Then rotate the new eyelid into place

FIGURE 7.12 Rotate the top eyelid into position, then use *Tool > Subtool > Duplicate* to copy the eyelid. Then, rotate the new eyelid into place.

Now grab the ring part of the *Gizmo 3D* and rotate the eyelid until it shows the cornea and pupil. If you hold down the SHIFT key while you rotate, the object will turn in fixed increments of 5°. Duplicate the eyelids using *Tool > Subtool > Duplicate* and rotate this new eyelid to become the bottom eyelid.

Select the topmost eyelid in the *Subtool* menu and use *MergeDown* to merge the two eyelids into one subtool. These are still two separate models even though they are one subtool, at least until we dynamesh them together. Instead, let's go ahead and select the topmost model in our subtool list and *Tool > Subtool > MergeDown* again, which will unify our entire eyeball into one subtool. Go ahead and save your progress now. Click on *Tool > Save As* and save your eyeball into the same folder as your fish model. Remember to use a descriptive and iterative naming convention for your eyeball file. Something like "eyeball_v1_01.ZTL" should work.

If you are having trouble with that command because of the order in which your subtools are arranged, there is an easy fix for that. Immediately underneath the subtool icon area, you should see an up and down arrow. You can use these two arrows to change the currently selected subtool, going either up or down through the subtool icon list. Below these two arrows are another set of arrows with a curve in

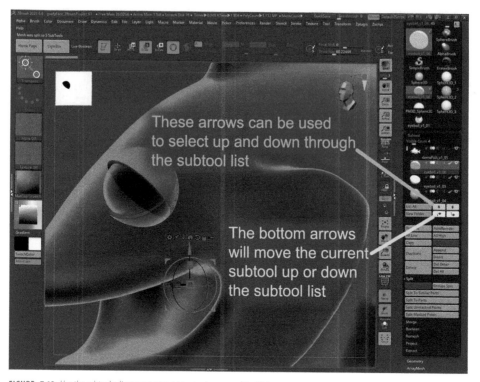

These arrows can be used to select up and down through the subtool list

The bottom arrows will move the current subtool up or down the subtool list

FIGURE 7.13 Use the subtool adjustment arrows to organize your subtool list.

them. Using the bottom set of arrows will actually move your currently selected subtool up or down the stack, depending on which curved arrow you use. These arrows will let you organize your subtools and make using commands like *Merge Down* a lot easier to manage.

Adding the eyeball models to the fish

In the *Tool* icon menu, select your fish to switch to that model. If you cannot find your fish model in the tool icon list, then use the *Tool > Load Tool* button to load the fish model back into ZBrush and select it. Your fish should now appear on screen. Use the *Tool > Subtool > Append* command to add the eyeball model to your fish model as a subtool. You can now use the *Gizmo 3D* to scale and move the eyeball subtool into place on your fish's head. Turn on the *Transp* button to make all of your inactive subtools partially transparent while you move and scale the eyeball into place. Just make sure that your eyeball does not cross the center of the fish. Keep in mind that the smaller the eye, the bigger the fish will look, while the bigger the eye, the smaller the fish will appear.

Spin your viewpoint around your fish while you work to make sure that your eyeball placement looks good from various viewing angles. Once

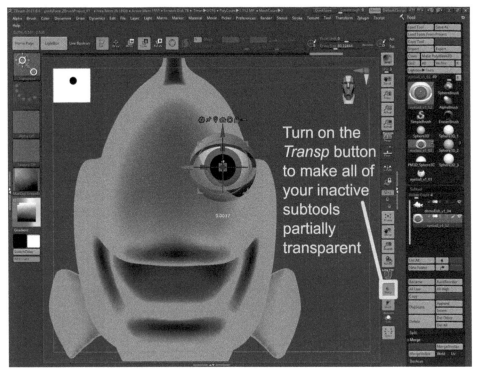

Turn on the *Transp* button to make all of your inactive subtools partially transparent

FIGURE 7.14 Turn on the *Transp* button to make all of your inactive subtools partially transparent.

you are happy with your progress, go ahead and save the fish model to have a backup handy in case something goes wrong later. After you have finished making a backup, use the *Tool > Subtool > Split > Split To Parts* command to separate all of the components of the eyeball. Since we never dynameshed the eye together, all of the pieces remained separate even though they were temporarily combined into one subtool.

Use the *Tool > Subtool > Merge > MergeDown* command to merge the eyeball, cornea, and pupil back together while leaving the eyelids out. If you have your *Gizmo 3D* active, you will notice that the center of the gizmo is now outside of the eyeball. If you want to move the gizmo back to the center of the eyeball, look at the small row of icons just above the gizmo. On the right side of the row of icons, you should see a small padlock icon, the *Lock/Unlock* toggle for the *Gizmo 3D*. If you click this icon, the lock will open up, and you can now move the Gizmo around in relation to the object. A few icons to the left of the lock, you should see an icon that looks like a teardrop with a small circle in it, which is the *Go To Unmasked Mesh Center* button. Click this icon, and the *Gizmo 3D* should now be centered inside your eyeball subtool. Repeat this process for the eyelids, and finish up by rotating the eyelids until you are happy with the results. Remember that you can always merge various subtools to make adjustments and then separate them

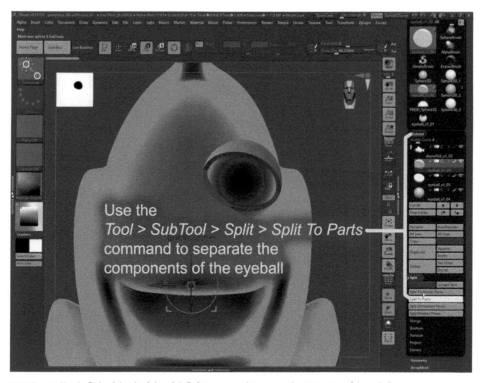

Use the
Tool > SubTool > Split > Split To Parts
command to separate the
components of the eyeball

FIGURE 7.15 Use the *Tool > Subtool > Split > Split To Parts* command to separate the components of the eyeball.

later to adjust each one individually. Another of ZBrush's quirks is that if you try to mix polymesh subtools and parametric subtools (i.e., subtools you haven't turned into a polymesh using the *Make PolyMesh3D* button), ZBrush will sometimes do unexpected things like deleting the parametric object. Another quirk to watch out for is that ZBrush is very serious when it says you cannot undo certain operations. If you try to undo an undoable action, ZBrush will usually crash immediately.

Make sure that you have merged all of the eye subtools together using the *Tool > Subtool > Merge > MergeDown* button. Now that the eye is a complete set of subtools, go to *Tool > Subtool > Duplicate* to make a copy of the entire eye. We can flip this copy of our eye using the *Tool > Deformation > Mirror* command. If you look at the top right corner of the *Mirror* button, you will see tiny *X*, *Y*, and *Z* characters. These little characters control the axis that the mirror occurs on. If you have created your fish facing forward, then the default X-axis should work just fine. If you have made your fish face a different direction, you may have to play around with these characters by clicking on them to turn them on and off until you get the right one. Note that the active axes are dark, and ZBrush will let you have multiple axes on at the same time to create some complicated mirroring possibilities.

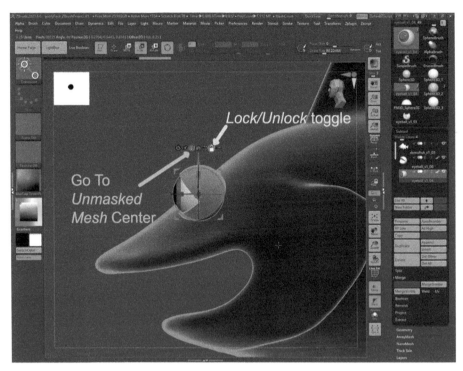

FIGURE 7.16 Using the *Lock/Unlock* and *Go To Unmasked Center* options on the *Gizmo 3D.*

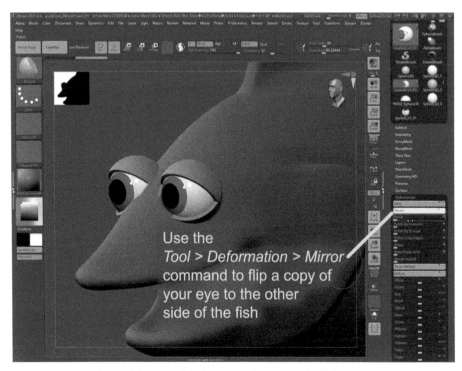

FIGURE 7.17 Duplicate the eye and then use the *Tool > Deformation > Mirror* command to flip the copy to the other side of the fish.

You can now split the two eyeball subtools into individual parts. Use the subtool arrows to arrange the eyelid components together, and then merge them. Then, arrange and combine the eyeball components (the sclera, cornea, and pupil) and merge these too. Remember to save your file frequently during this process. It can help when organizing subtools to name them. You can use the *Tool > Subtool > Rename* command to change the name of the currently selected subtool.

Select your fish model in the subtool stack and turn on transparency using the *Transp* button. Turning on transparency will not only help you see what you're doing; it will also ensure that you can sculpt the area underneath the eyeballs. If you don't turn transparency on, then the eyeballs will occlude part of the fish and prevent you from sculpting that part of the fish. Press the Q key on the keyboard to switch back to *Draw* mode (the button is on the *Top Shelf*). Select the *Standard* brush (or use the B S T keyboard shortcut) and use this brush to build up the back of the fish's head near the rear of the eyelids. Remember that you can hold down the ALT key to switch the brush from *Zadd* to *Zsub* while working. Work the surface up slowly by building up the surface and then smoothing it back and repeating this process until you get the exact shape you want. Save your tool. Always save your tool before you merge or split your subtools. Indeed, it is a good idea to save your tool before you do any sort of major operation on your model in case things go wrong.

FIGURE 7.18 Use the *Tool > Subtool > Rename* command to change the name of the currently selected subtool.

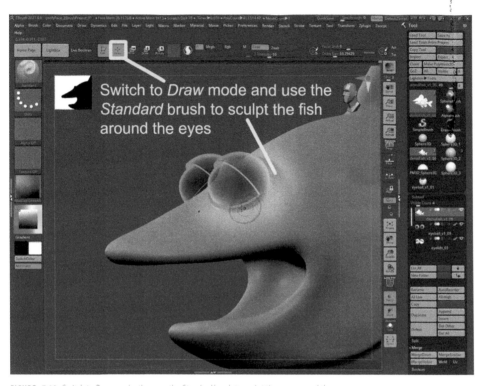

Switch to *Draw* mode and use the *Standard* brush to sculpt the fish around the eyes

FIGURE 7.19 Switch to *Draw* mode, then use the *Standard* brush to sculpt the area around the eyes.

Conclusion

Before we can call our sculpt finished, we will need to define the fish's tertiary details, such as the scales and fin rays, add a tongue and maybe some teeth, and any other features we can think of. After all of that, we can go in, paint our fish, and complete the model. For now, we should take a break. Hopefully, you are enjoying making a little cartoon fish and are becoming familiar with ZBrush and its workflow. If nothing else, it is important to just mess around with the program and explore it. Have fun with it and enjoy yourself. Set aside 15 minutes each day to play around with the program. It will turn into an hour because you'll have so much fun, but this is the way you master ZBrush. It is just that the first 2 weeks are a bit difficult as you wrap your head around ZBrush's odd workflow and terminology. Make sure that you watch the video associated with this chapter to help you understand all of the methods we have gone over.

Further reading

"ZBrush : Resource Center." Maxon Computer GMBH. https://pixologic. com/zbrush/downloadcenter/library/. Accessed 15 Dec. 2022.

8

The Fish, Part 4 – Tertiary Details

Welcome back! In this chapter, we're going to focus on adding more details to our fish model. We have previously created the primary forms of the fish's body, eyes, and fins, as well as some secondary forms, such as the gill covers. Additional secondary forms still missing include the tongue and maybe some humorous tonsils or teeth. After finishing these elements, we can move on to the tertiary details and add the scales and fin rays. Let's go ahead and start by adding a tongue. Like many models in ZBrush, we will begin with a sphere.

Creating the tongue

Go to the Tool menu, click on the large golden *S* icon (or your currently loaded model), and choose the *Sphere3D* tool icon from the pop-up menu. Click and drag on the document to draw the sphere on the screen, and then immediately press the T key to activate *Edit* mode. You can now go to the *Tool > Initialize* palette and increase the *HDivide* and *VDivide* sliders to increase the resolution of the sphere a bit. Afterward, click on the *Tool > Make PolyMesh3D* button to convert the sphere into a sculptable object. Press W on the keyboard to bring up the *Gizmo 3D* and proceed to scale the sphere until you make a sort of fat sausage shape.

Select the *Move Topological* brush using the B M T keyboard shortcut. Next, activate *Symmetry* by pressing the X key or clicking on *Transform > Activate Symmetry*. The default *X Symmetry* axis should be fine for crafting the tongue. After doing this, you can create a tongue shape out of the sausage model.

DOI: 10.1201/9781003215288-8

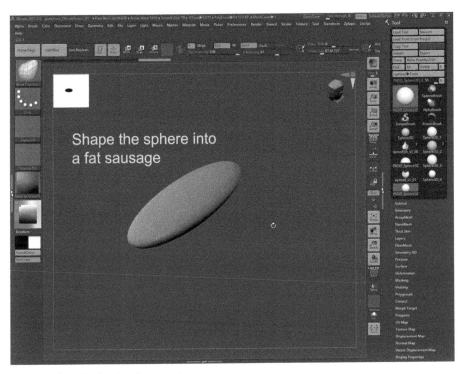

FIGURE 8.1 Shape the sphere into a fat sausage shape.

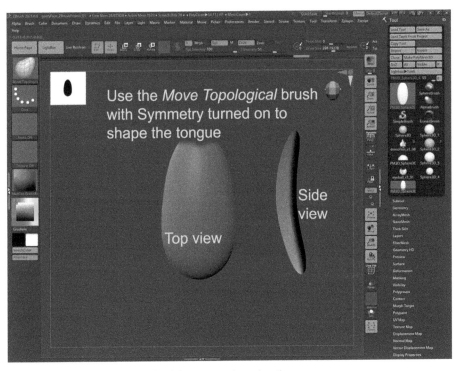

FIGURE 8.2 Use the *Move Topological* brush with *Symmetry* turned on to shape the tongue.

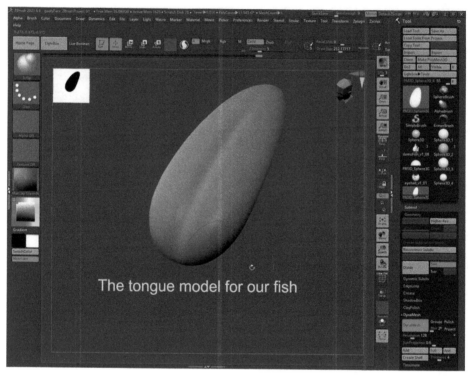

The tongue model for our fish

FIGURE 8.3 The tongue model for our fish.

If the model begins to show weird patterns in its geometry, fix it using the *Tool > Geometry > DynaMesh > DynaMesh* button, followed by judicious use of the *Smooth* brush. Next, use the *Inflate* brush (B I N) to puff up the tip and sides of the tongue. When using the *Inflate* brush, you will want to set the *Z Intensity* setting pretty low. For example, I used a *Z Intensity* of 5 for this part. *Inflate* is a very powerful tool, and it only takes a little of it to affect the model. Now, switch to the *DamStandard* brush (B D S), decrease your *Draw Size*, draw a crease right down the middle of the top side of the tongue, and then smooth the resulting line out a bit. The combination of the *Move, Inflate, DamStandard*, and *Smooth* brushes is a very powerful one in ZBrush. Continue using these brushes until you have shaped your tongue model to your satisfaction. Save your tongue model using the *Tool > Save As* command and place the resulting model into the same folder as the file for your fish model.

Adding the tongue to the fish model

Switch back to your fish model by using the Tool Palette icon list. You can use the *Tool > Load Tool* command to load the file from the hard disk if you do not see the fish model in the Tool Palette icon list. Use the *Tool > Subtool > Append* command to add the tongue model as a subtool to your fish model.

FIGURE 8.4 Use *Tool > Subtool > Append* to add the tongue to your fish model.

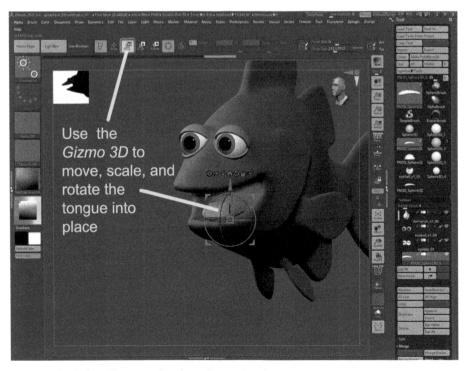

FIGURE 8.5 Use the *Gizmo 3D* to move, scale, and rotate the tongue into place.

Make sure that you have the tongue subtool selected in the subtool icon stack, then use the *Gizmo 3D* to move, scale, and rotate the tongue into place.

With the tongue subtool selected, click the *Tool* > *Subtool* > *Rename* button and change the name of the tongue subtool to "tongue_01". Use the *Tool* > *Save As* button to save an iteration of your ZBrush tool file.

Sculpting details in the mouth

Now that all of the major pieces of our fish are complete, we can begin adding details to our fish model. Zoom in to get a good view of the back of your fish's throat. Make sure that you have the fish subtool selected in the *Tool* > *Subtool* palette. Turn on transparency by pressing the *Transp* button on the lower right side of the document. In order to see the back of the fish's throat more clearly, it can help if you turn off the visibility of the other subtools by going to the *Subtool Palette* and clicking on the little eye icon on the far right side of the subtool, which will toggle the eyeball off and hide that subtool from your view. To unhide the subtool, simply click on the eye icon again to toggle that subtool back to visibility. Use this technique to hide all of the subtools that you do not need at the moment.

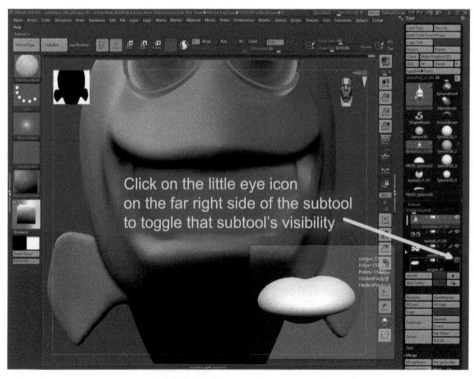

FIGURE 8.6 Click on the little eye icon on the far right side of the subtool to toggle that subtool's visibility.

Note that ZBrush only hides unselected subtools. This behavior can cause a bit of confusion if you aren't used to it, but it enables a very useful little trick. Hold down the SHIFT key and click on the subtool eye icon, which will hide all of the subtools except for the currently selected subtool, even though it turns off the eye icon for this subtool as well. Hold down SHIFT and click on one of the subtool eye icons to unhide all of the subtools.

After you have hidden any subtools that might get in the way, use the B D S shortcut to select the *DamStandard* brush. Draw in the uvula (the little dangly bit) and the throat in the back of the mouth, and then press the 1 key on the top row of numbers on your keyboard to repeat the brush stroke, which will carve the tonsils in deeper each time that you press the 1 key. Afterward, use the *Tool > DynaMesh > DynaMesh* button to remesh and clean up your fish's geometry.

Use the *Standard* brush while holding down the ALT key to push down the raised ridges in the throat area, which will start forming the throat behind the uvula. Clean up the geometry using a combination of the *DynaMesh* command and *Smooth* brush whenever the surface begins to look a bit too rough. You can use the *DamStandard* brush to carve the surface inward whenever needed. Recall that you can use the *Stroke > Lazy Mouse > Lazy Mouse* button to turn the *Lazy Mouse* feature on or off of your current brush.

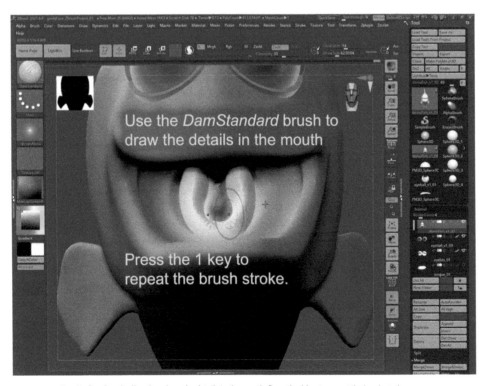

FIGURE 8.7 Use the *DamStandard* brush to draw the details in the mouth. Press the 1 key to repeat the brush stroke.

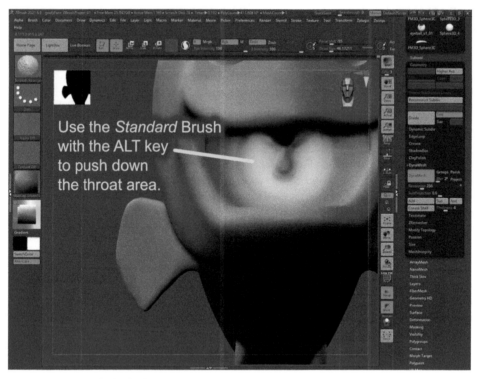

Use the *Standard* Brush with the ALT key to push down the throat area.

FIGURE 8.8 Use the *Standard* brush with the ALT key to push down the throat area.

We now need to pop the uvula out a little bit and shape it. Use the *Move Topological* brush (B M T) to pull the little dangly piece in the middle of the throat forward a bit. *DynaMesh* the results to rebuild your geometry. Use the Inflate brush (B I N) to add some bulk to the uvula, then *DynaMesh* the model again. You have probably noticed by now that we use *DynaMesh* pretty frequently. Whenever the surface begins to look rough or stretched, it is a good time to break out the old *DynaMesh* and use it to resurface your model. This approach is known as concept sculpting and is one of the more approachable workflows in ZBrush, but it is by no means the only workflow in the program. Concept sculpting with *DynaMesh* is, however, one of the easiest workflows in ZBrush and one that does not require the use of any other 3D program. For that reason, this approach is the one that we will be most focused on in this book. If you try to look up information online about ZBrush, you will need to be aware of what type of workflow you are dealing with. Not all of the various available workflows are compatible with each other. If you find a tutorial that seems at odds with what you have learned so far, that is most likely because they are using a different workflow. To really see what you are doing with the uvula, you can use CTRL+SHIFT+ALT with the *SelectLasso* brush to draw a selection area and hide any unwanted sections of your model.

While portions of the fish are hidden, you can use the *DamStandard* (B D S), *Move Topological* (B M T), and *Inflate* (B I N) brushes to sculpt the

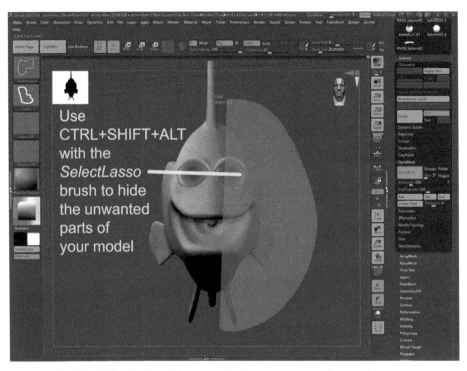

FIGURE 8.9 Use CTRL + SHIFT + ALT with the *SelectLasso* brush to hide the unwanted parts of your model.

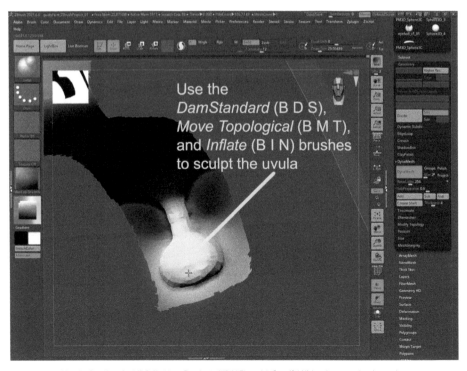

FIGURE 8.10 Use the *DamStandard* (B D S), *Move Topological* (B M T), and *Inflate* (B I N) brushes to sculpt the uvula.

uvula. Do not *DynaMesh* your model while a portion of it is hidden. That will yield some unexpected results if you do it now. Instead, remember to unhide the rest of your model (CTRL + SHIFT + click on the background) before you *DynaMEsh* things. Remember to smooth out any rough areas with the Smooth brush and to save your tool frequently.

Detailing the fins

We can now proceed to add some detail to our fins. Fish fins contain rays, and we need to sculpt those into our fish fins. Switch back to the *DamStandard* brush (B D S) and turn the *Z Intensity* down to around 20. Now, you can simply carve in the fin rays with a lovely degree of precision and control.

For the paired fins on the side and bottom of the fish, you will need to isolate the fins by using the *SelectLasso* brush by pressing CTRL + SHIFT and dragging a selection area over the fin you need to isolate. Try to make the surface you are sculpting perpendicular to your viewpoint. ZBrush brushes are sensitive to the angle at which you try to use them. Brushes typically function better the more of a right angle the surface forms with the view angle you have of the surface you are sculpting.

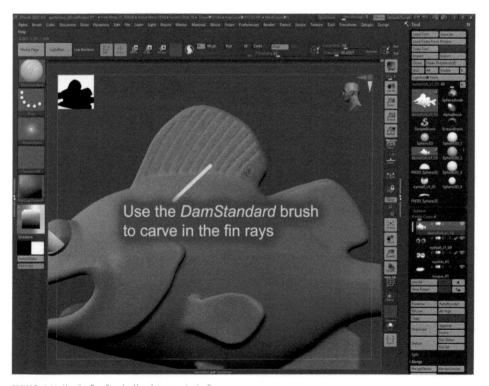

FIGURE 8.11 Use the *DamStandard* brush to carve in the fin rays.

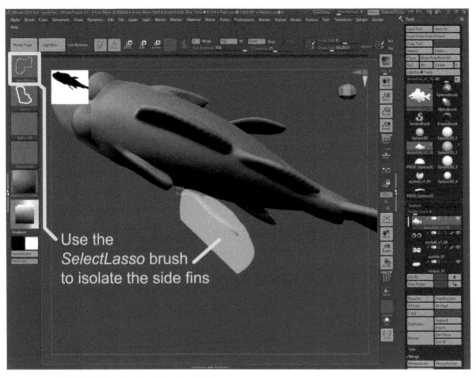

FIGURE 8.12 Use the *SelectLasso* brush to isolate the side fins.

Another approach is to make your current camera view parallel to the surface you are sculpting. Repeat this process of isolating your fins and then carving in the rays using the *DamStandard* brush until you have added some detail to all of your fins.

The thing to remember about these brushes is that even though the brush appears as a circle on your screen, the brushes are actually spheres, and with a thin object like these fins, the brush will actually go all the way through the model to the other side. To change this behavior, turn on the *Brush > Auto Masking > BackfaceMask* button. Note that having backface masking on can change the behavior of certain brushes. If you have a brush that is doing unexpected things, it can be useful to check this setting. Remember to save your progress.

To add a bit more random detail to the fins, we can now switch to the *Rake* (B R) brush and turn the *Z Intensity* down very low to around two or so. Gently go in and brush along the length of the rays we have already carved into the fins, which should add a teensy bit of extra rays to the fins. Save frequently. The autosave function is only partially reliable.

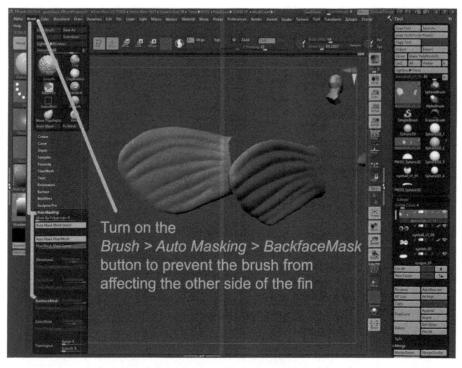

FIGURE 8.13 Turn on the *Brush > Auto Masking > BackfaceMask* button to prevent the brush from affecting the other side of the fin.

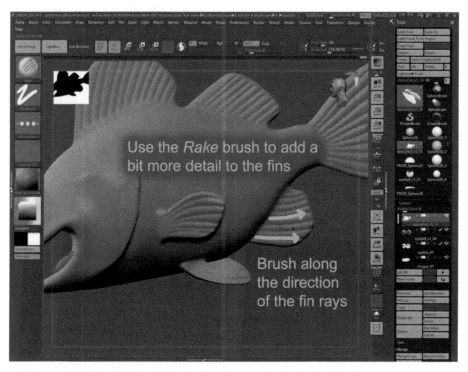

FIGURE 8.14 Use the *Rake* brush to add a bit more detail to the fins. Brush along the direction of the fin rays.

Making fish scales

Now that we are done with the fins, we can add the scales. Before we sculpt on the scales, we should mask off the areas that we do not want to have scales. Hold down the CTRL key to access the *MaskPen* brush and paint a mask over our fins. Pay close attention to the paired fins when creating your mask, and be sure to clean up any mistakes. Remember that you can hold down CTRL + ALT to erase parts of the mask if you need to. You should also mask off the inside of the mouth and the throat since these areas do not need any scales either. Use the *Tool > Subtool* palette to hide any subtools you do not currently need, using the tiny eye icons as a visibility toggle. Make sure that the *MaskPen* brush doesn't go all the way through your fish's mouth and accidentally mask off an unwanted area. If you hold down the CTRL key and tap on the masked-off area, it will blur the mask.

To sculpt in the scales first, choose the *Standard* brush (B S T). In addition to selecting the brush, we can also set the stroke and the brush alpha. The stroke controls how the brush is applied to the surface, while the brush alpha manages the shape of the brush tip. Click on the blank square that has the *Alpha Off* label on the left-hand side of the interface. The *Alpha* palette will pop up, and you can now use this to

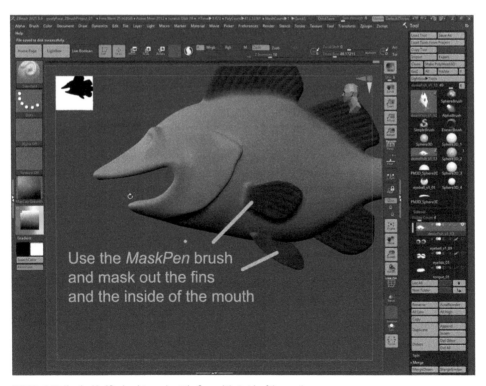

FIGURE **8.15** Use the *MaskPen* brush to mask out the fins and the inside of the mouth.

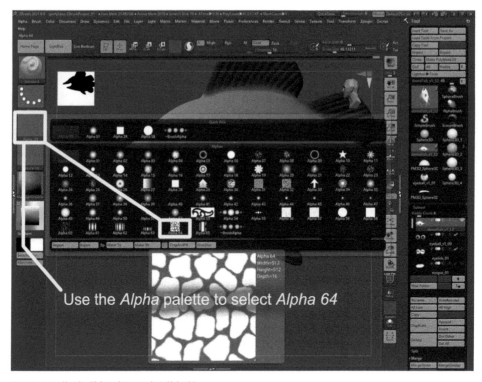

Use the *Alpha* palette to select *Alpha 64*

FIGURE 8.16 Use the *Alpha* palette to select *Alpha 64*.

choose *Alpha 64*, which is a nice, somewhat scaly-looking alpha for our brush. Make sure that you save your model now.

Try painting with your brush now to see what it does. Undo that stroke, and now click on the *Dots* icon just above where you set the brush alpha. A pop-up window will appear that allows you to access the *Strokes* palette. Select the *DragRect* brush and try it out. Undo those brush strokes. Now, try out the *Freehand* stroke in the palette and see what that does. Then, use the *ColorSpray*, *Spray*, and *DragDot* strokes to get a feel for what each of these different types of strokes does. Play with some of the other brush alphas and see what they do with various brush strokes. You can combine a given brush with one of the many strokes and different brush alphas to create an enormous range of differing effects while sculpting. If you mess up, there is always the undo (CTRL + Z) button, or you can load up your model file from a few minutes ago – that is why we saved it!

Switch to the *Color Spray* stroke and the *Alpha 64* brush alpha. Set the *Z Intensity* to a low value, say around 6, and paint in the scales on the rear of the fish. The size of the brush and the angle you paint on the object will also affect the result. This approach will let you add a scale texture to your model very quickly. Change to the *DragRect* stroke and up your *Z Intensity* to around 12 to add in some larger scales to

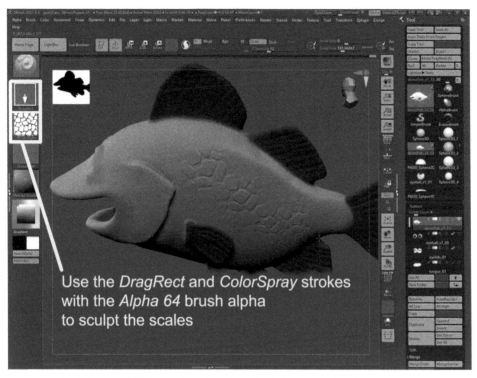

Use the *DragRect* and *ColorSpray* strokes
with the *Alpha 64* brush alpha
to sculpt the scales

FIGURE 8.17 Use the *DragRect* and *ColorSpray* strokes with the *Alpha 64* brush alpha to sculpt the scales.

complement the smaller pattern you have already painted on the
fish. To use the *DragRect* brush, simply click and drag on your model
to place a brush stroke. The *DragRect* brush gives you an incredible
amount of control over where to place each brush stroke.

Since we are sculpting a cartoon fish, we can just keep using the default
alphas that come with ZBrush. You can actually make alphas and use
them in ZBrush to create a really unique look for your sculpture. In fact,
you can go to the ZBRush Resource Center and download a bunch of
freely usable brush alphas (pixologic.com/zbrush/downloadcenter/
alpha/). Use the *Import* button at the bottom of the brush alpha palette
to load external brush alphas into ZBrush if you want to try this out.

Merging the eyelids with the fish

Right now, the eyelids are not quite matching up with the rest of
the fish, and we should fix that. I think that we need to merge the
eyelids with the rest of the fish. First, save your model. It is always
a good idea to have a backup. We need to make sure that our eyelids subtool is immediately underneath the fish model. Use the
Tool > Subtool > Move Up or *Move Down* command to arrange your
subtools, or you can just select your eyelids subtool. Hold down the

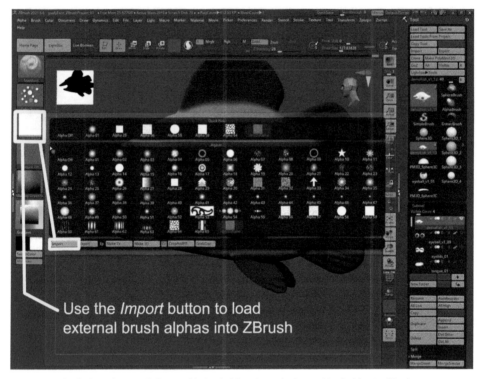

Use the *Import* button to load external brush alphas into ZBrush

FIGURE 8.18 Use the *Import* button at the bottom of the brush alpha palette to load external brush alphas into ZBrush.

CTRL key and use the up and down arrows on your keyboard to move your subtool around within the subtool stack. Once you have the eyelids underneath the fish subtool, select the fish subtool, and use the *Tool > Subtool > Merge > MergeDown* command to merge your fish with your eyelids. Next, use *Tool > Geometry > DynaMesh > DynaMesh* to create a unified surface out of the fish and the eyeballs. Make sure that the *Tool > Geometry > DynaMesh > Resolution* slider is set to an appropriate value, something like 256, for instance. If the *Resolution* slider is set too low, you will lose some of the detail that you have just added to your model. Now you can go in and smooth the eyelids into the fish model a bit and add some fine-scale texture to the back of the eyelids. If you need to add even more fine detail to your model, you can try to *DynaMesh* the model with a higher *Resolution*, say 366–512. Just make sure that you use a reasonable resolution and do not end up with a model that slows your computer down. If you ever apply a command that begins to take too long, you can press the ESC key to cancel that operation – just be aware that doing so can cause ZBrush to crash.

Continue using the *Smooth*, *Standard*, and other brushes to refine the details on your fish's ocular area. If the eyeball starts to peek through the back of the eyelids, you can use the *Move Topological* brush to pull the eyelids out a bit and cover the eyeball back up.

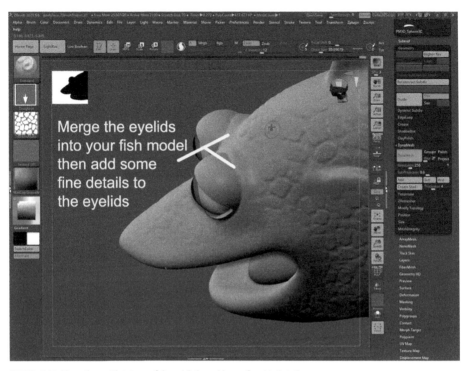

FIGURE 8.19 Merge the eyelids into your fish model, then add some fine details to them.

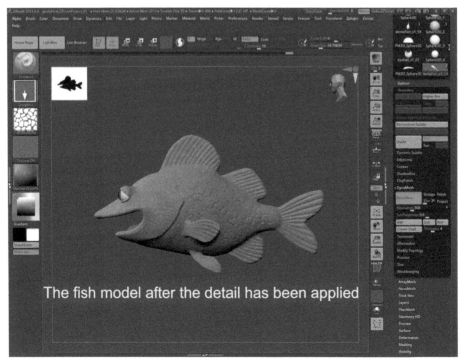

FIGURE 8.20 The fish model after the detail has been applied to it.

Save your model using the *Tool > Save As* button. Okay, so now we have got our fish model, and we have saved it. Make sure that you watch the video associated with this chapter to help you understand all of the methods we have gone over so far. Next up, it is time to paint this thing.

Conclusion

ZBrush is a wonderful software package. It can be a lot of fun, but it does have a steep initial learning curve due to its non-standard interface and workflow. Keep in mind that it takes a while to get to grips with this program. Having taught ZBrush for well over a decade now, I can say with some conviction that it will not be the first model you make that looks good, or even the second. It is usually sometime in the range of model number 6 to model number 12 that you attempt to believe that things will really start coming together for you. So remember to be patient. If things don't work the first time, don't sweat it. Just sit down later on and try it again. For now, just see how far you can get. If you really want to challenge yourself, then get a mirror and see if you can do a self-portrait in ZBrush. That is really hard to pull off, but if you're up for a serious modeling challenge, a self-portrait is a very good one. Next time, we are going to finish up our cartoon fish. We will paint this little guy, and then we're going to move on to a more difficult project and cover even more material. That is the way the rest of the book will continue as I progress through various projects. Every time I show you something, I take things a little bit further. I hope you are enjoying ZBrush so far.

9

The Fish, Part 5 – Painting the Fish

Welcome back and setting preferences

Welcome back! In this chapter, we are going to paint our fish. First, if you get tired of the ZBrush screensaver popping up all of the time, you can turn it off by toggling off the *Preferences > ScreenSaver > Screen-Saver On* button. You can find all of ZBrush's preference settings in this menu and tweak it however you like, but be aware that some of the settings could be clearer. You may also want to toggle off the *Preferences > LightBox > Open At Launch* button if you find that particular feature annoying. While I do not want to do a deep dive into all of ZBrush's preferences at the moment, it is important to know where to find these settings if you need help with how ZBrush behaves.

Materials for painting

Go ahead and load your fish model back into ZBrush using the *Tool > Load Tool* command, draw the tool onto the document, and turn on the *Edit* button to pick back up where we left off at the end of the last chapter. Take a look at your subtools. The eyeballs should already be colored in and ready to go, but the fish and the tongue need coloring. Go ahead and select the tongue and look at the material icon to see what material is currently on that object. When you are painting, you do not want to use any of the pre-colored materials. Materials that have a lot of color or dark tones are poor choices for painting, as the embedded color in the material will pollute anything that you paint onto the object. It can be very challenging to gauge how the different colors you apply will cooperate with these colored materials.

DOI: 10.1201/9781003215288-9

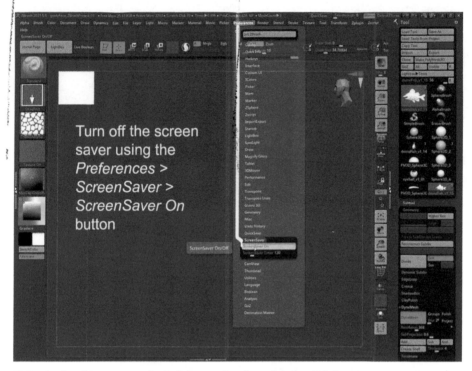

FIGURE 9.1 Turn off the screen saver using the *Preferences > ScreenSaver > ScreenSaver On* button.

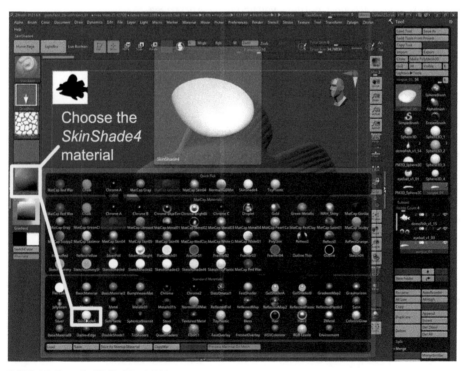

FIGURE 9.2 Choose the *SkinShade4* material.

As such, it is usually best to choose a material that is very pale or white as a base from which to work when painting. Go ahead and select the *SkinShade4* material from the Material Palette. The tongue should automatically update to the new material.

You may see the fish model auto-update as well. Remember that ZBrush tools will auto-update to the currently selected material and color by default until you permanently assign a material and color to that subtool. Now, choose a nice red color from the *Color Palette*. Don't worry if the fish changes color. It is just automatically updating. You will notice that the eyeballs don't change color and material. That is because we assigned a material and color to the eyeballs earlier. To permanently give your chosen color to the tongue subtool, make sure that you have the *Mrgb* button turned on at the top, the *Rgb Intensity* slider set to 100, and then use the *Color > FillObject* button. You should see over in the *Subtool* sub-palette that the tongue has changed color.

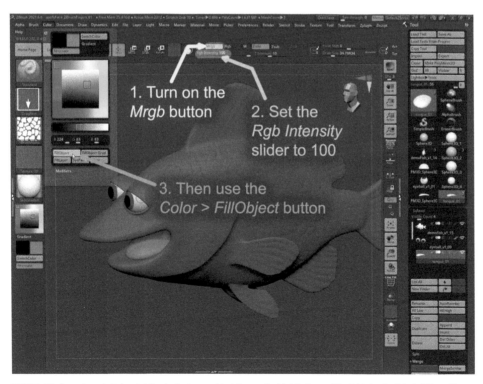

FIGURE 9.3 To apply a selected material and color to your object. Turn on the *Mrgb* button, set the *Rgb Intensity* slider to 100, and then use the *Color > FillObject* button.

Filling in a base color

Select the fish subtool in the *Subtool* sub-palette. Now we get to decide what color of fish we want. Well, we started the project by making a cartoon of a yellow perch, so our fish should be … yellow. Let's make our particular cartoon fish a bit more golden-orange than the real yellow perch. Cartoons are supposed to be a bit exaggerated, after all. With that in mind, pick out a bright, warm yellow color. In the demo, I used $R=208$, $G=195$, and $B=91$, but you can use whatever color you want. This time, we will just assign the color to the fish and leave the material unassigned. Turn on the *Rgb* button at the top. Leave the *Rgb Intensity* set to 100 and use the *Color > FillObject* button, which will embed just the yellow color but not the material. Later on, we can go in and still change the material using the current material auto-update feature. This approach will let us try out a bunch of materials to see how they look with our paint job.

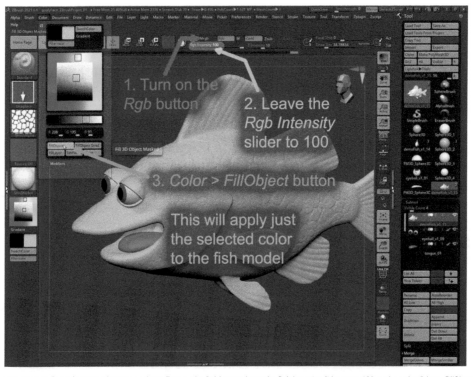

FIGURE 9.4 To apply just a color to your object. Turn on the *Rgb* button, leave the *Rgb Intensity* slider set to 100, and use the *Color > FillObject* button.

Hand painting the model

Now that we have applied a base color to our fish, we can start painting the model by hand, which is where masking comes in very handy. To set up your paintbrush, choose the *Standard* brush (B S T) and set the stroke to *ColorSpray*. We can start off using the same *BrushAlpha*, "*Alpha 64*." Make sure the *Rgb* button is on. Now, turn off the *Zadd* button at the top. Do this because if we have *Zadd* or *Zsub* on when we are trying to paint, we would be sculpting as well as painting at the same time, and that can be confusing. As such, we have split up creating the fish into a modeling portion and then a painting portion. Keep the *Zadd* and *Zsub* buttons off while you are painting, unless you want to sculpt your model. Note that if you use the SHIFT key to access the *Smooth* brush, it will have *Zadd* turned on by default. ZBrush remembers the settings for each brush independently by default, which means that you will have to pay attention to the status of the *Zadd* and *Zsub* buttons whenever you switch brushes.

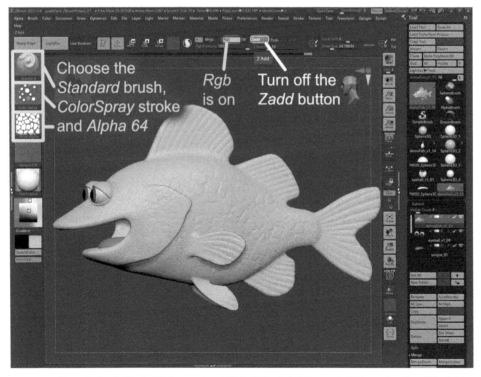

FIGURE 9.5 Choose the *Standard* brush, *ColorSpray* stroke, and "*Alpha 64*" brush tip. Make sure the *Rgb* button is on. Turn off the *Zadd* button.

Go ahead and turn down the *Rgb Intensity* slider to around 40. You can press the I key shortcut to make the *Rgb Intensity* slider pop up immediately under the mouse cursor. Now press the S key to get the *Draw Size* pop-up, and set the brush size to around 150. Change the current color to a pale tint of yellow. At this point, you can start painting the belly of the fish in lighter colors. Countershading is where the top of the animal is darker, and the bottom is a paler color. Countershading is extremely common in the animal kingdom and is a good concept to remember if you are ever trying to design realistic monsters. Our cartoon fish is no exception.

We will add more details later on. Right now, we are just applying our first coat of paint as we build up the color of the fish in various stages. A yellow perch has a little bit of brown coloration, too. Go ahead and choose a warm, mid-tone brown from the *Color Palette*. Since I do not want to paint the side fin at the moment, I can use either the masking tools (via the CTRL key) or the *SelectLasso* brush (CTRL+SHIFT keys) to hide the side fin for the time being. To quickly access the most commonly used settings, you can simply hold down the SPACEBAR. Doing so will pop up your *Color Palette*, *Draw Size*, brush selector, and a whole

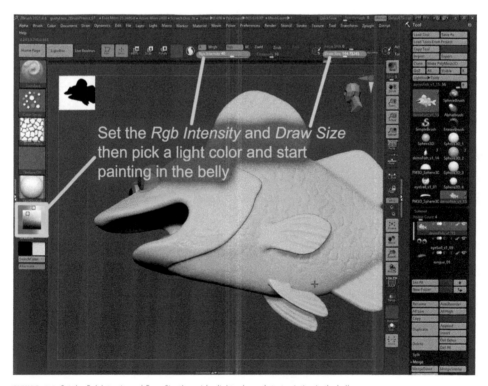

FIGURE 9.6 Set the *Rgb Intensity* and *Draw Size* then pick a light color and start painting in the belly.

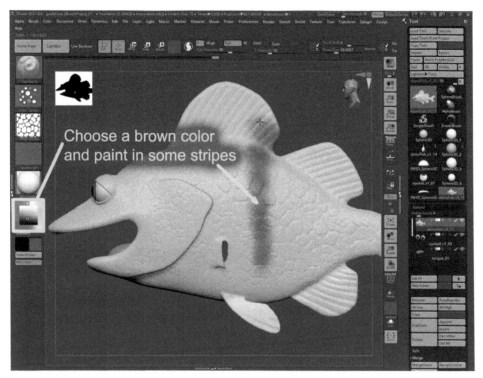

FIGURE 9.7 Choose a brown color and paint in some stripes.

bunch of other commonly used controls. Reduce your *Draw Size* just a bit and start painting some stripes on your fish. I prefer to gradually paint things in using multiple passes of a brush with the *Rgb Intensity* set fairly low to around 40.

Go ahead and use the brown to paint quite a bit of the top, or dorsal, part of the fish as part of the fish's countershading. If you want to avoid going through to the other side of your fish when painting it, for instance, if you don't want to paint the inside of the mouth, turn on *Brush > Auto Masking > BackfaceMask*. This option basically masks off the reverse side of what you are currently painting on. The *BackfaceMask* button is one of the more useful options in ZBrush, but it is buried in the interface, and there is no hotkey to it by default. Luckily, you can create new hotkeys in ZBrush.

First, let's take a look at all of the existing hotkeys in ZBrush by taking a look at the ZBrush Shortcuts and Mouse Actions Document that you can download from here (http://docs.pixologic.com/wp-content/uploads/2021/08/ZBrush-Shortcuts.pdf). You want to avoid accidentally overwriting an important existing hotkey. To create a new hot key, simply hold down the CTRL + ALT keys and click on the *Brush > Auto Masking > BackfaceMask* button. Now, press the key (or keys) on your

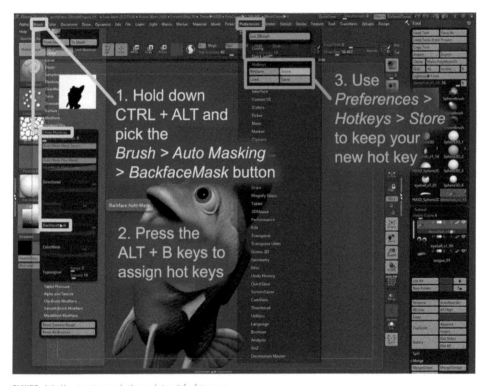

FIGURE 9.8 How to set a new hotkey and store it for future use.

keyboard; that will be the new hotkey, I used ALT+B on my computer. If you would like ZBrush to remember your new hotkey, click on the *Preferences > Hotkeys > Store* button. Alternatively, you can save your new hotkey(s) into a file using the *Preferences > Hotkeys > Save* button, and then use the *Preferences > Hotkeys > Load* button to bring your saved hotkeys back into ZBrush when you want them.

Go ahead and finish painting the stripes on the fish. Remember that your fish doesn't need to look like the one in the book if you do not want it to. If you make a mistake and paint a bit too much brown on a given area, you can easily fix it. First, we will need to grab the yellow color off of the fish. To use the eye dropper command to sample a color from the model, you can place your mouse cursor over the color you want and press C on the keyboard, or you can go to the *Color Palette* and then click and hold down the left mouse button over the color square and drag over the model to pick a color. You can now touch up the underlying color. When you are done, you can use the same technique to sample the brown color and keep painting on the stripes.

Using this approach, you can go ahead and add a touch of green to the fish (or whatever color you like). If you are painting with the *Rgb Intensity* set low, you can blend the colors you are painting with on the

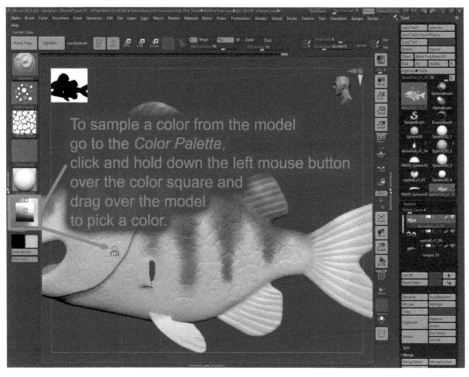

FIGURE 9.9 *To sample a color from the model, go to the Color Palette, click and hold down the left mouse button over the color square, and drag over the model to pick a color.*

object while you paint to create a rich, layered effect. Try adding color variation to your surface by using the *ColorSpray* stroke while painting with various colors. The *ColorSpray* stroke will shift your color around a bit as you paint. For example, I used yellow, orange, brown, and green to paint in the rough colors on the example fish shown in the book with the *Standard* brush set to *ColorSpray* with the "*Alpha 64*" *Brush Alpha*. Remember to unhide all of the pieces of your fish using the *Tool > Visibility > ShowPt* command or by holding down CTRL + SHIFT and clicking on the background.

We still need to paint the inside of the mouth. Use the color sampler technique to sample the tongue's red color. Rotate your view and zoom in until you can see the inside of the mouth clearly. Make sure that *Back-faceMask* is on. Now, start painting the inside of the mouth. You can turn on the *Transp* button to allow you to see and paint under the tongue, or simply hide the tongue using the subtool eye toggle. Change your viewpoint periodically to make sure that you get all the spots. After you have completed one coat of pale red, choose a darker shade of red and start painting in the back of the throat and any other areas you would like to be darker, like the roof of the mouth and under the tongue. Next, pick an almost black color and paint in the area behind the uvula.

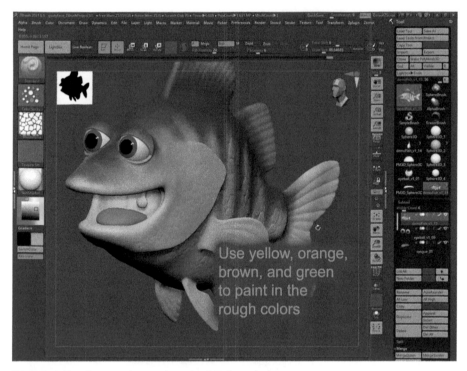

FIGURE 9.10 Use yellow, orange, brown, and green to paint in the rough colors.

FIGURE 9.11 Remember to change your viewpoint occasionally so you don't miss a spot. Use the subtool eye toggle to hide the tongue.

FIGURE 9.12 Make sure that the *Zadd* button is turned off whenever you use the *Smooth* brush while painting.

You can use the *Smooth* brush to blend the colors on the model together, but you need to pay close attention to make sure that the *Zadd* button is turned off whenever you do so. The different brushes remember their settings, and if you are not careful, you will end up smoothing out all of the detail that you spent so much time sculpting onto your model.

Adding touches of the various colors you have used so far on different areas of your model will help visually unify the color scheme and look of your model. For example, I use the red from the mouth to add some subtle coloration to the fins of the fish and warm up the browns a smidge. Unhide your tongue and turn off the *Transp* button to see how everything looks together once you have finished painting. If you are happy with how the fish looks, go ahead and save the tool using the *Tool > Save As* button.

Applying shading

As a final touch, we are going to make our fish look a whole lot better by applying some shading. Simply put, we are going to paint in some shadows and highlights, which is a classic technique that plastic model and miniature figurine painters have long used to enhance the look of their subjects. It is an approach that works equally well for a digital sculpture like ours. Back to the first chapter, I mentioned using the "How to Paint Citadel Miniatures" book and some old plastic model and diorama magazines such as "Fine Scale Modeler," "Scale Aviation Modeller," "Airfix Magazine" to help you explore this technique in full.

First, choose a dark color for your shadow and set the *Rgb Intensity* to around 5. Next, click on the *Tool > Masking > MaskByCavity > Mask By Cavity* button, which should mask off all of the creases in your model. Under the *Mask By Cavity* button is *Cavity Profile*. If you click on *Cavity Profile*, it will open up into a graph, which you can use to adjust how much of the model the *Mask By Cavity* command will mask. Simply click on the graph to place a control point, and slide that around until you get a graph profile that you like. You can get rid of the control point by simply sliding the control point off of the graph to one side or the other. You can add multiple control points to create complicated curves or slide a control point off to one side and then back onto the graph again to create a sharp angle on that control point. If you mess up, there is a small *Reset* button immediately under the graph to restore the graph to its original state.

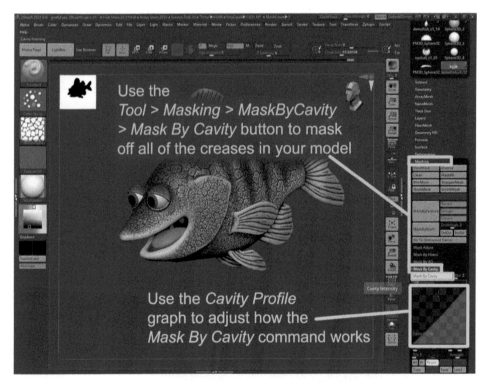

FIGURE 9.13 Use the *Tool > Masking > MaskByCavity > Mask By Cavity* button to mask off all of the creases in your model. Use the *Cavity Profile* graph to adjust how the *Mask By Cavity* command works.

After you create the cavity mask, use the CTRL+I shortcut to inverse the mask. Remember that you can find all of the mask commands under the *Tool > Masking* menu if you need them. Next, blur the mask using the *Tool > Masking > Blur* command. I prefer to turn off the *Tool > Masking > ViewMask* button so I can see what I am painting, but it isn't a strictly necessary thing to do. The whole point of doing the cavity mask is so that we can add some dark shading to the crevasses of our model. You can paint these shadows by hand using the brush, or you can use the *Color > FillObject* command to fill in the unmasked areas in one go. The results will be subtle because we have the *Rgb Intensity* set very low (to 5), so you may need to press the *FillObject* button several times to get the effect that you desire.

Use the *Tool > Masking > Clear* button to get rid of the existing mask. Now go ahead and use the *Mask By Cavity* button again, and follow that with the *Tool > Masking > Inverse* button. This time, we won't blur the mask before we use the *FillObject* button, which will darken the deeper parts of the cracks in our model. The whole idea is to paint in the shadows, meaning that the cracks and creases have dark shading, which fades away the further you get from the crevasse. This approach

FIGURE 9.14 Use the *Color > FillObject* command to fill in the unmasked areas.

mimics the way you would paint shadows on a figurine using a wash of very diluted paint, which naturally seeks out the low-lying areas of the figure. Practically speaking, this picks out the details in our model. It is important to understand that we aren't trying to paint in all of the shadows on the model, just the minor shadows that accentuate the details. The big shadows that appear on the model along the bottom and inside the mouth will be automatically generated by the 3D lighting setup within the program itself. All we are doing is artificially exaggerating the lighting with paint.

If you need to soften the shading that you have created, get rid of the mask first using either the *Tool > Masking > Clear* command or by just holding down CTRL and LMB and dragging in the background, and then use the smooth brush. Just make sure that the *Zadd* button is turned off so you don't affect the sculpt. You also need to make sure that the *Rgb* button is turned on. Otherwise, you won't affect the paint job.

Adding highlights

Now that we have successfully painted in the shadows, we still need to create some highlights on the fish. The method we use for this mimics how an artist would drybrush highlights onto a plastic model kit or miniature. Clear any masks that you have on the model. Use the *Tool > Masking > Mask By Cavity > Cavity Profile > Reset* button to clear any modifications you have made to the *Cavity Profile* graph. Now click on the *Tool > Masking > Mask By Cavity > Mask By Cavity* button to create a new cavity mask. Click the *Tool > Masking > Blur* button several times to really give the mask a strong blur. Make the mask invisible by toggling the *Tool > Masking > ViewMask* button off. Go to the *Color Palette* and select a very pale, bright shade of yellow. The color should be very white, with just a bit of yellow in it. At this point, you can either use the *Color > FillObject* command to affect the entire object or use a large, soft brush to paint in the highlights. I prefer using a large brush for this part since it provides more control over where the highlights appear. For the demo fish, I used the *Standard* brush with a *ColorSpray* stroke and the "*Alpha 01*" brush alpha. The *Rgb Intensity* was set to 3, *Zadd* was turned off, and the *Draw Size* was set to around 125. Once your cavity mask, brush, and color are set up, just go into the top of the fish and brush in some highlights on anything that would naturally catch the light: the top of the fins, the forehead, the top of the bottom lip, and the top of the gill flaps, for example. Gently brush in the highlights until you are happy with how the fish looks. The effect should be a subtle one. You are not trying to change the color of the fish significantly. The cavity mask that we created will protect the shaded areas. If you overdo the shadows or highlights, you can tone down their effect by selecting a color off of the body of the fish and painting over the shading or highlights a bit.

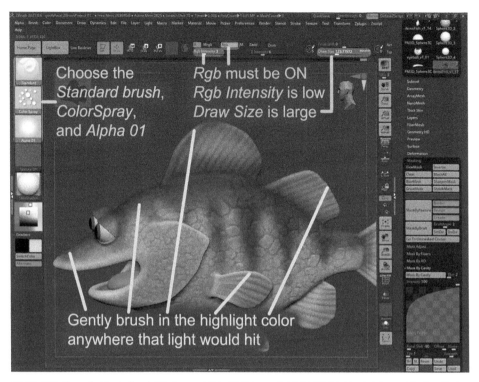

Choose the Standard brush, ColorSpray, and Alpha 01

Rgb must be ON Rgb Intensity is low Draw Size is large

Gently brush in the highlight color anywhere that light would hit

FIGURE 9.15 Choose the *Standard* brush, *ColorSpray*, and *Alpha 01*. Make sure that *Rgb* is ON, *Rgb Intensity* is low, and the *Draw Size* is large. Gently brush in the highlight color wherever light would naturally strike the object.

All you need to do at this point is keep working on your fish until you are happy with the results. Just make sure that you are having fun with the process. As long as you're having fun and enjoying yourself, then everything will work out great.

Rendering out a final image

The very last thing we need to do is render out some good images of our fish. First, move your viewpoint around until you find a good-looking pose for your creation. Next, turn on the *Persp* button (or press the P hotkey). It is a little icon with a receding grid on it that lives in the middle of the icon bar on the right side of the ZBrush document. By default, ZBrush works in an orthographic view (objects do not shrink as they get further away), but when it comes time to render your final image(s), folks usually turn perspective on since it more closely matches how the human eye perceives the world. Now save your tool using the *Tool > Save As* command. Look in the top right-hand corner of the document and find the *BPR* button. Press this *BPR* button (or use the SHIFT+R hotkey) to create a Best-Preview Render.

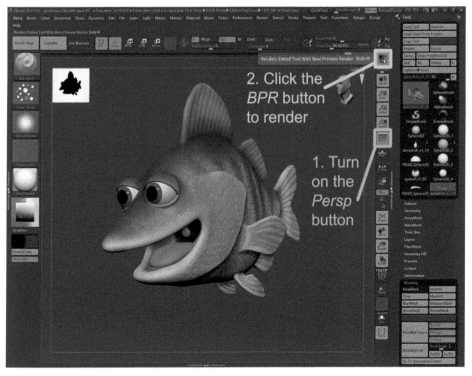

FIGURE 9.16 Turn on the *Persp* button and then click the *BPR* button to render an image.

The Best-Preview Render adds lighting and shadows to our object in the document window. If you like the results, use the *Document > Export* button to save an image file of the render.

A file window will pop up, and you should give your file a good name and make sure that you are saving the file in a location that you can find later on. Choose JPG as the file type to save as.

Use the *Export Image* interface to crop the image. Grab the small red circles at the border of the image and drag them to define the outer edges of your picture. You can also change the settings of the JPG if you choose. I suggest setting the *Quality* slider to 100 to maximize the quality of your JPG image. Click the OK button once you are finished to save the image to your hard disk.

You can use the *Document > Export* command to export the document anytime you like. The only thing you should be aware of is that you need to refrain from using the *Document > Save* or *Save As* buttons by mistake. If you save the document using either the *Document > Save* or *Save As* button, ZBrush will write out a.ZBR (ZBrush Document) file. Unfortunately, the only program in the world that will read this file format is ZBrush itself, which makes the ZBR file format less than useful. Use the *Document > Export* command instead. The export command is

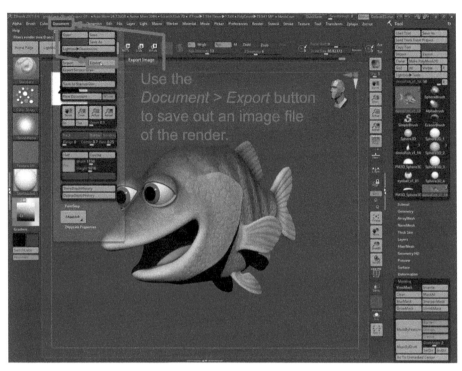

FIGURE 9.17 Use the *Document > Export* button to save an image file of the render.

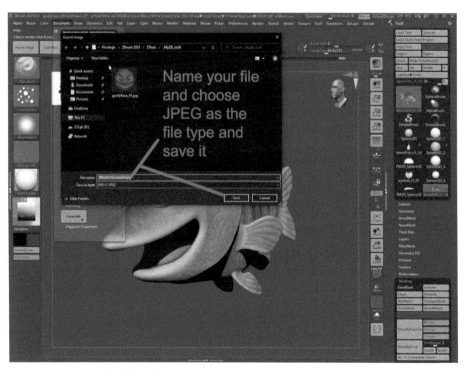

FIGURE 9.18 Name your file and choose JPEG as the file type.

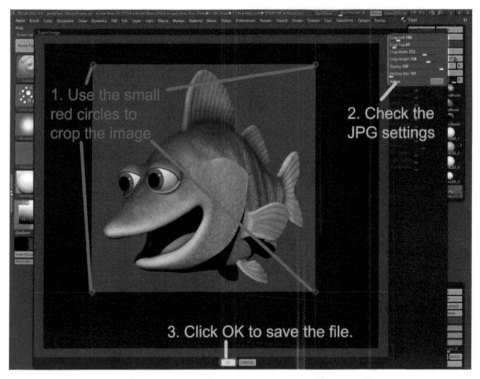

FIGURE 9.19 Use the small red circles to crop the image, check the JPG settings, and click OK to save the file.

capable of saving out BMP, JPG, PNG, PSD, and TIF file formats, which are all very common and useful file types. After you have exported your rendered image, ZBrush will get rid of all the shadows and go back to normal as soon as you begin to change your view. We will talk a lot more about rendering, shadow quality, and lighting later on, but this is a good place to wrap things up for now.

Conclusion

You should now know how to create a fairly simple model and have a fair understanding of some of the brushes and how they work. You have now learned the basics of masking, hiding objects, working with subtools, and rendering. Hopefully, you have begun to enjoy working with the program and have mastered the basic concept of sculpting workflows using *DynaMesh*. Make sure that you save a copy of your ZBrush tool. Keep playing around with the program and trying out various brushes and techniques to expand your knowledge of ZBrush and enhance your familiarity with it. In the next few chapters, we will start working on a more ambitious project and showcase a whole new slew of techniques.

Further reading

"Airfix Model World | Key Model World." Key Publishing Ltd. https://www.keymodelworld.com/airfix-model-world. Accessed 15 Dec. 2022.

"Fine Scale Modeler." Kalmbach Media. https://finescale.com/. Accessed 15 Dec. 2022.

Priestly, Rick, et al. *How to Paint Citadel Miniatures*. Nottingham, Games Workshop, 2003.

"SAMMI Latest Issue." Scale Aviation & Military Modeller. iHobby. https://www.i-hobby.co.uk/webshop/scale-aviation-military-modeller-international/sammi-latest-issue/. Accessed 15 Dec. 2022.

"ZBrush Shortcuts and Mouse Actions." Maxon Computer GMBH. https://docs.pixologic.com/wp-content/uploads/2021/08/ZBrush-Shortcuts.pdf. Accessed 18 Dec. 2022.

10

The Planning Stage

Pre-production, production, and post-production

This chapter discusses and explains the various elements and stages involved in creating a complicated project. This process breaks down into three phases: pre-production, production, and post-production. When you are beginning any sort of large project, it helps to engage in some sort of pre-production. Pre-production involves planning out the steps that you will need to accomplish and also describing the various elements that you will need to create to realize your creative vision. Depending on the size and scope of your project, the pre-production stage can be anything from a fairly simple outline to very in-depth documentation. Think of it like outlining a paper that you need to write. Since this is simply a concept sculpt and derived illustration, the pre-production process for us will be brief. We need some sort of idea of the subject for the illustration that we will be doing. Once we have our concept firmly in hand, we can turn to gathering all of the reference materials that we will need. After we have fleshed out our idea and gathered together all of the reference materials, we will be ready to begin production. During production, we will build all of the digital models that we need for the illustration, paint them, pose them, and render everything out. Last comes post-production, the stage where we combine all of the rendered elements into a cohesive whole and finish the work. In a professional setting, after everything has been completed and you have published the work, there will be one final step known as the post-mortem. In creative endeavors, a post-mortem is where you go back and analyze what went wrong and right with your production process. A post-mortem allows you to improve how things work for the next time. While it may seem a bit overzealous to

DOI: 10.1201/9781003215288-10

do all of this with a small project like this, having these formal steps in your creative process can help give your work a sense of structure and allow you to take on more ambitious projects than you would otherwise be able to accomplish.

Pre-production overview

The first step in development is to come up with some idea of what you want to do. Let us begin by deciding on the type of project that you will create. Are you making a concept sculpture, a 3D video game character, a television or movie model, an illustration, or a 3D-printed model? The answer to this basic question will determine what exact path you take for creating your ZBrush model, and each route has its own unique set of requirements and production pipeline to make it. Since this is an introductory-level book, it is appropriate to keep things simple. As such, we will keep our focus on concept sculpting since it is a widely used and practical approach that has a number of applications. Digitally sculpting a concept model is the first step in many professional production processes and covers all of the critical areas of ZBrush that you must know to make full use of the program. Concept sculpting fits the bill as something both broadly applicable and appropriate for a novice audience. After we build the model, we can refine it, pose it, and create a scene that we can render out and turn into a nice illustration. The final result will make a good addition to our artistic portfolio. Now that we have settled on our goal, the next step is to get creative and do some brainstorming about what exactly we want to create.

Ideation

To start, we should engage in a spell of creativity to work up a feasible concept. When ideating, you want to start as broadly as possible with as many different ideas as you can manage. Coming up with great ideas can be challenging, but your mind is a great source of inspiration in and of itself. Working up a good concept requires a lot of imagination and effort, but there are a number of techniques that can help you create a bunch of great ideas. Once you have a wide range of good concepts, you can then narrow these ideas down to just one excellent concept you want to pursue to completion. Let's examine some useful techniques for ideation now.

Sketch book

One of the most useful approaches to coming up with ideas is to purchase a small notebook or sketchbook that you can always have on you. You can use this sketchbook to record any interesting thoughts that you have. Any time some random thought strikes your fancy, take

FIGURE 10.1 Sketches from sketchbook.

a moment and record it in your sketchbook. These random musings and drawings can serve as the basis for further idea development once you have time to sit down and fully flesh these ideas out. In addition to recording your thoughts, you can use the sketchbook to engage in the fine art of doodling. Doodling is a way of accessing the power of your subconscious mind. To doodle, just sit down and start drawing whatever comes to mind. Don't consciously try to control what you draw. Let go and draw whatever you feel like. It doesn't matter what you draw, abstract patterns, little cartoons, scribble circles, or whatever. Once you have finished, look through what you have made and see if what you have drawn causes any interesting thoughts to spring to mind. Another fine use for a sketchbook is to simply sit down and sketch whatever you see any time you have a minute. Sketching trains your hand and eye to work together and will make you a better artist. Unlike most 3D programs, ZBrush cares about your drawing skills – a lot. If you have a knack for drawing, that will translate directly into skill with ZBrush once you get used to using the program.

Image and photo journals

Keeping an image journal is an easy way to give yourself some food for thought. The way this works is that anytime you see an interesting picture, just save a copy of it for later reference and inspiration. A photo journal works the same way, except in this version, you take the images yourself. Taking photos is easy to do since everyone has a mobile phone with a camera. Any time you see something interesting or inspiring, take a snapshot of it. Old cars, funny clouds, sunsets, cracks in the sidewalk, or whatever engages your imagination are all worthy photography subjects. Simply place the interesting photos you have taken into a folder for easy reference later on. Once you have the time to do so, sit down and go through your image and photo journals to see if they inspire you to create something great. I have entire external hard drives full of interesting reference images that I have built up over time!

FIGURE 10.2 Photo journal of clouds.

Dream journal

A lot of artists find it useful to keep a notebook next to their bed. When you first wake up, roll over and write down any dreams that you have had. Doing so creates a dream journal, and it is a powerful way of tapping the creativity of your unconscious mind. Do this every night, and you will also start remembering your dreams much better as well. When you need a great idea, just go through and read through your dream journal and see what it inspires you to think about. Your journal and other ideation notes may appear rather rough. They do not have to look nice. After all, you are the only person who will ever see this material. You just have to be able to understand the notes that you have written down when you re-read the material later on.

Free writing

In free writing, simply get out a sheet of paper and start writing down words and sentences non-stop. Don't worry about grammar, spelling, the subject matter, or even if it makes any sense. Just continue writing non-stop until you fill up a few pages. The important thing is not to inhibit yourself in any way. Just let the ideas flow onto the page and try to keep writing for as long as you can manage in a pure stream of consciousness. No one else needs to see what you write down, so make sure that you don't filter out any of your ideas. This technique is especially good at emptying your head of any preconceived ideas or notions that might be lurking around and enabling you to push through to some

FIGURE 10.3 Sample dream journal page.

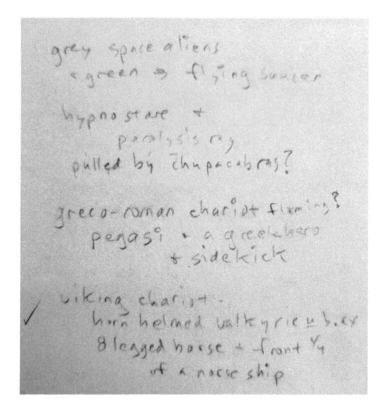

fresh ideas. There is a good chance that somewhere in the written ramblings this technique produces will be something that you can take and develop into a strong idea using the methods described in this chapter.

Randomization

In this ideation technique, simply find a random word and see if you can somehow weave it in to the idea you are working on. Any word will do. You can find a word by flipping to a random page in a book, closing your eyes, and pointing to the page. You can try using a random object you find lying around your house or one of the ingredients from a food item in your pantry. A quick internet search will turn up any number of random word generators if nothing else works. Just remember that the more completely unrelated the new word is to your topic, the better!

Mind mapping

For this writing exercise, go get a large sheet of paper and write down a topic you'd like to explore in the middle of the page. Next, write down all of the words that come to mind around your chosen topic, then draw a connection between each of these words and the original topic. Now, repeat this process for each of these new terms. Doing so

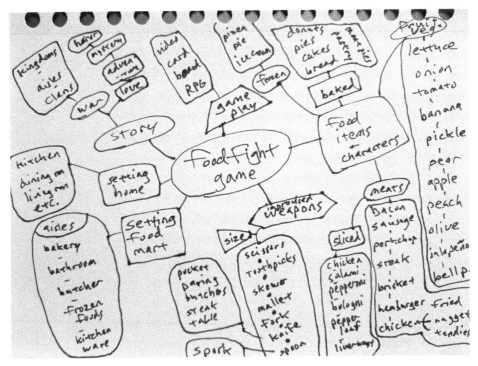

FIGURE 10.4 Example of mind mapping.

creates a tree-like structure, with the original topic serving as the tree trunk. Make things visually interesting. Use pictures or symbols, as well as words, in this process, as well as different colors, shapes, and types of lines to help organize your topic. Keep working at this until you have filled the page. Afterward, take a look at what you have done. Are any of the subjects interesting and worth further development? You can take any of the words or topics that you have generated and use them to start a new mind map, or you can roll that subject into one of the other ideation methods contained in this chapter.

Column mixing

Take out a blank piece of paper. Draw a line down the middle of the page. On the left side, write down a column of words derived from one of the other techniques in this chapter. Repeat this process on the right side. Try to make as diverse a set of words in each column as you can manage. Now, take one random word from the left side of the page and combine it with a random word from the right side. Does the combination work? Does this combination give you any new ideas? Try it again. Keep going until you have exhausted all of the different possibilities. Write down any interesting word combinations and save them for later. A variation on this approach is to put each word on a separate slip of paper, randomly draw words out of a hat, and see if any

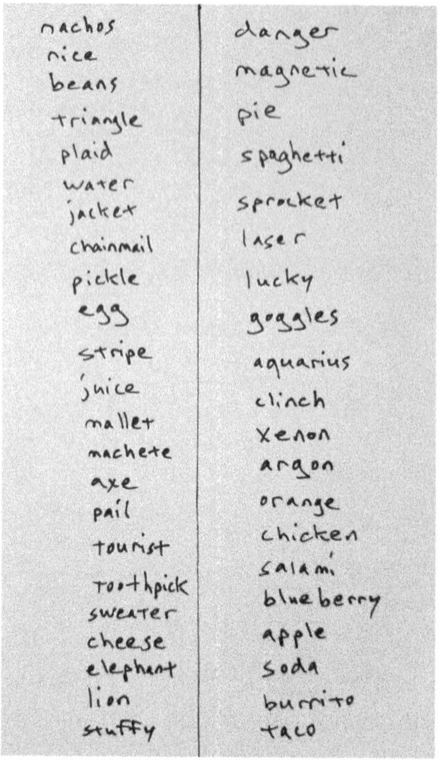

FIGURE 10.5 Example of column mixing.

nachos	danger
nice	magnetic
beans	pie
triangle	spaghetti
plaid	sprocket
water	laser
jacket	lucky
chainmail	goggles
pickle	aquarius
egg	clinch
stripe	Xenon
juice	argon
mallet	orange
machete	chicken
axe	salami
pail	blueberry
tourist	apple
toothpick	soda
sweater	burrito
cheese	taco
elephant	
lion	
stuffy	

combinations work. This technique works especially well in combination with random word generation.

Mixing it up and combining it all

Try out all of these methods to see which one works best for you. Once you have done that, go through and try combining your favorite approaches to see if you can develop your own best working method for developing new ideas. The key to all of these methods is to practice every day. Set aside 15 minutes a day to devote to ideation, sketching, doodling, or some other creative exercise. Exercising your mind like this will allow you to tap into your creative potential fully. Once you have come up with a number of interesting ideas, it is time to narrow these ideas down into one workable proposal.

Now that we have a large body of ideas to work with, it is time to compile them, analyze them, and select the best one for production. We need something that will be appropriate for an introductory level yet still visually interesting enough to make for a good concept model and, later on, an illustration. Creating a fun cartoon character model should fit the bill. Cartoon characters are relatively easy to make because there is no real-world object to compare them to. No one can say, "You got this bit wrong here," since the character is derived from your imagination. This design freedom makes a cartoon character an ideal subject for our first character model. We can add some peripherals and accouterments to the model to help flesh out the illustration and add some extra challenges to the model. While mechanical objects are more difficult to sculpt than organic models in ZBrush, we can still cover the basics, which ought to provide a fun and achievable demo that covers all of the critical elements in ZBrush that you will need to know. The goal is to make something fun that teaches you all of the basic aspects of the program that you need to know in order for you to introduce yourself to the more advanced techniques later on.

A general rule of thumb in ZBrush is that the more realistic you make something, the more difficult the process becomes. The most challenging models to sculpt are hyper-realistic human characters. The reason for this is that people are trained from birth to read and understand subtle non-verbal cues in human expression that help relay another person's mood and emotional state. The upshot of that training is that ANY flaw in a human model is immediately apparent to even untrained viewers. On the other hand, if the model is of an elf, orc, or ogre, it is easy just to say that since the model isn't human, that is the reason why it doesn't look quite right. If your goal is to become a character artist for video games or movies, then you will have to create at least one well-executed, hyper-realistic human character that conveys an emotion and a sense of place and time. That is to say, a character that makes the viewer feel something and immediately informs the viewer about the setting and what sort of game or movie the character is in. If you want to build this type of character, you will need to have an excellent knowledge of human anatomy and very good drawing skills and then devote considerable time to the endeavor. It normally takes anywhere from 6 to 12 attempts at building a professional, quality, hyper-realistic human character before you succeed. A lot of continuous practice is required. After you successfully create your first cartoon character, you can try something harder, like a self-portrait. All you need is a small mirror, and you can try your hand at sculpting your head in ZBrush. You will find creating a self-portrait a very challenging project the first time you do it! The important thing is not to be discouraged. It is easy to take a look at the excellent work posted on ZBrush Central and get disheartened. Just remember that all of those artists once began at the same place you are, so don't give up and just keep practicing!

Concept document

Now that we've explored various concepts and options, we should decide on the exact idea we want to pursue. I would like to sculpt a new character that will be the focus of the illustration, recycle the fish model we have already created, and then use both assets in an illustration. Maybe a cartoon with a good dose of humor? I quite like the sketch of the angry pie character I doodled in my sketchbook, so let's use that. How do I involve the fish model we did as a demo? Perhaps a fish pie? I know; how about having the angry pie character standing triumphantly over the defeated fish? Maybe have the character standing on a cutting board on a kitchen counter or stovetop? That is visually odd and could be humorous if done right. The idea has the added benefit of parodying a bunch of standard fantasy book cover paintings of the triumphant hero-type person standing over their defeated foe. Sounds good!

It helps to have some sort of development document to guide us through the creation process and further clarify our end goal. In the classes that I teach, we always start with a concept document. I find that putting the idea down on paper and answering a series of detailed questions helps refine a person's vision for any given project. We can adapt the questionnaire I normally use for pitching video games into a generic concept document that we can use for any type of serious project. A concept document is simply a brief, one- or two-page written summary of a project idea. This type of document is frequently used as a starting place for developing a professional project, be it a video game, movie, or other type of product. We can use the concept document to help us develop a viable idea that we can create in ZBrush. This approach leverages various critical approaches in creativity, digital sculpting, and illustration that are broadly useful in a number of industries.

Concept document worksheet

Name: Your name goes here.
Title: What is the name of your project?
Type: What type of project is this?
Genre and Theme: Describe the project's genre and theme.
Description: Provide a brief description of your project.

- Elevator Pitch:
- Comparison Pitch:
- Additional Information:

Audience: Who is your target audience?
Selling points:

- What is the feature set of this product?
- What will make people want to buy this product?
- What makes your product stand out against the competition?

Market information: What similar products already exist?
Completion date: When will you be finished with this project?
Cost: How much will it cost to complete this project?
Challenges: Are there any obstacles to completing this project? What are they?

Let's explore each of the questions on the worksheet in turn.

Name: Your name goes here

OK, so this one is a bit self-explanatory. Still, you might be surprised at the number of pieces of artwork out there that the creator needs to appropriately credit themselves on to ensure that the artwork can be linked back to their website or portfolio. It is always a good idea to put your name on your work and include some means for interested parties to link to your portfolio, website, or business.

In my case, the answer would be Greg Johnson, (*GregTheArtist.com*).

Title: What is the name of your project?

While "a rose by any other name would smell as sweet" might be true for Shakespeare, for the rest of us, we will need something a bit catchier that will show up well when searched for on Google or another search engine. You really do not want to have any brand confusion regarding your work. In other words, don't name your creation or project something similar to an existing product. No names like Gooble, Koka-Kola, McDonelds, or anything like that. Doing that sort of thing just ensures that you will get a cease-and-desist letter in the future. Take your time and do your research. Get creative and use the brainstorming techniques we have already talked about to find a really unique name for your product!

For the book project, we can simply name the illustration after the book itself, "Getting Started in ZBrush." That way, the illustration can be tied into the book's branding and publicity efforts. It's not the most fun or creative name, but a perfectly apt one, and having the image tie in with the book overrides any other concerns as a practical measure. As such, I don't have to do the normal internet search to find out if my project name brings up any other intellectual properties (IPs). Even though it isn't much of a concern for this image, normally it is obligatory to see if any other IPs sound or look similar. I cannot stress how important it is for your work to be uniquely identifiable on both legal and marketing grounds.

Type: What type of project is this?

Technically speaking, this is an illustration that serves as an introductory example of ZBrush concept sculpting and illustration work. If it turns out well, I may use the illustration, or part of it, as the cover for this book. Normally, I have students pitch a video game idea for the concept document and then try to derive a model they want to sculpt from their game idea. A movie, comic book, or illustration idea would work equally well in this regard.

Genre: Describe the project's genre and theme

The illustration I am proposing falls under the genres of humor and parody. An angry, animated piece of pie armed with some homemade weapons standing triumphantly over a defeated piscine foe seems rather funny to me on the face of it. This theme will let me poke some good natured fun at all of those classic fantasy illustrations of the big barbarian hero posing atop their defeated foe. If you have never seen one of these paintings, then try a Google image search for "Frank Frazetta" or "Boris Vallejo" to see some examples of what is considered classic fantasy artwork. I think the pie character should make for a humorous parody of the whole genre of fantasy illustration.

Description: Provide a brief description of your project
Elevator pitch

An elevator pitch is a simple, one-sentence summary of your idea that does not compare your idea with anything else. The elevator pitch is just a descriptive sentence. Look to the end of this paragraph for some video game elevator pitches to serve as examples.

Comparison pitch

The comparison pitch takes your idea and compares it to the closest well-known intellectual property you can think of. The point is to provide an immediate point of reference for your creative idea. Again, the examples follow below.

Additional information

If you think that the elevator pitch and comparison pitch don't quite do your idea justice, then you can use this segment to flesh out your thoughts and provide a few more relevant details. Only write a few pages about it. Showing someone a wall of text in a presentation is a surefire way to lose the attention of your audience. Just add in a few concise sentences if you need to.

Example pitches

Here are some examples. Each consists of an elevator pitch, then the comparison pitch, followed by any additional information required.

1. A video game featuring cowboy penguins riding polar bears in the Wild West of Antarctica. Think of Red Dead Redemption with penguins cast as cowpokes.
2. Medieval opossums in a fantasy adventure quest game. Imagine *Skyrim* using opossums and the wonderful marsupials of Australia. It might be visually impressive to use some of the wonderful natural scenery available in Australia as well.
3. Happy Space Amoebas, the musical. Picture "Star Trek TOS" meets "Hamilton" but with singing amoebas. The amoebas could be an invading race set to bring music and joy to the galaxy.

If I were doing the illustration idea this way, then it would be something like this:

A victorious piece of cartoon bilberry pie stand triumphantly over his defeated fishy foe. Like a gladiatorial fight in the Roman Colosseum done in the style of Frazetta or Boris Vallejo. It is a parody of all of those classic fantasy illustrations that decorated the pulp fiction novels of the past few decades.

Audience: Who is your target audience?

Defining your target audience may seem like an odd requirement at first, but it is probably the most important thing to answer on the whole worksheet. Before you even begin to make any sort of product, you must evaluate and determine who your target audience is and whether or not a market exists for your product. For the demo illustration that I am making, the answer is pretty simple. The target audience for the illustration is everyone who buys the book that the illustration is for. This audience includes anyone who has a desire to learn ZBrush and how to sculpt 3D models digitally. The age group will likely be in the 14- to 50-year-old range. It would include younger people curious about digital sculpting as a career field, older professionals seeking to train up on ZBrush, and hobbyists in the digital arts and 3D printing arenas. For your project, you have to ask yourself what you are trying to achieve within ZBrush. If the work is simply for your education, then the target audience is yourself! On the other hand, if you are trying to make money off of what you create, then you need to spend some time researching the various ways of doing that. Numerous careers utilize ZBrush. In the entertainment industry, there are character artists, concept artists, and environment artists who frequently use ZBrush. In the simulation and visualization industries, there are jobs in the medical, pharmaceutical, forensics, paleontology, and rapid-prototyping fields. In the arts, ZBrush is popular amongst illustrators and jewelry makers. There are many more careers in addition to what I have already listed off the top of my head, and the list is growing at a staggering rate each year. Basically, any field that can use the sort of high-fidelity digital visualization that ZBrush can produce has an interest in a person who can use the program well. Once you have identified your objective, you can steer your work in the appropriate direction. A common goal might be to produce a lovely portfolio piece for your targeted career path.

Selling points:
What is the feature set of this product?

A feature set is composed of the major elements, events, and attributes of your proposal. A sample feature set for a video game might include hyper-realistic artwork, clever character story arcs, and competitive gameplay. In contrast, the feature set for a plastic toy might consist of things like bright colors attractive to a younger audience or a promotional tie-in to a movie release. To answer this question in full requires that you do some market research into similar products to the one you are proposing. If you are actually trying to offer a marketable item, crafting the proper selling points becomes a job in and of itself. For our purposes, we can almost gloss over this portion since you probably won't be selling your very first attempts in ZBrush. I included the section on selling points and market research so you could understand a professional approach to creating a product. While this information might not be much help while you are simply learning the program, it will be of immeasurable aid later on once you have mastered ZBrush and are trying to monetize your new skill set in some fashion.

What will make people want to buy this product?

The answer to this question isn't that important at the moment since you are really just trying to learn the software and the techniques that go with it. I cannot overstate the importance of answering this question in full if you are going to make a real product. Before a company or an individual, for that matter, invests significant time and effort into a project, they need to know what the payoff is going to be. If the goal is to make a product, then you really must have your target market clearly identified and do your research on what exactly that target market wants and requires. The book publisher has already done this work and has identified a proper target market, making this an easy question for me. Since this book is the follow-up revision to an already successful imprint, it looks like the publisher did a fine job on their market research! Make sure that you pay proper attention to this question and do your research before undertaking any sort of serious product development.

What makes your product stand out against the competition?

Again, I've included this detailed question more as an example for your later use than anything important for us right now. Analyzing the competition is one of those questions that a company will expect you to be able to answer before they agree to green-light your game proposal, movie script, or product idea. Luckily, I can go ahead and answer this one using this very book as an example. This book originated with the idea that there were very few introductory-level texts on ZBrush available, and these could have done a better job teaching the program at an appropriate level. While there are a number of very good artists using ZBrush, there are few who have the knack for educating other people. All too often, an expert in a subject will forget to go over some of the more basic aspects of their process in a tutorial. You can frequently see it on YouTube ZBrush demos where an amazing artist just flies through a complicated process without explaining things step-by-step. The truth is that often, they no longer even see some of the more elementary steps that they are taking. Aspects of their process become so ingrained and instinctual that they don't even know that they are doing them anymore. This habit makes their tutorials much more challenging to follow. Creating an easy-to-follow introductory-level book was the cornerstone of the pitch that landed me the original book contract. Hopefully, you can get the gist of what this question entails now. It is also worth noting that this question is relevant to any sort of product, be it a book, a game, a movie, a piece of jewelry, or whatever. It is that good a question.

Market information: What similar products already exist?

Another market question. Perhaps you are seeing a pattern here? Companies will only move forward with a proposal if you can prove to them that your idea will make that company money in some fashion. Greed is an excellent motivator when it comes to dealing with businesses. For my example illustration, I've already mentioned the illustrative references of Boris Vallejo and Frank Frazetta. Any cartoon strip, political cartoon, or "Monty Python" sketch will serve to illustrate the parody elements I seek. For your work, you will have to do some research to familiarize yourself with that field. Go out and study similar video games, movies, simulations, or whatever is closest to your proposed product. Weirdly enough, this question is sort of a catch-22. Companies become very reticent to fund projects that have no clear antecedents or competing products. That could be an indication that your target market doesn't exist. Conversely, companies want to avoid entering a flooded market space or ending up competing with an industry giant who has deeper pockets or more resources than they can deal with. To answer this question, you have to find that particular sweet spot of market space that is underserved at the moment but has an established fan base. It's a tough thing to do since every company is looking for the same thing!

Completion date: When will you be finished with this project?

Figuring out how long a project will take can be a tough question to answer if this is your first time doing a project like this. One approach that I have found works quite well is to sit down and think about it for a while, and then take your best guess. Your goal is to establish a baseline for how long you think your project will take. Now, take your initial estimate and double it. Since this is the first time you have done this sort of project, you still have a learning curve to deal with, and you need to take that into account. It will take you some extra time as you try out various techniques and find out what works best for you. Now, double it again. This adjustment represents all of the dead ends you will reach, as some of the things you try just will not work out, and you will be forced to go back and redo that portion of the project. Having been teaching digital technology for over 25 years now, I believe this approach tends to provide a fairly accurate time estimate for the first time you try something. The good news is that the next time you do a project like this, it will take only half the time that it did on your first attempt. As you keep working and building up your proficiency, you will find that your work speed increases by leaps and bounds. Eventually, you will be able to knock out a professional product in no time at all!

Cost: How much will it cost to complete this project?

While this can be a tricky question to answer for a video game or movie project, for us, it should be a bit easier. There's the price of the book, the cost of a ZBrush license, and maybe a new Wacom tablet if you are really serious. That's about it, and you might be able to shave off a bit if you get an educational license. Simple!

Challenges: Are there any obstacles to completing this project? What are they?

The last question is a sort of catch-all for anything that might affect or delay your project schedule. If you are pitching a professional project, this might include licensing fees, talent scheduling conflicts, market instabilities, or any number of business or other factors. The smaller the project, the more predictable, and therefore manageable, this question becomes. Think through your next month or two and see if anything is coming up that might impact you. If so, write it down here.

The point of introducing this document to you is to show you how a business approaches idea development and to get you thinking about your project in professional terms. While a number of the questions in the concept document probably aren't huge concerns to you now, each one represents an aspect of professional project development that you need to understand. It pays to have a meaningful comprehension of the realities of pitching an idea and product development in the future. That said, go ahead and fill out the concept document as best you can. The goal is to clarify your vision for your project. Alternatively, you can follow along and create the same models that I do in the book. If you want to try creating your project, and I encourage you to do so, just keep in mind that when you are just starting, realistic things are harder to make than cartoon ones and that mechanical objects are very difficult to create until you have mastered the basics of ZBrush. It is best to start with something stylized and cartoony, like a caricature of a sea creature, bird, or animal. Cartoon characters are another good target, with examples found in the old Saturday morning cartoons or the stylized characters in the *World of Warcraft* and *Overwatch* games. If you start making a model and it gets too hard, or if you do not like the results, then feel free to scrap that project and try something a bit easier and work your way back up to the more difficult task. One fun ZBrush exercise is just to take a sphere and craft a little cartoon head out of it. Try giving it some sort of emotive expression or making it look like a cartoon of a celebrity, friend, or relative. These little projects are good exercises and will help you build up your skills quite quickly.

We should now have a firm idea of exactly what we are trying to create. If you are still trying to figure out what you'd like to do, feel free to continue reading anyway. You can mimic what I am doing in the book the first time you try this. It will serve as a good exercise for later when you have firmed up your concept. The ideation and concept development phase of our pre-production process is now complete. We can move on to gathering together all of the reference materials that we will need to execute our idea.

Reference images

Now that we have a clear goal in mind, it is time to start getting ready for production! We begin this phase of the process by making a list of assets that we will need to create for our project. It is a good idea to prioritize this list, placing those things that you must have first and less important or optional elements lower down the list.

Asset list

1. Cartoon pie character
2. Dead fish
3. Weapon(s)
4. Cutting board
5. Background elements
6. Secondary character(s)

Now that we have our prioritized asset list, we should go through the list and decide how to approach each asset. Anything that will be created in 3D should be either sketched out first or supported by plenty of reference materials. Now go back to the list and annotate the details of your process into it by individual asset.

Cartoon pie character

I already have the initial sketch of the character that inspired this whole madness.

To fully realize this model, I need more than just a single sketch. I need reference pictures. Luckily, I have on hand an old Canon SLR camera with a macro lens (OK, technically speaking, it is a Canon EOS Rebel T2i with a Canon Zoom EF 17–40 mm lens and DCE 77 mm Closeup Macro lens). Though the camera body is a bit old, it still takes nice pictures, but you do not need anything fancy to take reference images. Any cell phone camera will suffice. To add some detail to my pie character, I simply went to the grocery store and bought a fresh blueberry pie,

FIGURE 10.6 Sketch of an angry pie slice.

took it home, and proceeded to photograph a slice from every angle I could think of. When you are taking reference images, especially if you are doing so for potential 3D texture references, it is important to take the photos in diffuse light. Diffuse light is just any non-direct light. It is a light that has an obscure source. Outdoor objects on a cloudy day, subjects illuminated by light bounced off of a rough surface, or photos taken on the shadow side of a building are all examples of diffuse lighting. Diffuse light is soft and doesn't create harsh shadows that you will have to paint out by hand if you use the picture for a texture map later on.

Dead fish

We already have the fish model that we built as our introductory lesson. We can take that model and change it into something we can use for our illustration with a few tweaks and a new paint job.Weapon(s)

Here's a question for the ages: what sort of weaponry should an animated cartoon slice of pie use? My original sketch has a pie slicer. While a bit funny, the idea of having a sliced-up opponent seems a bit excessive. Maybe some sort of homemade bow or crossbow? Toothpicks would work for arrows, especially those with the little plastic frill at one end. Perhaps a bow built out of clothespins or a wire hanger, plus a bit

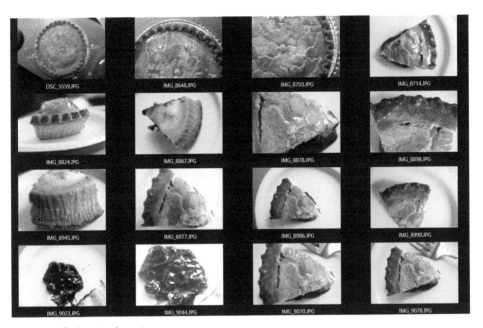

DSC_5559.JPG IMG_8648.JPG IMG_8703.JPG IMG_8714.JPG

IMG_8824.JPG IMG_8867.JPG IMG_8878.JPG IMG_8898.JPG

IMG_8945.JPG IMG_8977.JPG IMG_8986.JPG IMG_8990.JPG

IMG_9023.JPG IMG_9044.JPG IMG_9070.JPG IMG_9078.JPG

FIGURE 10.7 Blueberry pie reference images.

of dental floss for the bowstring? Sounds neat. Now, it is time to take a few dozen reference pictures for it.

Cutting board

I know there are a few cutting boards in my kitchen somewhere. Preferably an old and beat up cutting board with some "character" to it. Easy.

Background elements

I think some photos of the kitchen stove top would work well here. The trick is to take hundreds (no, really) of photos from many different angles. It might be easier to do this portion after I have the rest of the illustration built so that I have more of an idea of what exact angle I am looking for. That will reduce the required number of photos somewhat.

Secondary character(s)

It might be fun to have some supporting cast members for the illustration. Maybe an animated slice of cheesecake, a Vienna sausage, a lemon meringue pie slice, or a cheese wedge? Perhaps several of these? It's time to buy a cheesecake from the store and take a lot of photographs of it for my reference pictures.

Though it may seem a bit overboard to go and amass the number of photo references that I have, there are practical reasons for doing so.

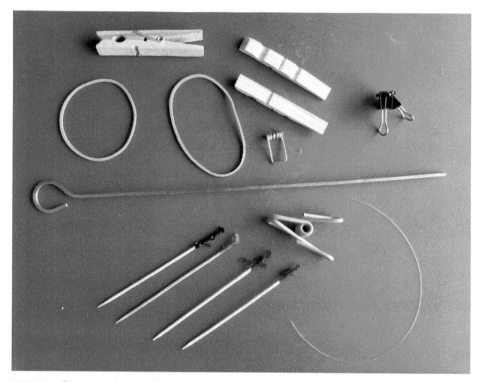

FIGURE 10.8 Tiny improvised weapons reference images.

First, if you just create things directly from your brain, you will inevitably get some of the details wrong. Most people aren't able to recall the finer details of an object that they have seen. Unfortunately, those same details are what make your model believable and enable your viewers to understand the object correctly. Second, digital photos are cheap! There really is no overhead to taking hundreds of photographs of an object. My general rule is to over-document an object. That way, if there is some detail that you need a reference for, then you will probably already have it. It can be extremely frustrating to travel to a museum or other location and photo document an object only to realize later that you missed some critical element once you have returned home from your vacation. Friends in the game industry have related how their company would keep actual copies of various military gear in a physical reference library so that the artists could go check out items, place them on their desks, and model directly from the reference object. Third, you need proper reference images to avoid making up the details. Someone will ultimately bust you on it if you just wing it. I have had clients count the rivets and look up the serial numbers on the tail fins of historic airplanes I've illustrated! These little details matter if you are making any sort of realistic item. Even though this is a cartoon character, it will still help to get the details right.

FIGURE 10.9 Cutting board reference images.

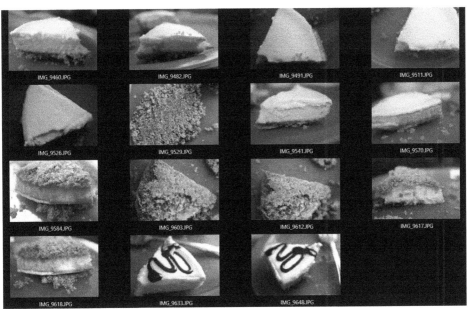

FIGURE 10.10 Cheese cake reference images.

Conclusion

We have now completed our pre-production process. You have fully developed and fleshed out your initial idea, turning it into an actionable concept document. In the process, you have gone through and analyzed your concept, identified competitors and similar products, and developed a sense of your target audience and potential marketing strategies based on your project's relative strengths. You should now have a clear idea of what you intend to create and have gathered together all of the reference images the project might require. Hopefully, the pre-production process has demonstrated its usefulness to you as we shift gears into the production stage. While we only have limited room to cover the topic in this book, and our project is a relatively small one, the pre-production process can be a lengthy and very involved affair when you are talking about a video game, movie, or other large project. It always pays off to do some really deep thinking before you invest a huge amount of time into a project, so you can accurately assess the costs and benefits of undertaking a major effort. With a modicum of pre-production effort, it is easier to underestimate the amount of time and resources that a project will demand.

11

Re-Making the Fish

Introduction

In our previous chapter, we decided to make a fun illustration, and I would like to repurpose our fish model toward that end. In order to do that, I need to make some changes to the fish, which is what today's lesson will be about. This lesson could be considered a form of "kitbashing," which is where you take a bunch of existing pieces of various models and combine them into a new model. Kitbashing is a very common form of creating models and levels. For example, a big game studio will keep a whole bunch of pre-existing assets such as fence posts, fire hydrants, window shutters, fences, and so forth from previous games in a large database so that game levels for the next project can be cobbled together quite quickly. The same principle works for 3D models and illustrations as well. In the accompanying science fiction space battle illustration, the green ship in the foreground got its missiles, guns, fuel pod, nobs, and details from a Soviet Mig-21 model. The blue spaceship in the mid-ground got its engine pods from a B-52 bomber. The turrets and engine come from a different sci-fi model. The planet itself is salvaged from a different scene. Reusing assets in this way can dramatically speed up your production process. In order to reuse our fish from the previous example, we will need to make some big changes to it. Fortunately, ZBrush will enable this, and I think you will be amazed at how straightforward and quick we can make enormous changes to our fish model.

First off, go ahead and use the *Tool > Load Tool* command to get your fish model back into ZBrush. Go ahead and draw the fish on the screen, and press the Edit button to enable sculpting. So, this fish is going to be our defeated opponent in the new illustration that we will create, which means that we will have to do a few things to make the fish

DOI: 10.1201/9781003215288-11

FIGURE 11.1 A science fiction illustration showcasing some examples of kitbashing.

look thoroughly vanquished. Since this is going to be something of a cartoonish take on the subject, we can avoid any serious grossness and simply strive to make things humorous. If your fish turns red, that means that we forgot to assign a material permanently to the model. To fix this, make sure that you have the body of the fish selected in the *Tool > Subtool* menu, turn on the M button at the top of the screen, select the *SkinShade4* material, and then use the *Color > FillObject* command to assign the material to the object. You can skip the *FillObject* command if you want to change the object's material only temporarily. To make our fish look thoroughly beaten, I think we should tone down the colors a bit and make the tone a bit bluer and grayer so the fish looks less lifelike. We certainly can't have the fish smiling!

Making the fish frown

Go ahead and turn on the *Transform > Activate Symmetry* on the *X* axis if this setting isn't already on. If you have modeled your fish aligned with the small positional head visible in the upper right-hand corner of the screen, then the X-axis should be the correct axis. If you modeled the fish facing a different direction, you might have to use either the Y or Z axis instead for the *Symmetry* command or use the *Gizmo 3D* to rotate your object. We can use the *Move Topological* brush to reshape the fish's face. Press the B-M-T shortcut keys on your keyboard to quickly

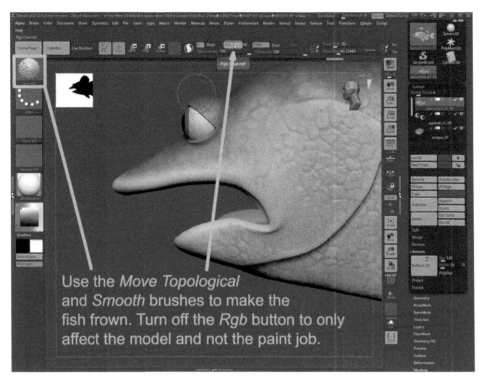

Use the *Move Topological* and *Smooth* brushes to make the fish frown. Turn off the *Rgb* button to only affect the model and not the paint job.

FIGURE 11.2 Use the *Move Topological* and *Smooth* brushes to make the fish frown. Turn off the *Rgb* button to only affect the model and not the paint job.

access that brush. Pull the corners of the mouth down into a frown and press SHIFT on the keyboard to access the *Smooth* brush and get rid of any unpleasant-looking geometry. Notice how the *Smooth* brush affects both the paint and the sculpture at the same time. If I turn off the *Rgb* or *Mrgb* button and keep the *Zadd* button on at the top of the screen, it will just smooth the model without actually changing the paint job. You can also smooth the paint job without actually moving any of the polygons by having the *Rgb* or *Mrgb* buttons turned on with the *Zadd* and *Zsub* buttons turned off.

Remaking the eyeballs

Now, it is time to adjust the eyes. We can delete the iris and pupil parts of the eyes easily enough. Select the eyeball subtool under *Tool > Subtool*, then use the *Move Down* button to shift the eyeball subtool to the bottom of the subtool list. While optional, this helps organize your subtool list for the next step. Now, use the *Tool > Subtool > Split > Split To Parts* command to separate the various pieces of the eyeballs. You will have to confirm this operation in a small pop-up window. Next, you can select one of the resulting pupil subtools and use the *Tool > Subtool > Delete* button to get rid of that component. Now go and choose

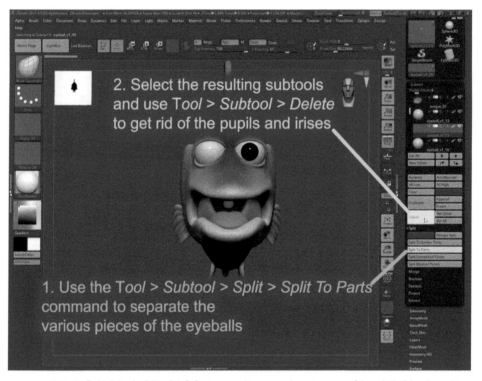

2. Select the resulting subtools and use *Tool > Subtool > Delete* to get rid of the pupils and irises

1. Use the *Tool > Subtool > Split > Split To Parts* command to separate the various pieces of the eyeballs

FIGURE 11.3 Use the *Tool > Subtool > Split > Split To Parts* command to separate the various pieces of the eyeballs. Select the resulting subtools and use *Tool > Subtool > Delete* to get rid of the pupils and irises.

and then delete the remaining pupils and irises one by one until you have gotten rid of all of those pieces, leaving behind just the white part of the eyeball.

While the fish looks a lot deader than it did just a bit earlier, I think we can enhance the effect somewhat by adding an extra cartoon effect to the eyes. After all, we aren't trying to make the fish gruesome or anything like that – so something cartoony should do. Go ahead and delete one of the white eyeballs. We only need to work on one eye since we can duplicate and mirror our modified eyeball later. We can now put a big "X" on the eyeball since that is a somewhat universal cartoon symbol for being dead. To do so, adjust your viewpoint so that you have a good view of the eye. Hold down the CTRL key to access the *MaskPen* brush. Reduce the *Draw Size* of your brush. I used 23 for the example, though you may need a different value depending on the size of your model. Harden the edge of your brush by lowering the *Focal Shift* of the brush. Remember that your brush settings are tied to the brush you have selected. Now, go in and paint an "X" on the eyeball.

To create the "X" shape, simply go to the *Tool > Subtool > Extract* menu and set the *Thick* value to 0.005 (again, your settings may need a

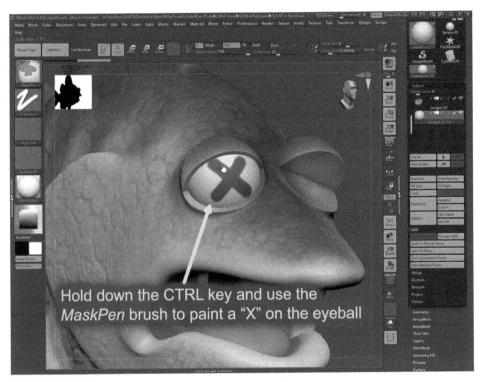

Hold down the CTRL key and use the
MaskPen brush to paint a "X" on the eyeball

FIGURE 11.4 Hold down the CTRL key and use the *MaskPen* brush to paint an "X" on the eyeball.

different value). Now click on the *Tool > Subtool > Extract > Extract* button, which will turn the masked-off area into a thin 3D shape. Once
you are happy with how the X model looks, go ahead and press the
Tool > Subtool > Extract > Accept button to turn the X model into a new
subtool.

After making the X shape, make sure that you get rid of the masks
on both the original eyeball and the new subtool. Go ahead and
DynaMesh your new subtool. I used a DynaMesh *Resolution* of 512 for
the demo model. You can smooth the X a bit using the *Smooth* brush
if you like. Alternatively, you can use the *Tool > Deformation > Smooth*
slider to apply a subtle smoothing to the entire X shape by simply
dragging the *Smooth* slider to the right, which will bevel the edge of
our new X shape just a smidge.

With the X subtool selected on the *Subtool* menu, go to the *Color*
palette and pick a very dark color. Remember that you can use the
Color > R G B sliders to set a precise color if you would like to. Make sure
that you have the *SkinShade4* material selected and the *Rgb Intensity*
slider set to 100. Afterward, use *Color > FillObject* to assign the chosen
material and color to the X subtool.

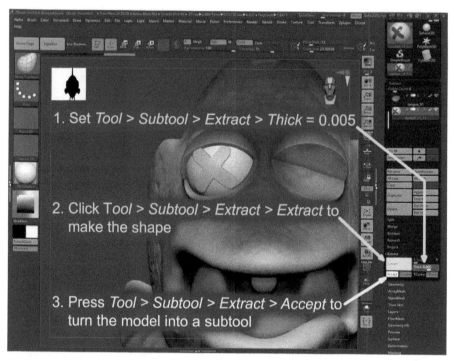

FIGURE 11.5 Set the *Tool > Subtool > Extract > Thick* to 0.005. Then click *Tool > Subtool > Extract > Extract* to make the shape. Finally, press *Tool > Subtool > Extract > Accept* to turn the model into a subtool.

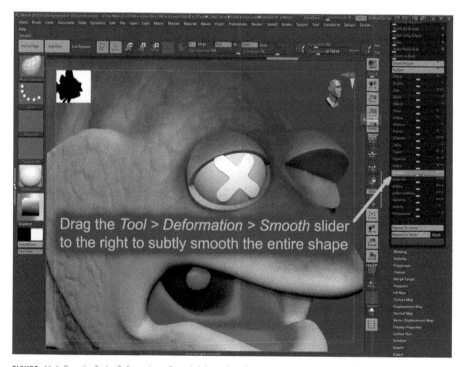

FIGURE 11.6 Drag the *Tool > Deformation > Smooth* slider to the right to subtly smooth the entire shape.

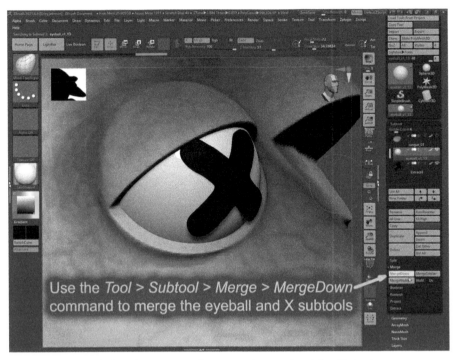

Use the *Tool > Subtool > Merge > MergeDown* command to merge the eyeball and X subtools

FIGURE 11.7 Use the *Tool > Subtool > Merge > MergeDown* command to merge the eyeball and X subtools.

Finally, we need to merge the X shape with the white part of the eyeball. Select the eyeball subtool and use CTRL + the UP ARROW or DOWN ARROW on your keyboard to place the eyeball subtool immediately on top of the X subtool in the *Subtool* menu. Use the *Tool > Subtool > Merge > MergeDown* command to merge the eyeball subtool with the X subtool.

Use the *Tool > Subtool > Duplicate* command to make a copy of the completed eye subtool to create the other eye. Next, click on the *Tool > Deformation > Mirror* command on the *X*-axis, which will replace the missing eyeball on the other side of the fish. That should complete the work on the eyeball itself.

Adjusting the eyelids

We also need to alter the eyelids in order to give our deceased fish that dead-eye stare. Make sure that you have the fish subtool selected from the *Subtool* palette. Hold down the CTRL key and click on the *MaskPen* brush to bring up the extended set of masking brushes available to us. Choose *MaskLasso* from the icons. With the CTRL key held down, use the *MaskLasso* brush to select the eyelid.

CTRL + click on the masked area to blur it, then CTRL + click on the background to inverse the mask. Switch to the *Gizmo 3D* by tapping

211

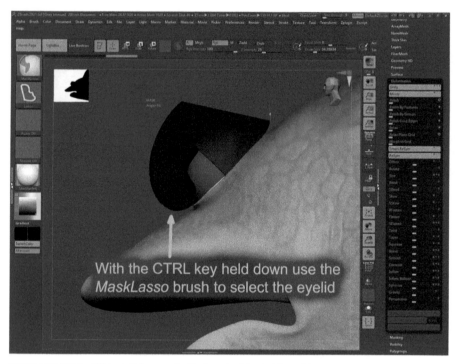

With the CTRL key held down use the *MaskLasso* brush to select the eyelid

FIGURE 11.8 With the CTRL key held down, use the *MaskLasso* brush to select the eyelid.

the R key on your keyboard. Do you remember how to unlock the gizmo and move it around on screen? No worries if you don't. Click on the small lock icon just above and a bit on the right of the gizmo. Now, you can click on the small circle-teardrop icon above the gizmo to center it on the unmasked area. If you need to adjust the gizmo some more, just grab one of the corners of the gizmo and drag it around. Place the widget in the center of the eyeball. Close the lock icon. Now, use the gray circle on the *Gizmo 3D* to rotate the eyelid back and open the eye up.

We can use the *MoveTopological* brush to fix the gap that now exists behind the eyelids. First, press Q on your keyboard to switch from the *Gizmo 3D* back into sculpting mode. Next, press B, then M, and then T to switch to the *MoveTopological* brush. Grab and drag the open edges until they overlap with the eyelid. Alternatively, you can use the *ClayTubes* or the *Inflate* brush to get the same effect. It is perfectly okay if the results are a little rough.

To finish fixing the eyes, go to the *Tool > Geometry > DynaMesh* menu. Once you are in the *DynaMesh* menu area, turn on the *Project* button and reduce the *Blur* slider to 0. Make sure that your *Resolution* is set fairly high, say 368, like in the demo, and click on the big *DynaMesh* button, which should close the gap completely while preserving your existing paint job. Use the *Smooth* brush with only *Zadd* on to smooth

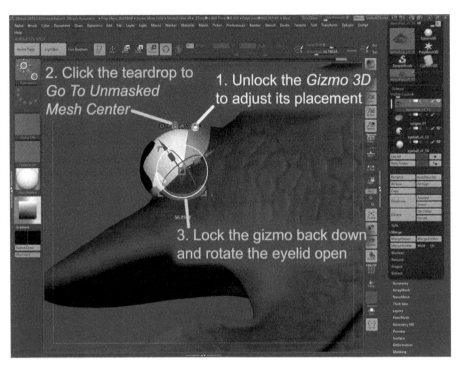

FIGURE 11.9 Unlock the gizmo, then click on the teardrop icon to center the gizmo on the unmasked area. Then, lock the gizmo back down and rotate the eyes open.

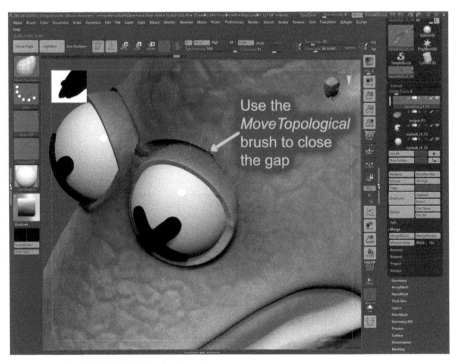

FIGURE 11.10 Use the *MoveTopological* brush to close the gap.

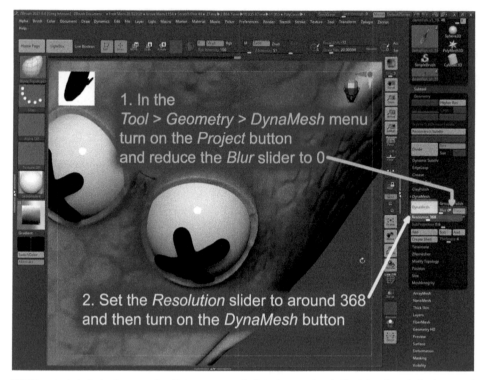

FIGURE 11.11 In the *Tool > Geometry > DynaMesh* menu, turn on the *Project* button, reduce the *Blur* slider to 0, set the *Resolution* to 368, and then turn on *DynaMesh*.

out any remaining blemishes around the eye. If you need to touch up any details or apply a few new wrinkles, simply use the *DamStandard* brush to do so.

If you like, you can now switch back to the *Gizmo 3D*, center the gizmo on the eyeball, and rotate each eyeball into a more aesthetic position. Suppose you want the eyeballs to mirror one another perfectly. In that case, you can simply delete one of the eyeballs, tweak the remaining eyeballs, and then duplicate and reflect them back into place after you have made your alterations. Remember to save your model periodically using the *Tool > Save As* command. Because we have made a bunch of drastic changes to this model, I suggest changing the name of the file to something like "deadFish_v1_01.ztl".

Repainting the fish

Currently, the color of our fish is a bit too bright and lively for a moribund cartoon critter. To fix that, we can make the color a bit bluer. A cooler color palette should zap the life right out of our fish. To change our colors, go ahead and switch to a *Standard* brush (B S T), make sure that Rgb button is turned on, and turn off the *Zadd* button. I also like to turn off the *Stroke > LazyMouse > LazyMouse* button as well. Now use

214

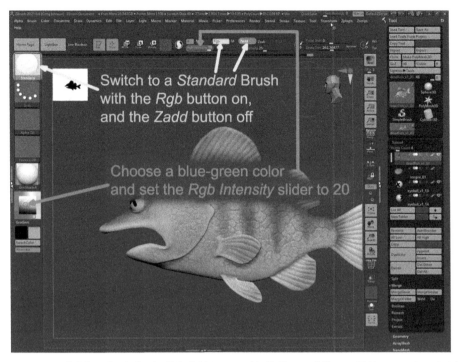

FIGURE 11.12 Switch to a *Standard* brush with the *Rgb* button on and the *Zadd* button off. Choose a rich blue-green color and set the *Rgb Intensity* slider to 20.

the *Color Palette* to choose a rich blue-green color and drop the *Rgb Intensity* slider down to around 20.

Using a large brush, I can now paint in some greenish-blue color on the fins and around the mouth and gills. The idea is just to tint the fish a different color without destroying the existing paint job. If you start to lose the stripes on the fish, simply switch to a darker blue color and paint the stripes back in. It only takes a little new color to get the fish looking a lot sadder and less lively. Suppose you want to make changes to all the fish at once. You can choose a mid-tone gray and use the *Color > FillObject* command to apply a uniform layer of new color to the fish model. Just keep in mind that the *FillObject* command uses the *Rgb Intensity* slider to set the opacity of the fill it applies to the object. On the demo fish, I have the *Rgb Intensity* set to 7 for the gray fill.

You may notice that adding all of those grays and blues has painted out some of our previous details. We can now recreate those details using the same techniques that we originally used in the last chapter. Switch to the *Standard* brush (B S T) and the *DragRect* stroke with the *Alpha 64* alpha. Make sure that you turn on *Zadd* and set your *Z Intensity* low; around 15 should work, as well as turn off the *Mrgb* or *Rgb* buttons if either button is on. After setting up the brush, you can simply paint in more fish scales on any part of your fish that has gotten a bit smoothed out.

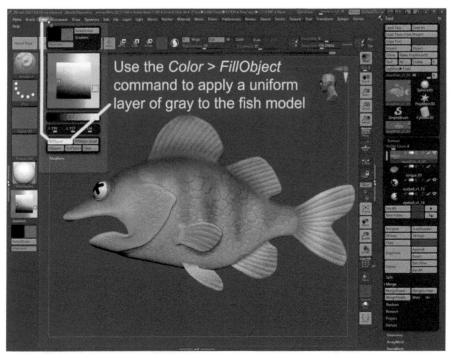

FIGURE 11.13 Use the *Color > FillObject* command to apply a uniform layer of gray to the fish model.

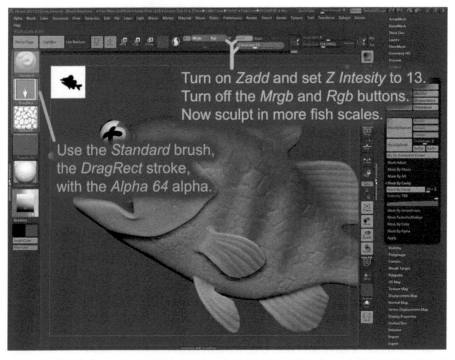

FIGURE 11.14 Use the *Standard* brush (B S T), the *DragRect* stroke, with the *Alpha 64* alpha. Turn on *Zadd* and set *Z Intensity* to 15. Turn off the *Mrgb* and *Rgb* buttons. Now sculpt in more fish scales.

After fixing the details, you can use *Tool > Masking > Mask By Cavity* to create a mask from the tiny surface creases in the model. Follow this with a quick *Tool > Masking > BlurMask* command to soften the mask a bit. Use the *Tool > Masking > Inverse* command to reverse the mask on the fish, and turn off the *Tool > Masking > ViewMask* button so that you can see what you are doing to the paint job next. Now, set your color to something cool and dark; a desaturated blue-black should work nicely. Next, turn the *Rgb* button on and the *Zadd* button off at the top of the screen. Set your *Rgb Intensity* to a low value, say around five or so. Finally, use the *Color > FillObject* command to add some shadow definition to the existing creases and fine details of your model. You can always click the *FillObject* button several times to achieve the intensity of the shadows that you are looking for.

Use *Tool > Masking > Clear* to get rid of this blurry mask, and then click *Mask By Cavity*, followed by Inverse, to create a new version of the mask, which will create a sharper version of our previous mask and let us paint in the very bottom of all of the creases. Turn off the *Viewmask* button and use *Color > FillObject* again to fill in the darkest part of the crease shadows. You can also use the *Standard* brush with *Rgb* turned on and *Zadd* turned off to simply paint additional shadows in any area you think needs a bit more.

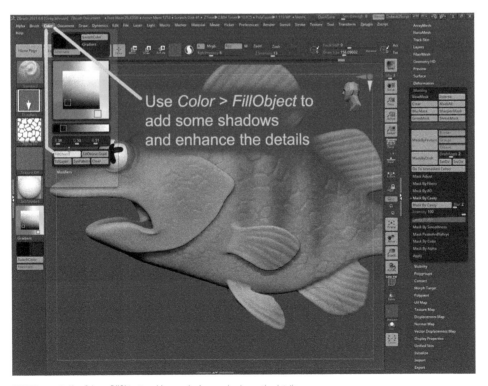

FIGURE 11.15 Use *Color > FillObject* to add some shadows and enhance the details.

Once you have the shadows dark enough, use the *Tool > Masking > Clear* command to get rid of the mask. If you need to, you can hold down SHIFT to activate the *Smooth* brush, turn off *Zadd* while leaving *Rgb* on, and smooth the shadows out a bit if you think the shadows in some parts are too strong. Remember that you can use the *Rgb Intensity* slider to control the strength of the smoothing effect.

This methodology is the same process we used in the last chapter. The process of hand painting a texture is a rather straightforward one once you understand the basics, and there is little variation to it. It really helps if you have done some real-life painting on either miniatures or models, too, as suggested earlier. Don't forget to save your tool using the *Tool > Save As* command frequently so you don't accidentally lose your work if ZBrush crashes.

Symmetry and asymmetry

One of the final steps when making a model is to go in and make the object more asymmetrical. While having symmetry turned on is very useful in the initial stages of model creation, at some point, it can become counterproductive. Actual living creatures are not perfectly symmetrical. There are always small imperfections, eccentricities, and unsymmetrical aspects to everyone and everything. An excellent way of seeing this is to take a photo of yourself and mirror the sides using a photo-editing tool like Adobe Photoshop or something similar.

The results of mirroring one side of your face can vary, but they always look a bit strange. Because faces and creatures aren't ever truly symmetrical, including a subtle bit of asymmetry will help your model look all the more real. Some artists even go through the extra process of simply always leaving symmetry turned off, even though that means doing a lot of extra work and running a high risk of the results not looking even.

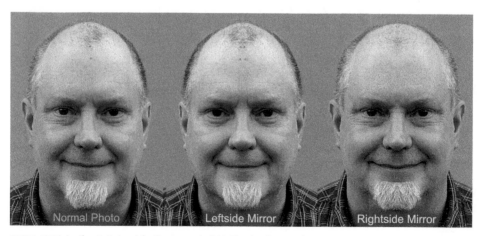

FIGURE **11.16** A self-portrait plus a left-side mirror and a right-side mirror for comparison.

More commonly, character artists will include some major asymmetrical elements in the character's costume and armor. For our fish model, this means that at some point, we need to turn off the *Transform > Symmetry* button and work on some unique features on both sides. The only exceptions are when the viewer will never get to see both sides of the model at the same time. In that case, you might be able to get away with skipping adding asymmetry to the model. Remember that a cardinal rule of creating artwork is that you do not make work that will never be seen. After all, if no one will ever see it, why create it in the first place? Taken to an extreme, this can mean just creating one side of an object and not the other. A great example of this sort of approach comes from Hollywood. A television town would consist of just flimsy facsimiles of the storefronts and nothing else. When the actress went into a building, the camera would cut to an entirely different set and simply create the illusion of continuity for the audience.

Introducing the transpose line

For this particular fish model, we need the fish to be lying on a counter-top, which means that the fish should be flat on the side facing the countertop and a bit curved on the other side. First, make sure that you have turned off the *Transform > Symmetry* button. Next, we need to mask off the side fin that sticks out from the side that will be lying on the countertop. We want to fold this side fin inwards toward the fish so that the fin lies flat against the fish's body. Hold down the CTRL button and use the *MaskLasso* brush to mask off the side fin.

Hold down CTRL and click on the background, or use the *Tool > Masking > Inverse* button to invert the mask, which should leave us with just one side fin unmasked. Now, go to the Move button at the top of the screen, or you can just press the W keyboard shortcut. While I could just use the standard *Gizmo 3D* for doing this kind of work, sometimes it is easier to use the alternative *Transpose Line* interface to Move, Scale, or Rotate an object. To switch from the *Gizmo 3D* to the *Transpose Line* interface, simply go to the top of the interface and turn off the *Gizmo 3D* button, or you can press the Y keyboard shortcut toggle.

Once you turn off the *Gizmo 3D*, you will get the *Transpose Line* instead. The *Transpose Line* is a really funky and weird three-circle thing connected by a dashed line. For many years, this wildly nonstandard device was the default interface to transform objects, and while the *Transpose Line* is quite powerful, it does take quite a bit of getting used to. We will use it to deform our fin as a means of introducing this unusual interface to you. First, click on the base of the fin where the mask begins and hold down the left mouse button while you drag the *Transpose Line* down the length of the fin. If you mess up, don't worry. You can just try again. The circle at the base of the fin, where

219

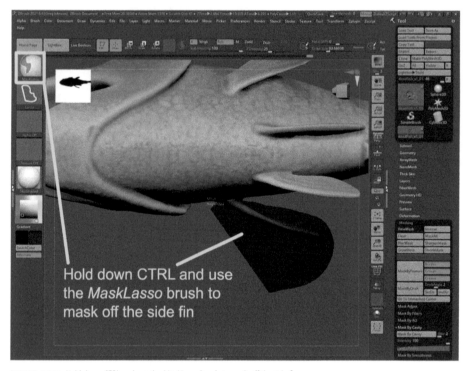

FIGURE 11.17 Hold down CTRL and use the *MaskLasso* brush to mask off the side fin.

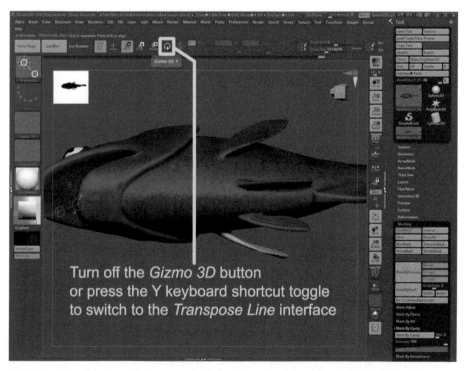

FIGURE 11.18 Turn off the *Gizmo 3D* button or press the Y keyboard shortcut toggle to switch to the *Transpose Line* interface.

we started from, is now the pivot point. The circle at the far end will act as our control and turn the *Transpose Line* into a sort of lever. This control interface contains quite a lot of various effects within it. If you want to move the *Transpose Line* around or adjust it, you grab one of the orange circles or the orange line by clicking and dragging on the line itself. If you place your cursor over the center of any of the orange circles, you will see a white circle appear. If you click and drag on the white circle, you will activate the *Transpose Line* and scale, move, rotate, clip, or deform the model, depending on whether you click on the top, middle, or bottom circle. Yes, it isn't very clear, and the exact effect varies depending on whether you are using *Move*, *Scale*, or *Rotate* and based on which circle you use. The best way to get used to the tool is simply by experimenting with it. Try using the *Transpose Line* as a lever with the *Move* button active first, then *Undo*, and try it again with the *Rotate* button turned on instead. You should see a difference in how the object reacts. Using *Rotate* and the *Transpose Line*, you can draw the controller from the base of the fin to its tip. Then click on the inside of the orange circle at the tip of the fin and slowly move the last circle toward the body of the fish so the fin lies flat against the fish's body. If using the *Transpose Line* interface is too confusing, you can achieve the same effect by simply using the *Move Topological* brush on the fin with the rest of the body masked out.

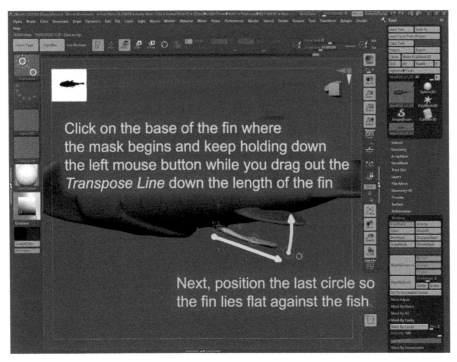

FIGURE 11.19 Click on the base of the fin where the mask begins and hold down the left mouse button while you drag the *Transpose Line* down the length of the fin. Next, position the last circle so the fin lies flat against the fish.

Clicking the small white circle at the tip of the *Transpose Line* will center the *Transpose Line* on the unmasked portion of our model. Clicking on one of the *X*, *Y*, or *Z* colored axes on the *Transpose Line* will align the *Transpose Line* with that axis. The *Transpose Line* has a very strange interface, but it is very powerful once you get used to it, much like ZBrush itself. When it comes to posing extremities and appendages, the *Transpose Line* can make your life much easier if you understand how it works. Make sure that you save a copy of your tool now as a backup.

Since our fish will be lying on its side, we should adjust the overall shape of the fish. Go ahead and merge the eyeballs into the rest of the fish model using the *Tool > Subtool > MergeDown* command. Leave the tongue subtool alone for now. We will adjust the tongue later on. With the fish subtool selected, go to *Tool > Deformation > SBend* with the *Y* axis active, and use this slider to bend the fish a little bit. A value of around −3 worked for the demo fish.

Use SHIFT + P or click on the *Floor* button to turn on the floor grid. The problem now is that we need to rotate our fish so that it lies flat on the floor. Press the R key on the keyboard to activate *Rotate* and make sure that the *Gizmo 3D* icon is turned on. You can press Y to activate the *Gizmo 3D* button if it isn't already there. Now, simply rotate the fish until it lies flat on the grid floor. One of the odd things about ZBrush is that the location of the floor is based on the lowest part of the model, so you may have to fool around with rotation a bit until it looks correct.

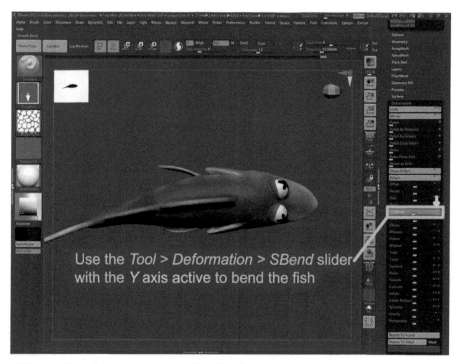

FIGURE 11.20 Use the *Tool > Deformation > SBend* slider with the *Y* axis active to bend the fish.

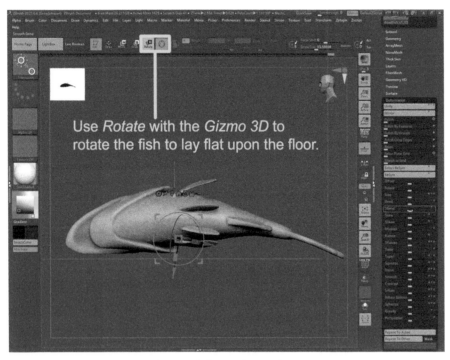

FIGURE 11.21 Use *Rotate* with the *Gizmo 3D* to rotate the fish to lay flat on the floor.

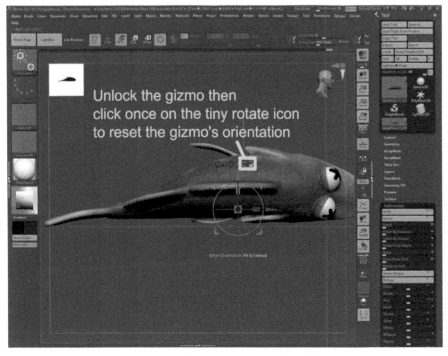

FIGURE 11.22 Unlock the gizmo, then click once on the tiny rotate icon to reset the gizmo's orientation.

You can now switch back to the *Gizmo 3D* in *Rotate* mode (press R on the keyboard). To realign the gizmo with the world axis, simply unlock the lock icon, then click once on the tiny rotate icon next to it on the gizmo, which should straighten up the gizmo and reset its orientation.

Press the Q button to go back to the *Draw Pointer* and switch to a very large *Move Topological* brush. Use this brush to adjust the fish's extremities and fins down a bit to flatten out the fish some more. Don't worry about messing up the details on the bottom of the fish because, honestly, it will be resting against a surface, and you won't see any of those details anyway. Go ahead and tweak the fish using this brush as much as you see fit. You can also use the *Tool > Deformation > Gravity* slider to refine the fish further and accentuate its flatness even more.

Mask out the two fins on the top of the body – that is, the dorsal side of the fish. Remember that you can simply CTRL + click on the background to inverse the mask. Now, you can alter the fins without accidentally affecting any other part of the fish. Turn off the *Gizmo 3D* button (Y on the keyboard) and switch to either *Move* or *Rotate* (W or R, respectively). Now, adjust your viewpoint so that you are looking at the front of the fish. Drag a new *Transpose Line* from the base of the top fin to its tip, and click inside the outer orange ring to bend the fin down toward the floor. Unmask the next fin and bend it into shape as well.

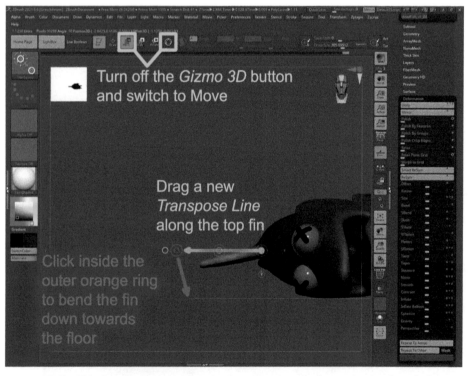

FIGURE 11.23 Turn off the *Gizmo 3D* button and switch to either *Move or Rotate*. Drag a new *Transpose Line* along the top fin. Click inside the outer orange ring to bend the fin down toward the floor.

Continue to mask out and use either the *Move Topological* brush or the *Transpose Line* to move all of the fins into the shape you like. There are usually several different ways to do any given task in ZBrush. Over time, you will discover which approaches you find the most useful and effective for your own workflow. If any of your tweaks to the fins and fish create new imperfections or flaws in the fish, you can simply switch to the *Smooth* brush by holding down SHIFT, making sure that you have *Zadd* on and both the *Rgb* and *Mrgb* buttons turned off, and blurring out any problem areas. Go ahead and save your tool using the *Tool > Save As* command.

Adjusting the tongue

We still need to fix the tongue. Select the tongue subtool layer from the *Tool > Subtool* palette and make sure that the model is visible – the tiny eye icon on the right side of the subtool layer should be a bright gray. You will need to turn the *Transform > Activate Symmetry* button off if it is on. Activate the *Move* button. Next, activate the *Gizmo 3D* button by pressing the Y key on the keyboard if you need to. Unlock the *Gizmo 3D* lock icon, and then click the pin icon to center the gizmo on the tongue model. Now close the *Lock* icon and use the *Gizmo 3D* to position and rotate the tongue model into the mouth. If you have trouble seeing the tongue inside the fish's mouth, you can turn on the Transparency button.

While there are always a number of ways to accomplish any given task in ZBrush, it is almost always a good idea to start with the easiest method you can think of, and if that doesn't work, then you can try more complicated approaches. With that in mind, simply load the *Move Topological* brush (B M T), increase the *Draw Size* of your brush, and move the back end of the tongue into the rear of the mouth. You can use this brush along with the gizmo to place the tongue exactly where you want it.

The last thing we need to do to finish making our fish look most moribund is to change the color of the tongue from a living pink to a more post-life like color. Choose a red-purple color from the color palette. Set your *Rgb Intensity* slider to around ten, and make sure that the *Rgb* button is turned on. Next, use the *Color > FillObject* button to apply a few coats of this new color to the tongue model. Now, use the *Tool > Masking > Mask By Cavity > Mask By Cavity* button to create a new mask and then soften the mask using several *Tool > Masking > BlurMask* commands. Click the *Tool > Masking > Inverse* button to invert the mask. Remember to turn off the *Tool > Masking > ViewMask* button if you want to see what you are doing. Now, choose a dark blue color from the color palette and use the *Color > FillObject* command to apply some dark blue to the recesses of the tongue.

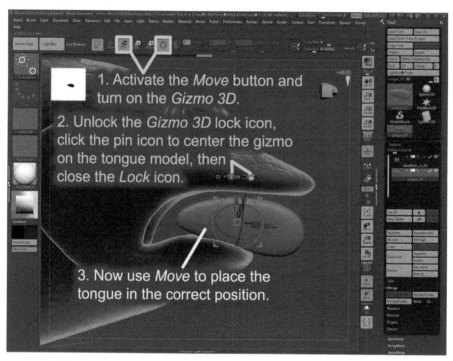

FIGURE 11.24 Activate the *Move* button and turn on the *Gizmo 3D*. Unlock the *Gizmo 3D* lock icon, click the pin icon to center the gizmo on the tongue model, and close the *Lock* icon. Now, use *Move* to place the tongue in the correct position.

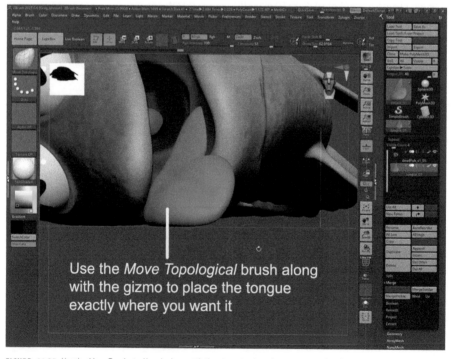

FIGURE 11.25 Use the *Move Topological* brush along with the gizmo to place the tongue exactly where you want it.

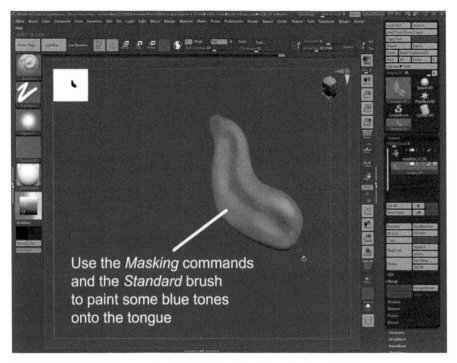

Use the *Masking* commands
and the *Standard* brush
to paint some blue tones
onto the tongue

FIGURE 11.26 Use the *Masking* commands and the *Standard* brush to paint some blue tones onto the tongue.

Remember that you should not try to paint using one of the *Move* brushes. Choose an icy blue color. Switch to the *Standard Brush*, make sure that the stroke is set to *Freehand* and the brush alpha is set to *Alpha 01*, and now paint some blues onto the tongue. Remember that you can use the *Smooth* brush to blend the colors, but you will need to deactivate the *Zadd* button on the *Smooth* brush before you try to blend the colors. You can go into the *Subtool* menu and turn off the fish layer's visibility by clicking on the tiny eye icon on that layer to see the tongue model more easily. If you are having trouble with the masking commands, you can always simply paint the colors directly by hand.

The tongue in the demo is still a little low resolution, coming in at only 24,500 polygons, so let's increase the resolution a little bit. While we could just *DynaMesh* the tongue again, this time, let us just click the *Tool* > *Geometry* > *Divide* button. Every time you press the divide button, it multiplies the total number of polygons in the model by four by splitting each polygon in the model both horizontally and vertically. This action will turn the model into what is called a subdivision surface with different levels of subdivision that you can work on. To change the current subdivision level, simply use the *Tool* > *Geometry* > *SDiv* slider. Using the *SDiv* slider, you can work on different subdivision levels at correspondingly different resolutions. This ability is one of the wonderful things about subdivision surfaces. That said, for this project, we

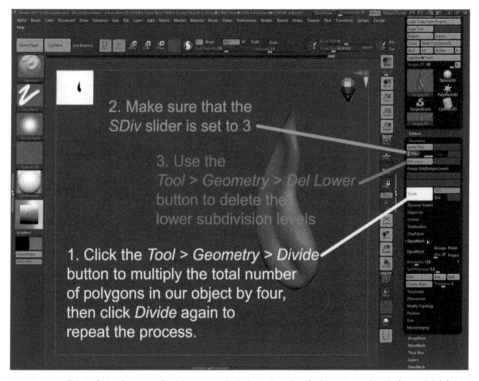

2. Make sure that the *SDiv* slider is set to 3

3. Use the *Tool > Geometry > Del Lower* button to delete the lower subdivision levels

1. Click the *Tool > Geometry > Divide* button to multiply the total number of polygons in our object by four, then click *Divide* again to repeat the process.

FIGURE 11.27 Click the *Tool > Geometry > Divide* button to multiply the total number of polygons in our object by four, and click *Divide* again to repeat the process. Make sure that the *SDiv* slider is set to 3, then use the *Tool > Geometry > Del Lower* button to delete the lower subdivision levels.

really do not need to change our *SDiv* levels back and forth, so I can use the *Tool > Geometry > Del Lower* button to delete the lower subdivision levels since there is no point in us preserving them for this particular model – we just need the high-resolution model to help us paint. Remember that since ZBrush paints directly onto the polygons of the model, you must have a fairly high number of polygons if you want the paint job to look nice.

To finish up, we just need to add some touches of blue and purple to the fish's mouth. Turn on the *Brush > Auto Masking > BackfaceMask* button so you don't accidentally paint through to the fish's face, and go ahead and add some of the same blue and purple colors to the mouth. Remember that you can click and drag from the color palette onto the tongue to sample the colors there. Remember to save your work using the *Tool > Save As* button, and to iterate the number on your file name so you have multiple backups just in case something goes wrong with your model files.

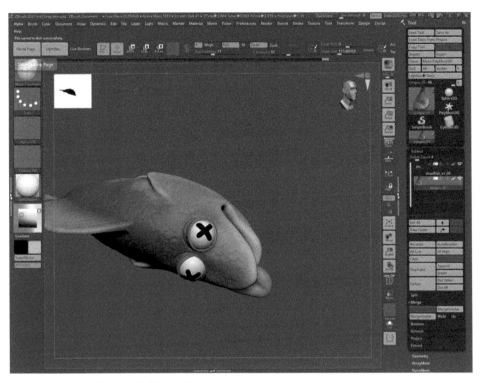

FIGURE 11.28 A parting look at our final fish model.

Conclusion

Congratulations! Our fish now looks rather dead or, at least, severely life impaired. We have successfully taken our demo model and turned it into a prop for our final painting. Remember that no fish were actually harmed in the production of our model. I hope that you are having a lot of fun so far in this process. In the next chapter, we will start creating our main character.

12

Creepy Pie Guy, Part 1

Introduction

Our final goal is to make a fun illustration out of our ZBrush models. While we already have a wonderful prop in our dead fish, we still need to produce a good character. Luckily, we already have a good sketch of a fun blueberry pie person. As part of my visual research for this model, I went out and bought a very tasty blueberry pie. I then proceeded to photo-document every slice of that pie – before eating it. These photos will serve as reference points and as photographic textures that I can use to paint the character model later on. Refer back to Chapter 10 – the Planning Stage to take a look at these images. Now, all we have to do is create the model based on our sketch and reference photos. It is a good idea to bring up your reference images on a separate monitor if you have a two-monitor workstation setup. Now, go ahead and start up ZBrush on your main monitor.

Making the basic pie shape from a cylinder

A cylinder seems like a great place to start making a digital pie. Select a *Cylinder* from the *Tool Palette* and draw it on the screen. The cylinder icon should be just to the right of the golden "S" *SimpleBrush* icon. Don't forget to press the "T" key to go into *Edit* mode immediately after drawing the cylinder on the screen. Next, go into the *Tool > Initialize* sub-palette and set the *Z Size* to 14, *HDivide* to 200, *VDivide* to 60, and *TaperTop* to 18.

DOI: 10.1201/9781003215288-12

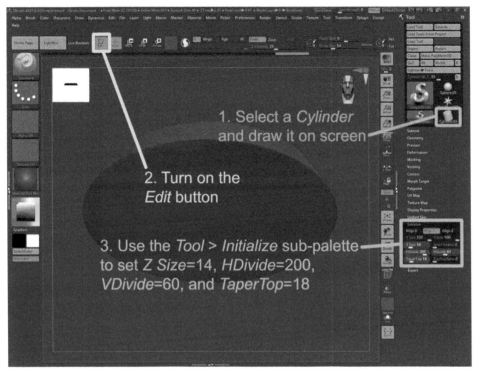

1. Select a *Cylinder* and draw it on screen

2. Turn on the *Edit* button

3. Use the *Tool* > *Initialize* sub-palette to set *Z Size*=14, *HDivide*=200, *VDivide*=60, and *TaperTop*=18

FIGURE 12.1 Select a *Cylinder* and draw it on the screen, and then turn on the *Edit* button. Under the *Tool* > *Initialize* sub-palette set *Z Size* = 14, *HDivide* = 200, *VDivide* = 60, and *TaperTop* = 18.

Using the *TrimCurve* brush

Now that we have a very basic pie shape, we should turn this into an editable polygon mesh by clicking on the *Tool* > *Make PolyMesh3D* button. Next, we need to slice our pie model into pieces. While there are several ways of doing this, I want to show you a new set of tools. As such, the first thing we should do is go ahead and use the *Tool* > *Geometry* > *DynaMesh* > *DynaMesh* button to resurface our model. After that, hold down the CTRL and SHIFT keyboard buttons. Normally, this brings up our select rectangle, but you can click on the *SelectRect* icon and pick one of the other specialty brushes. Today, we're going to be talking about the *TrimCurve* brush, so hold down CTRL+SHIFT and select the *TrimCurve* brush. The *TrimCurve* brush is one of the really neat brushes in ZBrush. Use the *TrimCurve* brush by simply holding down CTRL and SHIFT and then clicking and dragging the mouse to create a line with one shadow side to it. If you drag this line across your model, it will trim the portion of the model on the shadow side of the line completely off. Once you have started drawing the *TrimCurve* line, you can actually let go of CTRl and SHIFT without messing up the operation. If you hold down the SPACEBAR while creating the *TrimCurve* line, you can adjust its position. Make sure that you draw the line completely across the object you are cutting. If you only draw the trim curve line part of the way across the object, then you can get irregular results. If you tap the ALT button while you are drawing the line, you will add a control point that will let you bend the line. Basically, it turns the straight trim curve line into a spline that you can then adjust. Doing so can, however, create problems since curves are a bit harder for ZBrush to calculate, and you can get some odd results that way where the cut surface bulges in or out. It can sometimes be easier just to make lots of smaller straight cuts rather than try to fix any irregular bulges a curved trim line creates. Play around with the brush a bit until you get comfortable with it. If you double-tap ALT while drawing the curve, it will make a sharp corner point in the trim curve line. The *TrimCurve* brush is useful, but it can be rather sloppy in the results that it creates as you force ZBrush to guess what sort of surface it should create based on the shape of the cut.

To cut a piece of pie out, simply position your viewpoint so that you are looking at the top of the shape. Then, hold down CTRL + SHIFT and, starting at the bottom of the pie, draw a trim curve line all the way through the middle of the pie and completely through to the other side.

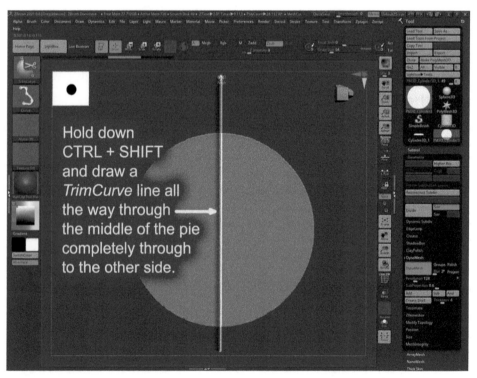

FIGURE 12.2 Hold down CTRL + SHIFT and draw a *TrimCurve* line all the way through the middle of the pie completely through to the other side.

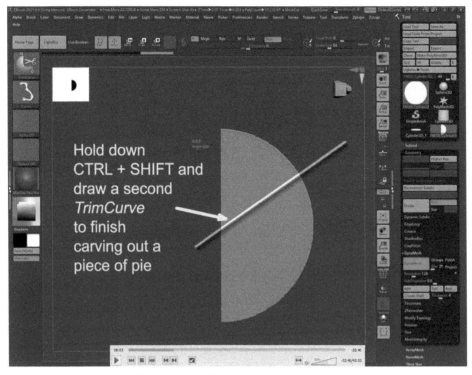

Hold down
CTRL + SHIFT and
draw a second
TrimCurve
to finish
carving out a
piece of pie

FIGURE 12.3 Hold down CTRL + SHIFT and draw a second *TrimCurve* to finish carving out a piece of pie.

Next, draw another trim curve at an angle to create the piece of pie. Make sure that you pay attention to which side of the trim curve line the shadow is on so that you know which side will be cut off of the model.

Using the *Gizmo 3D* to align your model correctly

Use the *Gizmo 3D* to rotate your piece of pie so that it is aligned to the tiny reference head in the upper right-hand corner of your ZBrush document. If the *Gizmo 3D* gets out of alignment with the model, you can reset the gizmo's rotation by unlocking the gizmo's *Lock* icon and then clicking on the tiny rotate icon. That will reset the gizmo's orientation.

You can now place the gizmo at the bottom point of the pie slice and make sure that the model is aligned to where the top of the pie is facing toward the front. The top of the pie should be visible when looking directly at the reference *CamView* icon (the little head in the upper right-hand corner). Since we are going to sculpt a face into the top of the pie, we will want that part to face toward the front. Once you have the pie slice oriented correctly, go ahead and save your model using the *Tool > Save As* command.

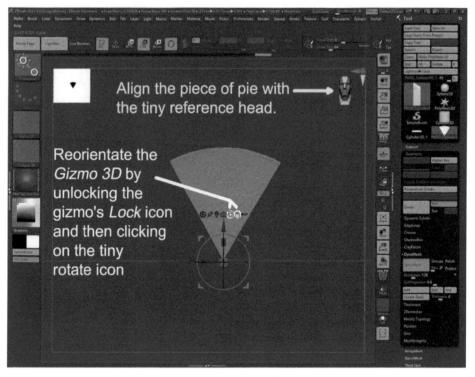

FIGURE 12.4 Align the pie piece with the tiny reference head. Reorientate the *Gizmo 3D* by unlocking the gizmo's *Lock* icon and then clicking on the tiny rotate icon.

Reference images and primary forms, secondary shapes, and tertiary details

Next, we can check out some of our reference pictures and take note of the details therein. To get these reference images, I mounted an expedition to the local bakery and purchased a lovely blueberry pie to serve as a photo reference. Over one hundred pictures later, I had finally taken all of the reference shots I needed and was full of blueberry pie.

The appearance of our model consists of primary forms, secondary shapes, and tertiary details. The primary form of our model is the large, basic shape that determines the model's silhouette. In our immediate case here, it is the triangular pie slice form. Secondary shapes are the crimped edges of the pie crust and the way the top and bottom crusts overhang the filling. These secondary shapes dramatically change the look of the item. Tertiary details consist of various fine details, such as the flaky texture of the crust and the granularity we see on the bottom of the slice. These tertiary details will be the finishing touches that we put on our model at the end of the process. When you are creating a model, the most critical elements to get right are the primary and secondary forms. No amount of clever detailing will make a bad model

FIGURE 12.5 A small selection of reference images for this project.

any better. We have already knocked out our primary form, and now we can move on to the secondary shapes of our model, consisting of the crimped edges, blueberry filling, and such.

Making the crust

To start creating the crust shape, you should first mask off the top edge of the circular portion of the crust. Simply hold down the CTRL key to access the masking brush and paint in the mask. You can use the *Tool > Masking > GrowMask* button to expand this new mask as needed. Click the *Tool > Masking > Inverse* button to invert the mask, then press the W key to bring up the *Gizmo 3D*, and move the crust edge up and forward to create the desired shape.

Make sure that you still have the *Transform > Activate Symmetry* button and the *-X-* option button turned on. Use the B I N shortcut to select the *Inflate* brush and gently inflate the unmasked portion of the crust until it starts to look like the reference photos.

Go ahead and get rid of the mask. In the *Tool > Geometry > DynaMesh* palette, set the *Resolution* slider to 256 and press the *DynaMesh* button to rebuild your geometry. Switch to the *Standard* brush (B S T) and sculpt in the zig-zag shape on the edge of the crust.

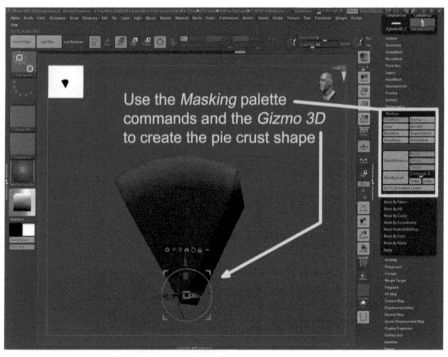

Use the *Masking* palette commands and the *Gizmo 3D* to create the pie crust shape

FIGURE 12.6 Use the *Masking* palette commands and the *Gizmo 3D* to create the pie crust shape.

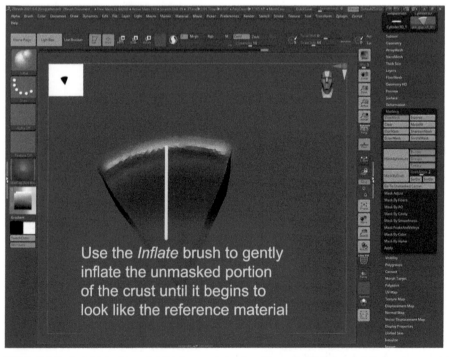

Use the *Inflate* brush to gently inflate the unmasked portion of the crust until it begins to look like the reference material

FIGURE 12.7 Use the *Inflate* brush to gently inflate the unmasked portion of the crust until it begins to look like the reference material.

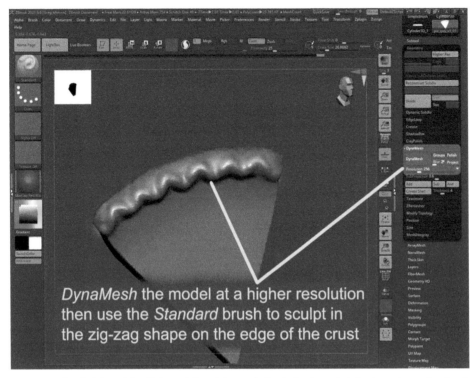

DynaMesh the model at a higher resolution then use the *Standard* brush to sculpt in the zig-zag shape on the edge of the crust

FIGURE 12.8 *DynaMesh* the model at a higher resolution and then use the *Standard* brush to sculpt in the zig-zag shape on the edge of the crust.

Creating the sides of the pie slice

We need to create the sides of the pie slice next. Re-orient your viewpoint to get a good look at the side of the pie slice. Go ahead and take a look at the reference pictures, and note the shape and flaky texture of the top and bottom crusts and the details of the gooey middle. Switch to the *Dam Standard* brush (B D S) and outline where the filling will go on our pie slice model. Since this is a blueberry pie, go ahead and draw some circles to represent the blueberries. While this looks a bit different than our reference photos, we need the model to read as a blueberry pie. It does us no good to make things hyper-accurate if the final model doesn't look like a blueberry pie to our audience. Sketch in some lumps to represent the goo between the berries while we are at this stage.

Switch to the *Move Topological* brush (B M T) and push the front edge of the filling inwards a little bit to create a lip where the crust meets the filling.

Hold down the CTRL key and switch to the *MaskLasso* brush. Use it to mask out the bottom and back of the pie. Make sure that you remember to blur the mask a bit to avoid creating any harsh seams. You can now use the *Move Topological* brush to puff out the front side of the pie

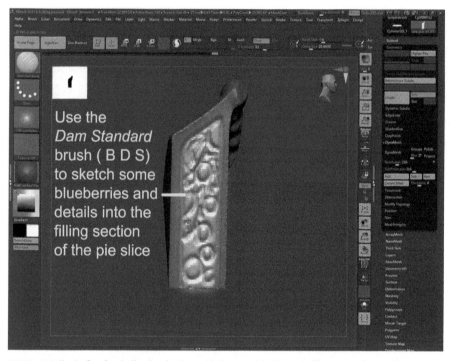

FIGURE 12.9 Use the *Dam Standard* brush to sketch some blueberries and details into the filling section of the pie slice.

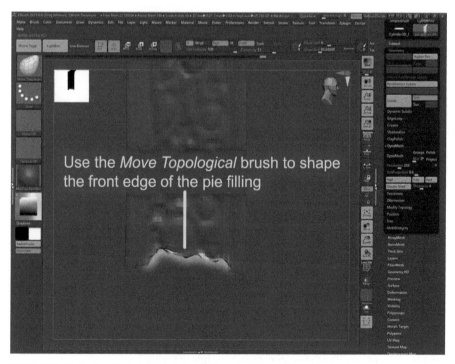

FIGURE 12.10 Use the *Move Topological* brush to shape the front edge of the pie filling.

a bit, giving the center of the pie slice the sort of half-bell curve shape a good pie should have.

Go ahead and mask off the crust of the pie, leaving just the gooey filling bits unmasked. You can use a combination of the *MaskPen* and *MaskLasso* brushes to do so. Remember that you should hold down the CTRL keyboard button to access these brushes. Once you have finished masking the crust off, you can use the *Gimzo 3D* to scale the pie filling down a bit to accentuate it.

DynaMesh and SDiv

Make sure to occasionally *DynaMesh* your object to fix any geometry issues that crop up. In fact, you can increase the *DynaMesh Resolution* slider to 256 or even 512 to increase the polygonal resolution of your model. Another way to increase the number of polygons in your model is to subdivide it. First, turn off the *DynaMesh* button if it is still on. Next, go to *Tool > Geometry* and click on the large *Divide* button. The *Divide* button splits each quadrilateral polygon, or quad, in your model into four polygons by cutting edges down the middle of each existing polygon, which turns your model into a subdivision surface. Use the *Tool > Geometry > SDiv* slider to go to your model's subdivision levels

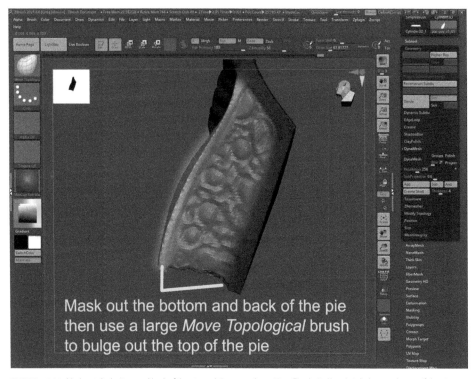

Mask out the bottom and back of the pie then use a large *Move Topological* brush to bulge out the top of the pie

FIGURE 12.11 Mask out the bottom and back of the pie, and then use a large *Move Topological* brush to bulge out the top of the pie.

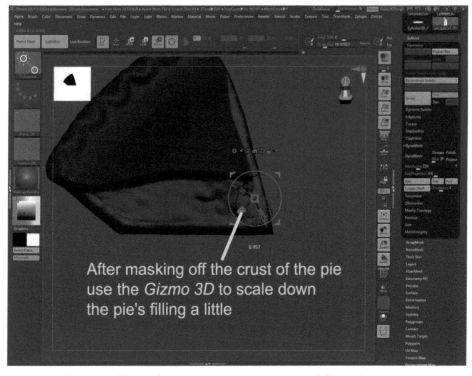

After masking off the crust of the pie use the *Gizmo 3D* to scale down the pie's filling a little

FIGURE 12.12 After masking off the crust of the pie, use the *Gizmo 3D* to scale down the pie's filling a little.

to work at different levels of polygonal resolution. For our immediate purposes, we just want the higher resolution level, so make sure that the *SDiv* slider is set to 2 and use the *Del Lower* button to remove the bottommost subdivision level. Be careful when using the *Divide* button. Remember that each time that you press *Divide*, it multiplies the number of polygons in your model by roughly 4. It is very easy to press *Divide* too many times and end up exceeding ZBrush's polygon limit of around 100 million, which will crash the program.

Now that we are working with a lot more polygons, you will probably want to swap out the standard Smooth brush for the *Smooth Stronger* brush. Remember that you should hold down the SHIFT key, click on the *Smooth* brush to pull up the *Brush* palette, and then use the *Load Brush* button to load the *Smooth Stronger* brush from the "\ZBrushes\ Smooth" folder in your ZBrush install directory. If you have trouble finding this file, you can use your operating system's search function to look for the "Smooth Stronger.ZBP" file to determine the brush's location on your system. I like to copy all of the specialty brushes that I use into an easily found folder on my machine so that I don't need to go digging through the installation directories when I want to load up a brush from the hard drive. Go ahead and switch to the *DamStandard* brush and use it to carve some extra detail back into the pie filling.

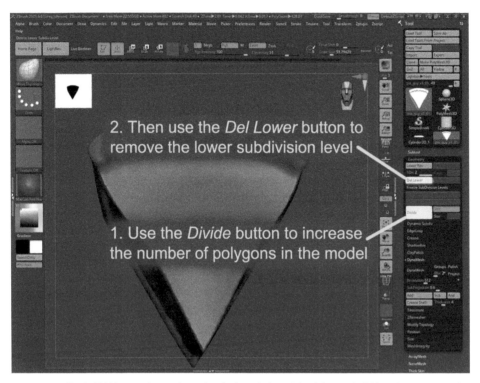

2. Then use the *Del Lower* button to remove the lower subdivision level

1. Use the *Divide* button to increase the number of polygons in the model

FIGURE 12.13 Use the *Divide* button to increase the number of polygons in the model, and then use the *Del Lower* button to remove the lower levels of subdivision.

One important consideration to take into account is that you do not want your model to be too symmetrical. If you want to breathe life into your characters, you will need to make them somewhat asymmetrical. It will look unnatural if things are perfectly symmetrical. No living creature in real life is like that. With that in mind, go ahead and switch the *Transform > Activate Symmetry* button off. Now, carve some unique details into your pie filling on both sides.

Fixing problematic spikes

You also have to watch out for spikes developing in your model. These sharp little projections can become a real nuisance when sculpting in ZBrush. If you get one sticking out of your model, simply switch to the *MoveTopological* brush and shrink the *Draw Size* of the brush down to a very small size. Now, use the brush to move the tip of the spike back inside the rest of the model. It does not have to look pretty. The spike just needs to be squashed flat. After you have shoved the spike back into the model, a quick *DynaMesh* should obliterate the spike. Note that you may need to increase the *Resolution* of your *DynaMesh* to preserve your polygon count. I have the demo *Resolution* slider set to 1,024 for my model, but yours may require a lower or higher number depending on the size of your sculpture. Afterward, you can carve some more blueberries into the filling, refine the details on the crust, and tweak a few asymmetrical flourishes in the model. Remember to save periodically.

Creating the eyeballs

This character also needs eyes, which we should go ahead and make now. We will use the same process that we did in Chapter 7. Select the *Sphere3D* tool from the *Tool Palette*, draw it on the screen, and turn on the *Edit* button. Go to the *Tool > Initialize* palette and increase the *HDivide* and *VDivide* sliders until the sphere looks nice and smooth. Convert your sphere into an editable polygonal mesh using the *Tool > Make PolyMesh3D* button now. Make sure that you have the *Mrgb* button activated at the top of the page, choose a pale yellow color, and assign the *ToyPlastic* material to your sphere using the *Color > FillObject* command. Next, use the *Tool > Subtool > Duplicate* button to create a copy of the existing sphere and assign this new sphere whatever color you like. Switch to the *Gizmo 3D*, scale this new sphere down a bit, and translate it up to create the cornea. Duplicate the cornea sphere, assign it a black color, and then scale and move this pupil sphere into

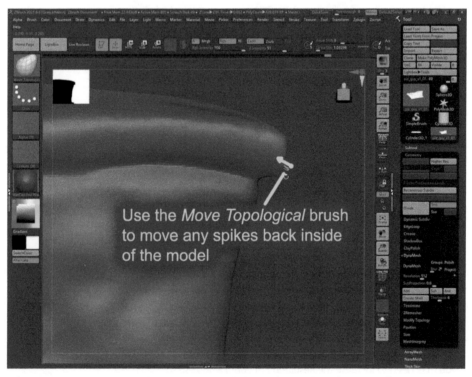

FIGURE 12.14 Use the *Move Topological* brush to move any spikes back inside of the model. A quick *DynaMesh*, afterward should eliminate the problem area.

place. I made the cornea of this new eye a bluish purple to mimic a blueberry's color.

To make the eyelids, simply duplicate the largest sphere in the eyeball and scale it up until it hits the rest of the eyeball. The last time we created eyelids, we masked out the bottom half of the eyelid sphere and used the *Gizmo 3D* to scale the sphere into a hemisphere. You can refer back to Chapter 7 for a more detailed breakdown of the entire eye creation process if you want to do things that way. This time, I would like to introduce a new way of creating the eyelids using the *TrimCurve* brush. To access the *TrimCurve* brush, simply hold down the CTRL and SHIFT keys and click on the default *SelectRect* brush. In the resulting *QuickPick* pop-up palette, select the *TrimCurve* brush. Now, hold down the CTRL and SHIFT keys, and while pressing the left mouse button, drag a *TrimCurve* line across the eyelid sphere. Remember that you can hold down the SPACEBAR to adjust the position of the *TrimCurve* line.

After you have trimmed the sphere in half, you can delete the existing material on the eyelid by assigning the *Flat Color* material to the eyelid subtool. Simply select the *Flat Color* material, make sure that you have the *Mrgb* button active, and use the *Color > Fill Object* command. Afterward, you should be able to switch to any material you like and see the

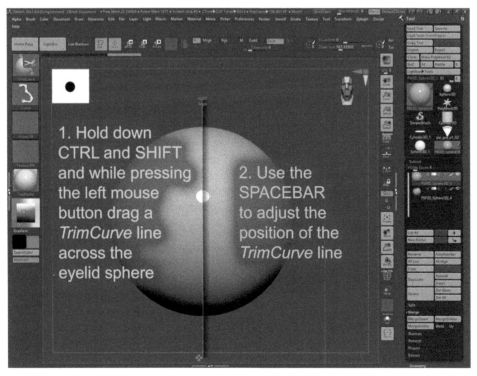

FIGURE 12.15 Hold down the CTRL and SHIFT keys, and while pressing the left mouse button, drag a *TrimCurve* line across the eyelid sphere. Use the SPACEBAR to adjust the position of the *TrimCurve* line.

eyelid automatically update to whatever material you have currently selected. Applying the *Flat Color* material erases the current material on an object.

Activate the *Gizmo 3D* to rotate the eyelid into position, and then use the *Tool > Subtool > Duplicate* command to make a copy of the eyelid. You can now rotate the second eyelid into position. Once you have the eye looking the way you want, select the uppermost subtool in the *Subtool* palette and use the *Tool > Subtool > Merge > MergeDown* command several times to merge all of the eyes subtools together. Now use the *Tool > Save As* command to save your eyeball.ZTL file.

Appending the eyes to the pie slice

Select your pie model in your *Tool* palette, which should automatically switch the current tool back to the pie model. Now, use the *Tool > Subtool > Append* command to add your new eyeball model as a subtool to the pie model. Make sure that the eyeball subtool is selected in the *Subtool* palette, switch to the *Gizmo 3D*, and use it to scale and position your eyeball on the pie model. At least, that is what I would normally do. In my demo model, it turns out that I had made the slice of pie quite small – which is why I need such crazy high numbers in my *DynaMesh Resolution* slider and why the eyeball model came into the scene so much bigger than the pie model. As such, I kept the pie model selected and used the *Gizmo 3D* to scale it up instead. Only after I had scaled the pie model up did I choose the eyeball subtool and use the *Gizmo 3D* to rotate, scale, and move the eye into position. Remember that you can turn on the *Transp* button to get a better sense of where each subtool is in relation to each other.

Once you have placed the first eyeball, use the *Tool > Subtool > Duplicate* button to create a second eyeball, and then use the *Gizmo 3D* to put it on the pie slice. In the demo version, I made one of the eyeballs significantly smaller to accentuate the asymmetry of the character and to give the pie model a certain "crazed" look. To help you keep track of the subtools, use the *Tool > Subtool > Rename* button to change the name of your subtools.

Go ahead and turn off the *Transp* button and see how your model looks. If it seems a bit freaky – that is excellent! After all, we are trying to create a scary cartoon character. We have now defined the basic shape of our main character. Go ahead and save your file using the *Tool > Save As* command. Make sure that you are iterating over the last number of the file name and not just saving over your existing files. Next time, we will start by adding in the arms and legs as well as the secondary level of detail, including the mouth, eye sockets, and other information that will give our character a bit more personality. Once

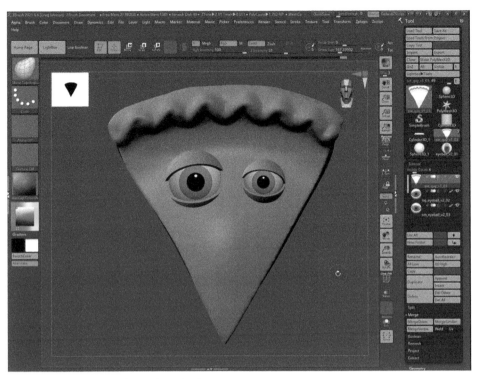

FIGURE 12.16 The final version of our pie during this chapter.

our secondary details have been added, we can then move on to the final tertiary details, such as the flaky bits of crust, blueberries, and other fine details.

Conclusion

In many ways, this chapter is more of a review of the techniques, tools, and processes that we have already learned. We are simply taking this knowledge and now applying it to the creation of proper cartoon characters rather than the relatively simple fish model. As we move forward with the character creation process, these are the techniques that you will be revisiting time and again since they serve as the fundamental basis for most concept sculpts in ZBrush. In our upcoming chapters, we will build upon this practical foundation and expand your repertoire of techniques dramatically as we work toward our final illustrative goal.

13

Creepy Pie Guy, Part 2 – Secondary Details

Introduction

It is time to pick up where we left off and add all of the secondary shapes to our pie character. These secondary details will include all of the things that will provide the form with a real sense of character, such as the mouth, eyelids, wrinkles, and other essential shapes. Since we are adding personality to the character, I need to decide what sort of character we want to create. Honestly, I think it would be fun to have a rather angry character. Right now, I believe that the face looks kind of sad. So we're going to need to change the face's expression. I think that it's about time that we get started.

Creating eye sockets

Go ahead and use the *Tool > Load Tool* button to add your existing model to the active tool palette and draw the model on screen. Press the *Edit* button to allow you to keep working on this model. Since we may want to work behind the eyeball subtools, we should go ahead and turn on the *Transp* button. We can start by using the *ClayTubes* brush, so press the B C T combo on your keyboard to access that brush quickly. Hold down the ALT key and start carving out the eye socket behind the eyeball. The nice thing about the *ClayTubes* brush is that it works in a one-level-at-a-time method, which gives you a wonderful amount of control over how much digital "clay" you are adding or subtracting from the model with each brush stroke. So long as you keep holding down your left mouse button and applying the brush stroke, the *ClayTubes* brush will simply keep working at the same depth of application. A typical workflow consists of drawing one brush stroke, smoothing that stroke down, then adding another stroke and

DOI: 10.1201/9781003215288-13

smoothing it, and repeating the process until you have managed to build up your shape into the desired form.

While using our brush to build up a form like this slowly works perfectly well, it can be more efficient to use another approach if you want to make big changes to the model. With that in mind, let's hold down the CTRL key and access the *MaskPen* brush. Now, set your *Focal Shift* slider to a negative number, like –75 or so, making the edge of the masking brush a bit harder. Now mask off the eye socket area. Remember that you can hold down the CTRL + ALT keys to erase the mask if you mess up.

Now go to the *Tool > Masking* palette and use the *Sharpen* button to refine the mask a bit. You can now use the CTRL + I shortcut or the *Tool > Masking > Inverse* button to invert the mask. Next, press the W key to activate the *Gizmo 3D*, and then drag along the Y axis, that is, the green arrow, to pull the eye sockets into existence.

DynaMesh and scaling factors

You can now clear the mask by using the *Tool > Masking > Clear* button or by simply right-clicking and dragging a small square on the document background. We can now apply *DynaMesh* to the model to

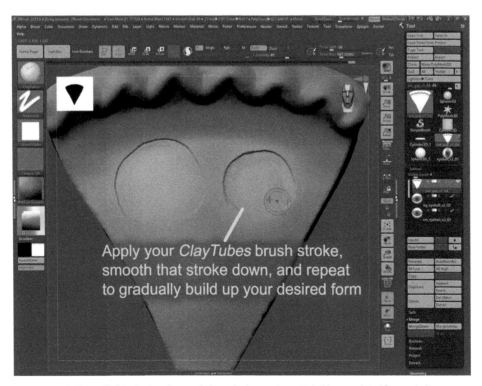

Apply your *ClayTubes* brush stroke, smooth that stroke down, and repeat to gradually build up your desired form

FIGURE 13.1 Apply your *ClayTubes* brush stroke, smooth that stroke down, and repeat to build up your desired form gradually.

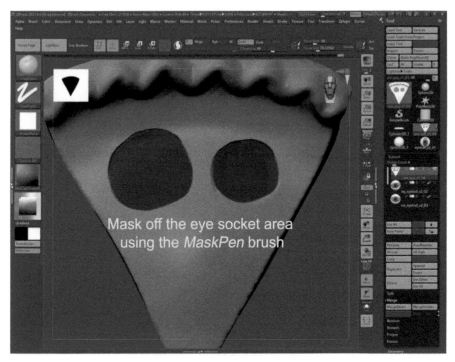

FIGURE 13.2 Mask off the eye socket area using the *MaskPen* brush.

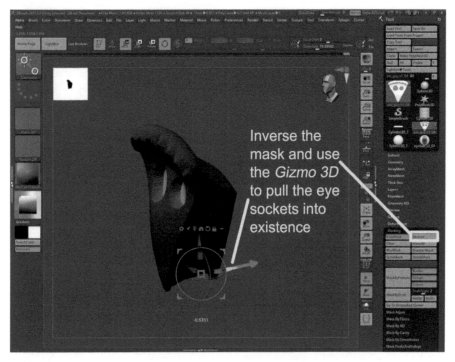

FIGURE 13.3 Inverse the mask and use the *Gizmo 3D* to pull the eye sockets into existence.

rebuild our geometry and give our eye sockets the polygons we need to sculpt and refine them. If you have scaled up your model, you may need to check the value of your *DynaMesh Resolution* slider. Remember that the size of the object factors into the *Resolution* slider setting to determine the final polygon density of the resulting dynameshed model. Since we have scaled this particular character model up significantly since the last time I applied a *DynaMesh* to the model, I ought to adjust the *Resolution* slider down to around 256 or so. If you *DynaMesh* your model with the *Resolution* slider set too high, you can inadvertently crash ZBrush. On the other hand, if the slider is set too low, you may lose some of your model's details. Generally speaking, it is better to err on the side of too low rather than too high. You can always undo, adjust the *Resolution* a bit, and try again if the *DynaMesh* results aren't detailed enough. However, if you have the *Resolution* slider set too high, you may crash the program and lose whatever progress you have made recently on your model. Remember that you can check the number of polygons in your model by simply resting your mouse cursor over the model icon in the active Tools palette. After applying our *DynaMesh* at a *Resolution* of 256, the number of polygons we end up with is roughly 3.5 million, which is a perfectly acceptable amount for right now. *DynaMesh* drops a fixed-size grid on the model to calculate the model's new geometry. How many polygons you get in the result depends on how big the model currently is in the ZBrush universe. Since we scaled the model up so much bigger, we can lower the *DynaMesh Resolution* and still end up with a model that has a lot more polygons!

DynaMesh will also patch up holes, unify overlapping geometry, and fill in seams, which can be a very useful feature or a significant challenge if you are trying to work on fine details. If you want *DynaMesh* to fill a seam, simply make sure that your surfaces overlap, and *DynaMesh* will do the rest. For example, I moved the back of the eye sockets forward a bit and then used the Move Topological brush to overlap the back of the eye socket with the sides. Now, when we *DynaMesh* the model, it will seal off and remove any redundant geometry and give us a clean back side of the eye sockets.

We can now go back to our *ClayTubes* brush to continue modeling. If you don't like the blocky look that *ClayTubes* creates by default, you can swap the square *BrushAlpha* shape for a round shape, say *Alpha 01*, instead and get a totally different effect.

Add a few more details

Now, we can swap to our *DamStandard* brush (B D S) and start carving in some blueberry pie-filling shapes in our character's eye sockets, which is the same technique we used when we created the pie filling on the sides of our pie slice. The goal is to make the eye sockets look

FIGURE 13.4 Use *DynaMesh* to clean up problematic geometry.

FIGURE 13.5 You can swap the *ClayTubes* brush's default square *BrushAlpha* shape for a round shape to get a totally different effect.

like lumpy pie filling, showing through holes in the pie crust. The *Dam-Standard* brush is a very useful brush for carving in a few details, then smoothing the surface out a bit using the *Smooth* brush, carving in more features, and smoothing these out. Keep repeating this process to build up your model details gradually. This approach will give you a richer and more detailed result than simply carving things in only once.

A lot of this is going to be hidden behind the eyeballs, but the parts that peek through will significantly add to the look of the model. Turn off the *Transp* button and turn on the visibility of your eyeball subtools (the tiny eye icons on the subtool layer) to check out the results so far.

Split To Parts

To really adjust each element of the eyeballs independently, we now need to select our eyeball subtool and use the T*ool > Subtool > Split > Split To Parts* command. A prompt will pop up telling you, "This is not an undoable operation." Click on the OK button. This command will separate the different elements of our eyeball back into their subtools, which can only be done if you have not dynameshed that subtool. Once you have applied a *DynaMesh* to a model, you have

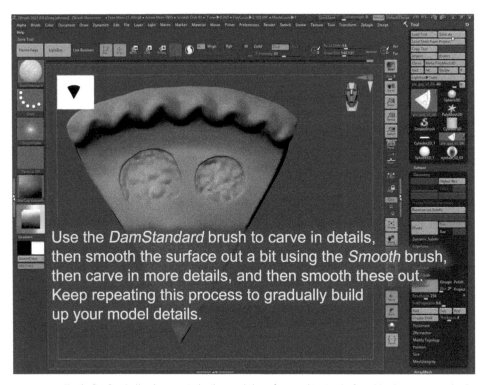

Use the *DamStandard* brush to carve in details, then smooth the surface out a bit using the *Smooth* brush, then carve in more details, and then smooth these out. Keep repeating this process to gradually build up your model details.

FIGURE 13.6 Use the *DamStandard* brush to carve in details, smooth the surface out a bit using the *Smooth* brush, carve in more details, and then smooth these out. Keep repeating this process to build up your model details gradually.

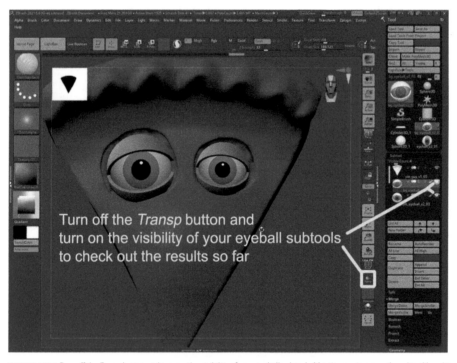

Turn off the *Transp* button and turn on the visibility of your eyeball subtools to check out the results so far

FIGURE 13.7 Turn off the *Transp* button and turn on the visibility of your eyeball subtools (the tiny eye icons on the subtool layer) to check out the results so far.

turned it into a unified mesh that cannot be separated back into its components in this manner.

Now that the eyeballs have been split into their components, you can select a specific subtool and use the CTRL+UP or DOWN arrow keys to arrange the position of that subtool on the *Subtool Palette*. Place the eyeball parts, the sclera, iris, and pupil together and use the *Tool > Subtool > Merge > MergeDown* command to merge these parts. Since we are only adjusting the eyelids, we don't need to mess with the actual ocular bits, so we might as well combine these so the subtool menu isn't so cluttered. Use the tiny eye icon on the subtool to hide it from view, though keep in mind that you can't hide an object if you have it currently selected.

Unfortunately, when you split a subtool into pieces, it resets your transformation center, which means that when you want to use the *Gizmo 3D* on a newly separated subtool, you will need to use the *Go to Unmasked Mesh Center* pin on the *Gizmo 3D* to recenter the gizmo on the object. You may need to *Unlock* the gizmo and adjust its position a bit to get the gizmo correctly centered on the eyelid. Once you have the *Gizmo 3D* positioned and aligned correctly, you can close the *Lock* and rotate the eyelid to exactly where you want it.

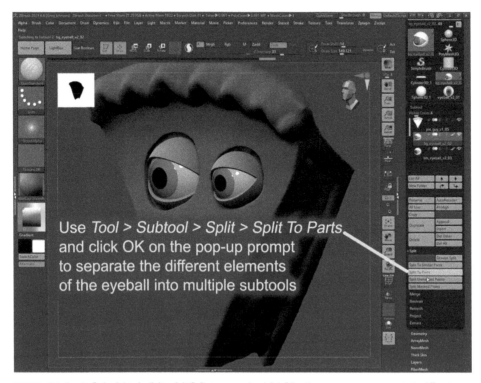

Use *Tool > Subtool > Split > Split To Parts*
and click OK on the pop-up prompt
to separate the different elements
of the eyeball into multiple subtools

FIGURE 13.8 Use the *Tool > Subtool > Split > Split To Parts* command and click OK on the pop-up prompt to separate the different elements of the eyeball into multiple subtools.

Repeat this sequence for the other eye and rotate the eyelids until you have quite the expression on your character that you are looking for. Afterward, merge your eyelid subtool using the *Tool > Subtool > Merge > MergeDown* command, and then use the *Tool > Subtool > Rename* command and give your eyelids a proper name, something like "eyelids_01". Remember to save your tool!

Making a crispy edge

Go ahead and use the *DamStandard* brush (B D S) to add a bit more detail to your pie filling on the side of the slice, making the filling a bit more complicated and hopefully visually interesting. You can use the *Inflate* brush (B I N) to puff up a few spots in the pie filling and turn these into blueberry shapes. If you press ALT while using the *Inflate* brush, you can create a few dimples and depressions to add even more variance.

I need to crispen one side of my pie crust. To do so, I simply mask off the area using the *MaskPen* brush (hold down CTRL), *Invert* the mask (CTRL+I), and then use the *Gizmo 3D* (W) to move the unmasked area up a small amount to create a new edge. Afterward, *DynaMesh* your model, and then use the *ClayTubes* brush to fill any rough patches.

253

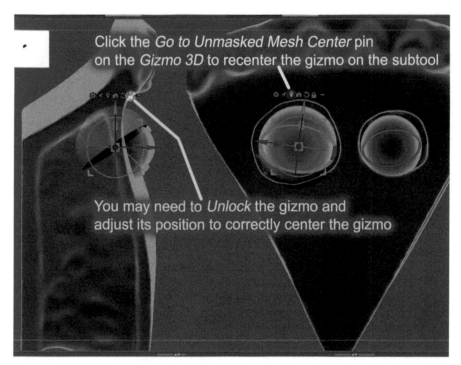

FIGURE 13.9 Click the *Go to Unmasked Mesh Center* pin on the *Gizmo 3D* to recenter the gizmo on the subtool. You may need to *Unlock* the gizmo and adjust its position to center the *Gizmo 3D* correctly.

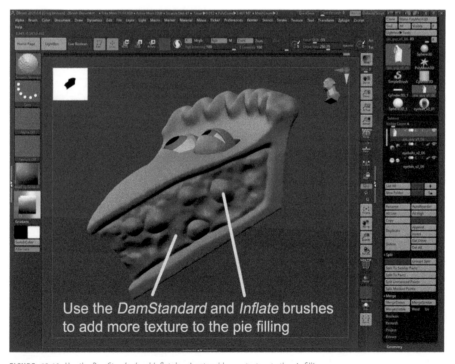

FIGURE 13.10 Use the *DamStandard* and *Inflate* brushes to add more texture to the pie filling.

254

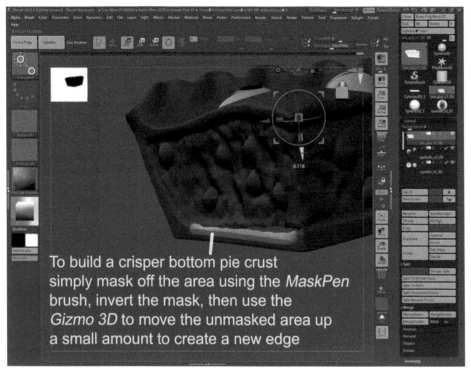

To build a crisper bottom pie crust simply mask off the area using the *MaskPen* brush, invert the mask, then use the *Gizmo 3D* to move the unmasked area up a small amount to create a new edge

FIGURE 13.11 To build a crisper bottom pie crust, simply mask off the area using the *MaskPen* brush, invert the mask, and then use the *Gizmo 3D* to move the unmasked area up a small amount to create a new edge.

Adding a mouth

The character now needs a mouth. To start carving a mouth shape into the top of the pie crust, first select the *DamStandard* brush (B D S) and then draw in your initial line. The *DamStandard* brush is great for sketching out the initial lines. Immediately after you make a brush stroke, press the "1" key along the top row of buttons on your keyboard, which will repeat the last brush stroke that you just made. Make sure that you press "1" immediately after completing the stroke. Otherwise, you might accidentally repeat a different operation.

Next, we can use the *MaskLasso* brush to mask out the bottom lip area of the mouth. Remember that you can use the *Tool > Masking* commands such as *BlurMask*, *GrowMask*, *BoostMask*, *ShrinkMask*, *SharpenMask*, and *DiluteMask* to help tweak the mask. You can also let go of the CTRL key, and then press down the SPACEBAR as you draw the mask to move the mask around, or you can also press the CTRL + ALT keys to subtract from the existing mask.

Now that we don't need to worry about affecting the other portion of the lip, we can dive in with the *Flatten* brush to shape the upper lip.

255

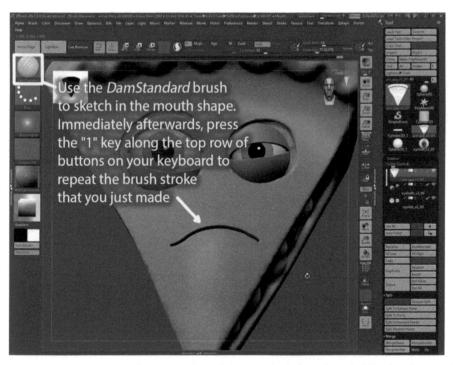

FIGURE 13.12 Use the *DamStandard* brush to sketch the mouth shape. Immediately afterward, press the "1" key along the top row of buttons on your keyboard to repeat the brush stroke that you just made.

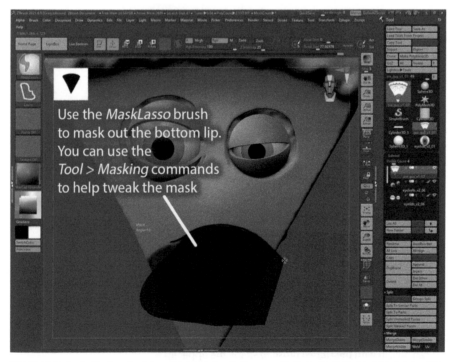

FIGURE 13.13 Use the *MaskLasso* brush to mask out the bottom lip. You can use the *Tool > Masking* commands to help tweak the mask.

After using CTRL +I to invert the mask, we can use the *Inflate* brush to puff out the lower lip. A bit of smoothing and a quick *DynaMesh* will then fix up our model. You can now use other brushes, such as the *Move Topological* and *hPolish* brushes, to refine the lips further. For this character, I think a sneer would be most appropriate and match the crazy eyes that we created earlier.

Adding wrinkles

We can now add a few wrinkles near the mouth to add a bit more character to our sculpture. The *DamStandard* brush is a great starting place for creating a wrinkle or crease. Simply create an initial stroke that you like. Then, use the "1" key to repeat the stroke a few times and strengthen that cut. Switch to your *Smooth* or *SmoothStronger* brush and really smooth down the beginning and end of the wrinkle while only gently softening the middle portion. Next, redraw the stroke and repeat the entire process. This methodology, where you add a few strokes, smooth them out, and then add some more strokes, will create a more subtle and realistic look for your model.

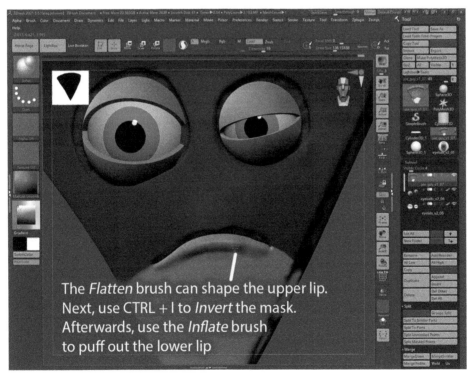

The *Flatten* brush can shape the upper lip. Next, use CTRL + I to *Invert* the mask. Afterwards, use the *Inflate* brush to puff out the lower lip

FIGURE 13.14 The *Flatten* brush can shape the upper lip. Next, use CTRL + I to *Invert* the mask. Afterward, use the *Inflate* brush to puff out the lower lip.

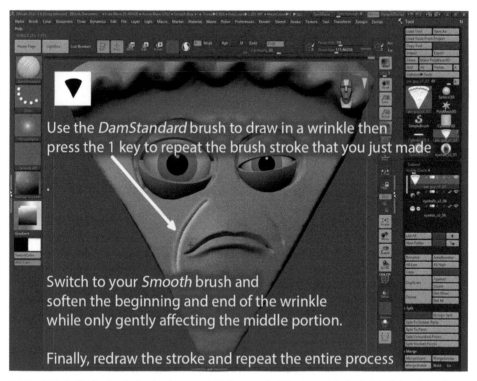

Use the *DamStandard* brush to draw in a wrinkle then press the 1 key to repeat the brush stroke that you just made

Switch to your *Smooth* brush and soften the beginning and end of the wrinkle while only gently affecting the middle portion.

Finally, redraw the stroke and repeat the entire process

FIGURE 13.15 Use the *DamStandard* brush to draw in a wrinkle, then press the "1" key to repeat the brush stroke that you just made. Switch to your *Smooth* brush and soften the beginning and end of the wrinkle while only gently affecting the middle portion. Finally, redraw the stroke and repeat the entire process.

Creating the lips and nose

Using the *DamStandard* brush, you can draw in the rest of the details on the face, adding in the philtrum (the little groove in the middle of the upper lip), a hint of a nose, as well as any other wrinkles you'd like to include for extra personality. The *Move Topological* brush can then be used to gently pull the lips a bit forward and shape the face. Quite a lot of detail can be added by just using a combination of a few simple brushes. The *DamStandard*, *hPolish*, *Inflate*, *Move Topological*, *Smooth*, and *Standard* brushes form a powerful tool kit that can accomplish almost anything in ZBrush. Now go ahead and mask out the area you'd like to turn into the nose. CTRL+I to *Invert* the mask. Now switch to the *Move Topological* brush (B M T) and pull the nose forward from the face. Afterward, shrink your brush down and smooth out any jagged parts.

Go in and finish up the nose area by using the *DamStandard* brush to finish carving in detail. A bit of the *hPolish* can be used to add definition to the new facial structures you have just added. The *hPolish* brush is very useful for flattening out puffy or over-inflated zones on your

FIGURE 13.16 Mask out the nose. Use CTRL + I to *Invert* the mask. Then, use the *Move Topological* brush to pull the nose out of the face.

model. Periodically, use the *DynaMesh* button to rebuild your geometry whenever it gets out of shape. If *DynaMesh* starts to lose any of the details that you have carved into your model, then you should try turning on the *Project* button just to the right of the bug *DynaMesh* button. Activating this button, along with raising the *Resolution* slider, should preserve all of the detail in your model quite nicely. Still, it will also increase the amount of time it takes *ZBrush* to calculate the *DynaMesh* function.

That constitutes the major feature of our pie character. We now have one funky-looking piece of pie! It is often easier to sculpt in extreme expressions rather than subtle ones.

Using a reference image with the *See-through* slider

It is now time to add some detail to the backside of our character. Luckily, I have a lot of good reference images that I took for this project. It is a simple enough process to find a good shot of the pie's crust to use.

A very useful trick is to bring up the reference image behind the ZBrush app and resize the image window so that it fits within the ZBrush document area. With ZBrush running in front of the image app, go to

FIGURE 13.17 Reference image for the back side of the pie.

ZBrush, and in the upper right-hand corner of the interface, find the *See-through* slider. Now, slide the *See-through* slider up a bit to around 20 in order to make ZBrush semi-transparent and view the reference image, which is a very handy trick that allows you to view your reference image while working in ZBrush.

Adding details

To carve the creases in the crust, we will again resort to the wonderful *DamStandard* brush. Simply making a nice brush stroke and then pressing the "1" key a few times will create a very nice mark in the crust. Varying the brush's Z intensity will also help the process along. We can mask off the parts of the pie we are not working on using the *Mask-Lasso* brush, so we don't accidentally mess up any of the work we have already done. Make sure that you have symmetry turned off for this part. You need a certain amount of asymmetry in order for a character to look real.

One of the big tricks to using ZBrush successfully is to keep going in and carving in details, then smoothing things out, then cutting in additional features, and repeating this process until you have built up a level of interesting surface details. Use the *DamStandard* brush to add that little extra smidge of detail anywhere on the model that needs it. Then add a touch of smoothing and a bit more detail.

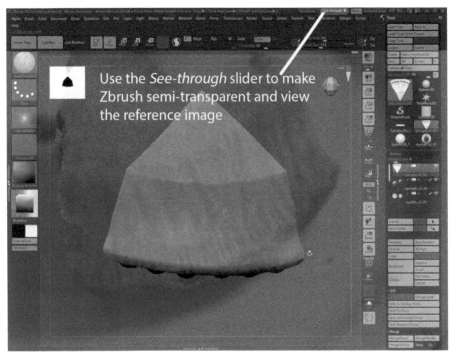

FIGURE 13.18 Use the *See-through* slider to make ZBrush semi-transparent and view the reference image.

FIGURE 13.19 Mask off the parts of the pie you are not working on. Then, use the *DamStandard* brush to carve some details on the pie crust.

Creating eyebrows

The model needs something else to help increase the character's expressiveness and convey emotion. I think that the character may need some eyebrows. While there are a lot of different ways to accomplish this, it is often best to simply use the most straightforward and unsophisticated approach to solving problems during production. It isn't enough to be really good at ZBrush to get a job doing this sort of work. You need to work quickly and efficiently. With that in mind, let's just start with a sphere. Switch to a *Sphere3D* tool, press the *Make-Polymesh3D* button, and use the *Gizmo 3D* to scale the sphere into an oblong shape.

After you make the initial spheroid shape, go back to your character tool and use the *Tool > Subtool > Append* command to add the spheroid to the character. Turn on the *Transp* button so you can easily see the new eyebrow spheroid subtool. Now, use the *Gizmo 3D* to move the spheroid into place above the character's eyeball. You can use the Inflate brush to round out the tips of the spheroid a bit, and then *DynaMesh* the spheroid to create the initial model for the eyebrow. Once you are happy with the eyebrow, use the *Tool > Subtool > Duplicate* command to copy the eyebrow subtool, and then use the *Tool*

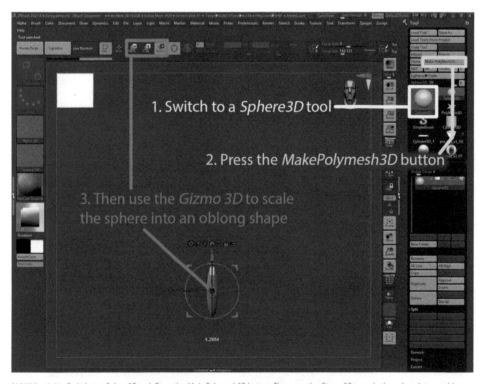

FIGURE 13.20 Switch to a *Sphere3D* tool. Press the *MakePolymesh3D* button. Then, use the *Gizmo 3D* to scale the sphere into an oblong shape.

>*Deformation* > *Mirror* command to flip the duplicate eyebrow to the other side of the face. Now select the top-most eyebrow subtool and use the *Tool* > *Subtool* > *Merge* > *MergeDown* command to merge the two eyebrows into one subtool. Now we can use the *MoveTopological*, *Inflate*, and *hPolish* brushes to shape the eyebrows until you are happy with their look.

After adding the eyebrows, you can use the *DamStandard* brush to add in a few more wrinkles on the forehead. Shape these wrinkles with the *Smooth*, *Inflate*, and *MoveTopological* brushes until you are pleased with the results. A few extra wrinkles added in this manner can really add a lot of emotional impact to the model and help convey the character's mood.

Conclusion

The process of adding features to our character is essentially the act of adding personality and emotion to our model. We have now defined all our major secondary features, such as the eyes, nose, mouth, and eyebrows, and we have begun the process of adding a few preliminary tertiary wrinkles. Much of what we did in this chapter simply used the tools that have already been introduced in previous chapters. Hopefully, you can now see that even these few simple tools are more than

FIGURE 13.21 The eyebrows and some additional wrinkles for added emotional impact.

adequate for much of the character creation process. Indeed, the most important aspects of character creation lie more in your artistic and aesthetic skills than in specific tools within ZBrush. We will complete our character by adding arms, hands, legs, and feet in the upcoming chapters. In the meantime, just keep practicing what you have learned so far and continue honing your ZBrush skills. Most importantly, have fun while you keep working in ZBrush!

14

Hands and Arms

Introduction

Welcome back! In this chapter of our fine book, we are going to create a suitable cartoon hand and arm for our crazed blueberry pie character sculpture that we have been working on. The process consists of first roughing out our forms with basic shapes. After this, we then merge all of our items and sculpt the model into its final form. Finally, we get the model ready to be imported into our main ZTool file.

Making a hand

To get started, draw a cube on the screen by clicking on the *Simple-Brush* golden "S" icon in the *Tool Palette* and selecting the *Cube3D* icon. Next, simply draw the cube on the screen and remember to press the *Edit* button immediately afterward. Then activate the *Gizmo 3D* and scale your object down on the Z-axis to create a flattened box shape.

After that, click on the *Tool > Make PolyMesh3D* button to convert the cube into an editable object. Finally, go to the *Tool > Geometry* sub-palette and click on the *Divide* button a few times to increase the number of polygons in our shape and smooth out the sharp corners. Now we can go ahead and *DynaMesh* this object, but you cannot *DynaMesh* a tool that has existing subdivision levels. This means that you need to press the *Tool > Geometry > Del Lower* button to get rid of the existing subdivision levels, after which you can go ahead and use the *Tool > Geometry > DynaMesh* button to resurface our model.

DOI: 10.1201/9781003215288-14

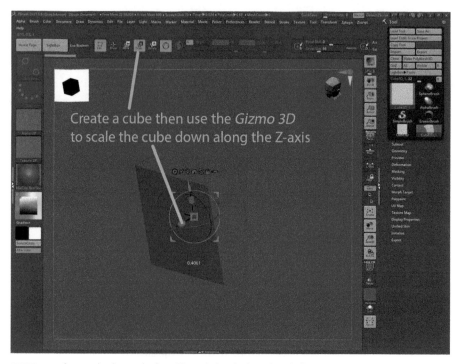

FIGURE 14.1 Create a cube, then use the *Gizmo 3D* to scale the cube down along the Z-axis.

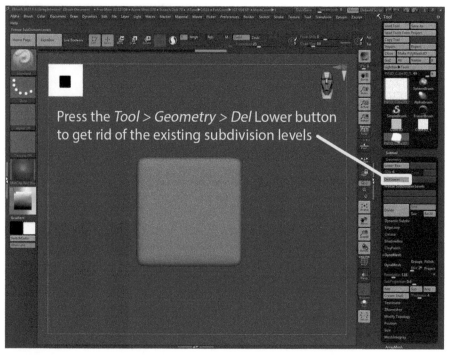

FIGURE 14.2 Press the *Tool > Geometry > Del Lower* button to get rid of the existing subdivision levels.

Switch to the *Move Topological* brush and start shaping the box. If you need a reference, simply look down and look at your hand. Modeling a hand is one of the easier things to find a reference for! Make your brush nice and large using the *Draw Size* slider and pull the box model into the shape of your palm, making generous use of the *Smooth* brush to round the model out.

You may notice that I first work on establishing the correct shape from one specific viewpoint before I move on to work from a different perspective, which is a great trick for working in 3D. You just need to be careful with the axis (or axes) you are moving the shape about. Specifically, in the initial side view I am working from, I only move the hand along the XY axis. In the next top-down viewpoint, I only work along the Z-axis while trying to avoid making any alterations on the XY-axis. Restricting the axis of movement like this allows you to establish a shape in one viewpoint and then refine that shape in the next view without messing up the original form that you created. Of course, it isn't quite so simple. You will find that you have to attack the project from a multitude of different angles. You get the silhouette right in one view, then switch to another view and get that shape correct, then switch back to fix any new problems, then switch to another view, and so on. That said, if you can pay careful attention to what axis you are adjusting in a given view, you can take care to make adjustments using a different axis in the next viewpoint.

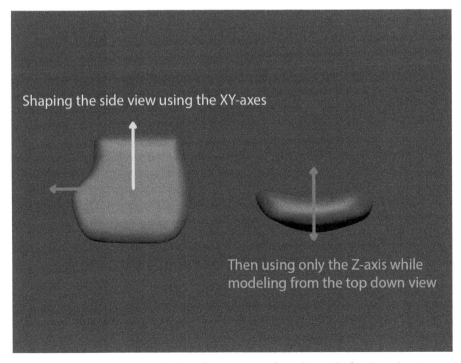

Shaping the side view using the XY-axes

Then using only the Z-axis while modeling from the top down view

FIGURE 14.3 Shaping the side view using the XY-axes. Then, using only the Z-axis while modeling from the top-down view.

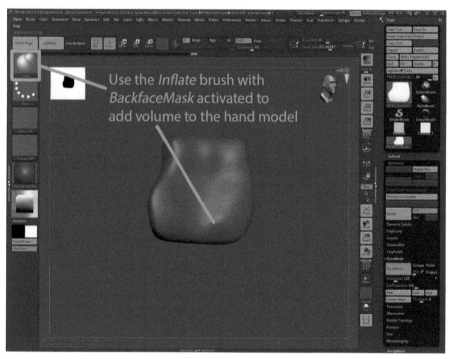

Use the *Inflate* brush with *BackfaceMask* activated to add volume to the hand model

FIGURE 14.4 Use the *Inflate* brush with *BackfaceMask* activated to add volume to the hand model.

Having established the general shape of the palm, we can now use the Inflate brush (B I N) to add some volume to the fleshy parts of our hand. Make sure that you turn on the *Brush > Auto Masking > BackfaceMask* button so you don't accidentally inflate both sides of your hand model. Now bulk up the lumps of tissue at the base of the fingers, thumb, and along the side of the hand. Now, switch to the other side of the hand and add some indicators of the knuckles. You will notice that I am creating a classic cartoon three-fingered hand, which is a time-honored tradition in animation when making cartoon characters for the simple reason that you end up with one less finger that you need to animate! Plus, most of your audience will only register the difference if it is pointed out. *DynaMesh* the model as required, and you can also swap the Smooth Brush out for the Smooth Stronger Brush if you need to do so.

One approach to creating the fingers

To create the fingers, we could just mask out the base of the fingers and simply drag the shapes out, which would be a straightforward approach. However, we're trying to show you some new stuff. In the spirit of discovery, let's go to our *Brush Palette* and choose

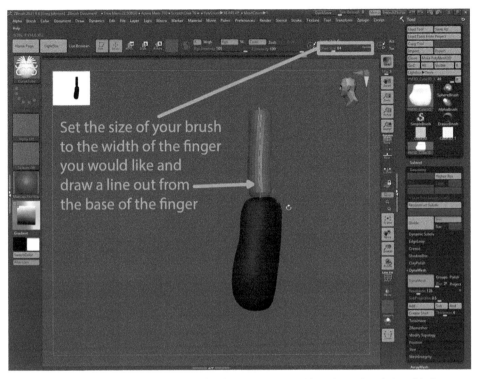

Set the size of your brush to the width of the finger you would like and draw a line out from the base of the finger

FIGURE 14.5 Set the size of your brush to the diameter of the finger you would like and draw a line out from the base of the finger.

the *CurveTube* brush, which is a fun little brush. This brush creates a curved tube based on the line that you draw while the button is pressed down. The size of your brush determines the diameter of the tube that is created. With that in mind, set the size of your brush to the diameter of the finger you would like and draw a line out from the base of the finger.

The *CurveTube* brush creates a new tube based on the size of your brush and the stroke you used on the canvas. The stroke itself will show up as a dashed line running through the middle of the tube. At the beginning and end of this dashed line, you will see a small green circle. This tiny green circle acts as a handle that you can use to control the position of the curve-tube itself. If you click and drag on the green circle at the start of the stroke, you can reposition the entire tube without editing its shape. On the other hand, if you click and drag on the green circle at the end of the stroke, you can reposition the curve tube and also change its shape.

Interestingly enough, the new finger isn't a separate subtool, but is instead an unmasked portion of the existing model. This means that if you want the new tube to be a separate object, you will need to use the *Tool > Subtool > Split > Split Unmasked Points* command to turn

269

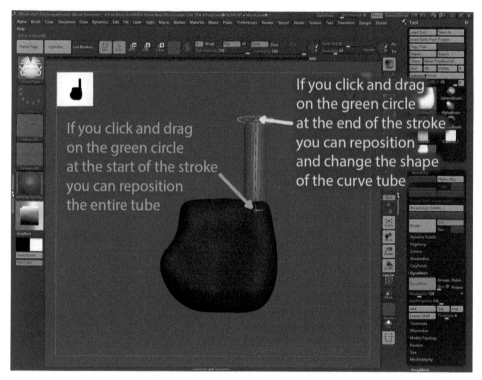

FIGURE 14.6 If you click and drag on the green circle at the start of the stroke, you can reposition the entire tube. If you click and drag on the green circle at the end of the stroke, you can reposition and change the shape of the curve tube.

the unmasked finger into a new subtool. Note that the initial tube is rather low-poly, and it is a good idea to go ahead and DynaMesh the new finger so that you have more polygons to work with. You can now go ahead and draw in a few new fingers and then use the Tool > Subtool > Split > Split To Parts command to break the new fingers into individual subtools.

You can now use the Tool > Subtool > Merge > MergeDown command to merge the fingers back into the rest of the hand. To work on just one of the fingers, you can simply hold down CTRL+SHIFT and tap one of the fingers to isolate that model from the rest of the hand, which only works before the fingers have been dynameshed into the rest of the hand. When you dynamesh a model, you turn it from a bunch of individual pieces into a single unified mesh. To bring the hidden models back, you can just CTRL+SHIFT and click on the document background.

Now press CTRL+SHIFT and tap one of the fingers to isolate that finger from the rest of the hand. Mask off the isolated finger. Use CTRL+SHIFT and tap the background to unhide the rest of the hand. CTRL+click on the background to invert the mask. Now, use the Gizmo 3D to tweak the position of the finger shapes.

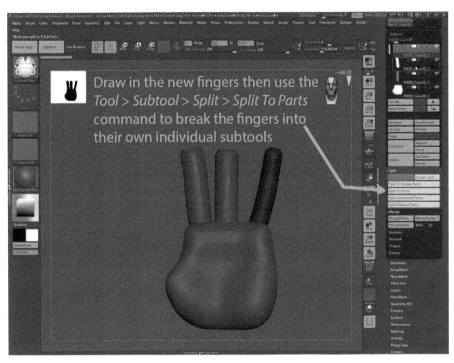

FIGURE 14.7 Draw in the new fingers, then use the *Tool > Subtool > Split > Split To Parts* command to break the fingers into individual subtools.

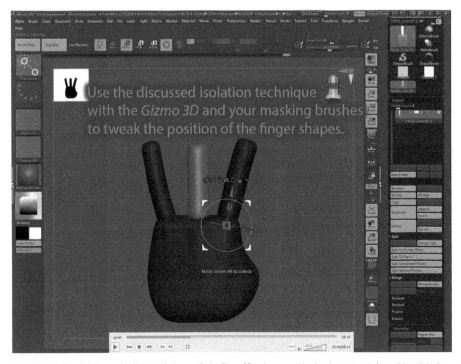

FIGURE 14.8 Use the discussed isolation technique with the *Gizmo 3D* and your masking brushes to tweak the position of the finger shapes.

A different approach to making the fingers

If we want to continue with these fingers, the next step would be to merge all of the finger and hand subtools, clear any remaining masks, and then *DynaMesh* the fingers together with the hand. Afterward, you can just sculpt the unified hand into a finished form.

An alternative way of going about completing the hand is to create one finger and then simply duplicate it to create the other digits. To use this approach, you only need to make one finger using the *CurveTube* brush. After making the tube, split it off of the palm model just like before, and then *DynaMesh* it to refine the finger's geometry. Now switch to the *Inflate* brush and bulk up the fingertips to make a nice cartoon digit, and then use the *Move Topological* brush to shape the finger. The *DamStandard* brush can be used to create creases in the finger. You may have noticed that quite a lot of work can be done using just a few simple brushes!

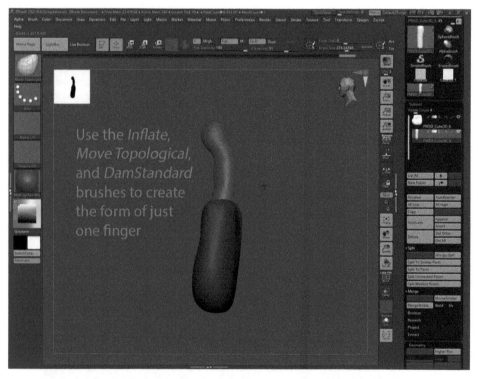

FIGURE 14.9 Use the *Inflate*, *Move Topological*, and *DamStandard* brushes to create the form of just one finger.

Creating the other fingers

To make the other fingers, simply use the *Tool > Subtool > Duplicate* command to create a copy of the finger that you have sculpted. Next, switch to the *Gizmo 3D* by pressing the W key, and then use the *Gizmo 3D* to position and scale the new finger. Finally, you can just repeat the process to make the next finger and the thumb as well.

Remember to check the position of the fingers from multiple different viewpoints, which will allow you to make certain that each finger is placed appropriately on the hand. Remember that once you have activated the *Gizmo 3D*, you can use it to move, rotate, and scale each finger. A useful trick is to unlock the *Gizmo 3D* and position it at the base of the finger you wish to adjust, which will make scaling the finger a bit bigger or smaller much easier.

Once you have finished positioning the fingers and thumb, select the topmost subtool and use the *Tool > Subtool > Merge > MergeDown* command several times to combine all of the fingers and thumb with the palm model. A quick *DynaMesh* afterward will create a unified

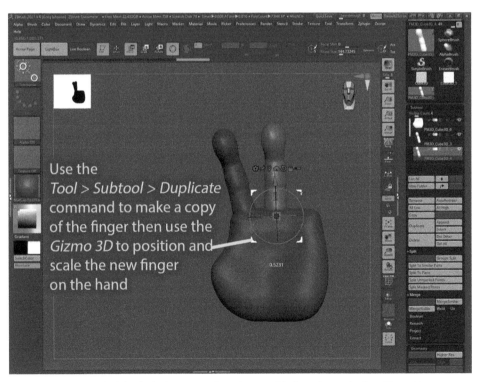

FIGURE 14.10 Use the *Tool > Subtool > Duplicate* command to make a copy of the finger, then use the *Gizmo 3D* to position and scale the new finger on the hand.

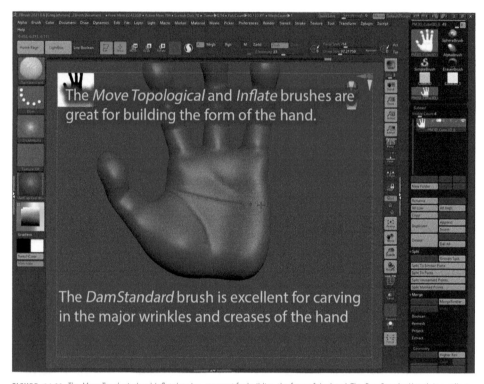

The *Move Topological* and *Inflate* brushes are great for building the form of the hand.

The *DamStandard* brush is excellent for carving in the major wrinkles and creases of the hand

FIGURE 14.11 The *Move Topological* and *Inflate* brushes are great for building the form of the hand. The *DamStandard* brush is excellent for carving in the major wrinkles and creases of the hand.

mesh from all of the various components that you can now sculpt into the final form of the hand model using the wonderful *Move Topological*, *Inflate*, and *DamStandard* brushes. Because this is a cartoon hand, it does not have to be a perfect replica of a human hand, but it does need to have certain elements, such as the fingertips being exaggerated a bit. The *DamStandard* brush is excellent for carving in the major wrinkles and creases of the hand. With these few brushes and a bit of smoothing, you can create almost anything! Remember to save your work occasionally.

Creating the arm

Now that we have created the cartoon hand, it is time to make the arm. Open up the brush palette again, and go back to the *CurveTube* brush. Set the brush's *Draw Size* to the width of the arm you want to create. Now click on the base of the hand where the wrist starts and drag up to set the length of the arm.

Next, adjust the placement of the arm using the lower green circle on the curve tube line. Then, use the *Tool > Subtool > Split > Split To Parts* command to separate the arm into different subtools. Select your hand

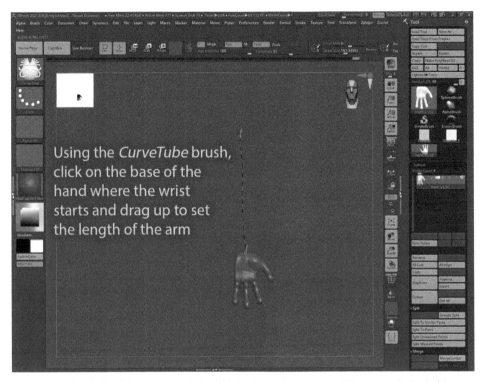

FIGURE 14.12 Using the *CurveTube* brush, click on the base of the hand where the wrist starts and drag up to set the length of the arm.

model in the *Subtool Palette* and get rid of the mask. Switch back to the arm subtool, *DynaMesh* the arm, and then use the *Smooth* brush to get rid of any unsightly seams and roughness. To shape the arm, select the *Inflate* brush (B I N), hold down the ALT key, and use this to deflate the arm near the wrist. You can then release the ALT key and simply inflate the top portion of the arm to add some muscle to this limb. Next, use the *DamStandard* brush to create a crease on the opposite side of the elbow. You can use the *MoveTopological* brush to pull out the elbow. You don't need a lot of definition since this is a cartoon character, but a bit of shaping helps a lot.

Adding a cartoon element to the hand

To accentuate the cartoonishness of the arm, we can go to the Tool palette and select the *Ring3D* shape, which will immediately swap out our arm model for a ring. No worries because the arm is still present in the tool palette, and we can switch back to it at any time. With the *Ring3D* on screen, go to the *Tool > Initialize* submenu and change the settings to *SDivide* = 85, *LDivide* = 246, and *SRadius* = 51. Next, click the *Tool > Make PolyMesh3D* button to convert the ring into an editable object.

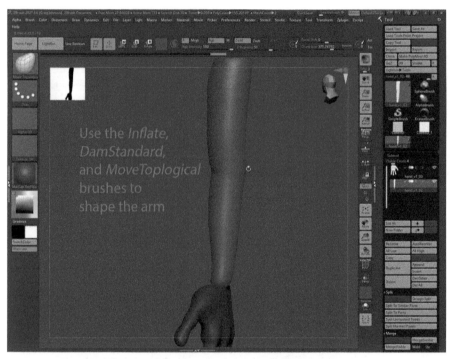

FIGURE 14.13 Use the Inflate, *DamStandard,* and *MoveToplogical* brushes to shape the arm.

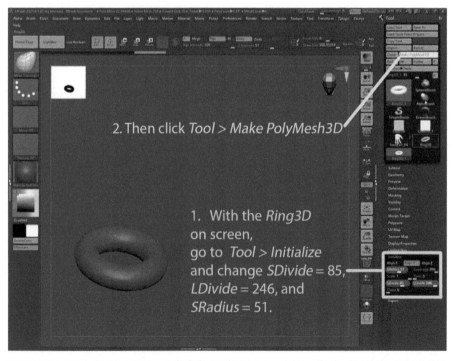

FIGURE 14.14 With the *Ring3D* on screen, go to the *Tool > Initialize* submenu and change *SDivide* = 85, *LDivide* = 246, and *SRadius* = 51. Then click the *Tool > Make PolyMesh3D* button.

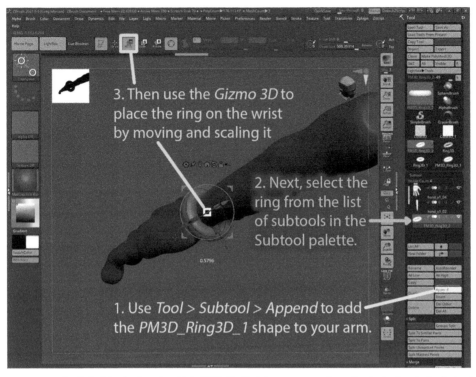

FIGURE 14.15 Use *Tool > Subtool > Append* to add the *PM3D_Ring3D_1* shape to your arm. Next, select the ring from the list of subtools in the *Subtool Palette*. Then, use the *Gizmo 3D* to place the ring on the wrist by moving and scaling it.

Go back to the *Tool Palette* and select your hand-arm tool from the list of 3D meshes there, which will reload your hand-arm model back onto the screen. Now use the *Tool > Subtool > Append* command and select the *PM3D_Ring3D_1* tool from the list of options that pop up, which should load the ring you just built into the scene. Next, choose the ring from the list of subtools in the *Tool > Subtool Palette*, and then use the *Gizmo 3D* to place the ring on the wrist by moving and scaling it, which will create a classic cartoon gloved hand look for the character we are building. Now, you can simply use the *MoveTopological* and *Inflate* brushes to fit the ring onto the arm and close up any gaps that exist between the ring and the wrist.

Finishing the hand and arm model

The result may be kind of strange-looking, but, as you have no doubt figured out by now, this is going to be a strange-looking project. I want to leave the hands manageable and avoid getting really finicky with the model because that would start taking away from the cartoony look of things. The other reason is that I want the attention of the viewer in the final illustration to be focused on the character's face or perhaps a weapon and not on a set of hyper-realistic hands.

To finish the model, simply select the topmost subtool in our *Subtool Palette* and then use the *Tool > Subtool > Merge > MergeDown* command a few times to merge all of the current subtool layers into one subtool. We can now *DynaMesh* the entire model, say at a *Resolution* of 256, and unify the mesh. To finalize everything, simply take a tour around your model and fix any problems that you find. I have found that the *MoveTopological* brush is great for making small tweaks to the model's shape at this stage. If you need to fill in a gap or close up a space, the *ClayTubes* brush is a great way of doing that. Just build up the surface until it overlaps and closes the area off, *DynaMesh* the results, and then use the *Smooth* brush to fix any irregularities. The Inflate brush is another great way of getting surfaces to overlap before dynameshing them as well.

The last step is to save your tool using the *Tool > Save As* command and remember to iterate your file name to create a new file rather than saving over an existing old file. That should finish the hand and arm model! Hopefully, you are doing OK so far. Next time, we will continue modeling our character by creating the feet and legs. Take care until then.

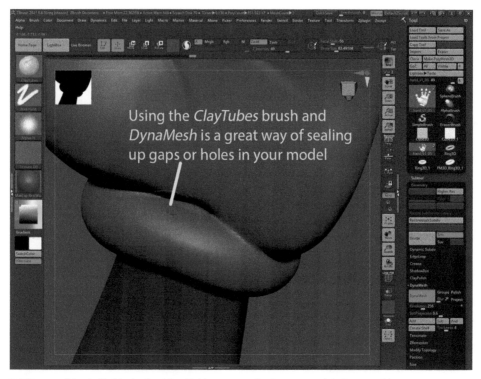

FIGURE 14.16 Using the *ClayTubes* brush and *DynaMesh* is a great way of sealing up gaps or holes in your model.

Conclusion

In this chapter, we learned how to create an arm and a hand for a cartoon character using just a few simple commands and brushes. Leveraging ZBrush to the fullest lies in understanding how the various features, commands, and brushes can be used together in diverse ways to create complicated forms. A large part of the learning process for this package involves slowly building up a degree of familiarity and comfort with using quite a small set of tools and then gradually expanding upon this functional base as needed. Keep in mind that it is perfectly OK to get stumped every so often. You will certainly run into problems when learning such a complicated and unusual software package as ZBrush. Remember to look things up using ZBrushCentral and the ZBrush documentation online when you need to. Fortunately, the ZBrush community is a welcoming and helpful one. Just make sure that you have read the available documentation first before asking questions on the forum. I hope you are enjoying the process so far!

15

Legs and Attachment

Introduction

Hello again, and welcome back! In this session, we're going to work up the legs. We will begin by trying the simplest approach possible to make what we need. Philosophically speaking, this brings up one of the fundamental principles of working professionally as a 3D artist – it isn't enough to be good; you must also be fast. You will frequently be working on a tight deadline, and you must be able to create content quickly. Practically speaking, this translates into building your model in the most time-efficient manner possible, which means using shortcuts whenever possible. Many artists choose to customize their interface to help speed up their workflow. Conversely, I have noticed over my many years of teaching that using a lot of shortcuts and a personalized interface has a horrible effect when teaching people new software skills. It is far better when teaching to start off using the plain vanilla version of things and slowly introduce shortcuts and other features after a basic proficiency in the software has been established. It is whole; you have to walk before you can run. That said, you are now entering the next phase, where you may want to learn all of the shortcuts and start speeding up your workflow. You can take a look at the list of ZBrush shortcuts on the official ZBrush website (http://docs.pixologic.com/user-guide/keyboard-shortcuts/shortcuts-by-palette/). If you feel you need more time to feel ready for that, that is perfectly fine, too. The list of shortcuts will be there when you need it.

DOI: 10.1201/9781003215288-15

Problems minimizing and maximizing ZBrush?

Once you have minimized ZBrush to the Windows taskbar, the program has the unpleasant habit of not restoring when you click on it. To fix this problem, if it should happen, you can hold down the WINDOWS key on your keyboard and press the various ARROW keys until you restore ZBrush. Another approach is to hold down the ALT key and use the TAB key to switch through all of the currently open apps, which can also work.

Making the leg

When making the leg, taking a speedy approach means using a cylinder as a starting place. First, select the *Cylinder3D* from the *Tool Palette* and draw it on the screen. Remember to press the *Edit* button after drawing the cylinder onto the document background. Then go to *Tool > Initialize* and set the following values:

    X Size = 11
    Y Size = 11
    HDivide = 133

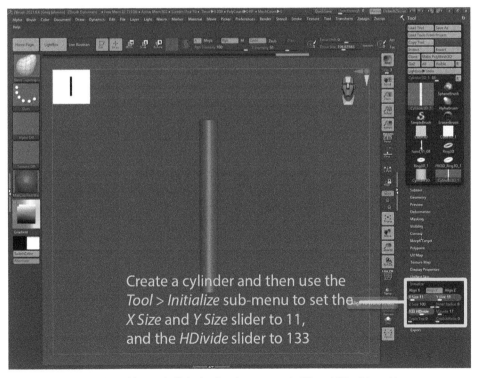

FIGURE 15.1 Create a cylinder and then use the *Tool > Initialize* sub-menu to set the *X Size* and *Y Size* sliders to 11 and the *HDivide* slider to 133.

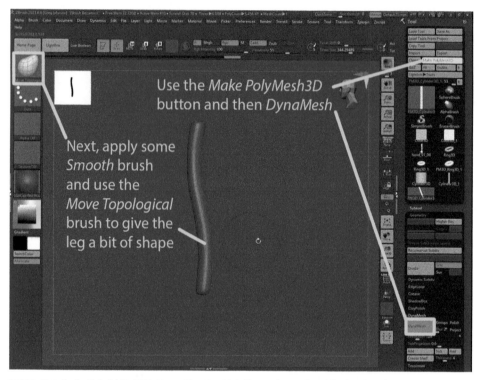

FIGURE 15.2 Use the *Make PolyMesh3D* button and then *DynaMesh*. Next, apply some *Smooth* brush and use the *Move Topological* brush to give the leg a bit of shape.

Next, click on the *Tool > Make PolyMesh3D* button to convert the model into an editable object. After that, use the *Tool > Geometry > DynaMesh > DynaMesh* button to rebuild the model's geometry. Switch to the *Smooth* brush and smooth the cylinder into a more rounded shape. Choose the *Move Topological* brush and give the leg just a bit of shape.

You can use the *Inflate* brush to puff up the leg muscles for a bit more definition as you like. Afterward, raise your *DynaMesh Resolution* to 256 and *DynaMesh* the model again. A bit of smoothing will always help, too. The final step is to save the ZTL model using the *Tool > Save As* button.

Making the shoe

To build the shoe, let's start with a sphere. Simply select a *Sphere3D* from the *Tool Palette*. When you choose the *Sphere3D* tool from the tool palette, the sphere should automatically replace whatever tool you had previously on screen. If it does not, then you can use the *Document > New Document* command, draw a new sphere on the screen, and then press the Edit button to get started. Next, go to the *Tool > Initialize* submenu and crank the *HDivide* and *VDivide* sliders up.

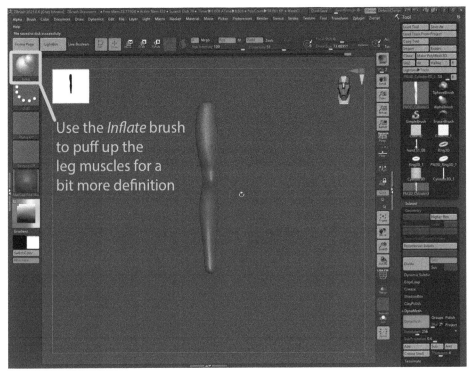

Use the *Inflate* brush to puff up the leg muscles for a bit more definition

FIGURE 15.3 Use the *Inflate* brush to puff up the leg muscles for a bit more definition.

I set my *HDivide* to 775 and my *VDivide* to 303, but the exact numbers do not matter so much as you simply make the model smooth and without visible seams. Then click the *DynaMesh* button as usual in the pattern of how we start off making a shape. Go ahead and rotate your view to where you are looking straight down upon the model. Remember that you can hold down the SHIFT key to snap the view into place while you change your viewpoint. Once you have set your viewpoint, go ahead and use the CTRL key to access the *MaskPen*, and then click and drag on the background to mask off half of the sphere with a masking rectangle. Press the W key to access the *Gizmo 3D*, move part of the sphere straight back, and then scale the sides of the sphere down a bit, which will make the basic shape of a cartoon shoe.

Go ahead and *DynaMesh* the shape we currently have to rebuild our model's geometry and smooth out the results. Switch your viewpoint back to the front view. You can click on the small blue circle in the upper right-hand corner of the document near the viewport *CamView* head. Hold down the CTRL and SHIFT keys and select the *TrimCurve* brush from the palette of *3D Sculpting Brushes* that pops up.

Now press the CTRL and SHIFT keys again, and click and drag a new *TrimCurve* on the screen across the middle of the model to cut off the bottom part of the shoe and flatten it out. Keep in mind that the

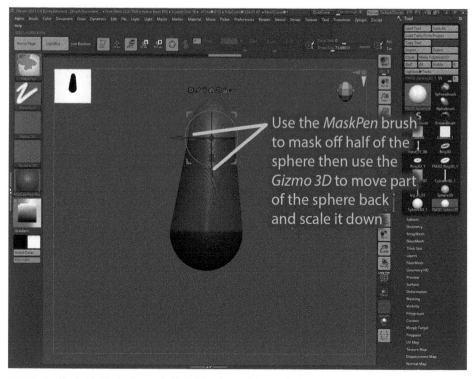

Use the *MaskPen* brush to mask off half of the sphere then use the *Gizmo 3D* to move part of the sphere back and scale it down

FIGURE 15.4 Use the *MaskPen* brush to mask off half of the sphere, and then use the *Gizmo 3D* to move part of the sphere back and scale it down.

shaded part of the trim line will be the portion of the model that is chopped off, and remember that you can hold down the SPACEBAR to reposition the trim curve as needed.

Use the *MoveTopological* brush to shape the shoe a bit, then *DynaMesh* and *Smooth* to clean things up a bit. If the bottom of the shoe gets bent out of shape, you can always re-trim it back to flat again. Because this is a cartoon shoe, we can keep our shape really quite simple.

Making the sole of the shoe

For the next step, we are going to make the sole of the shoe. The sole should have a small lip where the sole forms the bottom of the shoe. First, duplicate the shoe using the *Tool > Subtool > Duplicate* button. Now, move this copy of the shoe down a bit and determine the thickness of the sole you desire. Next, hold down the CTRL+SHIFT keys and use the *TrimCurve* brush to cut away the top portion of the duplicate shoe.

After that, switch to the *Gizmo 3D* and scale the sole up a bit to create the lip that we would like the bottom of the shoe to have. You can switch to the *MoveTopological* brush and a top-down view to make

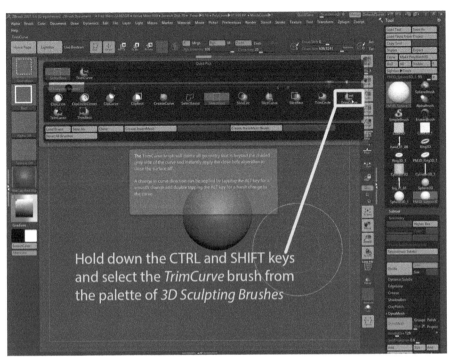

Hold down the CTRL and SHIFT keys
and select the *TrimCurve* brush from
the palette of *3D Sculpting Brushes*

FIGURE 15.5 Hold down the CTRL and SHIFT keys and select the *TrimCurve* brush from the palette of *3D Sculpting Brushes*.

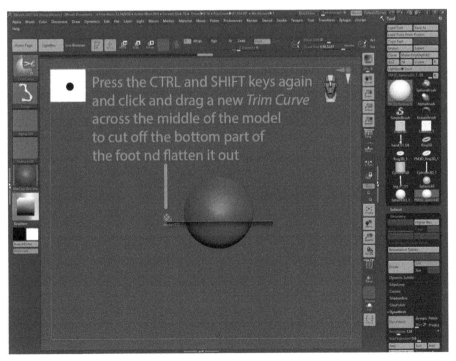

Press the CTRL and SHIFT keys again
and click and drag a new *Trim Curve*
across the middle of the model
to cut off the bottom part of
the foot nd flatten it out

FIGURE 15.6 Press the CTRL and SHIFT keys again and click and drag a new *TrimCurve* across the middle of the model to cut off the bottom part of the shoe and flatten it out.

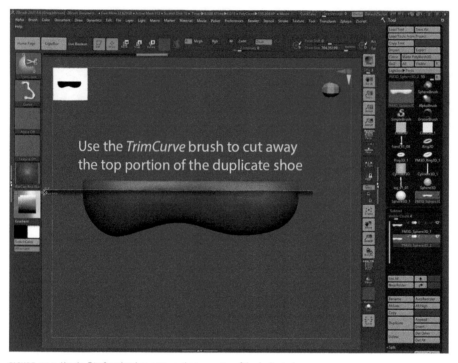

Use the *TrimCurve* brush to cut away
the top portion of the duplicate shoe

FIGURE 15.7 Use the *TrimCurve* brush to cut away the top portion of the duplicate shoe.

any final minor adjustments you might need to get the look you want. Once you are happy with how the shoe now appears, select the top-most subtool and use the *Tool > Subtool > Merge > MergeDown* button to combine the two subtools. Finally, use our old friend, the *DynaMesh* command, at a suitably high *Resolution* of around 256 to unify the two models fully. Add a light touch of the *Smooth* brush to ease away any roughness, and we now have the basic shape of the shoe completed!

Finalizing the shoe

It might help if you actually grab yourself a shoe to serve as a reference object. Go ahead and plop that shoe on your desk and study it for a moment. Notice where the shoe is a bit thicker or thinner, taller or shorter, and what have you. Now, go ahead and mask off the bottom half of the sole of the shoe, then use the *Move Topological* brush to adjust the height of the sole to match the look of our reference shoe better. Add a little bit of arch support in the middle, and remember to work on both sides of the shoe! Now that the shoe is asymmetrical, we can no longer rely on the *Symmetry* feature to keep both sides of our model in sync.

Use the *Tool > Subtool > Append* command to append the *PM3D_Ring3D* that we created for the hand to this model. If you didn't save that ring model, no problem. Simply create a new *Ring3D* shape and use that

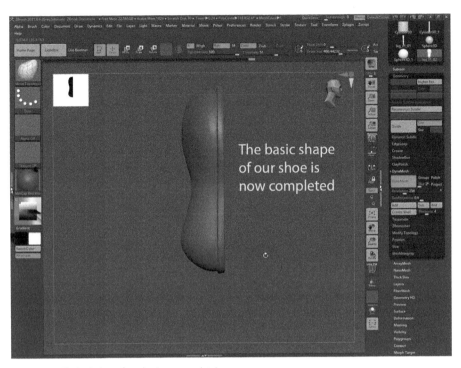

FIGURE 15.8 The basic shape of our shoe is now completed.

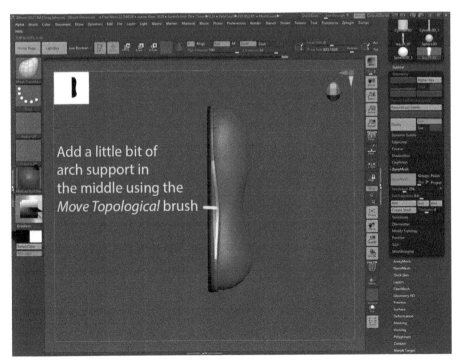

FIGURE 15.9 Add a little bit of arch support in the middle using the *Move Topological* brush. Remember to work on both sides of the shoe.

instead. You can refer back to the section on making the ring for the hand model in the last chapter if you need to see the values we used to initialize that particular *Ring3D* shape. Next, switch to the *Gizmo 3D* and move and scale the ring into position on our shoe where the ankle would be. After that, use the *Move Topological* brush to conform the ring to the shoe a bit better. You do not want any gaps between the ring and the shoe. Go ahead and save your tool using the *Tool > Save As* command. Always save your model before you merge your sub-tools. Finally, select the topmost subtool and use the *Tool > Subtool > Merge > MergeDown* to combine the two subtools and then *DynaMesh* the model.

Suppose you want to hollow out the center of the ring shape on the shoe. Mask out the middle of the ring. Invert the mask using the CTRL+I shortcut, then use the *Gizmo 3D* to move the unmasked center portion of the ring down deeper into the shoe. A bit of *DynaMesh* and smoothing later, and you now have a proper cartoon shoe!

If you feel up to it, you can add some detail to the bottom of the shoe. To begin, orbit your viewpoint so you are looking at the bottom of the shoe. Paint a mask over the center of the sole of the shoe, and then use CTRL+I to invert the mask. Next, use the *Gizmo 3D* to

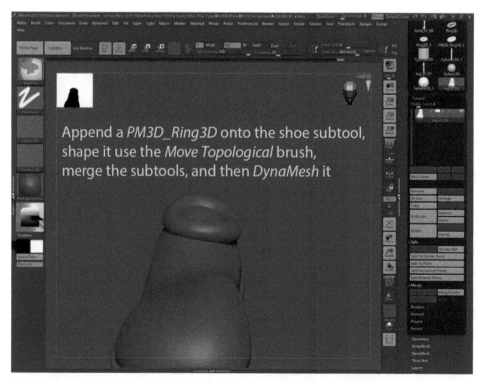

FIGURE 15.10 Append a *PM3D_Ring3D* onto the shoe subtool, shape it using the *Move Topological* brush, merge the subtools, and then *DynaMesh* it.

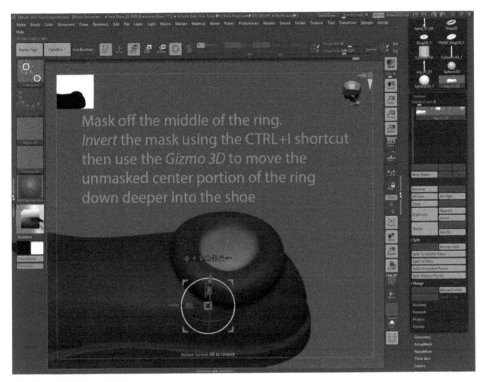

FIGURE 15.11 Mask out the middle of the ring. Invert the mask using the CTRL + I shortcut, and then use the *Gizmo 3D* to move the unmasked center portion of the ring down deeper into the shoe.

indent the unmasked area. Apply a bit of smoothing, and then use the *DamStandard* brush to add some tread to the bottom of the shoe. Follow up with a *DynaMesh*, a bit of smoothing, and then save your tool.

Combining the shoe and the leg

If the leg tool is not in your *Tool Palette*, go ahead and use the *Tool > Load Tool* command to bring it back into ZBrush. Select your shoe tool and use the *Tool > Subtool > Append* command to add the leg model as a subtool to the shoe tool. Select the leg subtool and switch to the *Gizmo 3D*. Unlock the *Gizmo 3D* and position the transform icon at the bottom of the leg. Close the *Gizmo 3D Lock*. Putting the *Gizmo 3D* here will make it much easier to scale the leg to fit the shoe.

Place the bottom of the leg subtool in the middle of the shoe ring, and then use the *Gizmo 3D* to scale the leg up until you are happy with its size. You can vary the scaling on all three axes until the leg looks exactly the way you want it to. To ensure a perfect fit into the shoe, go ahead and mask off the part of the leg outside of the shoe, and then use the *Inflate* brush to puff up the part of the leg inside of the shoe. The goal is to eliminate any gaps where the leg and the shoe join together.

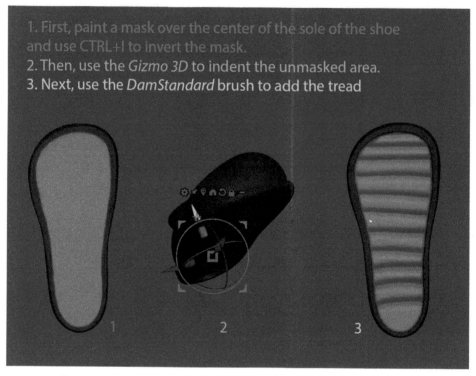

1. First, paint a mask over the center of the sole of the shoe and use CTRL+I to invert the mask.
2. Then, use the *Gizmo 3D* to indent the unmasked area.
3. Next, use the *DamStandard* brush to add the tread

FIGURE 15.12 First, paint a mask over the center of the sole of the shoe and use CTRL + I to invert the mask. Then, use the *Gizmo 3D* to indent the unmasked area. Next, use the *DamStandard* brush to add the tread.

DynaMesh the leg at a higher resolution if you need more detail in it. If you need to see the bottom of the leg as it fits inside the shoe, remember that you can turn on the *Transp* button to make the shoe semi-transparent.

Go ahead and merge the two subtools by selecting the upper subtool on the *Subtool* menu and then using the *Tool > Subtool > Merge > MergeDown* command. Now save the resulting tool. We will hold off using *DynaMesh* for now and keep the leg and shoe as is so we can split these models up later on if need be. Save your ZBrush tool so you don't lose it.

Putting all of the pieces together

Because creating the leg didn't take us very long at all, I think it's time for us to go ahead and start putting everything together. Use the *Tool > Load Tool* command to bring the pie model back into active memory. If the hand-arm model still needs to be added to your *Tool Palette*, go ahead and load it up as well. With the pie-guy model on screen, use the *Tool > Subtool > Append* command to add the hand-arm model as a subtool to the pie-guy. Switch to the *Gizmo 3D* and position

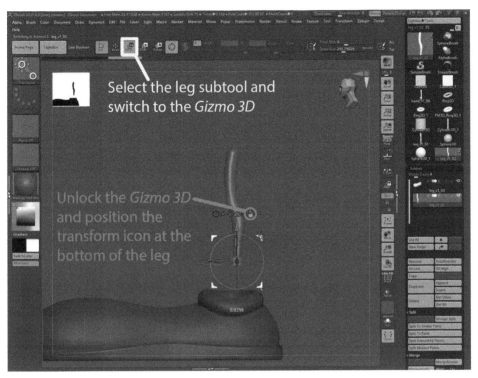

Select the leg subtool and switch to the *Gizmo 3D*

Unlock the *Gizmo 3D* and position the transform icon at the bottom of the leg

FIGURE 15.13 Select the leg subtool and switch to the *Gizmo 3D*. Unlock the *Gizmo 3D* and position the transform icon at the bottom of the leg.

the gizmo at the base of the arm, then rotate, scale, and position the arm where you like it on the pie-guy model. Save your progress.

Using the same process, append the leg-shoe model to the pie-guy as a subtool, and then activate Move and use the *Gizmo 3D* to move, rotate, and scale the leg into place. Remember to unlock the gizmo and place it at the top of the leg. You can activate the *Transp* button to make seeing the leg a bit easier if you need to. The leg doesn't quite match the proper angle of the side of the pie. To fix this, let's mask off the leg up to the knee. Now, hold down the CTRL key and left-click on the masked portion of the leg a few times to blur the mask.

Revisiting the transpose line interface

To pose the leg, turn off the *Gizmo 3D* by either pressing the active *Gizmo 3D* button or by using the Y shortcut to do so, which gives you access to the *Transpose Line* interface for moving, rotating, and scaling your model. After that is done, the *Move*, *Scale*, and *Rotate* buttons will bring up the *Transpose Line* interface instead of the *Gizmo 3D* on the top-shelf. Click on the *Move* button (W). You should see a small, complicated icon appear over your object. The icon consists of a series of three orange circles connected by a straight line with a small white

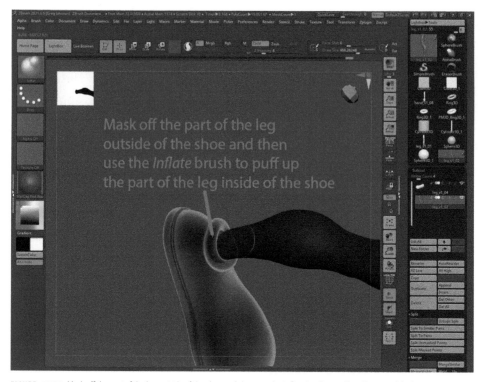

FIGURE 15.14 Mask off the part of the leg outside of the shoe and then use the *Inflate* brush to puff up the part of the leg inside of the shoe.

circle at the tip and an array of red, green, and blue lines tipped with tiny circles radiating from the origin point. The small red, green, and blue lines represent the coordinate axes – red for the X axis, green for the Y axis, and blue for the Z axis. If you click inside any of the tiny red or green circles, the orange circles will align themselves with the corresponding axis. If you click inside the small white circle at the tip of the *Transpose Line*, it will move the *Transpose Line* to start at the center of the object. You can adjust the position of the transpose widget by clicking and dragging ON the rings of the different orange circles. Clicking and dragging on the orange rings at either end of the *Transpose Line* will change the shape and orientation of the line. Clicking on the middle circle or the orange line connecting the orange circles will move the transpose tool around. If you click inside the orange circles, you affect the object in different ways depending on which of the orange circles you click and drag.

First, the leg

To use the *Transpose Line* on the leg, first turn on the *Move* button by pressing W on the keyboard. Then, click and drag the mouse pointer from the masked-off knee up to just a bit past the top of the leg. Next,

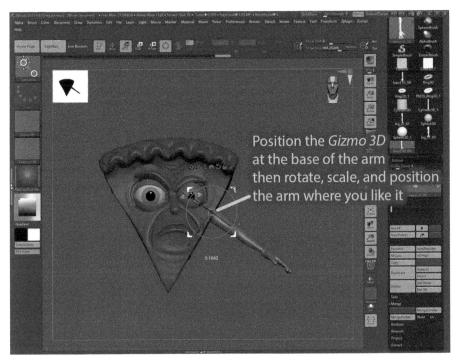

FIGURE 15.15 Position the *Gizmo 3D* at the base of the arm, then rotate, scale, and position the arm where you like it on the pie-guy model.

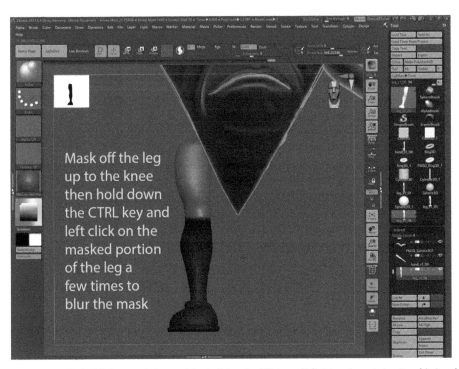

FIGURE 15.16 Mask off the leg up to the knee, and then hold down the CTRL key and left-click on the masked portion of the leg a few times to blur the mask.

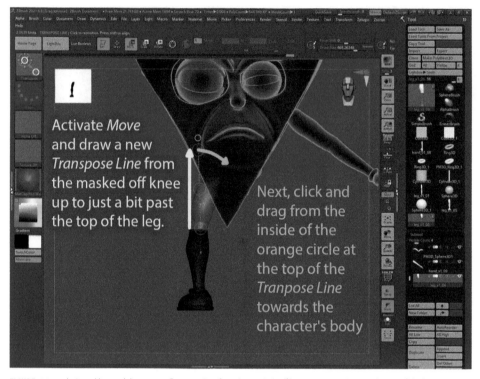

FIGURE 15.17 Activate *Move* and draw a new *Transpose Line* from the masked-off knee up to just a bit past the top of the leg. Next, click and drag from the inside of the orange circle at the top of the *Transpose Line* towards the character's body.

click inside the orange circle at the top of the *Transpose Line* and drag toward the character's body while holding down the left mouse button. This process will bend the top of the leg into the pie.

After that, turn your *Gizmo 3D* back on by pressing the Y key, and *Move* (W) the leg into its final place. Make sure that the leg lines up correctly with the body and the arms by changing your viewpoint frequently. Remember that it always helps when modeling to orbit your camera around and view your model from different angles to check your work so far. To finish the leg up, use the *Smooth* brush to get rid of any seams or imperfections created inadvertently by the *Transpose Line* and tweak the leg's shape using the *Move Topological* brush as needed.

And now the arm

You can repeat this operation on the arm. Go ahead and mask off the top of the arm down to the elbow, and blur the mask a bit. This time, switch to *Rotate* (R) and press the Y key to bring up the *Transpose Line*. Drag out a new *Transpose Line* from the elbow to the fingertips, and then click and drag from the inside of the orange circle on the

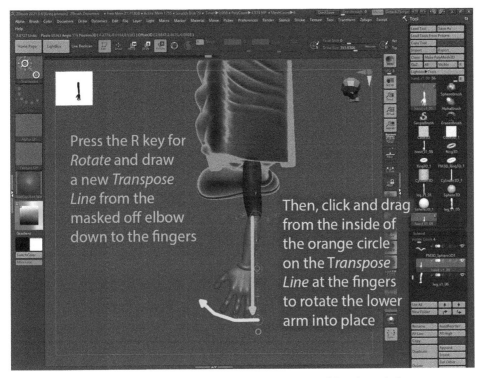

FIGURE 15.18 Press the R key for *Rotate* and draw a new *Transpose Line* from the masked-off elbow down to the fingers. Then, click and drag from the inside of the orange circle on the *Transpose Line* at the fingers to rotate the lower arm into place.

Transpose Line at the fingers to rotate the lower arm into place. This trick of using a simple mask with a bit of blur and the *Transpose Line* to *Rotate* a limb into position is at the heart of how we are going to pose the character later on. To be sure, there are other ways of posing a character in ZBrush, namely using a *ZSphere* rig, but the combination of masking, rotation, and the transpose line is by far the simplest and most reliable method available for use.

After using the *Transpose Line* on the arm, you can clean up everything using the same *Smooth* and *Move Topological* brushes that we have been using throughout the process. You can now tweak the arm into whatever final shape suits your fancy. For the demo project, I went ahead and created an armpit and a hint of a shoulder blade using a bit of masking, the *Move Topological* brush, and a touch of the *hPolish* and *ClayTubes* brush on the arm model. Keep in mind that for a cartoon character, you probably don't need a lot of detailed musculature, though. I also made the hand a bit bigger. To do this, I used the *Tool > Subtool > Split > Split To Parts* command to turn the hand into a separate subtool. I turned on the *Gizmo 3D* again by pressing Y and activated *Rotate* (R). I then unlocked the *Gizmo 3D* and moved it to the wrist, and then I locked the gizmo back down and scaled the hand up. Note that even though we have *Rotate* on, we can still

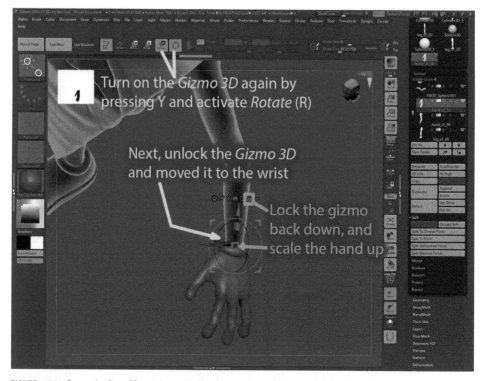

FIGURE 15.19 Turn on the *Gizmo 3D* again by pressing Y and activate *Rotate* (R). Next, unlock the *Gizmo 3D* and move it to the wrist, and then lock the gizmo back down and scale the hand up.

just click and drag on the yellow cube in the *Gizmo 3D* and scale the hand up. Merge the arm and the hand subtools using the *Tool > Subtool > Merge > MergeDown* command to finish up.

Duplicate and mirror both limbs

We now have a functional leg and an arm. Go ahead and save your progress, and remember to iterate your file name! We have made a lot of progress in this chapter, and we do not want to lose any of our work. Use the *Tool > Subtool > Duplicate* command to make a copy of the arm. Follow this by using the *Tool > Deformation > Mirror* on the X axis (which should be the default) to place the copy of the arm onto the other side of the character. You can then merge the two arms using the *MergeDown* command. Repeat the same process for the leg.

Take a good look at what we have wrought

Turn on the *Perspective* button and check out the model. Doing so will give you a better feel for how the final product will look than just the orthographic view that we have been using to build the model.

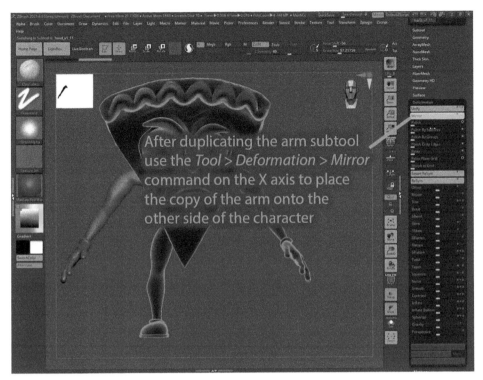

After duplicating the arm subtool use the *Tool > Deformation > Mirror* command on the X axis to place the copy of the arm onto the other side of the character

FIGURE 15.20 After duplicating the arm subtool, use the *Tool > Deformation > Mirror* command on the X axis (which should be the default) to place the copy of the arm onto the other side of the character.

You can also turn on the *Floor* button. With *Perspective* turned on, you will get a much more realistic view. We have created the stuff of nightmares!

We have reached a good stopping point for now. In the future, we still need to paint the character, add in a weapon or some other peripheral, and create our final pose – but all of that can be saved for the future. This project is going by fast, and I hope that you are having a lot of fun. Remember to save your model and make plenty of backups!

Conclusion

We have now finished making most of our characters. The character model has hands, feet, legs, and arms, as well as eyes and assorted details. There is still a lot of work to do. We need to apply some final details, then paint and pose the character. There is probably room to create some sort of interesting and appropriate implement for the pie character to hold. Finally, we will need to render and composite our final illustration. This chapter represents the conclusion of the basic techniques for sculpting and detailing a character that we have been

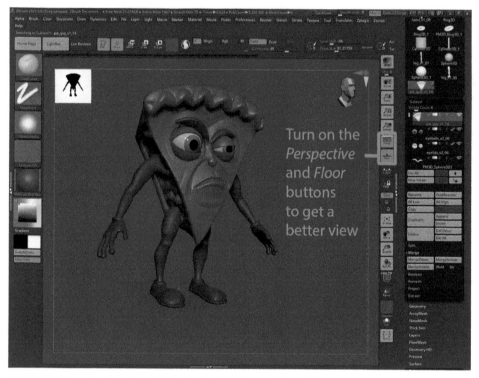

Turn on the *Perspective* and *Floor* buttons to get a better view

FIGURE 15.21 Turn on the *Perspective* and *Floor* buttons to get a better view of the model.

working with for the last few chapters. By now, you should be very familiar with the basics of creating a concept model using ZBrush. In the next chapter, we will apply our final tweaks and refinements to our creation before moving on to painting, posing, and alternate modeling techniques.

16

Pie Tweaks

Introduction

In this chapter, we are going to organize our model, check and fix any errors that we find, and then start painting the ever-so-creepy pie-person model that we have made. The first thing we need to do is check and make sure that there is enough resolution in all of our different subtools. Each subtool must be composed of enough polygons to support being painted. You need quite a high polygon count because ZBrush is a polygon painting program. That is to say, you are not painting onto a texture map; you are actually painting on the model's geometry itself and assigning a color to each polygon. Polypainting is a bit of an unusual approach in the realm of 3D software, but it alleviates the need for creating UV maps on the sort of high polygon count objects that ZBrush creates, and for the kind of concept sculpting that we are engaged in, it makes for an elegant solution to applying color information to our models. Remember that to check the polygon counts of one of our subtools, simply rest your mouse over that subtool icon in the *Tool > Subtool* menu.

Increasing the polygon count for painting

If you think that your subtool doesn't have enough polygons to support being painted, then go to *Tool > Geometry* and press the large *Divide* button. Each time you click the *Divide* button, ZBrush will add one subdivision level to your model, which multiplies the number of polygons in that subtool by roughly 4. Subdivision is a very quick and effective way to refine your model, but ZBrush will not *Dynamesh* an object with subdivision levels added to it in this manner.

DOI: 10.1201/9781003215288-16

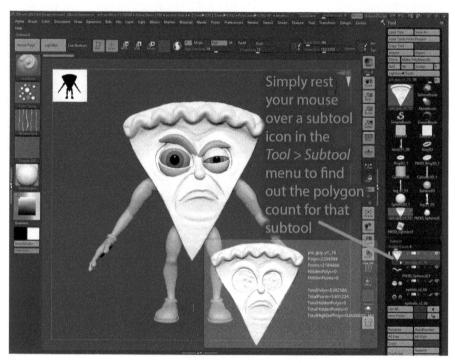

FIGURE 16.1 Simply rest your mouse over a subtool icon in the *Tool > Subtool* menu to find out the polygon count for that subtool.

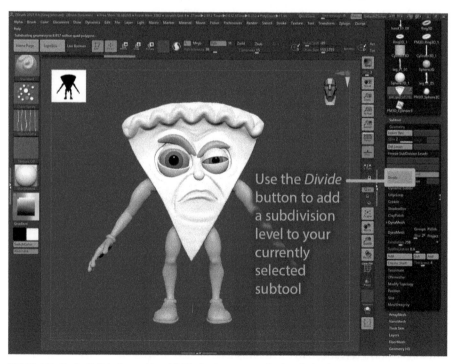

FIGURE 16.2 Use the *Divide* button to add a subdivision level to your currently selected subtool.

Keep in mind that subdividing your model can quickly build up extremely high polygon counts that can crash ZBrush if you overuse the *Divide* button. After subdividing your model, you can use the *SDiv* (*Subdivision Level*) slider to control which subdivision level you are currently working on. ZBrush will keep track of the details of each subdivision level separately. If you need to use *Dynamesh* again, you can delete any unused subdivision levels using either the *Del Lower* or *Del Higher* commands in the *Tool > Geometry* submenu, just above the *Divide* button. Just remember to be on the *SDiv* level you want to keep before using either delete command (I usually keep the highest level subdivision and just use the *Del Lower* button). Depending on your *Dynamesh* settings, you may lose some detail if the *Dynamesh Resolution* value is set too low.

The exact number of polygons you are seeking in each model is going to vary depending on the size of the subtool and how much detail you want the finished piece to have. Bigger models will require more polygons for painting than a small model. In our case, I have gotten the pie model up to around 8 million polygons, the eyelids at 1.5 million, and each arm and leg at about 2 million polygons. Play around with the *Divide* button until you are satisfied with the polygon resolution of each subtool.

Choosing a material

The next step is to pick a good material for our model. To do so, simply click on the *Material* icon on the left-hand side of the ZBrush interface right above the color swatch, which will open up the *Material Palette* and a whole bunch of different options. The top row in the *Material Palette* is your material *Quick Picks*. These are all of the materials that you have most recently used, grouped for your convenience. Next are the *MatCap Materials*. The *MatCap Materials* have lighting and texture information already baked into the material, which makes the *MatCap Materials* great for quick visualization of your objects but can play havoc with your renders if you try to use ZBrush's lighting system to illuminate your model. The middle row consists of the *Standard Materials*. These are ZBrush's default materials, and they work well with ZBrush's lights and default rendering engine. The *Standard Materials* are the ones that I will be using for all of the demos in this book. The next row introduces the newest addition to ZBrush's material inventory – the *Redshift Polypaint Materials* and the *Redshift Preset Color Materials*. These two sets of materials are part of the new Redshift renderer that ZBrush's new parent company, Maxon, introduced in the recent versions of ZBrush. While Redshift represents an important development in how ZBrush can render things, it is also a much more complicated process and a more advanced topic than is suitable for this particular book. If you are running an older version of Zbrush, you won't see the

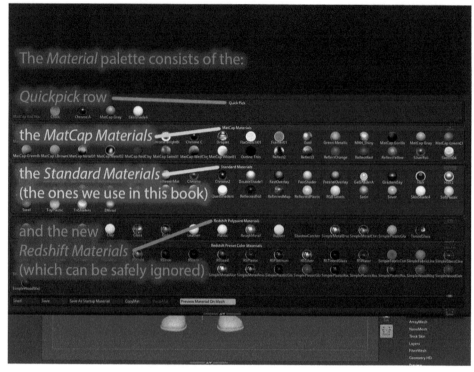

The *Material* palette consists of the:

Quickpick row

the *MatCap Materials*

the *Standard Materials*
(the ones we use in this book)

and the new
Redshift Materials
(which can be safely ignored)

FIGURE 16.3 The *Material Palette* consists of the *Quickpick* row, the *MatCap Materials*, the *Standard Materials* (the ones we use in this book), and the new *Redshift Materials* (which can be safely ignored).

Redshift Materials and options, but do not worry; we don't use them anyway in this book, and you can safely ignore them.

Previewing a material on your model

One of the unusual behaviors ZBrush sports is the ability to quickly preview a material by simply selecting it in the *Material Palette*. Whenever a material is selected, any object that has not had a material explicitly assigned to it will automatically update to the currently selected material, which is also true for colors as well! This quick previewing of materials and colors provides you with a quick and easy way of previewing different materials and colors to see what will look best on your model, but it can be a little confusing to get used to. Go ahead and try it! Select the *SoftPlastic Standard Material* and see what it looks like on your model. You can also set the current color to whatever you like by playing with the *Color* picker swatch. Try out any number of materials, such as the *Hair*, *JellyBean*, and *NormalRGBMat,* to name just a few. ZBrush will automatically switch to whatever material you have currently selected. Go ahead and have fun trying out various materials to see what they look like on your model.

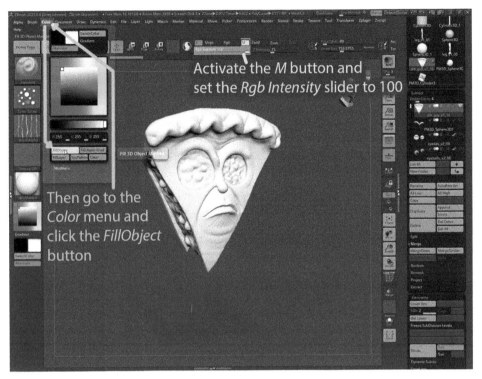

FIGURE 16.4 Activate the *M* button and set the *Rgb Intensity* slider to 100. Then go to the *Color* menu and click the *FillObject* button to embed the currently selected material into the subtool.

Assigning the material to the model

When you are ready to get serious again, go ahead and switch to the *SkinShade4* material. The *SkinShade4* material is a good choice for painting because it allows you to see the colors you are painting with clearly. Using materials with pre-existing colors will tint your results and make painting your model more difficult. Now activate the *M* button amidst the *Top Shelf* brush settings and set the *Rgb Intensity* slider to 100. Next, go to the *Color* menu and click the *FillObject* button to embed the currently selected material into the subtool you are working on.

Now, if you switch to a new material, you will see that this model no longer automatically updates its material. The material has been embedded into the subtool. We might as well go ahead and apply a color too. Choose a nice golden brown color that you think would look good as a pie crust, turn on the *Rgb* button (next to the *M* button we just used), and use the *Color > FillObject* button to flood the model with that color.

Painting color onto your model

Now that we have a base color and material applied to our model, we can start actually painting. Select the *ToyPlastic* material and a pleasing purple color. Activate the *Mrgb* button on the *Top Shelf* so you are working on both the material and color levels at the same time. Set the *Rgb Intensity* to 100. Switch to the *Standard* brush (B S T) because some brushes, like the *Move* brushes, do not work well when painting. Choose a good alpha for your paintbrush, like *Alpha 14,* and set your brush's *Focal Shift* and *Draw Size*. Once you are all set up, you can start painting the model. You can simply hand-paint the entire model this way!

If you need to grab material off of the model, you can simply left mouse click, hold down on the large *Material* icon, and drag the mouse *Pick* icon to the section of the model that you want to grab material from. Grabbing a color from the model works in the same way, and this is an easy way to find out what material you have previously used on the model.

One of the problems when painting the model this way is that there are no real transitions between different materials when polypainting. Unlike colors, which can be simply blended by using different levels

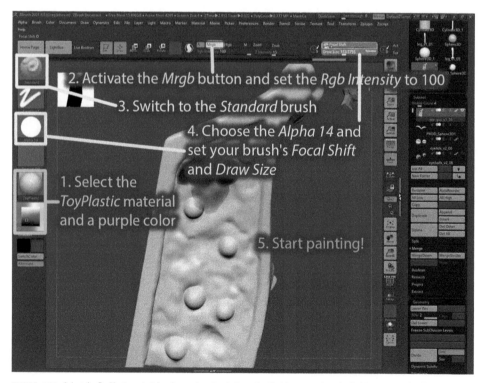

FIGURE 16.5 Select the *ToyPlastic* material and a purple color. Activate the *Mrgb* button and set the *Rgb Intensity* to 100. Switch to the *Standard* brush. Choose the *Alpha 14* and select your brush's *Focal Shift* and *Draw Size*. Now, start painting!

of *Rgb Intensity*, materials require extra effort to blend. The easiest approach to blending materials is to fake the effect when rendering out the final image. To turn material blending on, go to *Render > Render Properties* and set the *Materials Blend-Radius* value to around 5. Afterward, when you use the *BPR* button to render out your image, you will see the materials subtly blended at the edges. You can use this approach to avoid harsh seams between your different materials in your final rendered image.

Frequently, it can be easier to split the model being painted into different subtools and simply apply the color and material to the entire subtool. This approach works best on models that have clearly delineated areas of color and materials – which makes our pie guy model an eligible candidate for this approach. Let's go ahead and begin this process. First, choose a material. You can try sampling a material off of the model or just select the *SkinShade4* material. Make sure that you have the *Mrgb* button turned on and the *Rgb Intensity* set to 100. Then click on *Color > FillObject* to apply the material and current color to the model. Next, we need to mask off the piece of the model we want to split off of the model. Hold down the CTRL button, make sure that you have the *MaskPen* selected, and carefully mask off the gooey parts of the model. Remember that you can use CTRL + ALT to erase any mistakes. If you want to grab large areas of the model, you can hold down CTRL and click on the background to drag out a large mask rectangle. While time-consuming, you have to be precise, and precision takes time – especially if your model is asymmetric and you need to mask out both sides of the object. Working on a symmetrical model is much easier. However, too much symmetry in your final model is unrealistic. Real objects, places, and creatures are never perfectly symmetrical and do not have perfect angles. Nothing is ever perfectly level or straight, because that never happens in real life. Everything has flaws. If you forget to add in these imperfections, then the result will look fake and artificial. It is way too easy to leave that symmetry tool on and end up with an overly symmetrical model. Take your time and mask off the gooey sides and eye sockets of the pie character. Remember to save your model using the *Tool > Save As* button before you perform any big operations on it.

Separating pieces from the model

To separate the goo from the rest of the model, use the *Tool > Subtool > Split > Split Masked Points* button, which will chop off the masked portion of the model and turn it into a new subtool. This command will not work if the model has any subdivision levels. If your model currently has subdivision levels, you will need to get rid of them using the *Tool > Geometry > Del Lower* button, which will get rid of the lower levels of subdivision on your model and leave only the high polygon count object behind.

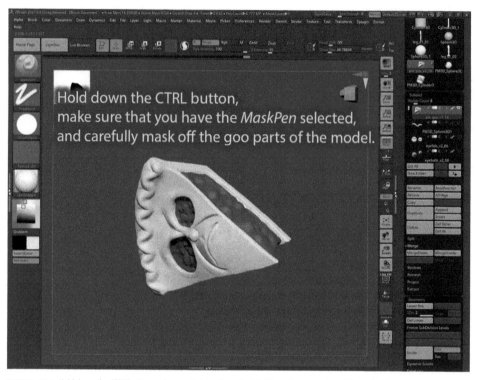

FIGURE 16.6 Hold down the CTRL button, make sure that you have the *MaskPen* selected, and carefully mask off the gooey parts of the model. Remember that you can use CTRL + ALT to erase any mistakes.

After using the *Split Masked Points* command, it will look like nothing has happened – until you check out the *Subtool* list and notice that you now have a new subtool there. This process will knock holes into your model. After all, you are carving out pieces of it, but you can use the *DynaMesh* command to close the resulting holes in the model.

Using the extract command

Go ahead and select the subtool for the gooey portions of the pie. If you need to clean up any small extraneous bits, you can simply mask any unwanted areas off and then use the *Split Masked Points* command to extract these bits into a new subtool. Next, use the *Tool > Subtool > Delete* button to get rid of the extra bits. The gooey subtool is mostly empty space. If you try to *DynaMesh* an object with a lot of holes or complicated spaces, it will give you poor results. ZBrush cannot intuit how you want the model to end up – you have to tell the program what to do specifically. You can use the CTRL + I shortcut to mask out the entire subtool, and then use the *Tool > Subtool > Extract > Extract* command with a *Thick* value of 0.01 to extrude the goo a bit and turn it into a proper 3D model. The extract results are shown as a preview. If you move your viewpoint, the preview will vanish. You need to press the

FIGURE 16.7 Use *Tool > Subtool > Split > Split Masked Points* button to chop off the masked portion of the model and turn it into a new subtool.

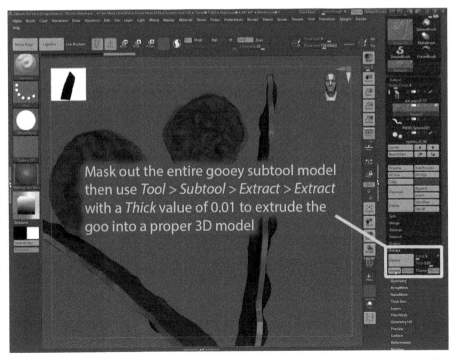

FIGURE 16.8 Mask out the entire gooey subtool model, and then use the *Tool > Subtool > Extract > Extract* command with a *Thick* value of 0.01 to extrude the goo into a proper 3D model.

Accept button in the *Extract* submenu to complete the operation, which will create a new subtool containing the extracted model. Alternatively, you could simply extract the masked-off pie-filling portion of the model into a new subtool, and then invert the mask and smooth out the gooey portion of the original model.

We can now switch the material to *SkinShade4* (or any other material you like) to get a better view of the resulting model, and then clear away any remaining masks on the model. Now go ahead and *DynaMesh* the goo model at a *Resolution* of 256. Next, I smoothed the jagged edges out on the model using the *Smooth* brush. Remember that you can always use the *DynaMesh* command to fix any small holes that may pop up when you are modeling.

Cleaning up the pie model

Once the jagged edges have been rounded off, we can go back to the pie subtool and see how the gooey filling fits on that model. You should still have the goo area masked off from earlier. Go ahead and inverse that mask. We can now smooth out this area of the pie model so that it does not poke through the goo subtool. You may want to swap to the

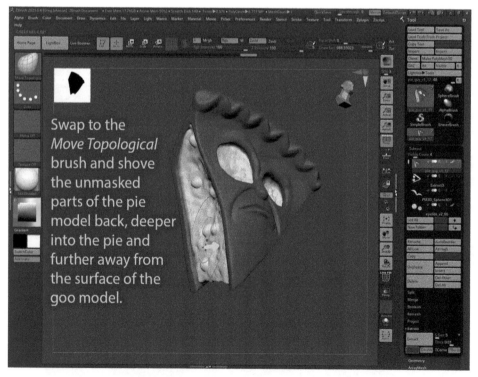

Swap to the *Move Topological* brush and shove the unmasked parts of the pie model back, deeper into the pie and further away from the surface of the goo model.

FIGURE 16.9 Swap to the *Move Topological* brush and shove the unmasked parts of the pie model back, deeper into the pie, and further away from the surface of the model.

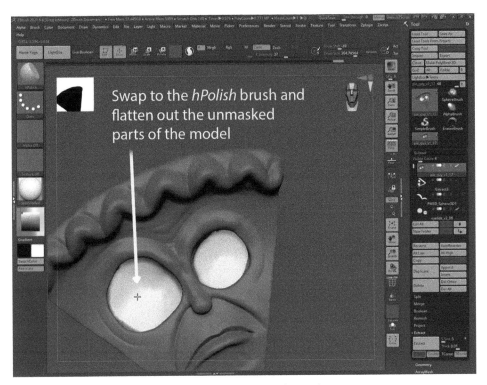

FIGURE 16.10 Swap to the *hPolish* brush and flatten out the unmasked parts of the model.

SmoothStronger brush for this. If you get tired of having to dig through the ZBrush install directory to find the *SmoothStronger* brush, you can simply use the Windows File Explorer to search for ".ZBP" to find all of the ZBrush brushes on the hard drive. Then, simply copy and paste the "Smooth Stronger.ZBP" brush file to a more easily accessible location. Make sure that you hide the goo subtool before you try to affect the pie model. If you need fast results, you can swap to the *Move Topological* brush and just shove the unmasked parts of the pie model back, deeper into the pie, and further away from the surface of the model.

Since the goal is to prevent the interior of the pie from poking through, we don't need to be worried about what the results look like terribly much. That said, you can swap to the *hPolish* brush and flatten out the unmasked parts of the model since this portion of the model does not require any detail.

Check for problems

Keep in mind that you do not want part of your model to become extremely thin, like a sheet of paper. Parts of the model that are extremely thin (i.e., two flat planes that are very close together) can create errors when using *DynaMesh* or during various ZBrush operations. A touch of the *Inflate* brush to puff up a thin edge is usually enough to correct this sort of problem whenever it occurs. Go ahead and save your tool again for safekeeping.

We should go in and smooth out the edges of the pie filling subtool. Select your pie filling subtool and mask off the two eye hole pieces of the model, then use the *Smooth Stronger* brush to refine the edges of the pie filling wherever you think the model requires it. Turn on the *Transp* button to be able to see the entire model without the pie subtool getting in the way. As you do this, you may notice the edge of the pie-filling model receding a bit. A little bit of shrinkage happens whenever you smooth a model. To get the edges of the gooey filling to overlap the pie crust without leaving any gaps, you can switch to the *Gizmo 3D* and then scale the pie filling up a small amount. Follow this up by using the *Move Topological* brush to make a few additional tweaks to ensure that the pie filling fits inside the pie crust seamlessly. You do not want any parts of the pie model peaking out from under the gooey filling. Now, you can invert the mask on the pie filling subtool and move the edges of the eyes up a bit until they also overlap underneath the main pie model as well.

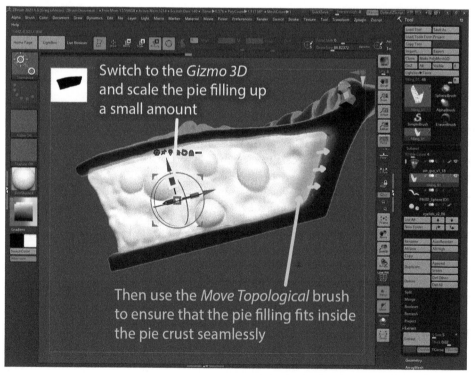

FIGURE 16.11 Switch to the *Gizmo 3D* and scale the pie filling up a small amount. Then, use the *Move Topological* brush to ensure that the pie filling fits inside the pie crust seamlessly.

Fixing a spike

Now is a good time to orbit around the model and check for any problems. Lo and behold, I find a small spike! A spike is when a small clump of polygons turns into a very pointy protrusion. Since spikes cannot be smoothed away, they can be a bit tricky to deal with. The two best approaches for fixing a spike are to grab the tip of the spike, smash it back into the body of the model, or see if *DynaMesh* simply obliterates it. Alternatively, you can mask out the spike and then use the *Tool > Subtool > Split > Split Masked Points* command to cut the spike off of the model. A quick *DynaMesh* on the main model will then fix the resulting hole in the mesh, and you can simply delete the spike subtool using the *Tool > Subtool > Delete* button.

It is worth looking at your model from a variety of different angles and just making sure that we don't have any major issues that need to be fixed before we move on to the next phase. One of the things that you will discover about 3D modeling is that problems need to be fixed as early as possible. Any issue with your model that you leave unresolved will snowball into a much bigger problem the longer you wait to fix it,

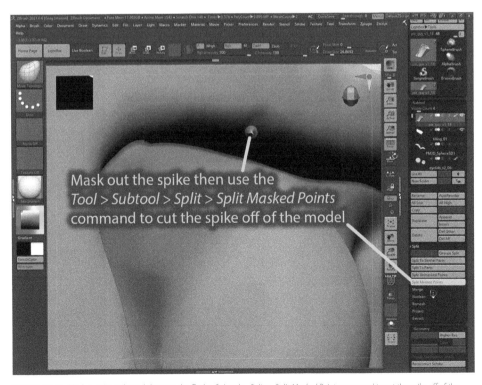

FIGURE 16.12 Mask out the spike and then use the *Tool > Subtool > Split > Split Masked Points* command to cut the spike off of the model.

which is why, if you watch the accompanying videos, you will notice that I frequently orbit my view around the model and check it for problems. Weirdness, like spikes and perfectly thin geometry, are issues that you need to fix whenever they crop up before they have time to evolve into much bigger problems, even though that means taking more time to do so. With effort, these good work habits will become second nature, and you won't have to think about it – you will just do these quick problem checks automatically as you work.

Finishing step

As the finishing step, let's select the *SkinShade4* material and a nice pie crust color, say a muted orange color, switch to *Mrgb* mode with an *Rgb Intensity* of 100, and use the *Color > FillObject* command to apply this color and material to the pie model. Next, turn off the *Transp* button, then select the pie filling subtool. Choose a nice blueberry color on the color palette and select the *Blinn* material. Use the *Color > FillObject* command to apply the blueberry color and *Blinn* material to the pie filling subtool. You can now unhide the rest of the subtools and apply whatever colors and materials you like to them as well. Remember that by default, ZBrush will display any model that has not had a color and

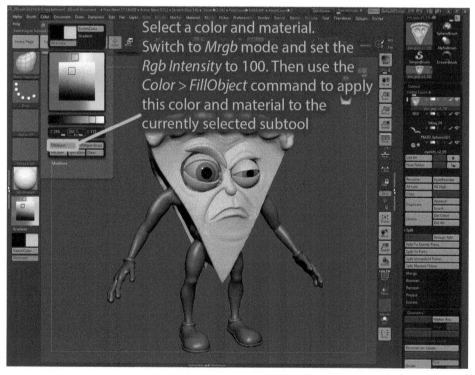

FIGURE 16.13 Select a color and material. Switch to *Mrgb* mode and set the *Rgb Intensity* to 100. Then, use the *Color > FillObject* command to apply this color and material to the currently selected subtool.

material specifically assigned to it with the currently selected material and color. You can always click on the currently selected material icon, hold down the mouse button, and drag to the model to choose a material that you have already used off of the model itself. The same trick works with the color palette.

We have now completed the overall form of our model and also established the basic colors and materials for it, which represents a good stopping point. When we pick up again, we are going to texture and detail the model.

Conclusion

In this chapter, we cleaned up and organized our model to make the next steps go smoother. Though it can be a time-consuming process, it pays huge dividends to have your model well organized into discreet subtools that provide for easy selection of key components. With that in mind, we split the pie filling from the pie crust and fixed any errors that we could find in the model. We also managed to apply a base coat of color and material to each subtool, which gives us a starting point for detailing and texturing the model in the upcoming chapters.

17

Pie Painting, Part 1

Introduction

With this chapter, we start properly texturing our main character. During this process, we will paint and detail the character by adding textures derived from photographs. While this can be a difficult process, it is absolutely essential to creating a successful 3D model. While painting and texturing your model, remember that a good model with a bad texture looks bad, while a bad model with a good texture looks good. In other words, do not scrimp on this part of the process! Creating a good texture for your model is at least as important as making the model itself, and you should allocate your time accordingly.

The ZAppLink plug-in

Luckily for us, our character is composed of fairly simple shapes and has a number of, essentially, flat planes in it, which will make our texturing job a bit easier. The first texturing approach that we will discuss is how to use the *ZAppLink* feature in ZBrush. *ZAppLink* connects ZBrush to an external image editing program. *ZAppLink* lets you paint textures onto your ZBrush models using a fully functional image editing and painting package, like Adobe Photoshop, for instance, to help you make your textures. When you are creating textures, one of the most important considerations to always keep in mind is the issues of polygon count and image resolution. The model you are painting needs to have enough polygons to support the texture that you are trying to apply to it. If the model is too low poly, the texture will de-rez and become pixelated, or if the image file that you are using as a source for the texture is too low resolution, then the results will also be substandard. There is a correlation between the number of polygons in

DOI: 10.1201/9781003215288-17

the model and the number of pixels in the image used for the texture. You need to have a good amount of both polygons in the model and pixels in the image file for texturing to work. Depending on the size of the model, anywhere from one hundred thousand to a few million polygons may be required. The image source used should be one or more megapixels in size. Painting on a low polygon model or using a low-resolution image as a texture source will both yield poor results. To rectify this problem when using *ZAppLink,* you need to make sure that the ZBrush document size is large and has a lot of pixels, that the image(s) you use as texture sources have a lot of pixels, and that the model you are trying to texture has a lot of polygons.

Adjusting the document size

First, increase the document size in ZBrush. You can use the *Document > Double* command to double the height and width of the *Document* simply. Since the default document size in ZBrush is fairly large, the *Document* size after doubling is more than adequate for texturing using ZAppLink. ZBrush will flash a warning saying that this is not an undoable operation. Just say okay to this and proceed. The ZBrush

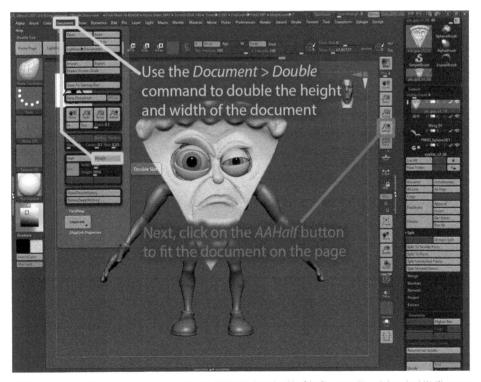

FIGURE 17.1 Use the *Document > Double* command to double the height and width of the *Document*. Next, click on the *AAHalf* button to fit the *Document* on the page.

image document will now be much bigger. Click on the *AAHalf* button on the side of the *Document* to zoom out and fit the *Document* back onto the page. While it may look like we have yet to accomplish much, the ZBrush document size has now been doubled. The *Document > Double* command and *AAHalf* work very well together to give your document more pixels. Alternatively, you can use the *Document > Width* and *Document > Height* sliders to set the document resolution to any pixel value you desire and press the *Document > Resize* button to alter the document size.

If you want even more pixels to work with, you can always repeat the process and double the document size again. You do need to be a bit cautious about increasing the size of your *Document* too much, though. The larger you make the *Document,* the more of your computer's memory gets used up. If you make the *Document* too large, it can make ZBrush unstable. When you resize the *Document* like this, whatever active tool you have on screen at the time will get dropped to the background and become inactive. You can use the *Layer > Clear* button to get rid of the old model and fix this problem when it occurs, and then simply draw the model back on screen and press the *Edit* button to activate the model to work on it again. Press the F key on your keyboard to *Frame* the model on your screen.

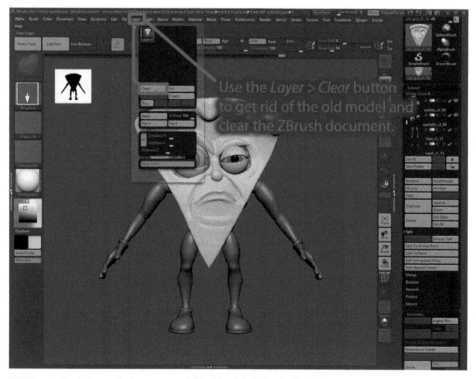

FIGURE 17.2 Use the *Layer > Clear* button to get rid of the old model and clear the ZBrush document.

Prepare the model for texturing

To prep the model for texturing, go into your *Subtool* list and turn off all of the arms, legs, eyes, and other bits of the model except for the pie crust component. Make sure that you have the pie crust component selected from the *Subtool* list. It is a wise precaution to go ahead and save your tool at this point as well. Take a moment and make sure that you have the *Mrgb* button turned on and the *Rgb Intensity* set to 100. You probably also want to turn off the *Persp* (Perspective) button to be in orthographic view mode. Press the F key on the keyboard in ZBrush to *Frame* your model and maximize it on the screen. Once you have completed all of the prep work, go ahead and click on the *Document > ZAppLink* button to start the texturing process.

Setting up ZAppLink

ZAppLink is a plugin for ZBrush that is part of the regular installation of the program. If it does not work at all, you may need to reinstall the program again. The first time that you use ZAppLink, you may need to connect the app to the image editing software that you want to use. To do so, click on the *Set Target App* button in the *ZAppLink* interface and use the file explorer that pops up to go into the install folder of the

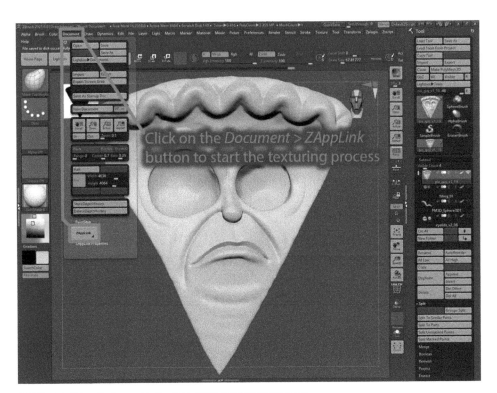

FIGURE 17.3 Click on the *Document > ZAppLink* button to start the texturing process.

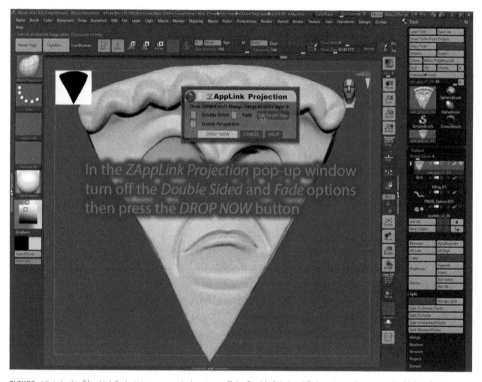

FIGURE 17.4 In the *ZAppLink Projection* pop-up window, turn off the *Double Sided* and *Fade* options, then press the *DROP NOW* button.

image editing program of your choice and select its main executable file to be the link target. In my case, I chose Adobe Photoshop and then went into the install folder for Photoshop to select the Photoshop.exe file to link Photoshop to the ZAppLink plugin. After you have ZAppLink set up, ZBrush will remember which program you have connected to the ZAppLink plug-in, and you won't need to set up the plug-in again. Next, press the *Document > ZAppLink* button, and a small *ZAppLink Projection* pop-up window will appear. Turn off the *Double Sided* and *Fade* options, then press the *DROP NOW* button.

Working with ZAppLink inside of Adobe Photoshop

ZAppLink now takes a screenshot of the ZBrush Document and throws this image into Photoshop. It may take a moment for Photoshop to open, so just be patient and wait for the computer to finish the process. Once the program completes opening, you should see a screenshot of ZBrush inside of Photoshop. In the Photoshop layers palette, you should see a *ZShading* layer, *Layer 1*, and a *Fill ZShading* layer. Both the *ZShading* layer and the *Fill ZShading* layer have "*(do not edit)*" next to their layer names. It is critically important that you leave these two

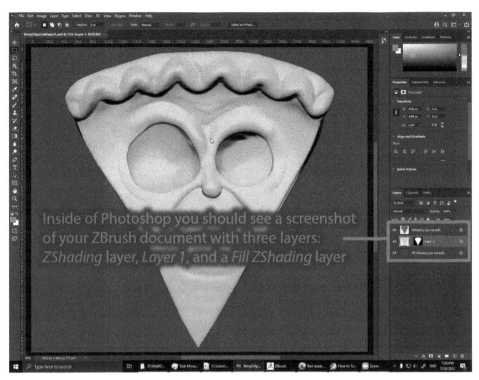

FIGURE 17.5 Inside of Photoshop, you should see a screenshot of your ZBrush document with three layers: *ZShading* layer, *Layer 1*, and a *Fill ZShading* layer.

layers alone and do not edit them at all. If you edit either the *ZShading* or *Fill ZShading* layers, then the ZAppLink process will not work. All edits that you make must end up as part of *Layer 1*. Basically, the final step you take inside Photoshop is to collapse all of the edited layers into Layer 1 while leaving the *ZShading* layer and the *Fill ZShading* layer untouched and then saving the file.

Now, load the image file that you want to use to paint into Photoshop. I have included several of the reference photos used in this demo with the materials of this book, and you can use one of these, or you can use a photo that you have taken yourself. You can use either the *File > Open* command or simply drag the image file you want to open from the file explorer onto the tab area at the top of the Photoshop document area. With your reference image on the screen, press the CTRL + A key combination to select the entire image. Double-clicking on the *Background* will convert the image into a new layer. CTRL + T will now allow you to rotate and transform the image. Press M on the keyboard to select the *Rectangular Marquee* tool and draw a rectangular selection around the area of the image that you wish to copy. Press CTRL + C to copy the selected image area. Switch to your TempZAppLinkExport.psd image inside of Photoshop and then use CTRL + V

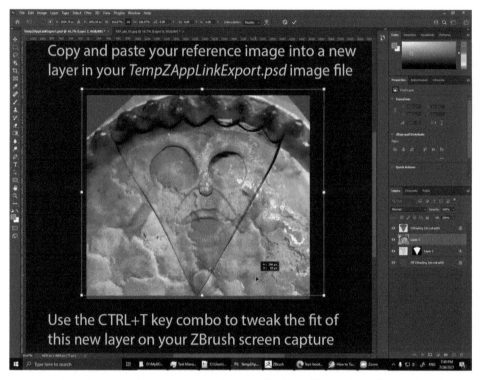

FIGURE 17.6 Copy and paste your reference image into a new layer in your TempZAppLinkExport.psd image file inside of Photoshop. Use the CTRL + T key combo to tweak the fit of this new layer on your ZBrush screen capture.

to paste the selected image area back down as a new layer, called *Layer 2*, in the ZBrush image file. Use CTRL + T again to tweak the scaling and fit of the image.

Click the three horizontal bars icon on the *Layer* palette and choose the *Duplicate Layer* command to copy your reference image layer. Then, use the *Move* tool to adjust the layer as you see fit.

You can rearrange the layer order in the *Layers Palette* as you like. You can also erase through the top layer to see the layer underneath. To do so, first choose the *Brush* tool from the *Toolbox*. Next, choose a brush tip type and set the size of your brush along the top command bar. Set the *Mode* to *Clear* and erase away. You can use the open and closed bracket keys, [and], to increase and decrease the size of your brush quickly – just like in ZBrush. As in most programs, the CTRL + Z key combo will undo if you mess up.

You can also use the *Clone Stamp* tool to copy part of the image. To use the *Photoshop Clone Stamp,* simply select the old-fashioned rubber stamp icon from the *Toolbox*. Hold down the ALT key and left-click on the part of the image you want to copy from. Move the mouse to a new area, hold down the left mouse button, and start cloning. Use the

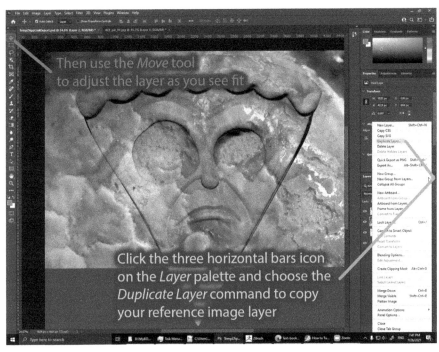

FIGURE 17.7 Click the three horizontal bars icon on the *Layer* palette and choose the *Duplicate Layer* command to copy your reference image layer. Then, use the *Move* tool to adjust the layer as you see fit.

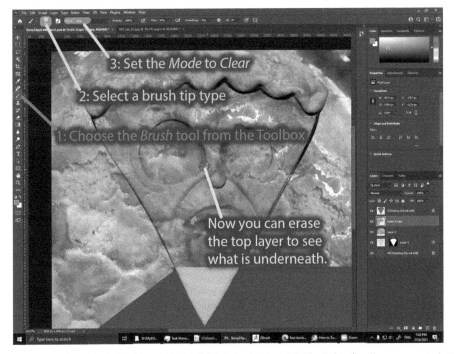

FIGURE 17.8 Choose the *Brush* tool from the *Toolbox*. 2: Select a brush tip type. 3: Set the *Mode* to *Clear*. Now, you can erase the top layer to see what is underneath.

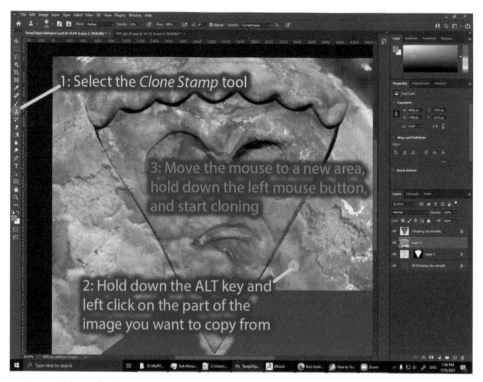

1: Select the *Clone Stamp* tool

3: Move the mouse to a new area, hold down the left mouse button, and start cloning

2: Hold down the ALT key and left click on the part of the image you want to copy from

FIGURE 17.9 Select the *Clone Stamp* tool. 2: Hold down the ALT key and left-click on the part of the image you want to copy from. 3: Move the mouse to a new area, hold down the left mouse button, and start cloning.

Clone Stamp to touch up areas that need a little bit of fixing up or even fill in an empty area.

Add extra layers from other reference pictures to the file as needed using the same procedure. Simply open up any additional image files you want to sample, select the area you wish to affect by using the *Rectangular Marquee* tool, and then copy and paste that area into your *TempZApppLinkExport* file. Adjust the fit using CTRL+T to transform the area, then use the *Clone Stamp* and *Eraser* to clean up any rough patches. You can use the *Polygonal Lasso* tool to select an irregularly shaped area to copy and paste rather than using the *Rectangle Marquee* tool if you want a bit more control over the shape of the selection area. Add the crust area to the *TempZAppLinkExport* file that we have been working on. Remember to keep all of the layers we are working on together in the *Layers* palette, and do not touch the *ZShading* and *ZShading Fill* layers at all.

About Adobe Photoshop

There is quite a lot of power lurking in Photoshop. It is the world's premiere image editing software at the moment, and it is well worth your time mastering this program – though doing so is beyond the scope of this book. If you would like to learn more about Adobe Photoshop, then I suggest visiting the official Photoshop tutorials website here (https://helpx.adobe.com/photoshop/tutorials.html). Since Photoshop has been around for decades, there are literally millions of useful tutorials and lectures about it that you can find on either Google or YouTube. While Adobe Photoshop is a wonderful image editing tool and a long-standing industry standard, other image editing software such as GIMP can also work with ZAppLink.

Going back to ZBrush

Once you have your image looking the way you want it to, it is time to head back into ZBrush. To do so, we first need to merge all of our paint layers. You must leave the *ZShading* and *ZShading Fill* layers untouched during this process! Select the topmost image layer and press the CTRL+E combo to merge the currently selected layer with the layer underneath. When you merge the last image layer down into *Layer 1*, a pop-up will appear asking what you would like to do with the *Layer Mask* and whether to *Apply*, *Preserve*, or *Cancel*. Choose *Preserve* to keep the layer mask active.

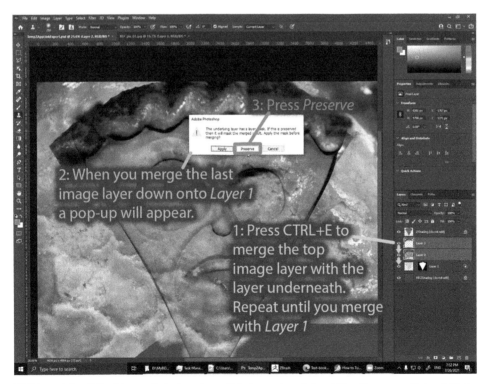

FIGURE 17.10 Press CTRL + E to merge the top image layer with the layer underneath. Repeat this until you merge with *Layer 1*. When you merge the last image layer down onto *Layer 1*, a pop-up will appear. Press *Preserve*.

After you have merged all of the image layers, you should see *Layer 1* next to its mask, along with the *ZShading* layer and *ZShading Fill* layer. Use the *File > Save* command to save the *TempZAppLinkExport.psd* file. Switch back into ZBrush and click on the *Re-enter ZBrush* button that pops up on the screen. The *ZAppLink Projection* pop-up will now appear, and you should click on the *PICKUP NOW* button to complete the ZAppLink operation. Note that if you select the *Double Sided* check box, ZAppLink will apply the texture from Photoshop to both the front and back of your model.

Give ZBrush a moment to think, and there you have it! The model should now have the texture that you created in Photoshop applied to your ZBrush model. If you have turned on the *Double Sided* option, the texture will be projected all the way through the object. Otherwise, ZAppLink will just paint one side of the model. Orbit around your model and examine it. Note how image pixels projected onto the edges of the model have created streaks along those sides. Go ahead and save your ZBrush Tool using the *Tool > Save As* command.

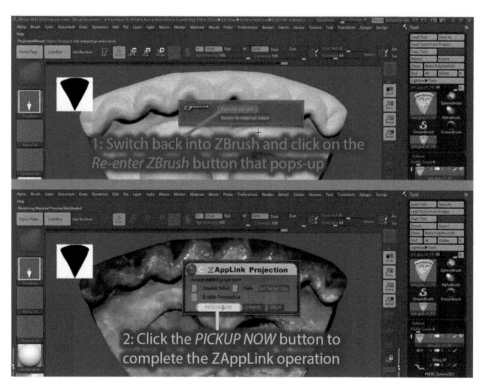

FIGURE 17.11 Switch back into ZBrush and click on the *Re-enter ZBrush* button that pops up on the screen. Click the *PICKUP NOW* button to complete the *ZAppLink* operation.

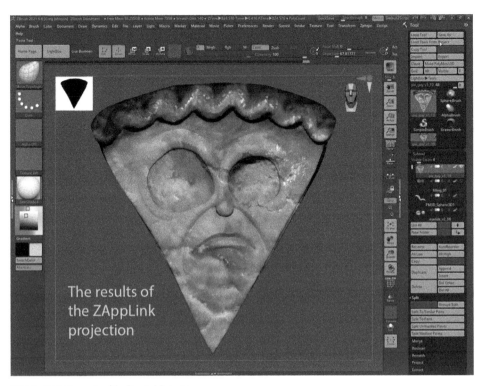

The results of
the ZAppLink
projection

FIGURE 17.12 The results of the *ZAppLink Projection*.

Creating a texture for the back of the model

Now, we need to create a texture for the back of the pie, which we can do using ZAppLink once more. First, let's mask off the previously painted areas on the front of our model that we want to preserve. Use the *MaskLasso* to mask off the front and sides of the model.

Flip the model around so that you are looking straight at the rear of the model. Press F to *Frame* the model in the *Document*. Now, go ahead and click on the *Document > ZAppLink* command. In the *ZAppLink Projection* pop-up window, turn off all of the checkboxes, and then click on the *DROP NOW* button.

Photoshop will open up. If you still have the old ZAppLink image file open, a pop-up will appear asking you to update the image file. Go ahead and click on the *Update* button.

From this point on, the process is the same as before, except this time we use photos of the backside of the pie. And yes, that is a photo of a piece of blueberry pie slapped upside down on a plate. Use the *Polygonal Lasso* tool in Photoshop to select the area of the pie's backside that you want to use, and copy and paste that into your

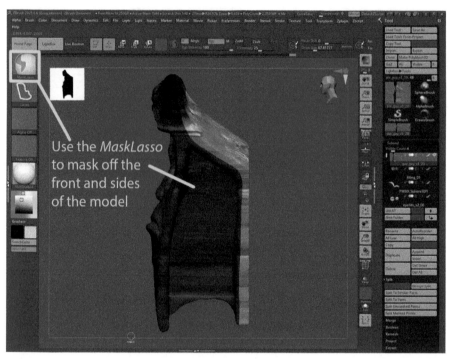

FIGURE 17.13 Use the *MaskLasso* to mask off the front and sides of the model.

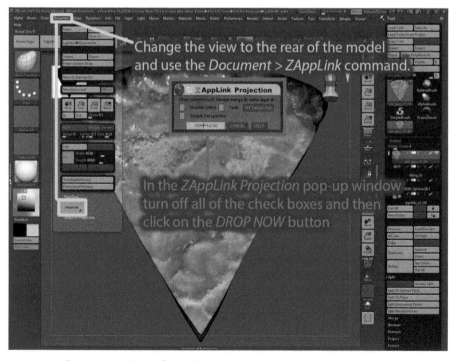

FIGURE 17.14 Change the view to the rear of the model and use the *Document > ZAppLink* command. In the *ZAppLink Projection* pop-up window, turn off all of the checkboxes and then click on the *DROP NOW* button.

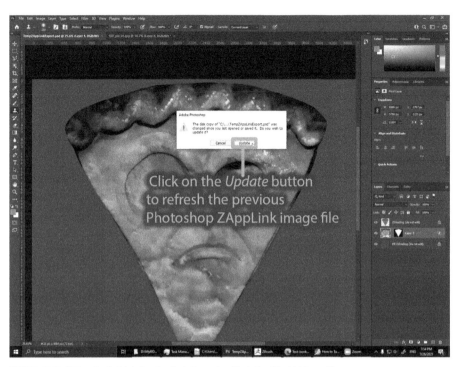

FIGURE 17.15 Click on the *Update* button to refresh the previous Photoshop ZAppLink image file.

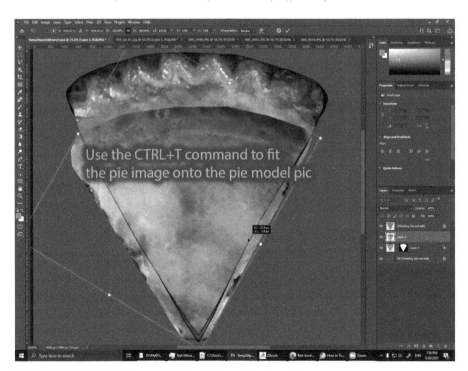

FIGURE 17.16 Use the CTRL + T command to fit the pie image onto the pie model pic.

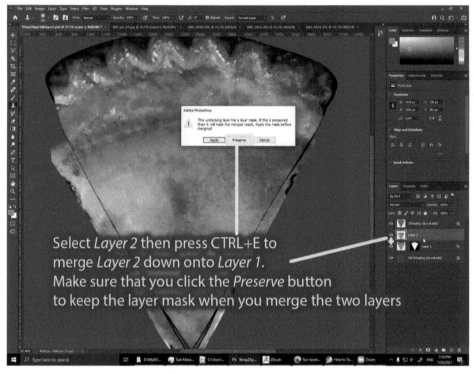

Select *Layer 2* then press CTRL+E to merge *Layer 2* down onto *Layer 1*. Make sure that you click the *Preserve* button to keep the layer mask when you merge the two layers

FIGURE 17.17 Select *Layer 2*, and then press CTRL + E to merge *Layer 2* down onto *Layer 1*. Make sure that you click the *Preserve* button to keep the layer mask when you merge the two layers.

TempZAppLinkExport.psd file. Make sure that the new layer you just pasted down sits right on top of the *Layer 1* layer. Use the CTRL+T command to fit the pie image onto the pie model picture.

Use the *Clone Stamp* tool to touch up any flaws that you need to fix. Once you are happy with the results, select *Layer 2,* then press CTRL+E to merge *Layer 2* down onto *Layer 1*. Make sure that you click the *Preserve* button to keep the layer mask when you merge the two layers. Next, save the Photoshop image file.

Going back into ZBrush again

Switch back to ZBrush. ZBrush should show you the ZAppLink dialogue box, and you should click on the *Re-enter ZBrush* button that pops up on the screen. Using big image files in ZAppLink will occasionally crash either ZBrush or the ZAppLink plugin. For instance, ZAppLink will sometimes fail to load the image file from Photoshop when re-entering ZBrush. If this should happen, try using the *Photoshop File > Save As* command to replace the *TempZAppLinkExport.psd* in the temp file directory. This action will force the ZAppLink plugin to reprocess and usually trick it into updating inside of ZBrush. Because ZAppLink can be a bit unpredictable at times, it helps to save your ZBrush tool after each use of ZAppLink. This way, if ZBrush crashes, you only lose a little bit of information and not a whole day's worth of effort. After clicking on the *Re-enter ZBrush* button, a different pop-up window will appear. You now need to click the *PICKUP NOW* button to complete the ZAppLink operation.

Next steps

Go ahead and mask off the bottom of the rear of the pie model now that we have painted that portion. This mask will protect our existing work and let us keep using ZAppLink without any fear of messing up the finished portions of our model. Orbit around your model, check it for errors, and then save your tool.

Switch to the rearview again and move the camera to the rear of the model. We need to orbit the viewpoint so that the angled portion of the pie crust is parallel to our view screen. Make sure that you press F to frame the model on screen, then go ahead and activate ZApp-Link just like we did the previous two times. Update the image inside Photoshop and open up a reference image that provides a good view of the part of the crust that we are working on. Use the same process as earlier to select, cut, and paste the reference image into Photoshop. Use the *Free Transform* tool (CTRL + T) in Photoshop to adjust the image layer and then merge it down into *Layer 1* while preserving the layer mask. Save the image in Photoshop, re-enter ZBrush, and pick up the ZAppLink again, just like in the earlier examples. Remember that Photoshop is a fully functional image editing program, and you can alter the image hues and colors, paint on the image, and do other image editing operations, too. You can work with as many image layers in Photoshop as you like – you just have to make sure that all of your various image layers are merged into *Layer 1*, and the *Layer Mask* must be preserved for ZAppLink to work. Any layers that are not merged into *Layer 1* will not show up when you go back to ZBrush. Under no circumstances should you mess with the *ZShading* layer or the *Fill ZShading* layer. Once you have updated the texture inside of ZBrush save the tool.

How to touch up the texture

At this point, we have created the majority of the texture for our model, but we still have to fix the heavily streaked sides of the model and a couple of seams where the various texture projections touch one

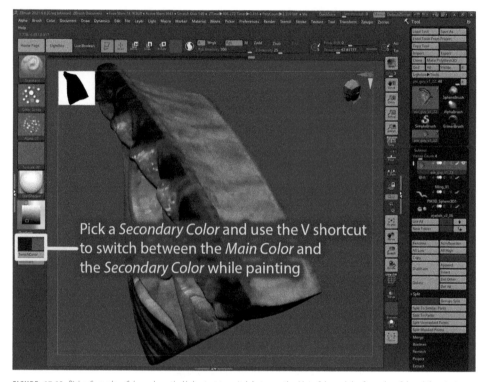

Pick a *Secondary Color* and use the V shortcut to switch between the *Main Color* and the *Secondary Color* while painting

FIGURE 17.18 Pick a *Secondary Color* and use the V shortcut to switch between the *Main Color* and the *Secondary Color* while painting.

another. We could continue using ZAppLink, but for touch-up work like this, it is often easier just to paint these areas. First, let's sample a color from the textured portion of our model. Rest your mouse over the *Color Picker*, hold down the ALT key, and sample your pie model to set your current color to a medium. You can also click on the *Secondary Color* swatch (the color swatch immediately to the left of the main color swatch), hold down the ALT key, and use the sample function to set the *Secondary Color* to a darker brown color. You can use the V shortcut key to switch between the *Main Color* and the *Secondary Color* while painting.

To start painting, switch to the *Standard* brush [B S T], set the *Stroke* to *Color Spray*, and set the *Alpha* to *Alpha 07*. Make sure that you have the *Rgb* button active and the *Zadd/Zsub* buttons inactive – you want to paint the model, not sculpt it. Set the *Rgb Intensity* to around 50, the *Draw Size* to roughly 100, and turn off the *Stroke > Lazy Mouse > Lazy-Mouse* button. Now, just paint over the seam where the two pie crust textures meet.

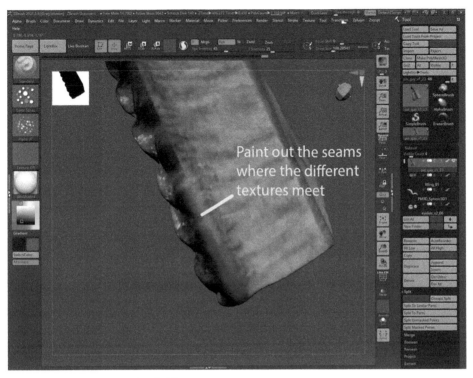

Paint out the seams where the different textures meet

FIGURE 17.19 Paint out the seams where the different textures meet.

Solving issues with lag

If you start to notice excessive amounts of lag while you are working in ZBrush, then you need to reduce the program's memory overhead. The first thing to do is to make sure that you have closed any unneeded programs running on your computer. ZBrush is a real memory hog and can be slow and rather unstable if it needs more free memory to play with. For example, an internet browser with a lot of open tabs can eat up a lot of your system's memory and should be closed when you run ZBrush. It can help turn off calculation intensive features like *Lazy-Mouse* as well. If you have done all of these things, and ZBrush is still a bit slow, try reducing the size of the current ZBrush document – which is what we are going to do in this case. Go to *Document* at the top of the screen and check that the *Width* and *Height* values are set to something reasonable, and then press the *New Document* button. You can now simply redraw your tool on the screen, press the Edit button [T], and go right back to painting your model. The model should now be much more responsive than it was earlier.

If freeing up extra memory does not fix all of ZBrush's memory problems, you can use the *Preferences > Init ZBrush* command to reinitialize ZBrush, which effectively restarts the program and should

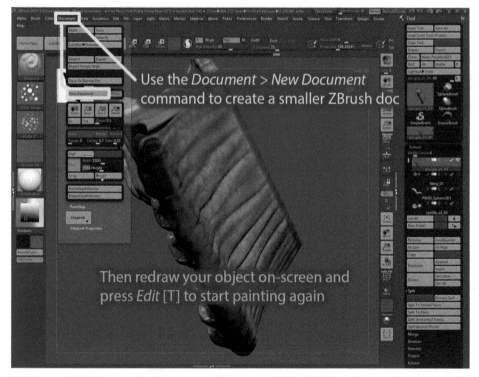

Use the *Document* > *New Document* command to create a smaller ZBrush doc

Then redraw your object on-screen and press *Edit* [T] to start painting again

FIGURE 17.20 Use the *Document > New Document* command to create a smaller ZBrush doc. Then, redraw your object on-screen and press *Edit* [T] to start painting again.

clear up any issues that you have. Using the *Init* button does mean that you will need to reload the tool, draw the model back on screen, enter *Edit* mode again, and redo all of your brush settings – but all of this should be second nature to you by now. If ZBrush is still unstable, then that is a strong indicator that your entire computer system has become unstable and needs to be restarted. Luckily, we have been saving our model frequently, so you won't lose any work when this happens.

Continuing the process

Beyond this point, the painting process becomes a repetitive process of sampling colors from the model, adjusting the brush *Draw Size* and *Rgb Intensity,* and touching up any flaws, seams, and imperfections that you can find. In particular, try to fix all of the streaks and the bright highlights that were part of the original reference files. I really like using the *Color Spray* stroke in combination with a grainy brush alpha because of the subtle color variations this introduces to the painted texture. Subtle changes are best when doing this sort of touch-up work.

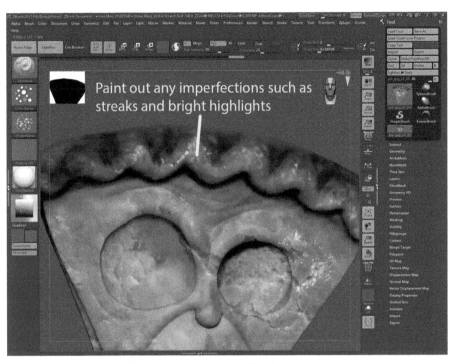

FIGURE 17.21 Paint out any imperfections, such as streaks and bright highlights.

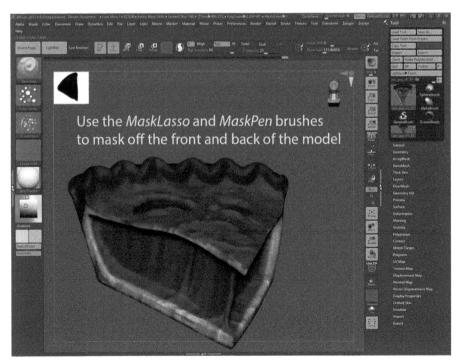

FIGURE 17.22 Use the *MaskLasso* and *MaskPen* brushes to mask off the front and back of the model.

Once you have finished touching up the front and the back, we can begin to deal with the sides of the model using *ZAppLink* once more. Use the *MaskLasso* and *MaskPen* brushes to mask off the front and back of the model to protect the parts that we have already painted.

Using ZAppLink for the side of the model

Orbit your camera until you get a good view of the side of the pie piece. The side of the model should be parallel to your view plane. Use the *Document > ZAppLink* command to bring up the *ZAppLink Projection* pop-up. In the pop-up, make sure that all of the boxes are unchecked, then click *DROP NOW*, which will open up Photoshop.

Using the same process as before, open up a reference image of the side of the pie and copy and paste it onto the *TempZAppLinkExport. psd* image. Use the *Free Transform* tool and *Clone Stamp* to adjust the fit of the image on the side of the model. Once you are happy with how it looks, merge your image layers down onto *Layer 1* and make sure that you preserve the *Layer Mask*. Remember that any layers that are not merged into *Layer 1* will simply not show up when you go back to ZBrush. Refrain from messing with the *ZShading* layer or the *Fill*

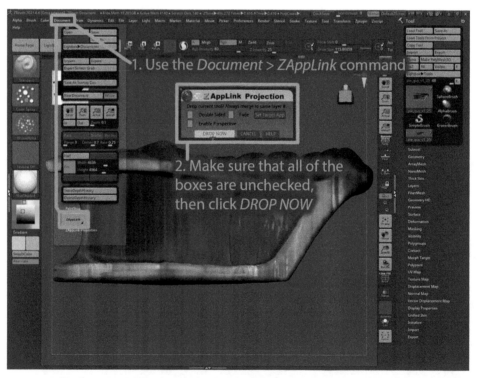

FIGURE 17.23 Use the *Document > ZAppLink* command. In the *ZAppLink Projection* pop-up, make sure that all of the boxes are unchecked, and then click *DROP NOW*.

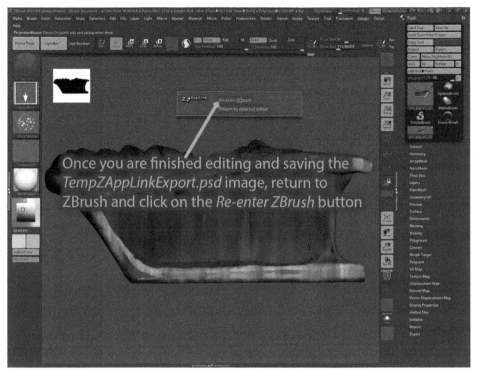

FIGURE 17.24 Once you are finished editing, save the *TempZAppLinkExport.psd* image, return to ZBrush, and click on the *Re-enter ZBrush* button.

ZShading layer. Once you are finished merging layers, go ahead and save the file. Return to ZBrush and click on the *Re-enter ZBrush* button to pick up the model again.

Check and make sure the ZAppLink texture application has worked properly by orbiting around the model. Go ahead and touch up the texture as needed. You will need to repeat this process for the other side of the pie crust, but you do not have to worry about the insides of the pie. Once you have finished texturing the other side of the pie, unhide the gooey filling subtool model. The gooey filling subtool should cover up the remaining unpainted portions of the pie model.

Last step

Go ahead and save your ZBrush tool. Now is a good time to pause and take a look at the progress that we have made. Even if your model does not look like the example model, that is perfectly fine! When you first start a complicated program like ZBrush, it takes a while to master the various procedures and techniques that the program uses. It probably won't be the very first model that you create that turns out absolutely fantastic, and it may not be the second or even the third

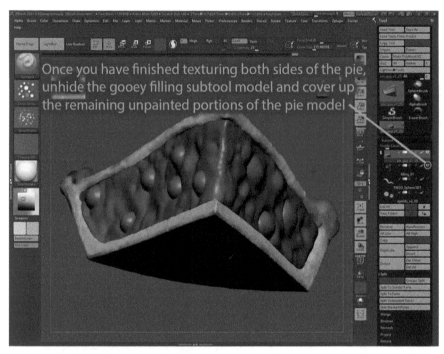

FIGURE 17.25 Once you have finished texturing both sides of the pie, unhide the gooey filling subtool model and cover up the remaining unpainted portions of the pie model.

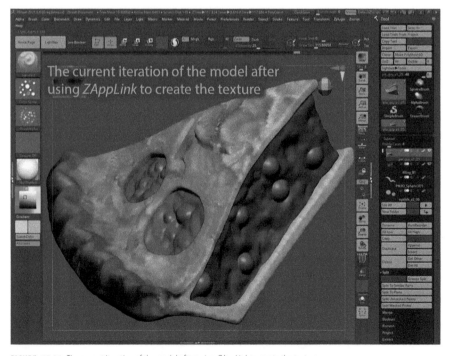

FIGURE 17.26 The current iteration of the model after using *ZAppLink* to create the texture.

attempt. It normally takes somewhere between six and twelve times before you develop enough control over the program to make it do exactly what you want it to do. The important thing is to keep working at it. Patience is key to mastering any complex task – such as making something in ZBrush. So just keep that in mind, and don't let yourself get frustrated.

Conclusion

This chapter covered how to texture a model in ZBrush using *ZAppLink*, along with some helpful tips about masking, touch-up, and problem-solving the process. While texturing a model using the *ZAppLink* plug-in is not an easy process, it does allow you to bring all of the power of a full-blown image editor like Photoshop to bear. Creating photorealistic textures is a challenging task by any means. It involves a good understanding of ZBrush, a usable model, working with the somewhat finicky *ZAppLink* plug-in, and a good set of reference photographs to work from. If you can manage it, the ability to create photorealistic textures will open up new vistas for your work. The results certainly warrant all of the effort!

18

Pie Painting, Part 2

Introduction

In this chapter, we are going to use a new technique to paint the eyebrows of our pie character model. The *SpotLight* is a texture projection function inside of ZBrush that provides a flexible way of painting textures directly onto your model without having to resort to using a separate app. Like many of the workflows in ZBrush, the *SpotLight* has an unusual interface that needs to be learned before this feature can be leveraged fully. The *SpotLight* system provides a useful alternative or addition to the *ZAppLink* plugin.

To begin, go ahead and load your model, draw it on screen, and press the edit button. Unhide any subtools that may be hidden by turning on the small eyeball icon next to the subtool layer in the *Tool > Subtool* palette. Now, something you may notice going forward in this book is that I am going to stop giving step-by-step instructions for things that we have already talked about. By now, you should be familiar with how ZBrush operates in general and can accomplish most things without explicit instruction, as you have now progressed to an intermediate level of proficiency with the program. If you need help following the tutorials subsequently, please go back and review the appropriate section in the book that goes over that material.

Setting up the work area

First, we need to set up our work area. Click on the *Divider Bar* to open up the *Left Tray* of the ZBrush interface. On the top menu bar, click on the word *Texture* and open up that menu. Now, left-click on and hold down the small icon in the uppermost left-hand corner of the texture

 DOI: 10.1201/9781003215288-18

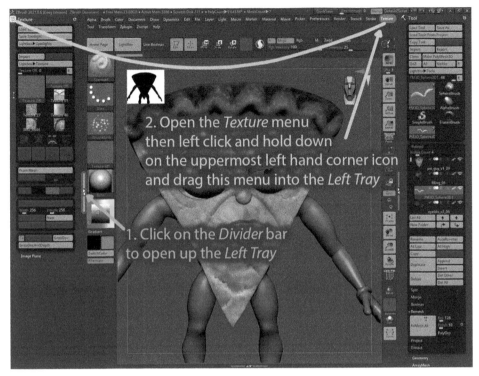

2. Open the *Texture* menu
then left click and hold down
on the uppermost left hand corner icon
and drag this menu into the *Left Tray*

1. Click on the *Divider* bar
to open up the *Left Tray*

FIGURE 18.1 Click on the *Divider* bar to open up the *Left Tray*. Open the *Texture* menu, then left-click and hold down on the uppermost left-hand corner icon and drag this menu into the *Left Tray*.

menu, the one that looks like a small circle with an arrow pointing up and out, and drag the texture menu to the *Left Tray*. The menu should snap into and fill the Left Tray.

Importing a texture map

Next, we need to import the texture map that we will use to paint the model. In our newly repositioned *Texture* menu inside the *Left Tray*, click on the *Import* button and use the file explorer that pops up to find and open the texture file that you would like to use on your computer system.

After you have imported the file, select the icon of the image that shows up inside the *Texture* menu in the *Left Tray*.

Adding texture to the SpotLight

Next, you need to press the *Add To SpotLight* button to load your texture file into the *SpotLight* function. Warning: the icon can be a bit hard to identify because there is no writing on it. As soon as we add our

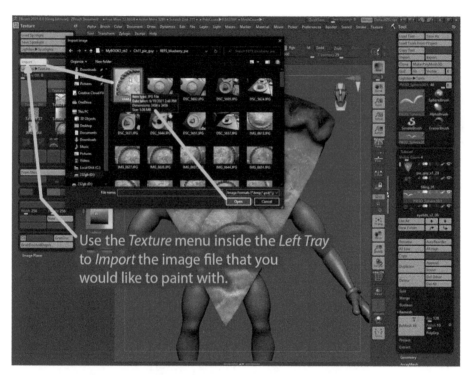

FIGURE 18.2 Use the *Texture* menu inside the *Left Tray* to Import the image file that you would like to paint with.

FIGURE 18.3 Select the image icon of your file from the *Texture* menu.

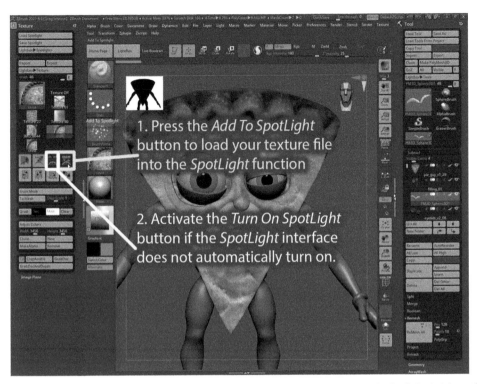

FIGURE 18.4 Press the *Add To SpotLight* button to load your texture file into the *SpotLight* function. Activate the *Turn On SpotLight* button if the *SpotLight* interface does not automatically turn on.

image to the *SpotLight* a weird interface should pop up. If you do not see the *SpotLight* interface, simply activate the *Turn On SpotLight* button or press Shift + Z as a shortcut.

One of the things you have probably noticed by now is the sheer number of non-standard and just plain odd interfaces in ZBrush. Frequently, these interfaces are poorly documented, unlabeled, and unintuitive. These unusual interfaces are found throughout the program. On the *SpotLight* interface, each of the small icons on the menu circle has a different function and will make various adjustments to your texture image and how it is applied to the model. If you rest your mouse over one of the icons, a small pop-up will display the name of the command the icon represents. Near the top of the *SpotLight* interface circle, you should see an icon that looks like a dot with an arrow circling it – this is the *Rotate* button. If you hold down the left mouse button, you can rotate the texture in the *SpotLight*. If you simultaneously hold down the SHIFT key while using the *Rotate* button, then the *SpotLight* will turn in 5° increments. The *Scale* button is immediately to the right of the *Rotate* button and will scale the image size for you. Three icons to the right of the *Scale* button, you should see an icon that looks like a person standing behind frosted glass – this is the *Opacity* button.

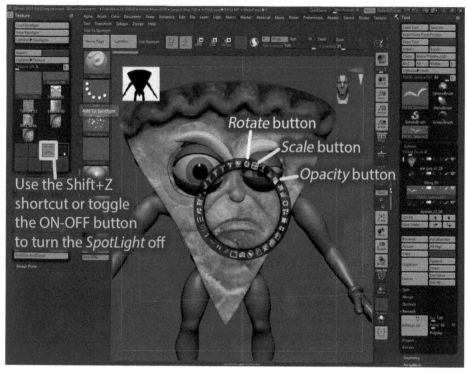

FIGURE 18.5 Use the *Rotate, Scale,* and *Opacity* buttons to adjust the *SpotLight.* Use the Shift + Z shortcut or toggle the ON-OFF button to turn the *SpotLight* off.

Hold down the left mouse button on top of the *Opacity* button and move the mouse around to adjust the opacity of the *SpotLight.* Making the *Spotlight* somewhat transparent will make it a lot easier to see what you are doing in relation to the model. Note that the *Opacity* slider does not alter how the *SpotLight* paints at all; it simply adjusts your view of the texture image. Unfortunately, the *SpotLight* interface does not possess the standard ZBrush help feature where you can hold down the CTRL key and get more information about the feature your mouse pointer is hovering over, which makes this particular interface a bit harder to understand.

Using the *SpotLight*

If you left-click on the screen, the *SpotLight* interface will reposition itself to where you clicked and then let you reposition the texture. You can also click inside the tiny central orange circle in the *SpotLight* interface and move it around. If you click inside the main ring of the *SpotLight* interface, you can reposition both the texture and interface. Go ahead and practice this for a minute or two and become comfortable with how moving the interface and texture around works. It can take a bit of getting used to, and you will need to play with and explore the *SpotLight* a fair bit to start understanding how it operates. The normal camera move, zoom, and orbit shortcuts become ineffective with the *SpotLight*, *although* the *Move*, *Zoom3D*, and *Rotate* buttons on the lower right side of the ZBrush document still work just fine. You can use the SHIFT + Z shortcut or the On-Off button in the *Texture* menu to deactivate the *SpotLight*, but when you turn it back on, the texture will reappear without the *SpotLight* interface, and you need to press the Z key to restore the SpotLight interface.

Once you have the *SpotLight* positioned where you want to apply the texture, simply press the Z key to turn off the *SpotLight* interface and paint with your brush onto the model. This act will paint the *SpotLight* texture onto the model. Now, of course, you need to have a brush capable of painting the model selected. Something like the *Standard* brush will do. You must have *Rgb* or *Mrgb* mode turned on, *Zadd* turned off, and your *Rgb Intensity* slider set above 0, or you will not be able to paint anything onto your model successfully. If you hold down the SHIFT key and click on the eyeball icon on a subtool layer, it will hide all of the unselected subtools and let you focus on the subtool you are currently working on.

FIGURE 18.6 Make sure that you have the *Rgb* mode turned on, *Zadd* turned off, and your *Rgb Intensity* slider set. Press the Z key to turn off the *SpotLight* interface and start painting.

Use the Shift + Z shortcut for toggling the *SpotLight* on and off, the Z key to turn on painting, and simply move the model around underneath the *SpotLight* to paint your texture onto any part of the model that you desire. *SpotLight* is a very powerful tool, but like much of ZBrush, it does have a learning curve to it and will take you some time to become comfortable with it. The really nice thing about *SpotLight* is that since it is built directly into ZBrush and isn't a plugin like *ZAppLink*, *SpotLight* is more robust and not as buggy as *ZAppLink*. The downside to *SpotLight* is the funky interface and process that you must use. Which one of the two methods you end up using more boils down to your own personal preference.

Mask By Polypaint

To finish detailing our character's eyebrows, we can try out the *Tool > Masking > Mask By Color > Mask By Polypaint* command. In the new interface, this command brings up, click, and drag from the topmost light gray box on the right-hand side. This gray box is a color swatch for the *Mask By Polypaint* command, and you use the *Color Picker* on your mouse pointer to choose the color you would like to mask off on your model.

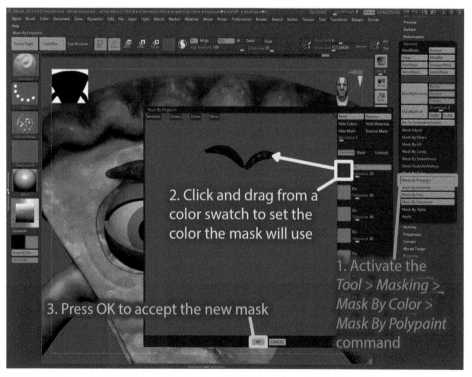

FIGURE 18.7 Activate the *Tool > Masking > Mask By Color > Mask By Polypaint* command. Click and drag from a color swatch to set the color the mask will use. Press the OK button to accept the new mask.

You can use the *Tolerance* slider to tweak the amount of color that the mask covers up. You can also use the other color swatches to add to the mask selection. After you have the object masked off in the preview window to your satisfaction, press the OK button at the bottom of the *Mask By Polypaint* interface to accept the mask and re-enter ZBrush's main interface. You can now use the mask like you would any other.

Painting the eyebrows

To paint the eyebrows, make sure that you have *Rgb* mode turned on, *Zadd* turned off, and your *Rgb Intensity* set how you prefer. You can now select the *Standard* brush, set the *BrushAlpha* to *Alpha 07*, pick a brown color, and paint the eyebrows. Use the *Mask By Polypaint* function to prevent ZBrush from painting over any color that you would like to preserve. Change your colors as you paint using the *Color Picker* to grab existing colors off of your model. Paint these colors into the eyebrows to achieve a unified color palette between the body of your character and the eyebrows. I want the eyebrows to be darker than the rest of the body, so I intentionally picked up colors off of the more burnt and well-cooked portions of the character model. After putting down a dark base color, I gently applied a few low opacity strokes using a lighter shade to create a stippled effect.

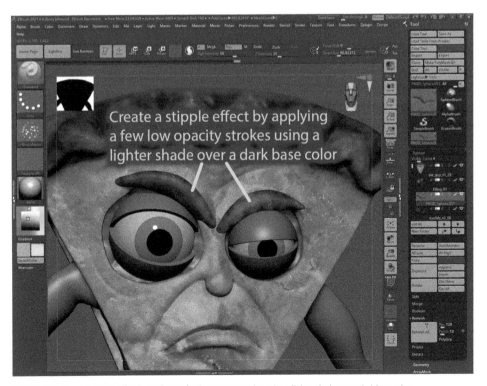

FIGURE 18.8 Create a stipple effect by applying a few low opacity strokes using a lighter shade over a dark base color.

Applying noise with the *NoiseMaker*

An alternate approach for applying fine details is to use the *Noise* feature found inside the *Tool > Surface* menu. Clicking on this button activates the *NoiseMaker* interface. Once you are inside the *NoiseMaker* interface, click on the *NoisePlug* button in the upper right corner. Doing so will bring up yet another new interface, which will let you choose from a list of procedural noise-making algorithms and adjust their settings to create a wide variety of different noise effects on the surface of your model.

Perlin noise

You can select one of the different patterns from this list and change the settings while looking at the results in the *NoiseMaker* window that displays your model. For this example, I used the *Perlin Noise* pattern and then just played around with the *Octaves*, *Frequency*, and *Amplitude* sliders until I got something that I liked in the *NoiseMaker* window. Press the OK button to accept the latest pattern settings that you have created. Finally, press the OK button at the bottom of the *NoiseMaker* viewer window to head back into ZBrush.

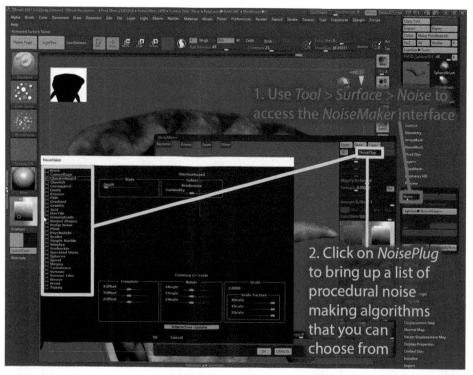

FIGURE 18.9 Use *Tool > Surface > Noise* to access the *NoiseMaker* interface. Click on *NoisePlug* to bring up a list of procedural noise-making algorithms that you can choose from.

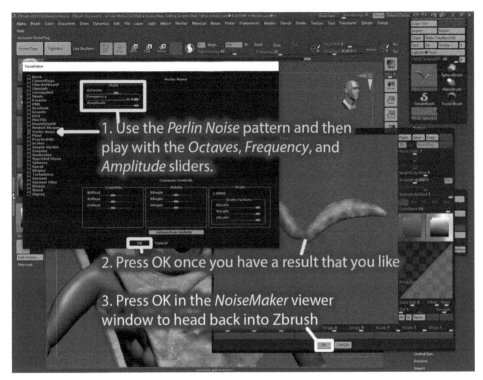

FIGURE 18.10 For this example, I used the *Perlin Noise* pattern and then just played around with the *Octaves, Frequency*, and *Amplitude* sliders. Press OK once you have something that you like in the *NoiseMaker* window. Finally, press OK again in the *NoiseMaker* viewer window to head back into ZBrush.

Once you are back inside the standard ZBrush interface, click the *Tool > Surface > MaskByNoise* button to convert the pattern that we created with the *NoiseMaker* into a mask that we can use to paint on top of. If you now turn off the *Rgb* button and turn *Zadd* on, you can now sculpt a fine stipple pattern onto the eyebrows. Alternatively, you can go to the *Tool > Deformation > Inflate Balloon* slider and use it to add just a smidge of detail to the eyebrow model.

Fractional Brownian Motion

Once you have finished using the *NoiseMaker*-created mask, simply press down CTRL, click, and drag a small selection box in the background to clear the mask. You can also use the *NoiseMaker* to create other types of masks using different algorithms. For example, I find the *FBM* (Fractional Brownian Motion) choice quite useful. Use *Tool > Surface > Noise* to pull up the *NoiseMaker* interface once more. Click on the *NoisePlug* command again, and this time, choose the *FBM* option.

With the *NoiseMaker* created mask active, adjust the *Tool* > *Deformation* > *Inflate Balloon* slider to add some detail to the eyebrow model

FIGURE 18.11 With the *NoiseMaker* created mask active, adjust the T*ool* > *Deformation* > *Inflate Balloon* slider to add some detail to the eyebrow model.

Set *Lacunarity* = 2, *Gain* = 2, and *Detail* = 2, then press OK. Press OK to close out the *NoiseMaker* window, and then click the *Tool* > *Surface* > *MaskByNoise* button. I also like to turn off the *Tool* > *Masking* > *View-Mask* button to let me observe what I am doing, but that is merely a personal preference. Now you can pick a brighter brown color and paint this into the eyebrow model while using the mask to protect the parts of the original paint job that you would like to keep. You can switch back to sculpting by turning *Zadd* on and *Rgb* mode off and adding some fine details to the model this way. If you want the sculptural grittiness of the mask to come through a bit more evenly, then use the *InflateBalloon* slider instead. Note that a little bit of *InflateBalloon* will go a long way, so keep your adjustments small when using that slider.

Finishing the eyebrows

To finish things off, use CTRL + I to invert the mask, choose a dark brown color, turn on *Rgb* mode, and set your *Rgb Intensity* to something low – say around 20 or so. Now, use the *Color* > *FillObject* command to apply this dark brown to the bottoms of the creases on the

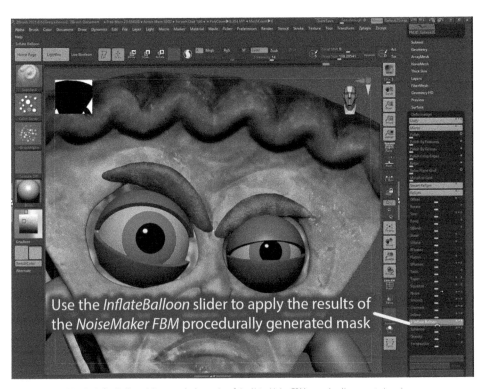

Use the *InflateBalloon* slider to apply the results of the *NoiseMaker FBM* procedurally generated mask

FIGURE 18.12 Use the *InflateBalloon* slider to apply the results of the *NoiseMaker* FBM procedurally generated mask.

eyebrows. This process will add a bit of "pop" to this model. Of course, once you have a level of 3D grit applied to a model, you can always simply use the *Tool > Masking > Mask By Cavity > Mask By Cavity* command to remask out the crevices in the model if you ever need to. The essence of what we have done here is to create a finely detailed mask and then use that mask to create a small variance in the surface of our model. Having done so, we paint the highest parts of the crevices in the model a pale color and the bottom of the crease a darker shade, which accentuates the three-dimensionality of the object. This basic painting technique is often used in painting miniature figurines for wargaming and plastic model kits. It is an excellent way of showing off the fine details of your model. If you are interested in seeing where these techniques come from, look up how to "dry brush" and create a "wash" on a plastic figurine or model. All we are doing is translating these classic painting techniques into the digital realm.

Conclusion

Using a combination of the *SpotLight* feature, the *Mask By Polypaint* command, and the *NoiseMaker* you can create all sorts of interesting fine details and patterns on your models. These functions add a fine set of techniques to your ZBrush knowledge and will enable you to mimic certain traditional painting techniques, such as dry brushing and applying washes to your model. A thorough understanding of the various commands and functions inside of ZBrush will empower your ability to bring your full artistic knowledge to bear within this powerful three-dimensional sculpting package. Once you are comfortable with how ZBrush operates, you should have no trouble figuring out how to apply real-world painting techniques through ZBrush's digital lens!

Oh, and don't forget to save your work!

19

Pie Painting, Part 3 – The Hands and Feet

Introduction

In this chapter, we're going to paint the gooey pie filling of our blueberry pie. As such, I think it would be useful to combine the different models that we currently spread out over several subtools. Merging all of the models that will end up with a gooey pie-filling material and texture will make painting the model much, much easier later on. Before I start merging things, it would be wise to check the number of polygons in each subtool to make sure that each subtool has a fairly even spread of polygons. You want to avoid merging one object that has a high polygon count with another object that has a low polygon count since the result can look uneven. When evaluating the polygon count of an object, you need to consider size – a big object will have more polygons in it than a small one. To check the polygon count for each subtool, simply rest your mouse pointer over that subtool, and a detailed account of the number of polygons and other relevant data should show up. You can use the *Move Up* and *Move Down* arrows to arrange the gooey subtools together. Remember to save your *Tool* before any major subtool operation!

Merging subtools

Merge the arms, legs, eyelids, and pie-filling subtools together by selecting the topmost subtool from this list and using the *Tool > Subtool > Merge > MergeDown* command to merge these subtools. If you SHIFT + click on the eyeball icon of the resulting merged subtool, you can turn off all of the unselected subtools and view them in isolation.

DOI: 10.1201/9781003215288-19

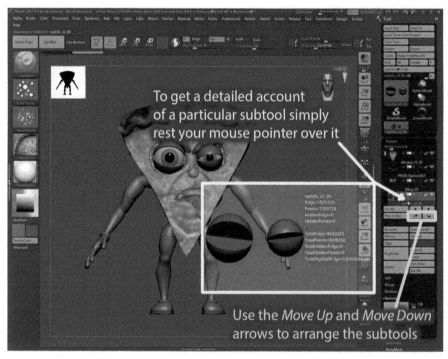

FIGURE 19.1 To get a detailed account of a particular subtool, simply rest your mouse pointer over it.

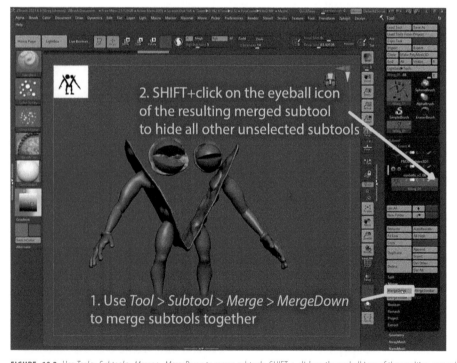

FIGURE 19.2 Use *Tool > Subtool > Merge > MergeDown* to merge subtools. SHIFT + click on the eyeball icon of the resulting merged subtool to hide all other unselected subtools.

Splitting out the hands and feet

Having done this, I now want to split out the hands and feet since they will eventually have a different material and paint job than the rest of the arms and legs. To split a subtool into its constituent parts, simply use the *Tool > Subtool > Split > Split To Parts* command (it is located immediately above the Merge command). Now, we can go into our subtool palette and move the hands and feet subtools above the other subtools. Finally, use the *Tool > Subtool > Merge > Merge-Down* command to merge the arms, legs, eyelids, and pie-filling subtools back together. The goal is to combine all of the models that will share the same material and color into one subtool. Grouping things using subtools in this way is a LOT easier than using masks to isolate the various pieces of the model for painting and applying materials. At the end of this process, the boots and the hands are in one subtool, the pie filling and other purple pieces are in a different subtool, the eyeballs are in another subtool, and the pie crust and eyebrows are each in their own subtools. Always, always, always save your file before you start splitting and merging subtools, just in case ZBrush gets mad and crashes.

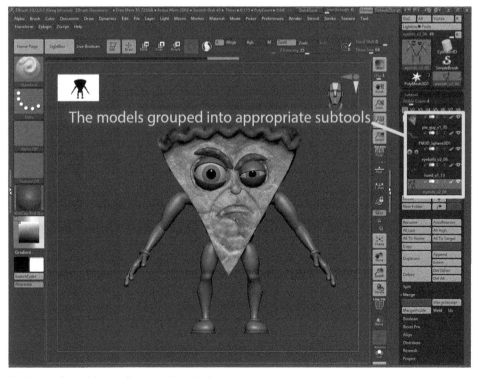

FIGURE 19.3 The models grouped into appropriate subtools.

Applying a base color to the hands and feet

With the hands and feet in the same subtool, I can now simply select that subtool, turn on the *Mrgb* button, set the *Material* to *Skin-Shade4*, *Rgb Intensity* to 100, and the *Color* to off-white, then use the *Color > FillObject* command to paint the entire subtool. We can now hide the hands and feet subtool by clicking on the eyeball icon on that subtool layer. Simply applying a good material and base color to the model can go quite a long way in establishing the look we are trying to achieve.

Introducing masks by cavity and the cavity profile graph

Select our gooey pie filling, arms, legs, and eyelids subtool. I have the demo model setup using the *Blinn* material and a rich purple color. You can set the material and color to whatever values you like and use the *FillObject* command to apply these settings to your model now if you haven't already. Once you have the base color and material applied, open *Tool > Masking > Mask By Cavity* and click on the *Mask By Cavity* button. Doing so will mask off all of the shadowy crevices in the model. You can control how much or little of the low-lying places on the mesh are masked off when you click on the *Mask By Cavity* command by clicking on the *Cavity Profile* bar and adjusting the *Cavity Profile* curve. This interface controls how the *Mask By Cavity* command is applied to the model. The left side of the graph is the low-lying part of the model, and the right side is the upper part. The dark color on the graph represents the masked-off portion of the model. That said, it is a bit more understandable if you simply play with the graph and try it out a few times to get the hang of it. You can adjust the curve and the results provided by the *Mask By Cavity* command by simply clicking on the curve and adding a control point to the graph. You can then move the control point around to shape the graph and the results as you see fit.

By controlling the shape of the curve on the *Cavity Profile*, you can mask off more or less of the model the next time you click on the *Mask By Cavity* button. You will notice that the control point provides the curve in a soft, rather rounded manner. If you click and drag the control point off of the graph entirely and then let go, you will delete the control point. If you click and drag the control point off of the graph entirely and then drag it back onto the graph, this will convert that control point to a hard edge type. The hard edge type of control point has a sharp and angular effect on the curve. Repeating this will change the control point back to a smooth curve type. You can also add more control points by simply clicking on other spots on the curve.

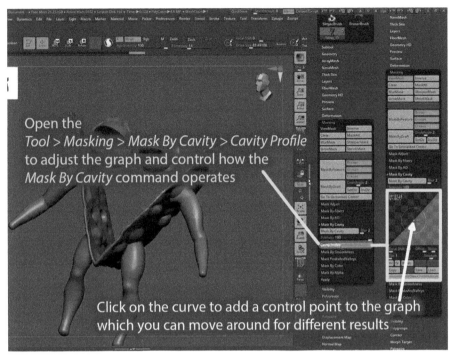

Open the
Tool > Masking > Mask By Cavity > Cavity Profile
to adjust the graph and control how the
Mask By Cavity command operates

Click on the curve to add a control point to the graph
which you can move around for different results

FIGURE 19.4 Open the *Tool > Masking > Mask By Cavity > Cavity Profile* to adjust the graph and control how the *Mask By Cavity* command operates. Click on the curve to add a control point to the graph, which you can move around for different results.

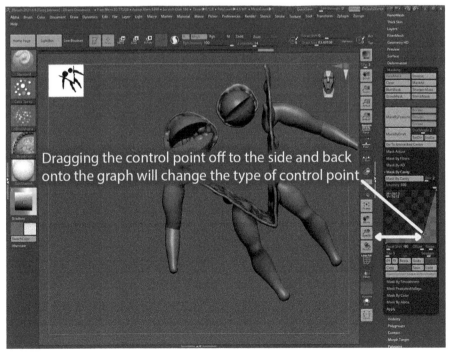

Dragging the control point off to the side and back
onto the graph will change the type of control point

FIGURE 19.5 Dragging the control point off to the side and back onto the graph will change the type of control point.

If you need to, clicking on the *Reset* button found underneath the graph will restore the graph to its default settings. In the area near the *Reset* button are a few other control settings that you can use to alter the graph as well. Try playing around with the *Focal Shift*, *Noise*, and *Strength* settings to see what effect these have on your final results. You can always reset the graph if you need to. By default, the *Focal Shift* is set to −90, which adds quite a lot of bend to the graph curve. It is important to consider this setting when you are playing around with the curve, as it is easy to overlook.

Using mask by cavity

To start with, you can simply use the default settings and press the *Tool* > *Masking* > *Mask By Cavity* > *Mask By Cavity* button to create your mask. Now, either press CTRL+I or simply click on the document background to invert the mask. You can blur the mask by either clicking on the *Tool* > *Masking* > *Blur* command or simply CTRL+clicking on the mask itself. I always prefer to turn off the *Tool* > *Masking* > *ViewMask* button so I can see the results of my operations more clearly. Next,

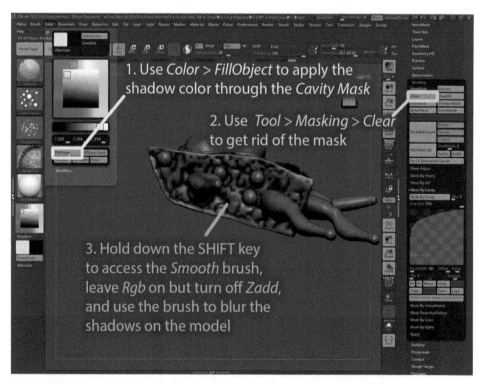

FIGURE 19.6 Use *Color* > *FillObject* to apply the shadow color through the *Cavity Mask*. Next, *Tool* > *Masking* > *Clear* to get rid of the mask. Hold down the SHIFT key to access the *Smooth* brush, leave *Rgb* on, but turn off *Zadd*, and then use the brush to blur the shadows on the model.

I select a darker version of the purple color I am using for the character. Set the *Rgb Intensity* to around 25. Finally, use the *Color > FillObject* command to apply this darker purple to the crevices of the model. You can now use the *Tool > Masking > Clear* button to get rid of the mask. Next, hold down the SHIFT key to access the *Smooth* brush, leave *Rgb* on, but turn off *Zadd*, and use the brush to blur the shadows you just created on the model.

Alternatively, you can CTRL+click on the mask to blur it a bit more, lower the *Rgb Intensity*, and apply a broad, thin layer of color to build up the strength of the shadows. Play around with the *MaskByCavity* and *FillObject* commands in combination with the *Smooth* brush to achieve an effect that you like.

Creating highlights

The procedure we can use to create the highlights on the model follows the same pattern – just with a different *Cavity Control* graph. Open up the *Tool > Masking > Mask By Cavity > Cavity Control* graph again and use what is essentially the inverse of the curve that we used earlier.

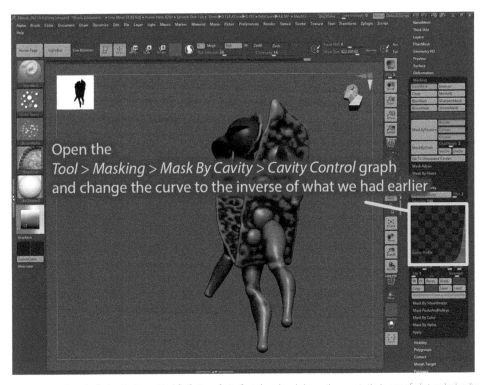

FIGURE 19.7 Open the *Tool > Masking > Mask By Cavity > Cavity Control* graph and change the curve to the inverse of what we had earlier.

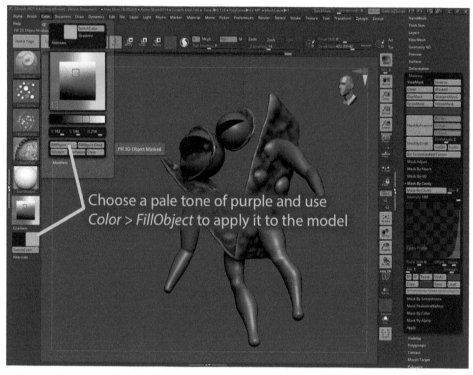

FIGURE 19.8 Choose a pale tint of purple and use *Color > FillObject* to apply it to the model.

Now proceed to use the *Tool > Masking > Mask By Cavity > Mask By Cavity* command to create the mask and blur the results. Choose a pale tone of purple that will look good as your highlight. Finally, apply this purple tint to the model using the *Color > FillObject* command. You can also get rid of the mask and then use the *Smooth* brush to blend the highlights out as you see fit.

Painting the shadows and highlights

Remember that you can also paint some highlights and shadows by hand, either by using the *CavityMask* or simply by freehand. Add a touch of highlight to any place on the model that catches the light. The goal with all of this is to create shadows and highlights on the model that pick out the details of the object. It is a simple trick that has been used for decades by plastic kit modelers and miniature painters. I find that the *Standard* brush, in conjunction with the *Color Spray* stroke and a fine dot pattern alpha like *Alpha07* works very well for adding just a little bit of color variation to a paint job. You can use a *Cavity Mask* to protect any areas that you do not want to paint over accidentally.

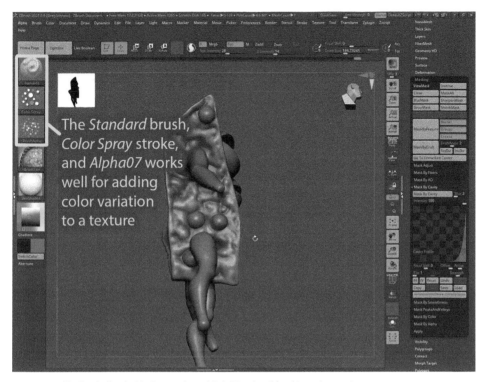

The *Standard* brush, *Color Spray* stroke, and *Alpha07* works well for adding color variation to a texture

The hands and feet

Next up, we need to paint the hands and the feet. We will use the same process that we used earlier on the gooey portions of the body. To start, select the subtool that contains the hands and feet. Just like our previous example, go to *Tool > Masking > Mask By Cavity* and use the *Mask By Cavity* command to mask off the low-lying portions of the hands and feet model. You may need to open up the *Cavity Profile* graph and adjust it to get good results. Use the *Tool > Masking > Blur-Mask* command to soften the mask to your preference. Turn off *Tool > Masking > ViewMask* to better observe what you are doing. Press the *Tool > Masking > Inverse* command to reverse the mask. Choose a dark color and set your *Rgb Intensity* to a low value; around ten works just fine. Finally, use the *Color > FillObject* command to add the shadow color to the hands and feet. Remember that you can always use the *Smooth* brush to blend out the shadows even more. Just remember to turn off the *ZAdd* while using the *Smooth* brush, or you will also smooth out your 3D details.

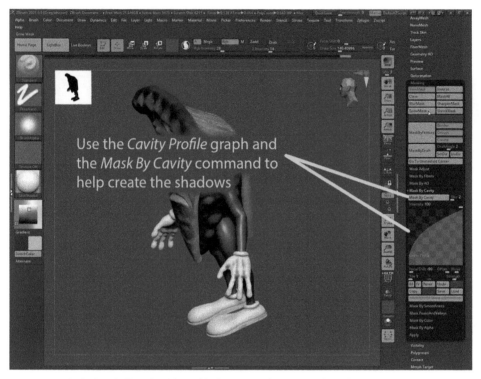

Use the *Cavity Profile* graph and the *Mask By Cavity* command to help create the shadows

FIGURE 19.10 Use the *Cavity Profile* graph and the *Mask By Cavity* command to help create the shadows.

Fixing a hole

You can also paint in some darker shadows by hand, as needed, using the *Standard Brush*. I added some extra shadows to the creases in the palm, around the base of the hands, and on the edge lines for the feet. While doing this, I discovered a small pit near the wrist of the character. To fix this, I switched to the *ClayTubes* brush with a small *Draw Size* (14) and simply bulked up the walls of the pit until it closed. Note that by just tapping once on an area, ZBrush will then orbit the camera around that point. This technique lets you easily focus on a specific area to work on. Follow up with a quick *DynaMesh*, and the pit is gone. You may need to adjust the *DynaMesh* resolution slider to preserve the details of your model.

Once you have fixed any problems that you find, you can go back to painting in your shadows. The bottoms of the shoes should be a bit dirtier than the rest of the model, so I painted the bottom of the shoes rather heavily as compared to the rest of the model. Whenever you are painting elements by hand, you always have to think about where these particular elements are on your character's body and how the light sources in your scene would interact with the model.

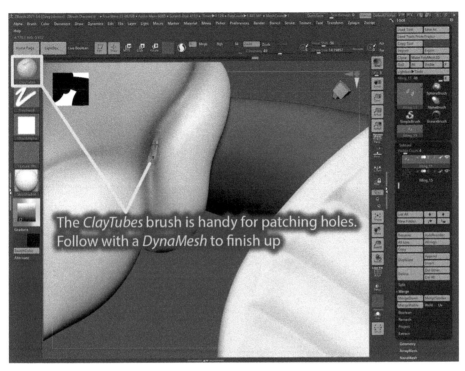

FIGURE 19.11 The *ClayTubes* brush is handy for patching holes. Follow with a *DynaMesh* to finish up.

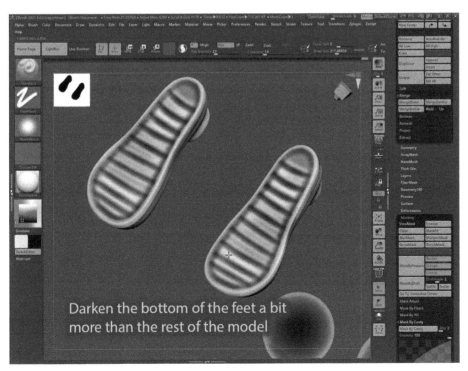

FIGURE 19.12 Darken the bottom of the feet a bit more than the rest of the model.

Use the *Cavity Mask* to paint in some shadows on the pie crust

FIGURE 19.13 Use the *Cavity Mask* to paint in some shadows on the pie crust.

The last bit of shading that we need to do is on the pie crust itself. Select that subtool and use the same process as before – using the *Mask By Cavity* in conjunction with the *Cavity Profile* graph to mask off the low-lying areas of the model, blur the mask, and then invert the mask (CTRL + I). Choose a dark color that will work for the shadows, and slowly fill these areas in with a low *Rgb Intensity* fill using the *Color > Fill Object* command. You can change colors, brushes, strokes, and brush alphas to create variation in the model's texture, too, if you like.

The techniques that you have learned in this chapter can be applied to any model that you are working on. It is a generally useful methodology that is broadly useful for any number of three-dimensional characters, environments, or objects.

Conclusion

Much of hand painting a model boils down to the repeated use of just a handful of rather simple techniques: *Mask By Cavity* along with the *Cavity Profile*, the *Color > Fill Object* command to apply uniform coats of paint, some painting using the *Standard* brush, and a fair bit of the *Smooth* brush – just don't forget to turn off the *Zadd* button when you smooth your paint job. A good habit to get into is to frequently

FIGURE 19.14 Our progress so far.

orbit the camera around your model just to make sure that you are treating both sides of the model the same. You always want to work on the whole of the model rather than focusing on just one small portion. Doing otherwise can lead to uneven-looking results in the final product. Adding an extra bit of shadow and highlights will bring out the details of the model and make the whole affair look even better. As long as you do not overdo it, this process of adding these extra shadows and highlights won't interfere with how the object's material interacts with the scene lights later on when we render out the final image.

I hope you have enjoyed this chapter on how to hand-paint your 3D model in ZBrush! Make sure that you try out all of these painting techniques on your model, and be sure to have fun. Remember to save your tool periodically and to back up all of your work.

20

Pie Painting, Part 4 – The Eyes

Getting a fresh perspective

We are now down to the finishing touches on our main character and getting the model ready for final assembly. After that, we just have to pose the character, light it, render it out, and then composite all of the renderings into our final image. But do not worry – none of this is as daunting as it might seem. To start, take an overall look at the model as it stands so far. Reanalyzing your work can help you get a fresh perspective on things because your eyes get used to what you are working on, and you stop really observing what is there. You just see what you expect to be there. To get this fresh perspective, try the following old artist's tricks:

1. *Flip it upside down*: Grab a screenshot of the work and flip it in Photoshop, or just turn your monitor upside down, if possible, without breaking it. Either way, this should force your eye to re-examine the work.
2. *Flip the work left-to-right*: This method requires a mirror or a screen grab and some Photoshop. Much the same as the first technique, this will clear out your preconceived notions about what the object looks like and give you a new perspective on things. Flipping the image (either horizontally or vertically) is a great way to check your proportions and the overall composition of a piece of artwork.
3. *Step back from the work and look at it from a different distance*: All too often, we sit at our computer workstations and maintain the same distance from the screen day in and day out. Stepping back a fair bit and taking a look at the work performs the same trick as flipping it.

DOI: 10.1201/9781003215288-20

4. *Squint your eyes and take a look at what you have on screen*: Squinting should blur the image. While this might seem counterproductive, it will force you to notice the overall patterns of lights and darks in what you have on screen, and you can see issues that you may not have yet to catch.

Go ahead and try these techniques out now and see if you notice any problems that you haven't yet seen. It is essential to find and fix any issues that remain in the model before continuing. The reason this is so critical is that any remaining problems will multiply the difficulty level of the following tasks. Problems in 3D tend to snowball quite dramatically. The model and paint job must be well and truly done before you proceed. Otherwise, you run a real chance of having the project turn into an unfinishable quagmire. This tendency for errors to quietly accumulate in the background until the project becomes untenable will undoubtedly make itself known to you as you work on this, your first ZBrush project. It is simply unavoidable that there will be a few problems that you miss. Just remember to learn from any mistakes you make. Luckily for us, the project we are working on in this book is a fairly straightforward illustration. A simple project like this provides a comfortable margin of error in which mistakes can be made and not completely derail the whole project. Creating a character for animation on either television or a video game is a whole lot more complicated and vulnerable to errors than what we have undertaken.

Fixing the eyes

The eyes are bugging me a little bit, so I am going to fix them. Putting that noise filter on the sclera of the eyeball has turned them too pink, I think. Select the eyeball subtool, hold down CTRL + SHIFT, and just tap the white part of the eyeball to isolate that piece of the model. Then select the *Standard* brush, the *Color Spray* stroke, and the *Alpha 01* brush tip. Set the color to a very pale yellow, make sure that the *Zadd* button is turned off and the *Rgb* button is turned on, and set the *Rgb Intensity* to about 50. Turn on the *Transp* button so that the eyelids and other objects don't get in the way. Now, paint the center of the sclera (i.e., the part that is around the iris and pupil) to brighten this part of the eye up. Having done this on one eye, hold down CTRL + SHIFT and tap on the background to unhide the rest of the eyeball subtool. Now CTRL + SHIFT and tap on the other eyeball to isolate and paint it, too. When you are done working, simply CTRL + SHIFT and tap on the background to unhide everything again.

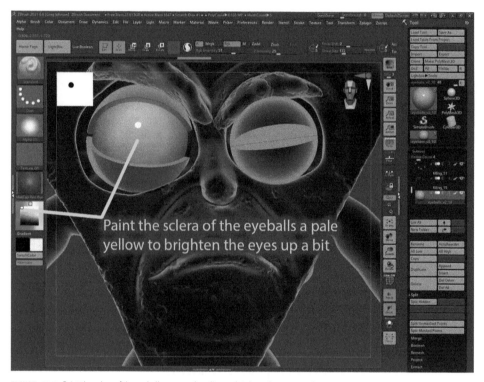

Paint the sclera of the eyeballs a pale
yellow to brighten the eyes up a bit

FIGURE 20.1 Paint the sclera of the eyeballs a very pale yellow to brighten the eyes up a bit.

Adding detail to the pupil

I also want to add some detail to the green pupils, so go ahead and
isolate the green pupil part of the eye model by CTRL+SHIFT tapping
on the green part. I would like to add a sort of chaotic ray pattern
radiating outward from the eyeball so it looks a bit more realistic than
just the flat color that it is now. I seem to recall a certain *LayerRoll* brush
that would be useful for this, but I cannot find it in the default palette
of available brushes. Never fear! ZBrush has a ton of brushes and other
resources hidden away in its install folder on the hard drive. To load
the *LayerRoll* brush, simply open up the *Brush Palette*, click on the *Load
Brush* button, and then navigate through the resulting pop-up file
directory to the ZBrush install directory and the ZBrushes\Layer folder.
On my machine, the path is C:\Program Files\Maxon ZBrush 2023\
ZBrushes\Layer, but the location on your machine may vary somewhat.
Now, double-click the LayerRoll.ZBP file to load it into ZBrush.

Turn on *Rgb* mode and make sure that *Zadd* is turned off. Remember
that ZBrush remembers the settings for each brush, so you need to
do this for each brush that you paint with. Now, pick a color (I used a
slightly darker green) and start painting. You can alter the stroke to

FIGURE 20.2 Load the *LayerRoll* brush from the ZBrush install directory on your hard drive.

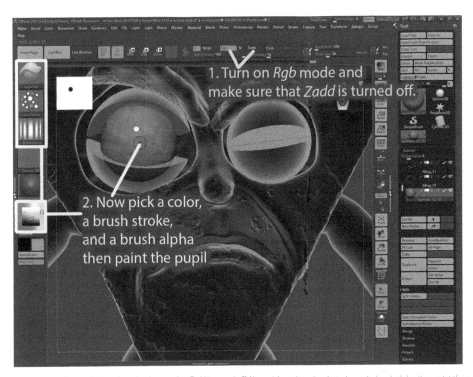

FIGURE 20.3 Turn on *Rgb* mode and make sure that *Zadd* is turned off. Now, pick a color, a brush stroke, and a brush alpha, then paint the pupil.

color spray, change the brush alpha, and vary your *Rgb Intensity* to try out different things until you are happy with the results. Once you have finished one eye, simply repeat the process for the other pupil. You can always adjust the *Rgb Intensity* and use the *Smooth* brush to blend colors and fix any small imperfections.

Go ahead and save your tool file so you can keep up with your work. Be careful when you do so, though. By default, ZBrush takes you to the last folder that we worked with – which in this case is inside of the *Layer* brushes directory inside of the ZBrush install folder. We certainly do not want to save our model inside of that folder! So pick a more useful folder to save your model to (probably where you have been saving your ZBrush tools previously). You really have to watch ZBrush carefully at times. Some of the program's default behaviors can create quite a lot of trouble for you if you aren't careful or don't pay attention to what it's doing.

Preparing the eyelids

For the next phase of operations, we can use the *Tool > Subtool > Split > Split To Parts* command on the purple gooey subtool that also contains the arms, legs, and eyelids. This command will split each piece of the model into a separate subtool, which will make isolating specific pieces much easier.

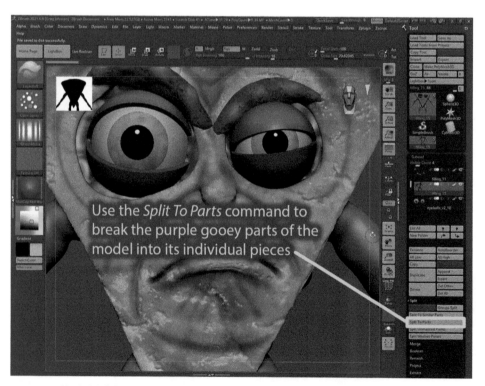

Use the *Split To Parts* command to break the purple gooey parts of the model into its individual pieces

FIGURE 20.4 Use the *Split To Parts* command to break the purple gooey parts of the model into their individual pieces.

Go ahead and use the *Tool > Subtool > Merge > MergeDown* command to unify the arms and legs back together into a single subtool. Use the *MergeDown* command again to merge the eyelids and the goo behind them into one component as well. This merged subtool is the part of the model that we are going to detail next. SHIFT-click the eye icon on the eyelid's subtool layer to switch off subtool visibility for all of the other subtools, which will effectively isolate the portion of the model that we are going to sculpt.

If you ever accidentally drop a tool into the background, either by accidentally pressing the T key, using the SHIFT+B combo, or whatever means – it can really help to know how to get rid of any unwanted background objects without having to restart the program or use the *Preferences > Init ZBrush* command. You can use the *Layer > Clear* command to get rid of unwanted elements in the background or use the *Document > New Document* command to replace the current document completely.

With the pieces of the eyelid merged into a single subtool, we can now use the *DynaMesh* command to unify the polymesh. You may need to adjust the *DynaMesh > Resolution* slider to get a good result – I set my *Resolution* to 256 in the demo video. Next, I can sample the purple color from the eyelid by simply resting the mouse over the object and pressing the C shortcut. Now, hold down SHIFT and apply a touch of smoothing to the eyelids. The whole point of this is to make the eyeballs look more integrated.

Detailing the eyelids

I think the eyelids need a few lumps so that they look a bit more oozy. To add these details to the eyelids, switch to the *Blob* brush and start sketching in a few new lumps on the eyelids so they match the gooey pie filling a bit better. Whenever parts of the eyelids begin looking a bit derezzed or when the polygons start showing, simply go in and *DynaMesh* the eyelids again and apply a touch of the *Smooth* brush. The *Blob* brush is one of those brushes that can be very useful in specific circumstances, such as this.

Press the B - I - N keys to switch to the *Inflate* brush and use it to puff up a few big blueberry lumps on the eyelids, and, if you hold down ALT while using it, shrink down some other areas.

Painting the eyelids

Now that we are done with sculpting the eyelids, we can paint them. To set up a paintbrush, switch to the *Standard* brush, turn off Zadd, turn on Rgb, and set the Rgb Intensity slider to a low value like 15. Now pick a nice pale purple color to serve as a highlight color, and gently apply this color to the tops of any lumps that you want to pick

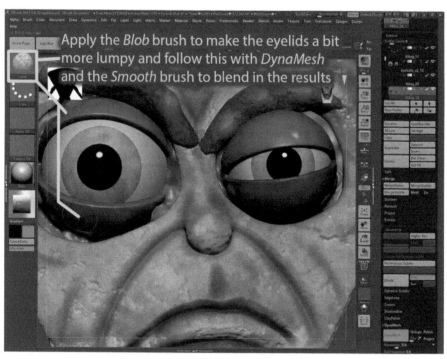

FIGURE 20.5 Apply the *Blob* brush to make the eyelids a bit lumpier, and follow this with *DynaMesh* and the *Smooth* brush to blend in the results.

FIGURE 20.6 Use the *Inlate* brush to add a few "berries" to the eyelids.

out from the base color a bit. After you have done the first pass, make the color a bit paler, and apply some more highlights. Keep doing this to slowly build up your highlights until you are happy with the result. Remember that if you use the *Smooth* brush, you will need to turn off the *Zadd* button, or the *Smooth* brush will affect your geometry and not just blend your colors.

To add some shadows, go to *Tool > Masking > Mask By Cavity* and use the *Mask By Cavity* command, which will grab the shadow areas of the model. Use the *Tool > Masking > BlurMask* command to soften the mask a bit, and then press the *Tool > Masking > Inverse* command to leave just the shadow areas unmasked. I like turning off the *Tool > Masking > View-Mask* switch so I can better see what I am doing. Now, choose a dark purple and a low *Rgb Intensity* setting, and use the *Color > FillObject* command several times to fill in your shadows. This process is the same approach that we used earlier when painting the model, so I hope that you are familiar with it by now. Remember that you can change the *MaskByCavity > Cavity Profile* curve to achieve different effects with the *Mask By Cavity* command and then use the mask to help apply lighting effects, and once you inverse the mask, some shadows as well. Go ahead and save your model now so that you don't accidentally lose it to a random power outage or surge.

Painting blood vessels

As a final touch to the eyeballs, I would like to try to draw in a few blood vessels in the eyeball's sclera. While I could just hand-draw the arteries, I think it might be more instructive to try to automate the process a bit. With that in mind, select the subtool that is the white part of the eyeball (the sclera). If you want to, you can isolate the sclera by SHIFT+clicking on the eye icon on the subtool layer, or you can simply press the *Transp* button. Once you have the eyeball subtool selected, click on the *Tool > Surface > Noise* command, which will open up the *NoiseMaker* pop-up window. Click on the *NoisePlug* to open up the plugin pop-up window. Put a checkmark next to *Erosion,* and then play with the different settings until you get something you like. For the demo, I set the *Magnitude* to 0.4, *Detail* to 3.0, and *Scale* to 1.1.

Once you have your settings in place, go ahead and press the OK button on the plugin pop-up window, and then press OK on the *Noise-Maker* window. Next, click on the *Tool > Surface > MaskByNoise* button, which will convert the *Noise* information that you just created into a mask on your currently selected subtool. After that, use CTRL+I to inverse the mask. I always like to turn off *Tool > Masking > ViewMask,* but this is optional. We are now ready to paint the eyeball while leveraging the mask.

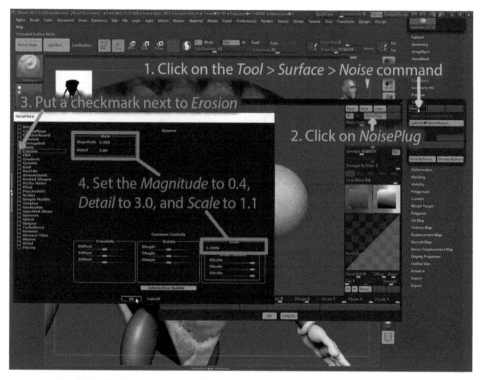

FIGURE 20.7 *To add a few blood vessels to the whites of the eye, click on the Tool > Surface > Noise command. Inside the NoiseMaker pop-up window, click on the NoisePlug to bring up another pop-up window. Put a checkmark next to Erosion and set the Magnitude to 0.4, Detail to 3.0, and Scale to 1.1.*

Pick a bright, blood-red color. Switch to your *Standard* brush and make sure that *Zadd* is off and *Rgb* mode is on. Set your *Rgb Intensity* to a high value and shrink your brush *Draw Size* down to a very small size (I used a *Draw Size* between 35 and 5 in the demo). Now, just gently brush in the red color, working from the back of the eyeball and then going forward. If you need to paint under the eyelids, you can turn on the *Transp* button to make the eyelids see-through. Remember that you are just creating a few spiderweb arteries in the eyeballs – not painting the whole thing red. It could be very difficult to draw this sort of spiderweb artery pattern by hand, but with the use of some basic masking tricks, it is no problem at all.

You can tone down the artery effect by sampling the color of the eyeball, lowering the *Rgb Intensity,* and painting some of the red out if you accidentally apply too much of it. Once you are finished with one eye, go ahead and repeat the process on the other eye. While you could theoretically duplicate and mirror the painted eyeball, the finished model will look better if you have some subtle variation so

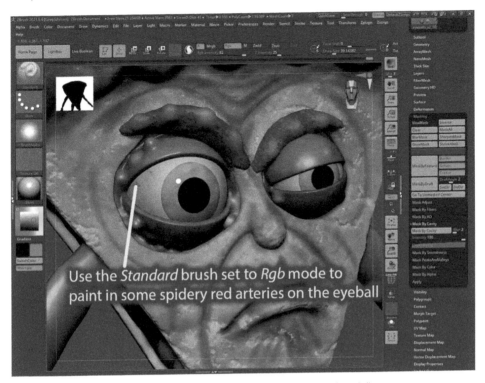

Use the *Standard* brush set to *Rgb* mode to paint in some spidery red arteries on the eyeball

FIGURE 20.8 Use the *Standard* brush set to *Rgb* mode to paint in some spidery red arteries on the eyeball.

that the two sides of your model are not perfect mirror images of one another. The other confounding factor to that approach is that we have our left and right eyeballs on this particular model scaled differently as well.

Organize your file

The last bit of preparation we should do before moving on is to go through our subtool list and make sure that all of the subtools are named appropriately. Use the *Tool > Subtool > Rename* command to rename any files that you need to. Basically, the goal is to be able to identify each subtool at a glance, so make sure that you have the hands and feet named "hands_feet_01" and the eyebrows named "eyebrows_01" for instance. Go ahead and merge any subtools that you need to, rename your subtools for easy identification, and then save your ZBrush model using the *Tool > Save As* command.

Conclusion

Take a moment and pat yourself on the back for a job well done! The model is now finished and complete. The character has been sculpted, the materials have all been applied, and the paint job is done. You have learned how to concept-sculpt a model using *DynaMesh*, as well as how to paint this model using a variety of different approaches. While there is certainly a lot more to be learned inside of ZBrush, you now have a solid foundation, which you can later expand upon at your leisure. That completes this chapter and the accompanying video session. Tune in next time as we completely shift gears and learn how to pose the character that we have built.

21

Posing

Introduction

This chapter describes the laborious yet straightforward process of combining everything and starting to pose the character. While there are a lot of different ways of doing this, the way I am going to show you is probably the easiest and most direct of all the methods that are out there. As always in ZBrush there are a multitude of ways and means of accomplishing anything – there are certainly faster methods, but the other approaches are a lot trickier or more difficult to set up. For instance, there is a whole *ZSphere* rigging process – but that can be rather frustrating to get correct. There is also the tried and true method of exporting your models into a third-party program such as Autodesk Maya for rigging and posing – but that gets you into the very complicated process of taking a high-resolution character and deriving a low-resolution version from it before you rig the model. This involved procedure is required because no other 3D package aside from ZBrush can handle the million-plus polygon count that ZBrush handles with such aplomb. Setting up the model correctly for that process takes a lot of work, and there is a high chance for things to go wrong the first time you do it. So, having tested all of the various methods, I thought a plain and simple process would be better for us at this point. While the approach we are going to use is a very robust solution that always works, it takes more work and effort. For an introductory-level book like this one, I thought it more appropriate to use something easy and reliable than something more advanced and complicated that runs a significant risk of malfunctioning. Now that you are really looking forward to things after that rousing speech, go ahead and load up your file, and let's get started using the *Transpose Line*.

DOI: 10.1201/9781003215288-21

Error checking

Let's take a look at our pie character and give the model a final once-over to see if any other errors still need to be addressed. For instance, whenever you *DynaMesh* a model, ZBrush will get rid of any assigned materials on that object. Since we dynameshed the eyelids in the last chapter, we can bet that ZBrush got rid of the material on the eyelids. Go ahead and select the eyelids subtool, and choose the material that you would like to use on this subtool. Now switch to the *Standard* brush, turn on the *Mrgb* button at the top of the screen, and then use the *Color > FillObject* command to fix the material on the eyelids. If you do not remember what material you used previously on the eyelids, simply hold down the left mouse button on top of the currently selected material icon and drag the mouse over to the purple gooey bits on your character to pick the material from the model on screen. An easy way to check and see if any of your subtools are missing materials is to click on the *Material* icon and pick one of the loudest and brightest materials on the material palette. I like to use the *NormalRGBMat* because its rainbow array of colors is very easy to spot, but you can use whatever material you like best. Just pick a material that is easy to notice. Once this material is chosen, any subtools that do not have a currently assigned material will show up as the bright material you have just chosen. In my case, I just have to see if any of the objects suddenly turn a rainbow bright.

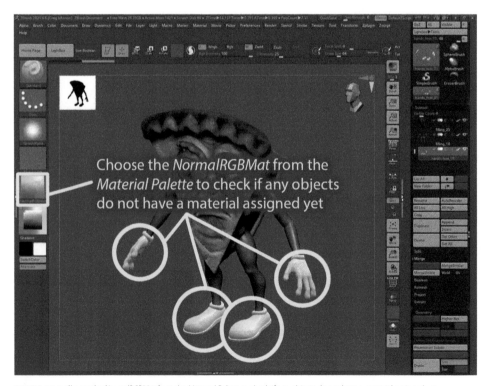

FIGURE 21.1 Choose the *NormalRGBMat* from the *Material Palette* to check if any objects do not have a material assigned yet.

If any object does turn into a rainbow, then simply select that object's subtool, pick the material that you want for the object, switch to your *Standard* brush, make sure that the *M* or *Mrgb* button is turned on, and use the *Color > FillObject* command to assign your chosen material to that subtool. If, for some reason, you want to remove the material from your model, all you have to do is assign the *Flat Color* material to it, which will get rid of any pre-existing materials applied to the model and restore the default behavior regarding materials to the object. However, you will need to switch to a different material to see the default behavior again.

Polygon count

One of the things that we have to be careful about when using the transpose method to pose a character is the total number of polygons, or polycount, in the model. If the polycount gets too high, then ZBrush can become sluggish or unresponsive. To check the polycount of a given subtool, simply rest your mouse icon over that subtool layer. A small pop-up window should appear, telling you exactly how many polys (i.e., polygons) the subtool has. If you find a subtool with way too many polygons, you can use *DynaMesh* to retopologize the model with a lower *Resolution* to reduce the number of polys in the subtool.

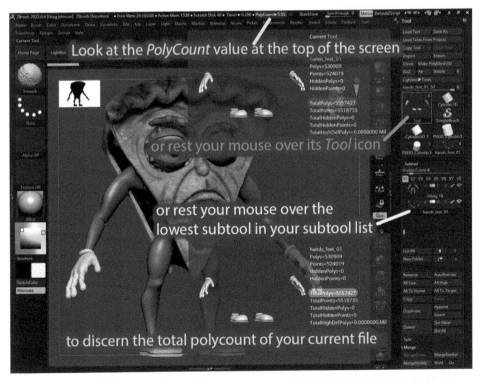

FIGURE 21.2 Look at the *PolyCount* value at the top of the screen, or rest your mouse over its *Tool* icon, or the lowest subtool in your subtool list, or to discern the total polycount of your current file.

To find out the total polygon count of all of your subtools, you can rest your mouse on top of the file's icon in the *Quickpick Tool Palette*, or you can select the bottommost subtool in your subtool list and rest your mouse icon on top of it. Either way will work. This action brings up a pop-up window that contains info about your subtool and model, including a *TotalPolys* amount for the entire file. Another simple way of finding out the total polycount is to just look at the very top of the ZBrush window. You should see a line of data there, including a *PolyCount* value.

The total polygon count of your model should come in under 30 million, which is probably a good deal lower than that. The pie character demo comes in at around 5.5 million, for example. ZBrush can handle some amazingly high polycounts. I once got one file with 99.9 million polygons! ZBrush was not happy about it, though. It is typical to end up with anywhere from 15 to 45 million polygons in the final assembled scene – but the higher that total polycount number rises, the more sluggish ZBrush becomes. If you get the total polycount number high enough, ZBrush will either become too unresponsive to work with or just crash. That said, no hard-and-fast number is the ceiling for your polycount. The exact maximum that your system will handle varies depending on how you have your computer set up, how much RAM it has, what other programs you are running in the background, and so forth. Still, these numbers should give you a sense of where the limits probably are.

You can use *DynaMesh* to drop the polycount of any subtool you choose by playing with the *DynaMesh > Resolution* slider and then dynameshing the model. You may need to make some tiny changes to the model to get *DynaMesh* to work. Sometimes *DynaMesh* will only update if the model has been modified in some way, shape, or form. You can always tweak something in a place no one will see. Even the smallest change usually works. Be careful that you don't reduce the polycount so much that you lose the detail that you have carved into the model.

The various pieces of your character should have the same polygon density – that is to say, the number of polygons should be evenly spread out across the whole of the model. If you turn on the *PolyF* button (SHIFT+f) you can see the polygon density for each subtool as you select them. You may have to zoom in a bit to get a good view. The wireframe should look the same for each subtool. Granted, some areas, such as the face or other high-detail parts, may need a bit more polygon density than others, but the overall polygon density should be more or less even across the model.

To sum up:

1. Make sure that your subtools do not have any problems.
2. Ensure that each subtool has roughly the same polygon density as the rest of the model.
3. Make sure that your computer can handle the total number of polygons in the scene.

Once you feel that your model meets these criteria, then it is time to proceed to the next step and unify your model's subtools. Save your tool just in case there is a problem during the next phase.

Merging subtools

To combine all of the subtools, you can simply select the topmost sub-tool and use the *Tool > Subtool > Merge > MergeDown* command. Successively merge each subtool down until all of the subtools have been merged. Alternatively, you can try the *Zplugin > SubTool Master > Merge* command.

After ZBrush takes its time calculating the results, it will create a new tool in the tool palette called "Merged_" plus the original tool name. You absolutely must keep in mind that ZBrush will sometimes place the result of a major operation into a brand new tool in the *Tool Palette* while leaving you with the old model still selected and on screen! If you forget this fact, then you can easily end up clicking on the same command multiple times, thinking that the operation did not work correctly. Each time you click the command, ZBrush adds another new tool containing the results to the *Tool Palette*. Whenever you execute

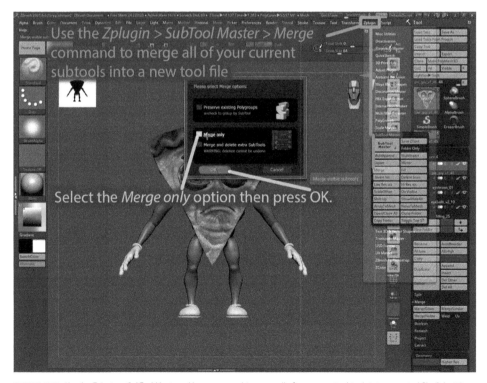

FIGURE 21.3 Use the *Zplugin > SubTool Master > Merge* command to merge all of your current subtools into a new tool file. Select the *Merge only* option, and then press *OK*.

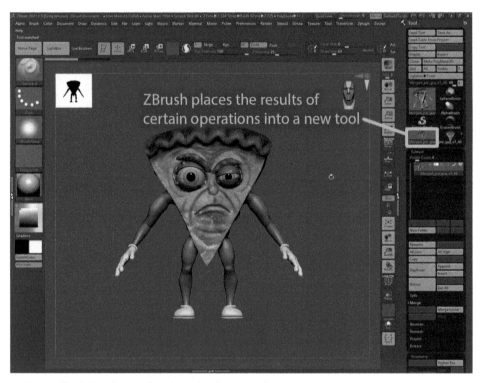

ZBrush places the results of certain operations into a new tool

FIGURE 21.4 ZBrush places the results of certain operations into a new tool.

a command in brush and do not see the results, check the *Tool Palette* and see if a new tool containing the output of the operation has been placed there. You will need to select the new tool to work on the results of the operation. For example, the *Zplugin > SubTool Master > Merge* command copies all of your subtools, merges everything, and then puts the result into a different tool. Go ahead and make sure that you have the new tool selected, and use the *Tool > Save As* command to save the file. When I do this, I usually start a new numbering sequence for the file using the same name. If "pie_guy_v1_21.ztl" was the previous file name, the new file containing the merged subtools will be "pie_guy_v2_01.ztl" or something similar to that effect.

Adding a model as a subtool

You can also merge a different model from another file into your current tool. To demonstrate, I will add a butter knife model that I created as part of the bonus video material for this book. You can find the video for how to make the butter knife inside of ZBrush on my website (www.GregTheArtist.com) or on the book publisher's website. To add in a new model file, you must first open up the file. Go ahead and use the *Tool > Load Tool* command to open up the "butter_knife_DEMO.ztl" file. Press *Open* once you have the proper file selected. The butter knife

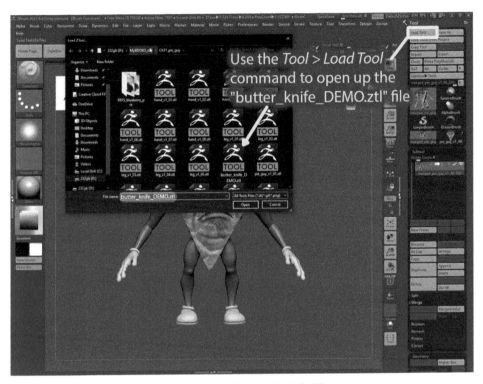

FIGURE 21.5 Use the *Tool* > *Load Tool* command to open up the "butter_knife_DEMO.ztl" file.

model will automatically replace the tool you are currently viewing once it loads up. No problem, though. Simply use the Tool Palette to switch back to your pie character tool.

Turn on the *Floor* button on the ZBrush sidebar so you can see the ground underneath the character, and check the small *CamView* head orientation guide in the upper right-hand corner of the background. Double-check that your character is facing the front, i.e., your character's face should be looking in the same direction as the *CamView* head, and the character's feet should be on the floor. If, for some reason, your model is not oriented correctly, then you can use the *Gizmo 3D* to reorientate your character now before things get more complicated. Click on the *Tool* > *Subtool* >*Append* command and select the "butter_knife" tool to add the butter_knife to your current scene as a new subtool.

This process will add the butter knife model to your pie character. You will quickly notice that you have a scaling problem and maybe an orientation issue, too, with the new subtool. These problems are easy enough to fix. To fix this scaling issue and set the character model and the butter knife to the same unified scale, I first need to know how big each item would be in real life. The butter knife from my kitchen measures about 7 inches (18 cm) long, give or take a bit. A standard pie ranges from 9 to 10 inches (roughly 23–25 cm) in diameter, which

Click on the *Tool > Subtool >Append* command and select the "butter_knife" tool to add the butter knife into your current tool as a new subtool

FIGURE 21.6 Click on the *Tool > Subtool >Append* command and select the "butter_knife" tool to add the butter knife into your current scene as a new subtool.

means that a slice of the pie should be somewhere in the 4–- to 5-inch range (10–13 cm) very roughly, which is enough to establish a basic size correlation between the pie character and the butter knife models. Basically, it means that the knife should be a bit bigger than the pie character. Of course, the so-called "Rule of Cool" trumps most measurements – if it looks good, go with it. To actually scale the knife, simply select the butter_knife subtool, switch to the *Gizmo 3D*, and then click and drag on the yellow square at the center of the gizmo to scale the butter knife. Go ahead and save your tool before we go any further.

Unlock the *Gizmo 3D* and reposition it relative to the model so that the gizmo is centered on the knife. Repositioning the *Gizmo 3D* will make it easier to maneuver and place into the character's hands. Take a moment and think about what pose you want your character to have. It might help to grab a broomstick and pose with it yourself for a few minutes. Get a friend to take a few pictures of yourself posing. You can then use your favorite picture as a reference for your character's final pose. With your reference image in mind, use the *Gizmo 3D* to move and rotate the butter knife into position. Remember to move your viewpoint around while you adjust the knife's position to make sure that it goes exactly where you want it to.

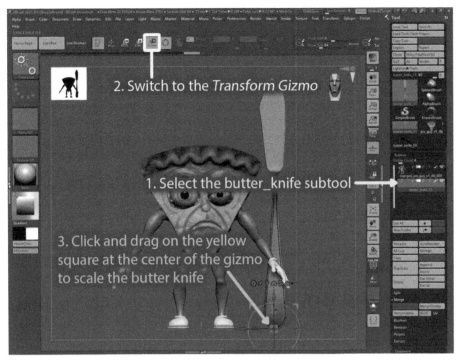

FIGURE 21.7 Select the butter_knife subtool, switch to the *Gizmo 3D*, and then click and drag on the yellow square at the center of the gizmo to scale the butter knife.

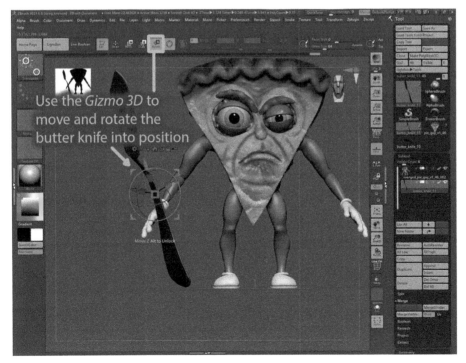

FIGURE 21.8 Use the *Gizmo 3D* to move and rotate the butter knife into position.

Posing the character

To pose the character, select the merged character subtool from the *Tool > Subtool* list, and then use the *Gizmo 3D* to rotate the character a bit. Generally speaking, people do not stand with equal weight on both feet. Folks tend to use one foot to carry their weight more than the other. With this in mind, rotate the character a bit to duplicate the angle of the hips that the character will need for the pose that you have chosen. When you are posing a character like this, it can be a good idea to start from the character's center of gravity (i.e., their hips) and work outward from there, posing each piece in turn. Make sure that you do not have any masks on the character when you are doing this – you do not want to leave a portion of the character behind when you rotate it.

Using the TransPose line

To start moving the character's limbs around, you first want to mask off everything that you are not trying to pose. Turn on *Rotate*, but then turn off the *Gizmo 3D* by pressing the Y keyboard shortcut, which will

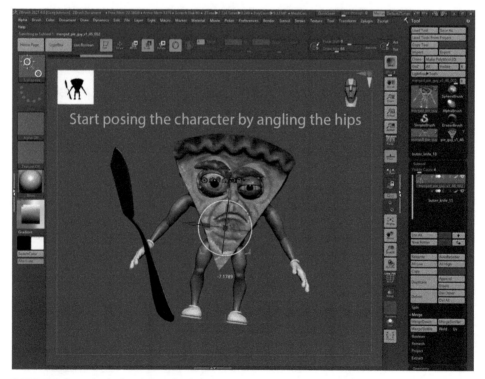

FIGURE 21.9 Start posing the character by angling the hips.

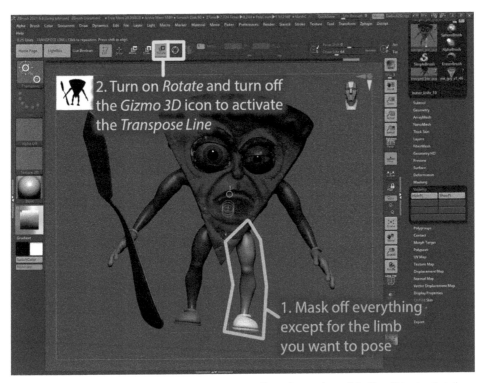

FIGURE 21.10 Mask off everything except for the limb you want to pose. Turn on *Rotate* and turn off the *Gizmo 3D* icon to activate the *Transpose Line*.

activate the *Transpose Line* interface. The *Transpose Line* is a powerful interface for positioning your object, but it does take a bit of getting used to due to its unique interface (which is why many users prefer the *Gizmo 3D* instead).

To use the *Transpose Line*, simply hold down the left mouse button and drag out the *Transpose Line*, starting at the hip joint and ending at the ankle. If you mess up, simply try again. Unlike using the *Gizmo3D*, it makes a huge difference which of the transformation buttons you have active, so make sure that you have the *Rotate* button active and not the *Scale* or *Move* button. You can move the *Transpose Line* itself by clicking and dragging on the dotted transpose line itself or the central orange circle – make sure that you click on the orange circle itself and not inside of it. Clicking and dragging on the orange circle at either end will let you reposition those circles. Clicking inside one of the end circles will rotate the object around the distant end of the *Transpose Line*. We can use masking plus this function of the *Transpose Line* to pose our characters.

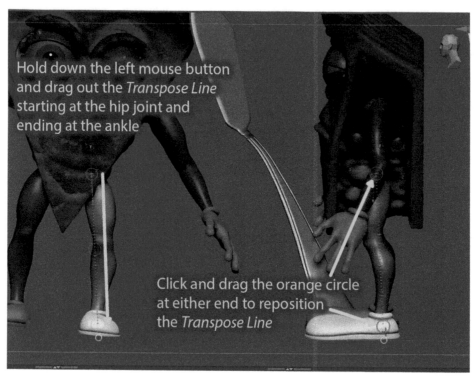

Hold down the left mouse button and drag out the *Transpose Line* starting at the hip joint and ending at the ankle

Click and drag the orange circle at either end to reposition the *Transpose Line*

FIGURE 21.11 Hold down the left mouse button and drag out the *Transpose Line* starting at the hip joint and ending at the ankle. Click and drag the orange circle at either end to reposition the transpose line.

There are a number of additional features built into the *Transpose Line*, which you can discover by holding down the ALT key while experimenting with the transpose line. If you rotate the object using the transpose line while holding down SHIFT, it will snap the rotations to 5° increments. If you have trouble with the *Transpose Line* you can opt to use the Gizmo3D instead. To do so, make sure that the *Gizmo 3D* button is active (you can use the Y shortcut toggle), hold down the ALT key, and click on the object where you want to place the *Gizmo 3D*. You can refine the position of the *Gizmo 3D* by unlocking it and changing its location as needed. Once correctly placed, just click and drag the circle portion of the *Gizmo 3D* to rotate the object.

Once you have positioned the *Transpose Line* properly, you can click inside of the orange circle at the foot end to rotate the leg into position. Alternatively, if you are using the *Gizmo 3D*, you can click and drag on one of the rotation circles to rotate the leg. Keep in mind that you cannot undo placing the *Transpose Line*, which means that you need to be careful and patient when adjusting it. Another issue to consider is that when you pose the model this way, you will inevitably need to clean up the geometry afterward and fix any problems posed by the model.

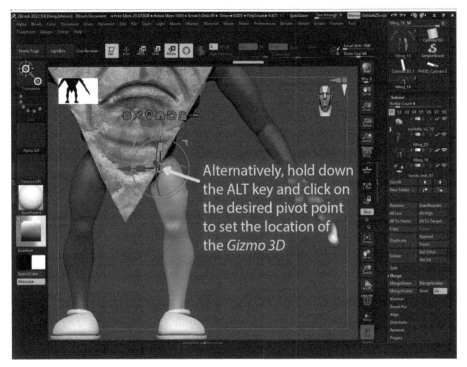

FIGURE 21.12 Alternatively, hold down the ALT key and click on the desired pivot point to set the location of the *Gizmo 3D*.

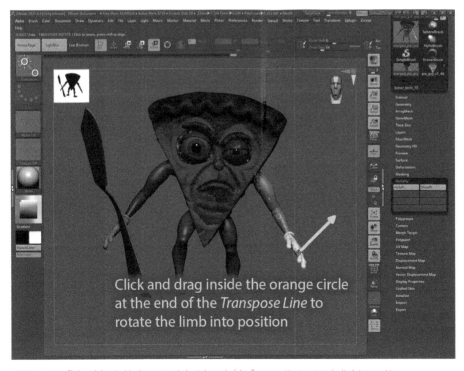

FIGURE 21.13 Click and drag inside the orange circle at the end of the *Transpose Line* to rotate the limb into position.

Posing process summary

To summarize the process:

1. Mask off the model, leaving only the part you wish to pose unmasked.
2. Turn on *Rotate* mode using the R shortcut key.
3. Use the Y shortcut toggle to turn off the *Gizmo 3D* button.
4. Draw out a *Transpose Line* starting where you wish the bend to occur. Usually, you begin at a joint in the limb and end at the distal end of the limb.
5. Click and drag inside the orange circle at the end of the *Transpose Line* to rotate the limb into position. Once you are done posing the limb, you can press the Q shortcut to switch back into *Draw* mode and clean up any problematic geometry.
6. Repeat this process for each limb of your model until you have finished creating the character pose that you desire.
7. Remember to save your progress frequently and iteratively.

It is quite easy to make a mistake while doing this. It pays to be cautious and patient while displaying your character. Remember to save frequently!

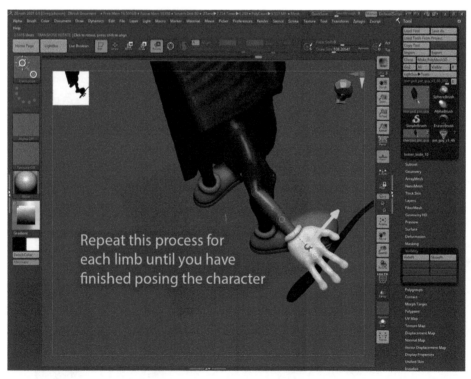

FIGURE 21.14 Repeat this process for each limb until you have finished posing the character.

Pay close attention to your masks while posing your model. It is easy
to miss masking a portion of the model and get unexpected results.
One easy method to avoid this issue is to mask out the portion of the
model you want to bend and then invert the mask using the CTRL+I
shortcut. Another useful trick is to move your viewpoint around while
placing the *Transpose Line* to ensure that you line up the *Transpose
Line* correctly. Typically, the *Transpose Line* takes the place of the bone
inside the limb. So, to rotate the arm, you would place one end of
the *Transpose Line* where the ball socket of the humerus lies and the
other end of the *Transpose Line* at the wrist joint. Then, you just grab
the *Transpose Line* at the wrist and rotate the arm into place. Next, you
would mask off the arm down to the elbow and draw a new *Transpose Line* starting at the elbow and ending at the wrist, then grab the
Transpose Line at the wrist again and rotate the lower arm into position. When posing, try to work from the center of gravity outward. So
you pose the character's body first, then begin rotating the limbs into
position, starting with the legs as a whole at the hip joint, then moving
to the knee joints, and finally to the ankles and feet. Similarly, you start
by positioning the entire arm, then the lower arm, then the hand, then
the fingers.

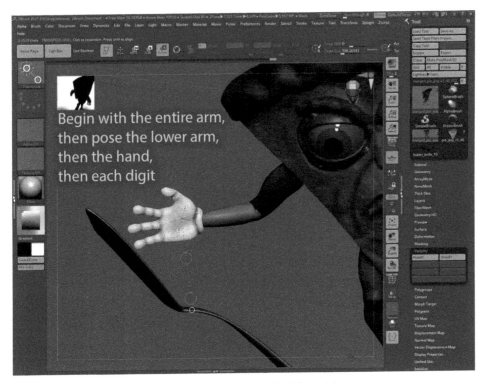

FIGURE 21.15 Begin with the entire arm, then pose the lower arm, then the hand, then each digit.

Forward and inverse kinematics

The process we are using is known as forward kinematics. Forward kinematics uses the position and orientation of the model and its various joints and pivot points to control the pose of the character. It is not the only possible approach to posing a character. In fact, there are numerous alternate ways to pose a character, including using inverse kinematics, where you simply place the ends of an articulated skeleton into position, and the rest of the model's position is automatically calculated. The benefit of using forward kinematics as covered herein is that it is very simple to implement. You just need a good degree of patience to get the masking and *Transpose Line* approach to work. Inverse kinematics, using a *ZSphere* skeletal rig, for instance, requires a great deal more setup and is much more prone to technical error – which is why we used the approach that we have. That said, I encourage you to explore the other methodologies for posing characters available at your own leisure.

We need to make the character hold onto the butter knife prop that we have created for him. Switch to the knife subtool and carefully place it into the character's hand using the *Gizmo 3D*. Once the knife has been correctly positioned, you can carefully wrap the character's fingers around the knife handle so that the character holds it properly.

FIGURE 21.16 Switch to the knife subtool and carefully place it into the character's hand.

Placing the dead fish model into the scene

Now would be an appropriate time to place the dead fish model into our scene to make sure that the character, the knife, and the dead fish all work together in a functional composition. If I were to continue posing the pie model, I could easily end up having to repose the character later to make the fish fit into the scene – and I hate having to redo work. Find your dead fish ZTL file and load it into ZBrush. Merge all of the subtool components of the dead fish to make it easier to import the model into the character file. Save this model as a new ZTL file so you don't lose it accidentally. Use the *Tool > Subtool > Append* command to add the dead fish model to the file containing our character model and butter knife. Select the dead fish subtool and use the *Gizmo 3D* to fix the model's scale and position the dead fish in relation to the character and the knife. Remember to save the combined ZBrush file.

Once you have the fish positioned, select the character subtool and finish posing it. I make liberal use of hiding and revealing different portions of the model while I mask off the various portions of the model by using SHIFT+CTRL and clicking. Adjust the character's right leg and foot so they rest on the top of the fish.

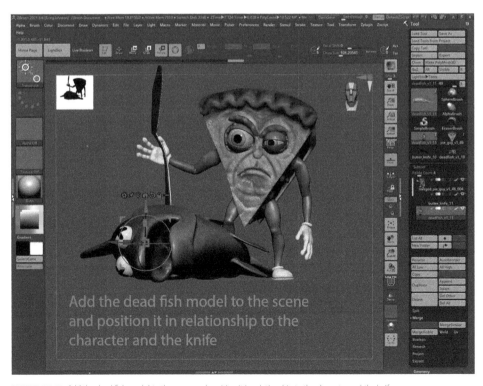

FIGURE 21.17 Add the dead fish model to the scene and position it in relationship to the character and the knife.

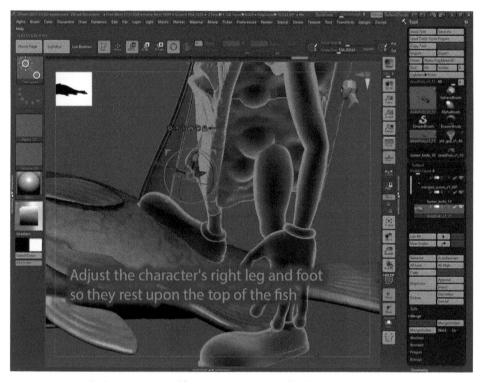

FIGURE 21.18 Adjust the character's right leg and foot so they rest upon the top of the fish.

Grabbing the prop

Next, I turn the knife around so that it is embedded in the dead fish, and then proceed to wrap the character's fingers around the knife handle. You can adjust the fingers as a group once you have them masked off, basically rotating the three fingers as a group and then tweaking each finger individually afterward. Unfortunately, there is no push-button solution for posing your character. No matter what technique you use, it always takes a certain amount of fiddling and massaging to get the results that you want. This particular approach just requires patience, care, and a substantial amount of tweaking.

Pose the fingers by progressively masking off the joints, working from the hand out to the fingertips.

Final touch up

Once you have finished posing the character, you should go in with the *Smooth* brush, *Move* brush, and *Inflate* brush to fix any problems with the geometry that you may have accidentally created while posing the character. The necessity of touching up the model is one of the significant downsides of the masking and transposing technique. Still, this approach is completely rock solid and free of the technical

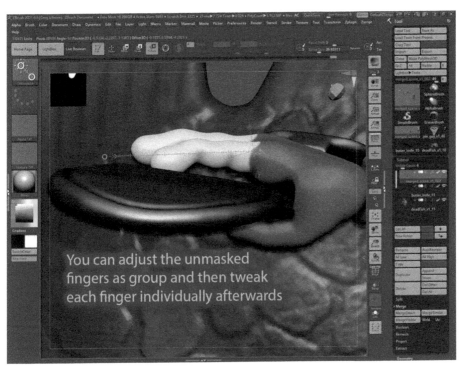

FIGURE 21.19 You can adjust the unmasked fingers as a group and then tweak each finger individually afterward.

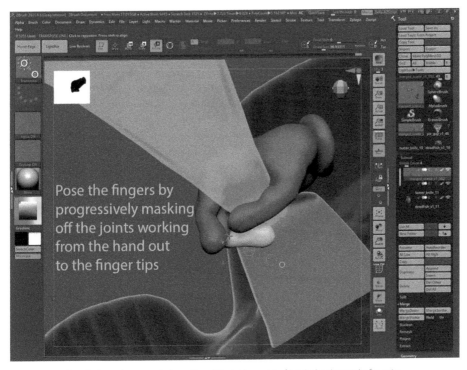

FIGURE 21.20 Pose the fingers by progressively masking off the joints, working from the hand out to the fingertips.

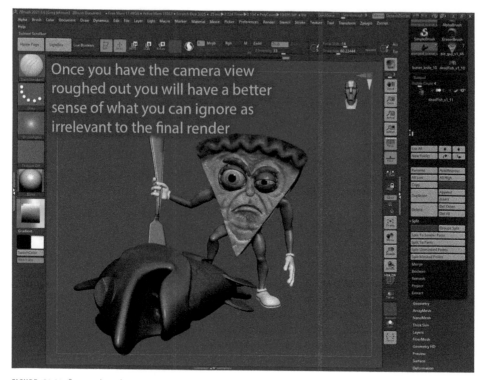

FIGURE 21.21 Once you have the camera view roughed out, you will have a better sense of what you can ignore as irrelevant to the final render.

glitches that can plague inverse kinematics. Take your time, pay attention to the details, and save your progress frequently. Keep in mind the general principle that if you aren't going to see it, you don't need to worry about it, which will save you from wasting time on aspects of the model that really aren't important to the final image. With this principle in mind, take a minute and sort out a good camera view for the final render. Once you have the camera view roughed out, you will have a better sense of what you can ignore as irrelevant to the final render.

Conclusion

Now that we have added the various props and posed the character, we are really getting close to the end of our project. Working in ZBrush is always a challenge. There are always unexpected things that come up when working in 3D, complex issues that you have to solve, but the more you practice, the better you will become at quickly resolving any problems that appear. Hopefully, you are enjoying this process and having lots of fun. ZBrush provides great power for artists to leverage and create whatever they can imagine – but the program does have a steep learning curve, and working in 3D can be quite difficult. Be patient, save your file frequently, and work diligently, and you will see great results.

22

Lighting

Introduction

In this chapter, we establish the camera and add lights to our scene in preparation for the final render. Working with cameras in ZBrush is quite a simple process and one that we can quickly accomplish. On the other hand, ZBrush's lighting system is a good bit more complicated and further hindered by the unusual and non-standard interface for managing lights that ZBrush uses. Nevertheless, we will navigate those treacherous waters and get you proficient with lighting inside of ZBrush by the end of the chapter. As part of the lighting process, we will explore a professional lighting setup widely known as three-point lighting and the various types of lights used in 3D rendering. By the end of this chapter, you should be ready to proceed to rendering and compositing, which form the final portions of the book.

Camera

Creating a good camera vantage point begins with creating a good composition of our scene objects. Luckily, we have already done most of this work while posing the character with the knife and the fish in the earlier chapter. Composition is one of the fundamental art skills that you MUST know if you want to be a good visual artist. While well outside the subject of this book, you can learn the critical concepts of composition in any good college course on 2D design fundamentals. I strongly recommend acquiring a copy of the book *Creative Illustration* by Andrew Loomis and reading pages 24–54 of part one, where Loomis writes about the principles of composition. This chapter will provide an invaluable aid to your art skills. In addition, some very

DOI: 10.1201/9781003215288-22

FIGURE 22.1 Press the *Draw* > *Store Cam* button, and then give the new camera a name.

interesting PDF books on composition, drawing, sculpture, and other art-related topics can be found at the Internet Archive (https://archive.org/) with a quick search of their "always available" collections.

More specific to ZBrush, establishing a camera is a fairly straightforward process due to the fairly new ZBrush *Universal Camera*. This camera is much improved over what ZBrush was capable of just a few versions ago. The *Universal Camera* will enable you to closely match the performance of a film camera with standardized camera settings in a way that the older camera system just really couldn't do. While an extended discussion of camera settings is outside of our purview for this book, suffice it to say that we simply want to store a camera view and come back to it later. To do so, first, you need to set up the shot that you desire by orbiting your current viewpoint until you have a satisfying view, then press the *Draw* > *Store Cam* button. A small pop-up window will appear asking you to "Please enter a new name" for your camera so that ZBrush can save that camera view. Name this camera "Painting1" and press enter to complete this task. Whatever name you used for the camera will now show up as a saved camera name in the *Draw* menu.

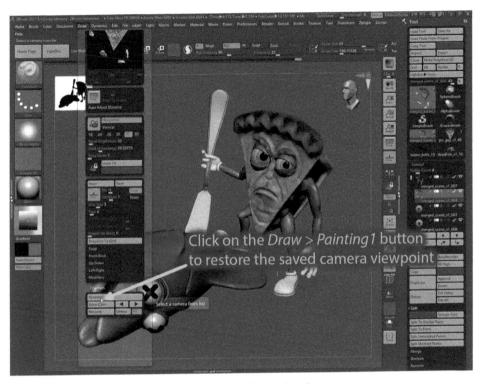

FIGURE 22.2 Click on the *Draw > Painting1* button to restore the saved camera viewpoint.

You can now change your viewpoint and take on whatever tasks in ZBrush you need to. To go back to the saved camera view, just click on the *Draw > Painting1* button.

Another useful camera trick is the ability to lock the camera in place so that you do not accidentally move it while you are working. To do this, activate the *Lock Camera* button to prevent the camera viewpoint from being changed. Locking the camera in place is extremely useful when you are trying to render out a sequence of images. It allows you to do things such as change the materials of your object, adjust the lights, and perform other similar tweaks without messing up your camera view.

There is, of course, a lot more to the camera in ZBrush. Inside the *Draw* menu, you can change the type of lens the camera uses, play with your focal length, and change the crop factor. All of these settings will allow you to really get in there and closely match the specific camera settings of a real camera. All of these are very useful if you are trying to do photographic compositing. When you save a ZBrush project using the *File > Save* or *Save As* button, ZBrush will embed the camera information into that saved file.

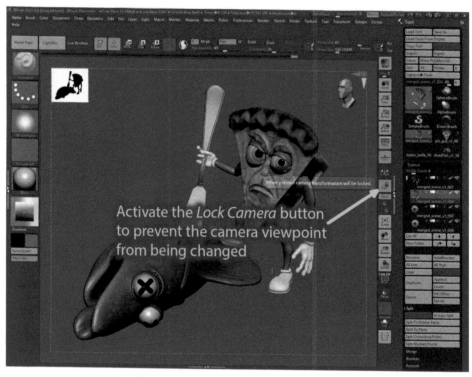

FIGURE 22.3 Activate the *Lock Camera* button to prevent the camera viewpoint from being changed.

The background image

We now need to check and see how this ZBrush image is going to be composites with a background image. To prepare for this step, I went out and took a bunch of photographs of an old stovetop I had access to. I thought the old stove looked kind of cool and would work well as an appropriate backdrop for the angry pie character. While taking these hundreds of photos, I moved around a bit for each photo, changing the viewpoint slightly between each shot. Since I wasn't sure what the ZBrush composition was going to be and because I didn't have access at the time to my ZBrush files to check the camera angles, I compensated by simply taking an enormous amount of photos from every conceivable camera angle that might work, figuring that one of the resulting images would serve our purpose. After coming home from that trip, I carefully reviewed the photographs that I had taken, and I found this image, which I think would be a perfect backdrop for our piece of pie.

To check and see if the background image will work with our model, you should first open up your background image and place it behind ZBrush. Now lock the camera in place inside of ZBrush. Then, use the *See-through* slider, located in the upper right corner of ZBrush, to make

FIGURE 22.4 Picture of an old stove top to be used as a background image for the final render.

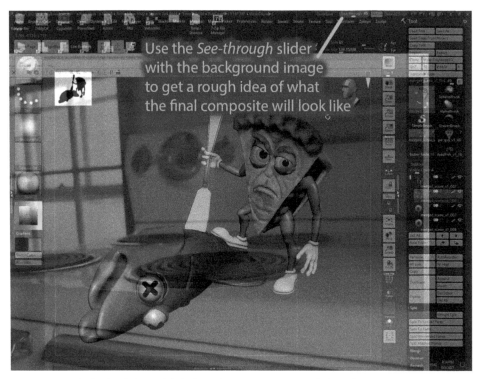

FIGURE 22.5 Use the *See-through* slider with the background image to get a rough idea of what the final composite will look like.

ZBrush transparent enough to see the image behind it. Next, you can adjust the position of the background image on your monitor behind ZBrush to get a rough preview of what that background image will look like when it gets composited behind the ZBrush model. Using the *See-through* slider provides a simple way to get a quick visualization of what the final rendering will look like after we composite everything together inside Photoshop.

Lighting setup

We now need to add lights to our scene. To get started, double-click on the left side *Divider* to open up the *Left Tray*, which will give us some space on the interface to place the lighting user interface elements.

After doing this, you should see the default *Brush* palette in the left-hand tray. To close this default palette, click on the small icon just to the right of the word *Brush* at the top of the palette. Now we have a nice black tray, which we can use for our purposes!

We shall now make use of this blank tray. Open up the *Light* palette, click and hold down on the small icon in the top left-hand corner of the palette, and then drag this palette into the *Left Tray*. Let go of the

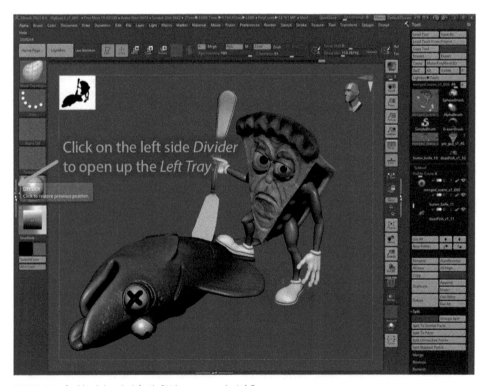

FIGURE 22.6 Double-click on the left side *Divider* to open up the *Left Tray*.

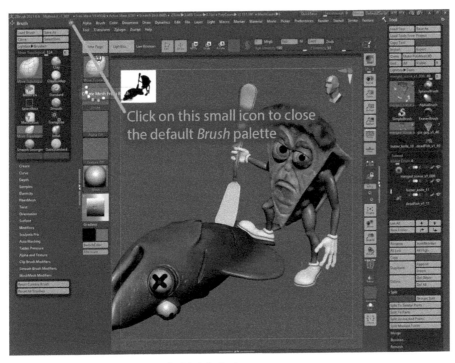

FIGURE 22.7 Click on this small icon to close the default *Brush* palette.

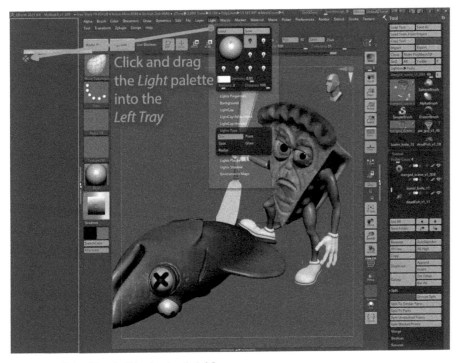

FIGURE 22.8 Click and drag the *Light* palette into the *Left Tray*.

mouse button to finish the job. We now have our *Light* palette placed in the *Left Tray*. Now, we can get down to the business of lighting and rendering.

Lighting basics

Lighting is rather complicated in 3-D, and ZBrush is no exception to this. In keeping with ZBrush's unusual nature, though, a lot of its lighting process is rather divergent from that found in other 3-D programs. At the top of the *Light* palette in our *Left Tray,* you should see a sphere next to a series of small lightbulbs. Each lightbulb represents a single light in the scene. Any lightbulb that is highlighted in orange is turned on and affects the ZBrush model in the scene. ZBrush can have up to eight active lights in a scene. The sphere provides a quick preview of each light's effect. Below these icons are the controls for *Intensity*, *Ambient*, and *Distance*. The lightbulb that has a thin gray border surrounding its icon is the light that is currently adjustable using the controls. Strangely enough, whether or not a lightbulb is turned on or not has no bearing on whether the light is now being adjusted. To select a light for adjustment, simply click on its lightbulb icon. You should see the thin gray border appear around that lightbulb. If you click on the same lightbulb again, it will be highlighted in orange and turn

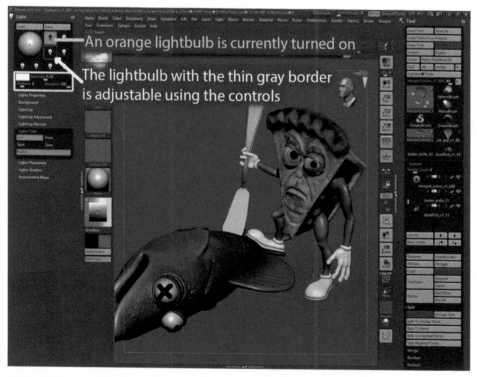

FIGURE 22.9 An orange lightbulb is currently turned on. The lightbulb with the thin gray border is adjustable using the controls.

on. Pressing the lightbulb a third time will turn it back off. I suggest taking a few minutes and familiarizing yourself with how the lightbulb buttons work. This interface is one of the many wildly nonstandard interfaces found within ZBrush and can take a bit of getting used to.

To change the position of a light, you first need to take a few steps so that you can see the results of your adjustments. Make sure that you have one of the *Standard Materials* on the object. A *Standard Material* can either be applied to your object or merely selected, but it must show up on the scene object. Remember that all of the *MatCap Materials* have their own lighting baked in, and any scene lights that you add will not affect an object with a MatCap material on it at all. Now, select the lightbulb and make sure that it is turned on. The lightbulb icon should turn a bright orange and have a thin gray border around it. Next, to move the light, click and drag on the small gray sphere in the *Light* menu, which will change the position of the light in the scene. You should be able to see the results in the main *Document* viewport. It is easier to see the effects of lighting with certain *Standard Materials* such as *BasicMaterial*, *Blinn*, *SkinShade4*, *SoftPlastic*, or *ToyPlastic*. There *are* a few *Standard Materials*, such as *NormalRGBMat* and *FlatColor* that will not display the lights no matter what you do. The small preview sphere in the *Light* menu will offer you a quick preview of what the scene will look like as you work.

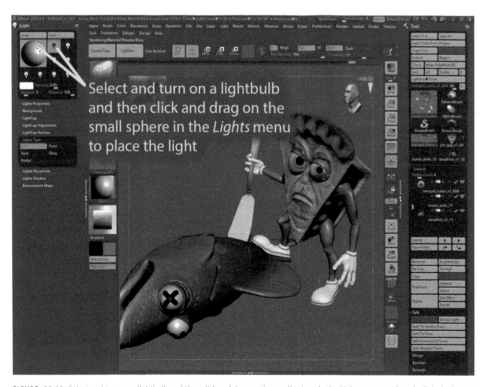

FIGURE 22.10 Select and turn on a lightbulb and then click and drag on the small sphere in the *Lights* menu to place the light in the scene.

Matching a photographic reference

Since we are going to be inserting our scary pie character into a photo-graph, it behooves us to take a look at the photograph I will be using so we can match the lighting in the photo. The light in the picture is com-ing in from three different locations. One light source is the window in the background. The other two sources show up as strong highlights in the metal rim of the stovetop burner. Being the person who took the photo helps at this point since I know that there was a window on both the right and opposite walls of the stove where those highlights came from, but you can still determine the lighting by simply observing those highlights. Now we have some idea of the lighting solution that we want to mimic in ZBrush for our character.

Three-point lighting

Coincidentally, the lights in the photograph offer a rough approxima-tion of a standard three-point lighting setup. Three-point lighting is a widely used technique that employs three different light sources strategically positioned to illuminate the subject. This approach pro-vides very effective control over the shading and shadows in the scene

FIGURE 22.11 One obvious light source is the window, while the highlights reveal the other light sources.

and can create a multitude of different results depending on how it is employed. The components of a three-point lighting setup include a key light, a fill light, and a backlight. Each of these lights will have different settings for color, intensity, position, and angle.

Key light

The primary light in a three-point lighting setup is the key light. The key light is the brightest light, is typically positioned at a 45° angle from the camera, and illuminates the subject directly from a raised position. You can move the key light around to get different effects – to either side or higher or lower.

Back light

The backlight acts to separate the subject from the background by creating a rim of light around the edge of the subject. The back light is usually placed behind and above the subject, pointing directly at it, usually from the directly opposite side of the key light.

Fill light

The fill light is a secondary light source, dimmer than the key light, that acts to fill in the dark shadows created by the key light on the other side of the subject. The fill light is positioned on the other side of the camera from the key light, usually at a 90° angle from the key light.

When using a three-point lighting setup, you will want to turn off the ambient light. Ambient light is artificial light that permeates the entire scene. It is meant to represent light bouncing off of other objects in the room. Ambient light can spoil an otherwise good lighting setup if not taken into account, so you will want to take firm control over it in your scene. Start by turning it off and seeing how the scene looks without it. Only if you think the scene needs some ambient light should you slowly bring it back in.

The last step is adjusting the lights. Once you have all your light sources set up, you can begin tweaking and adjusting the lights to achieve the sort of mood and ambiance that you are looking for in your scene. You can change the strength of the various lights, adjust their position, and even add some color to the lights – though be careful with color! A little bit of color goes a LONG way when lighting.

Types of lights

There are several different types of light in ZBrush available in the *Light > Lights Type* palette. *Sun* provides light coming in from infinitely far away in a bunch of parallel beams and is a good type of light to

Three Point Lighting

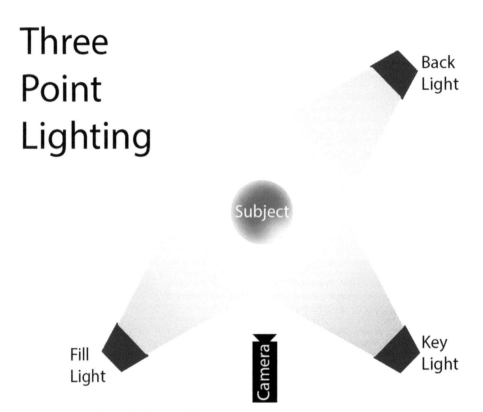

Back Light

Subject

Fill Light

Camera

Key Light

FIGURE 22.12 Layout for a standard three-point lighting setup.

work with as it's very quick and easy for the computer to calculate. Another type of light is the point light, so called because it is just a point in space emitting light. The spot-type light acts like a stage spotlight. The glow and radial lights are a bit weird. While you can find a sun light, a point light, and a spotlight in most 3D packages, glow and radial type lights are rarer. A glow light is rather like a point light, but with the addition of a glow radius setting that offers additional control over the illumination. A radial light affects the opposite side of the object rather than the side facing the light. Feel free to play with the different types of lights and see what they do and how each variety of light affects the lighting in the scene.

Create the key light

To mimic the lights in the photograph, I will start by placing the key light slightly up and to the right of the sphere. Doing so will make the light come in from an ~45° angle from the camera and a 45° angle from the horizontal. I will also drop the *Ambient* slider down to 0. The ambient light provides a sort of overall glow to the scene. When I'm

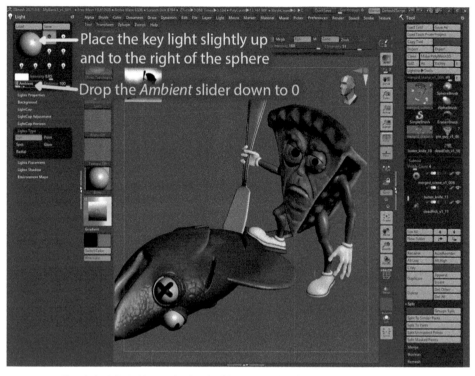

FIGURE 22.13 Place the key light slightly up and to the right of the sphere and drop the *Ambient* slider down to 0.

setting up lights, I turn the ambient light off to start with. You can always add some ambient light later on, if you think the scene needs it.

Add the back light

Start by turning off the key light. Simply click on the key light's lightbulb icon and turn the icon from orange to gray. That way, you can easily see what effect the backlight has once you turn it on. To add the backlight to our scene, simply turn on a different lightbulb in the *Light* menu. Make sure that this new light has its *Light Type* set to *Sun*. Go to the preview sphere in the *Light* menu, hold down ALT, and click on the background behind the *Light* menu preview sphere. Doing so will place the light behind the sphere, basically shoving the light behind your scene object. Now, the light will still point at your model – it will just do it from the far side of the model. This odd method is how you place a light behind an object in ZBrush. Next, move the light to the other side of the sphere, opposite to where you placed the key light. You can now adjust the backlight's *Intensity* slider. I used an *Intensity* of 0.7 for this demo. Remember to check and make sure that the *Ambient* slider is set to 0.

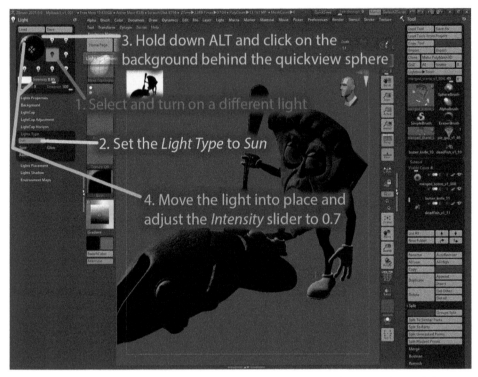

FIGURE 22.14 Select and turn on a different light for the backlight. Set the *Light Type* to *Sun*. Hold down ALT and click on the background behind the preview sphere. Move the light into place and adjust the *Intensity* slider to 0.7.

Make a fill light

To make a fill light, we should start by turning off all existing lights currently in the scene. Unfortunately, ZBrush lights aren't color-coded, named, or anything that might make each light easier to identify. You will just have to remember which lights you have used for the key light and the backlight. Select and turn on a third light in the *Light* menu. Set the *Light Type* to *Sun* once more. The *Ambient* slider should be set to 0. Change the *Intensity* slider to a value less than the *Intensity* of the key light. A low *Intensity* value for the fill light will look more dramatic, but a higher intensity may well look more aesthetically pleasing. Since we are trying to match a photographic background, I used an *Intensity* value of 0.2. Place this fill light on the opposite side of the sphere from the key light, but keep this fill light in the foreground (unlike what we did for the backlight).

You can click on the white color swatch next to the *Light > Intensity* slider and adjust the color of the selected light, but I recommend being really, really, really super careful when doing so. Strongly colored lights can easily overwhelm your scene very, very quickly. If you are going to color a light, it is best to be very subtle. That said, adding a slight blue

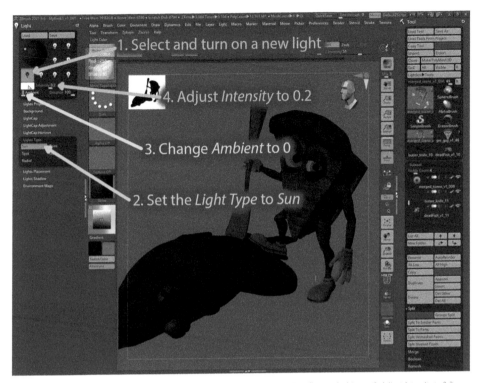

FIGURE 22.15 Select and turn on a new light for the fill light. Set the *Light Type* to *Sun*. Change *Ambient* to 0. Adjust *Intensity* to 0.2.

tint to fill light and a touch of warm yellow or orange to the key light can be quite efficacious. Try it out and see what you think!

Lighting results

Go ahead and turn on the key light, the fill light, and the backlight to see how these three lights work together to light your model. You can now go back into any one of the lights to tweak its intensity, color, or type. Do so a few times and observe how the changes affect the final lighting outcome.

Saving the lights

You can actually save out just the lights as a separate file using the *Light > Save* feature and then using the *Light > Load* button to bring your custom lighting setup back into ZBrush later on. Go ahead and save your lights now. Now would be a great time to use the *File > Save As* button to save a new iteration of your entire ZBrush scene to record your camera, model, materials, lights, and everything else. Remember that it is always a great idea to have multiple copies of your important files!

FIGURE 22.16 Turn on your key, fill, and backlight to see the final effect.

Conclusion

This lecture wraps up the demo on lighting in ZBrush. You have now learned how to set up a robust and functional three-point lighting scheme in ZBrush. ZBrush can do a fairly good job of lighting once you get used to its rather bizarre interface. Keep in mind that a good book on photographic or video lighting will go a long way toward improving your lighting results in any 3D program. I strongly suggest purchasing such a book if you are at all interested in lighting. Lighting is one of the most useful and underappreciated aspects of 3D digital art and can be a good job-getter once you master its intricacies. Congratulations are in order! You are very close to the end of our ZBrush adventure. Right now, if you want to, you can simply press the *BPR* button and then use the *Document > Export* command to save a final render and be done. That said, we have a few more tricks and tips to show you in the next couple of chapters that will let you really polish up the results we have achieved so far and produce a far more professional-looking end product. If you are game, then proceed on to the next chapter!

23

Rendering

Introduction

In this chapter, we introduce the concept of render passes (a.k.a. render layers) in ZBrush. The chapter teaches the reader how to use the various tools in the *Render* menu, including multiple settings and tools in the *Render Properties* and the *BPR RenderPass* menu panels, to create a series of render passes. Each render pass contains a single aspect of the final illustration, such as the shadows, lighting, color, specular highlights, and so forth. Finally, a few extra tips and tricks for creating additional refinements for the final illustration are discussed, along with how to execute those procedures.

We are now going to explore some of the finer points of how to render out a scene to an image in ZBrush using render passes (also called render layers in other software). Of course, you can simply press the *BPR* button and use the *Document > Export* button, but there is a whole lot more to rendering than just that. The techniques you are going to learn in this chapter have parallels in film and television production. In a professional studio, the rendering process will be broken up into a multiple-step process that renders out the different lights, shadows, specular highlights, glossiness, alpha channels, and other image aspects separately from one another. While using render passes is more labor-intensive in the set-up phase, it saves an enormous amount of time during the image compositing and polishing stage when you need to adjust one of these elements. For example, if the shadows are a bit too dark, using render passes allows you to quickly tweak the strength of the shadow pass layer in your compositing software in only a few seconds. However, if you are using the simple *BPR* method of rendering, you would need to go back into the *Light* menu to adjust

DOI: 10.1201/9781003215288-23

the strength of the shadows from there and then re-render the entire picture, which could take an hour or more of your time. When using render passes, making even huge changes to the lighting, shadows, and final look of your image takes no time at all. Now that the concept of render passes has been explained, we can dive into the practice of using render passes within ZBrush.

Getting started

Minimize the *Tool* menu inside the *Left Tray* by clicking on the word *Tool* at the top of the menu. Open up the *Render* menu, and click and drag on the small circle with a line in it icon at the top of the *Render* menu, and move it over to under the collapsed *Tool* menu in the *Left Tray*.

Render properties

Activate the *Best* button inside the *Render* menu. Under the *Render > Render Properties* header, we want to turn on all of the things to be included in our final image. Activate the following buttons: *AOcclusion* (ambient occlusion), *Shadows*, *Sss* (subsurface scattering),

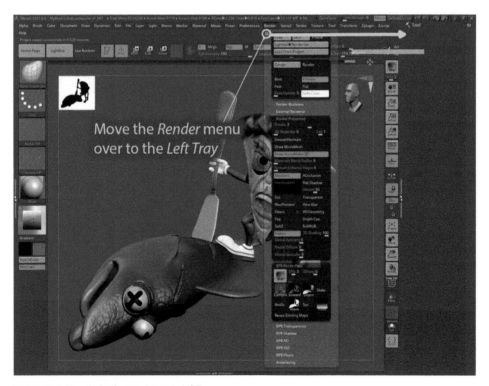

FIGURE 23.1 Move the *Render* menu over to the *Left Tray*.

WaxPreview, and *DepthCue*. Strictly speaking, the only options that we really need are *AOcclusion*, *Shadows*, and *Sss,* but the other options might provide something useful, so we may as well activate them and see what they produce. Leave the other buttons set to their default values. Now click on the *BPR* button and give ZBrush a few seconds to create the renders, which will create our final render. If ZBrush balks at anything, you may need to flip a switch somewhere, like turning on the *Sss* button under *Light > Lights Properties* to enable *Sss* rendering options. ZBrush is actually fairly decent at telling you what is wrong if you keep an eye out for pop-up windows and messages.

Now, we can start saving our rendered images. First, use the *Document > Export* command to save a TIF file type, which provides us with a baseline render of what you currently see on the screen. We can use this rendered image as a reference or as an extra render pass in our composite later on. We can name this file "complete_render_01.tif". It is important to use meaningful names when doing this sort of work so that when you go back to it in a week, a month, or a year, the names will still make sense and you can pick up where you left off.

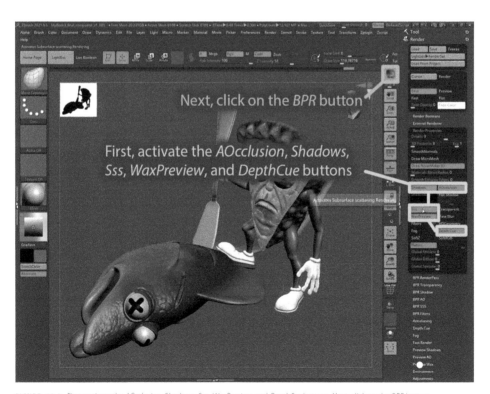

FIGURE 23.2 First, activate the *AOcclusion, Shadows, Sss, WaxPreview*, and *DepthCue* buttons. Next, click on the *BPR* button.

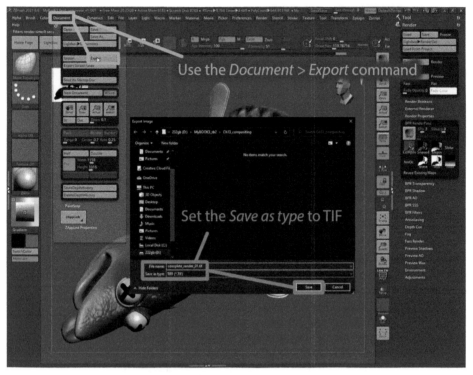

Use the *Document > Export* command

Set the *Save as type* to TIF

FIGURE 23.3 Use the *Document > Export* command. Set the *Save as type* to TIF.

Image file types

When saving out render image files for compositing work, you want to use what are known as lossless file types. These are file types that do not compress the image data. Lossless file types stand in stark opposition to what are known as the lossy file types that compress the image data. Compressing the image data provides you with a much smaller file size, but each time that you save the file, it compresses, i.e., removes, more data. Eventually, this will cause an image that you are working on to "rat out" and start showing compression artifacts and other errors, leaving you with a rather poor-looking image. Lossy file types include such common formats as JPG and PNG. While these lossy file types are great for the internet, they should be diligently avoided when working on the images in any editing or compositing software. Lossless file types, on the other hand, can be opened, edited, and saved any number of times without losing any fidelity. Common lossless file types include the PSD, BMP, and TIF file formats. All of these various image file formats are available for use in ZBrush. For our renders, either PSD, BMP, or TIF will do just fine.

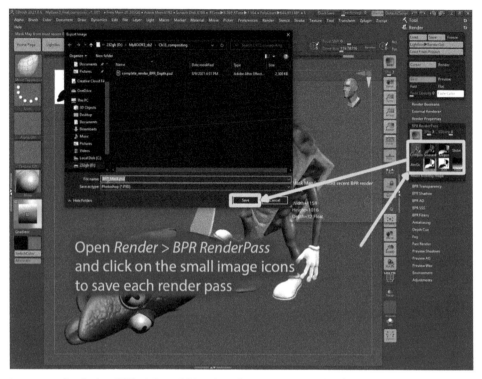

FIGURE 23.4 Open *Render > BPR RenderPass* and click on the small image icons to save each render pass.

BPR RenderPass

After activating all of the render options you desire in the *Render Properties* panel and pressing the *BPR* button, ZBrush will render out your render passes – but you won't see them – this is ZBrush, after all. Did you expect it to be obvious? Open the *Render > BPR RenderPass* panel, and you should see a series of small icons just above an abbreviation of each render pass's name. Clicking on each of these icons will save that specific render pass. ZBrush will even provide an appropriate default name for each render pass file. I suggest saving the images using either the PSD, TIF, or BMP image file formats.

Extra tricks

That is the basic process for creating render passes in ZBrush! There are a few other tricks to using render passes that you can try out if you want to. The first is to render out each light's render passes separately. To try this, go back into the *Lights* panel and turn off all of the lights except for the Key light. Now make sure that you have your render passes still active in the *Render Properties* panel, press *BPR*, and then save the resulting images from the *BPR RenderPass* panel by clicking on the small icons. This trick allows me to adjust the strength of each light individually from within Photoshop by simply changing the intensity of each individual layer on the final composite image file. It is just a series of small, extra steps that give you even more control over the final image.

The second trick is to go back into the scene and replace all of the colors and materials to get different levels of specularity, i.e., shine, on the model. To do this, make sure that you save a copy of your scene file (*File > Save As*) under a different name before you get started. You really want to avoid accidentally changing your final scene file with these tricks we are about to do! Next, select each subtool and fill it with the material of your choice. I started off with the *ToyPlastic* material, but also did a version with the *SoftPlastic*, *ReflectedPlastic*, *JellyBean*, *Hair2*, and *FlatColor* materials. Turn on all of your lights, press *BPR*, and render out your image again. You don't need the render passes for these renders, just the *BPR*, so making these variations will go quite fast.

One of the most useful variations to make is a shadow layer. To create this render pass, assign a white *SkinShade4* material to all of the objects in the scene and render an image. You may even want to render the shading from each light individually by using only one light for each render. Another useful variation to create is a highlight render pass. To make this variation, simply put a shiny black material on all of your objects and render an image. Again, it can be useful to create a separate render for each light. You can also try out some of the *MatCap Materials* for some extra pizzazz if you want to. Create as many of these material variations as you like. The goal is to create variations that have more extreme reflections, shadows, or other effects that you may want to composite into your final render inside of your image editing software. Once you have the basic concepts of how to use render passes down, you can revisit these tricks and see if you can make something useful out of them if you so desire.

Conclusion

That is really all there is to it! We have created all of the various render passes that we need for the next step in our image compositing program. You can now close ZBrush – you are done with it for this project. Go to a good image editing program, such as Adobe Photoshop, open up all of the different render layers that you created, and take a look at them.

In the next chapter, we will take these render passes and combine them all into our final illustration. Pat yourself on the back! You have learned an incredible amount of information in the past chapters and

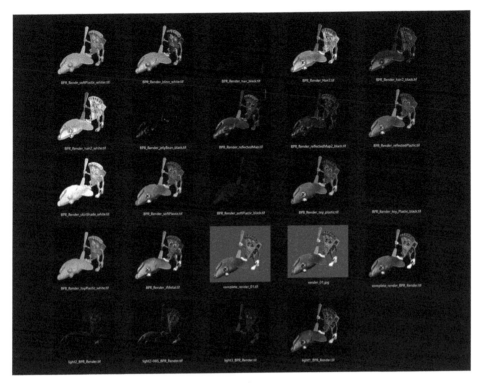

FIGURE 23.5 All of the various render passes that we created in this chapter.

are hopefully now proficient with ZBrush and its strengths and oddities. While there is a LOT more to ZBrush that I simply did not have room to go over in this book, you now have enough working knowledge about the program to go out and explore the rest of the package on your own without getting stymied by the weirdness of the ZBrush's interface or stymied by ZBrush's obtuse workflow. One last thing before the final chapter: make sure that you save the model that you have been working on so far. If you keep working on ZBrush, in a year or two, go back and look at the first model that you created and take note of how far and how fast you have progressed. You will no doubt be amazed!

24

Compositing

Introduction

Welcome to the final installment in our epic quest to construct a wonderful illustration using ZBrush. By this point, you have learned how to sculpt and paint a 3D model in Zbrush, as well as how to light and render out various render passes from those models. It is now time to leave ZBrush and learn to weld all of the components that you have created so far into a lovely final image using third-party image editing software. This chapter serves to reinforce the notion that no 3D application stands alone. Whether you are making movies, TV shows, video games, plastic figurines, toys, jewelry, or even automobiles, each 3D model eventually needs another piece of software to complete its transformation into a usable piece of entertainment. For us, in the last chapter, you learned how to output a series of render passes in ZBrush as image files. Now, we proceed to the final step of assembling all of these ZBrush images into a unified whole.

Getting started

Close out ZBrush and any other extraneous programs that you have running at the moment. Image editors are notorious RAM hogs, and you will likely need all of the computer memory available to complete this project. While I am going to use Adobe Photoshop for this demo, you can use whatever image editor you like and have available. Any professional-grade image editor will have the same sort of capabilities that Photoshop has, and the techniques I will employ in this demo have equivalent commands. I am going to keep this demo rather brief since this is a book about ZBrush and not Photoshop, but there should

DOI: 10.1201/9781003215288-24

be plenty of information in what is presented in this chapter to see you through to success in this project.

Render passes as layers

What we are going to do now is convert most of the render passes that we have created into layers, and then use the layer blending modes of each layer to composite the layers together in the layer stack. I promise it will make more sense when you see it in action. To begin, open the BPR render that contains all of the various elements – the picture that has all of the lights turned on and the normal materials on the models. This image will form the base layer in our Photoshop layer stack. Double-click the word *Background* in the *Layer* window to convert the image into a layer and name it "default_render."

Using a mask for transparency

Click on the small stack of four horizontal lines icon on the upper right of the *Layer* window and select the *New Group from Layers…* command, which will create a group consisting of our currently selected "default_render" layer.

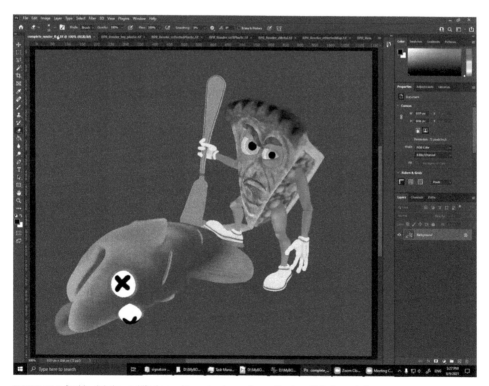

FIGURE 24.1 Double-click the word "Background Image", and name the resulting layer "default_render".

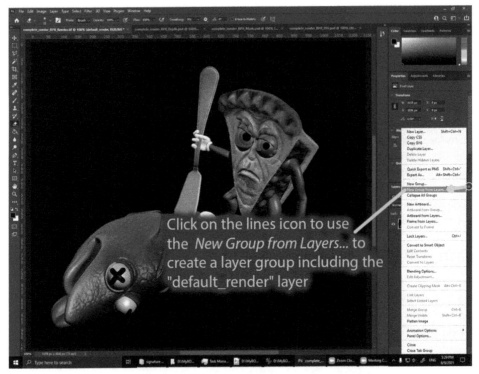

FIGURE 24.2 Click on the lines icon to use the *New Group from Layers*. . . command to create a layer group, including the "default_render" layer.

Click the *Add layer mask* button to create an alpha mask for the layer group.

Select the white box next to the folder icon on the layer's panel to select the mask. Now click on the *Channels* tab.

Once you are in the *Channels* tab, select the "Group 1 Mask," which should be at the bottom of the stack of different channels. Now, open up the mask render pass from ZBrush. It should look like a black background with a white silhouette of your character in the middle. Press CTRL + A to select the entire image, and then press CTRL + C to copy the mask image to the clipboard. Go back to your image with the chosen channel mask and use the CTRL + V shortcut to paste the render pass mask into the mask channel. You should see the background immediately turn pink and transparent. If you turn off the eye icon next to the "Group 1 Mask" channel name, the pink coloration will vanish.

Using the mask render pass from ZBrush as the alpha channel mask to isolate our character from the background is at the heart of this compositing technique. To become more familiar with alpha channels,

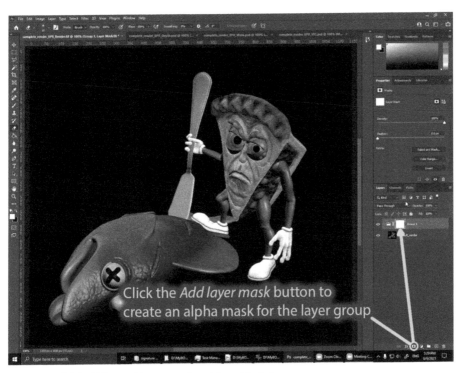

FIGURE 24.3 Click the *Add layer mask* button to create an alpha mask for the layer group.

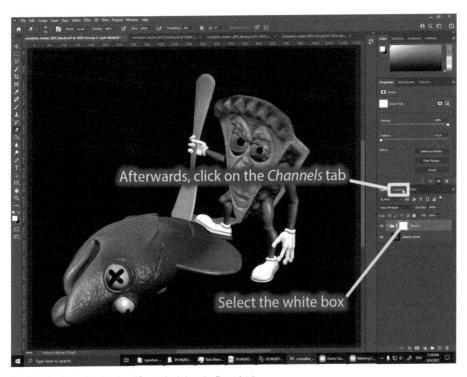

FIGURE 24.4 Select the white box. Afterwards, click on the *Channels* tab.

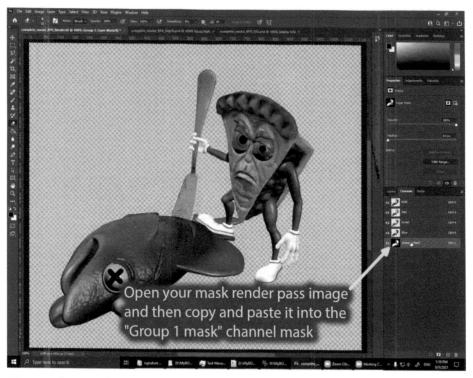

FIGURE 24.5 Open your mask render pass image and then copy and paste it into the "Group 1 mask" channel mask.

masking, layers, and channels in Photoshop, I strongly urge you to visit the official Adobe Photoshop help website (https://helpx.adobe.com/support/photoshop.html) to better familiarize yourself with these concepts and operations.

Placing the background image

Open up the background image of the stovetop, use CTRL+A to select the image, and then press CTRL+C to copy the image to the clipboard. Go to our main image with the character and make sure that you have the RGB channel selected in the Channels panel (otherwise, you might paste the background image into the mask by accident). Click on the *Layers* tab and press CTRL+V to paste the background stovetop image at the bottom of the list of layers. If it goes somewhere else in the layer stack, you can always simply click and drag the stovetop image to the bottom to move it there. If the stovetop image is too big, you can press CTRL+T to activate the *Free Transform* bounding box. Click and drag on the corner of the *Free Transform* bounding box to scale the stovetop image to fit the picture frame. Press the enter key once you are done to complete the transform operation.

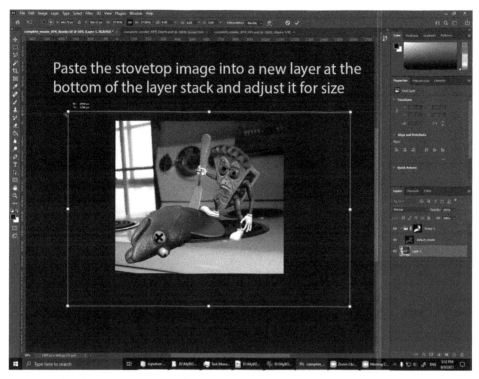

FIGURE 24.6 Paste the stovetop image into a new layer at the bottom of the layer stack and adjust it for size.

Add the depth cue render pass

Double-click on the layer name and change it to "Background." With this layer selected, click on the small lock icon at the top of the layer stack to lock this background image into place. This action will prevent us from accidentally moving the layer later on in this process. Go back to the *Channels* tab, click on the horizontal lines icon, and add a *New Channel* to the image. We can use this new alpha channel to store the depth cue render pass as a new alpha channel. Follow the same process that we used to add the original mask to the image file to add the additional depth cue render pass to the image.

Add the *sss* render pass

Do the same process for the sss (subsurface scattering) render pass and add it as a third channel mask to the illustration. This action will complete our setup for all of the channel masks that we might need for the compositing process. If you haven't already, you should save your file now using the *File > Save or File > Save As* commands or the CTRL+S shortcut to create a Photoshop PSD file type. It is important to use the PSD file type when working like this because it is the only file type

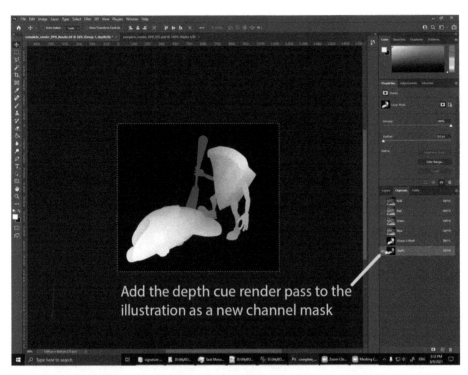

FIGURE 24.7 Add the depth cue render pass to the illustration as a new channel mask.

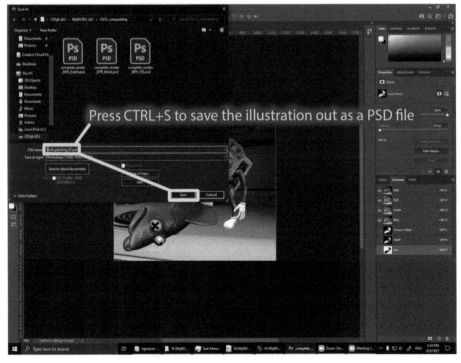

FIGURE 24.8 Press CTRL + S to save the illustration as a PSD file.

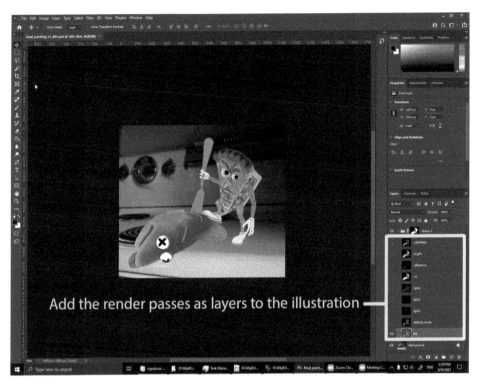

Add the render passes as layers to the illustration

FIGURE 24.9 Add the render passes as layers to the illustration.

that saves all of the various masks, layers, and channels correctly when you are working in Photoshop. Remember to name the file something meaningful and place it somewhere that you can easily find it later on your hard drive.

Open up the other render pass image files and copy and paste them into the illustration file as new layers on top of the "default_render" layer. Remember to name the layer containing each render pass after the render pass file name, i.e., the "light3.jpg" file becomes the "light3" layer, the "flatColor" render pass becomes the "flatColor" layer, and so on. The critical render passes to include are the three separate light render passes and the flat color render pass. These four render passes will become the basic building blocks for the final illustration. Next, include a selection of any additional render passes that you think are interesting. I added a couple of bright metal render passes, a basic white-shaded render pass, and a shiny reflection render pass. We may not use these render passes in the final illustration, but they will give me a few neat visuals to play around with and try some things out.

Including shading

You can use the small eye icons just to the left of the layer names to control the visibility of each layer. Turn off all of the ZBrush render pass layers except for the flat color layer and the white layer that has shading on it. Make sure that the flat color layer is at the bottom of the layer stack inside of "Group 1" but placed above the background image. Select the layer with the white character and shading and set the layer blend mode to *Multiply*, which will add the shading from the white shading layer onto the flat color layer!

Adjusting the lighting

You can now turn on the various light render passes and use the layer *Opacity* slider to dial in the amount of lighting you want to add from that render pass. Simply select the light layer that you wish to adjust and add the desired amount of lighting effect. Try using the *Lighten* or *Screen* blending modes and see how they compare with the *Normal*

FIGURE 24.10 Select the shading layer and set the layer blend mode to *Multiply*.

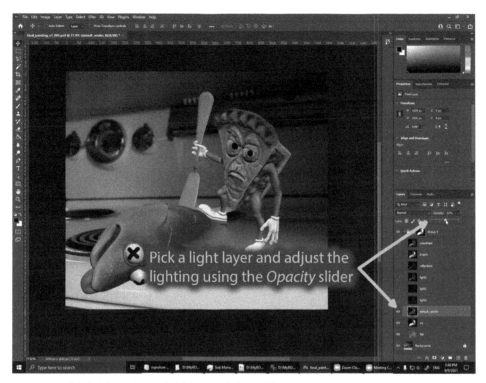

FIGURE 24.11 Pick a light layer and adjust the lighting using the *Opacity* slider.

blending mode. Typically, the *Screen* mode will give you a brighter result than the other modes, which is an extremely powerful approach to crafting images and lets you do the work in an image editor rather than go back into ZBrush, dig through the interface, and tweak the lights. Quick results are an obvious product of this approach, and it gives you a lot of control over the final product.

Using extreme render passes

The critical elements of the compositing technique include how to adjust the lights using either the *Screen*, *Lighten,* or *Normal* blending modes, plus adding shadow using the *Multiply* blending mode. If you use the default *BPR* render as the base image, you will be strengthening the existing lights and shadows, whereas if you use the flat color layer as the base image, you will be adding the lights and shadows from scratch.

With those critical aspects now done, we can turn to refining and tweaking the results using our "extreme" render passes that we created with the ZBrush material variations. If you have not done so already, add the shiny black render pass as the "highlights" layer and place it on top of the various light layers in the *Layers* panel. Set the blend mode

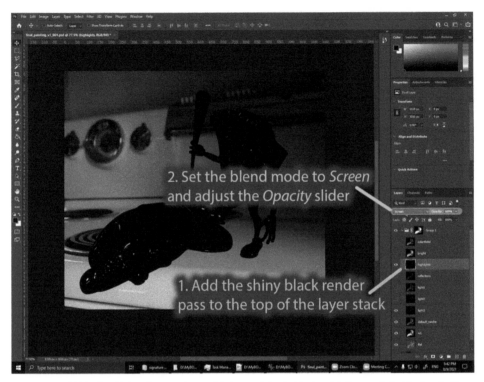

FIGURE 24.12 Add the shiny black render pass to the top of the layer stack. Set the blend mode to *Screen* and adjust the *Opacity* slider.

to *Screen* and adjust the *Opacity* slider to see how this adds new specular highlights to the model.

Adding reflections

Add the shiny metal render pass on top of all of the light layers and set its layer blending mode to *Lighten*. Next, go down to the bottom of the *Layers* window and click on the white rectangle icon with the hole in the middle. Doing so will add a mask to this "reflections" layer. Select the white rectangle on the layer so that you will affect the mask and not the layer itself. Switch to a large, soft paintbrush tool. Set the color to black. Now, paint out any reflections that you do not want on the mask layer. You can even reduce the *Opacity* of the brush for more subtle effects. Using this technique, you can leave the reflections on just the eyeballs and fish scales. Using layer masks in this manner allows you to adjust the image nondestructively. The nondestructive aspect is critical because it will enable you to go back in later and tweak things. You did not obliterate any of the original data. While working nondestructively may seem like a minor consequence, it is of critical importance when working in a professional environment. You can repeat this process for any of the "extreme" render passes that we created. Add the

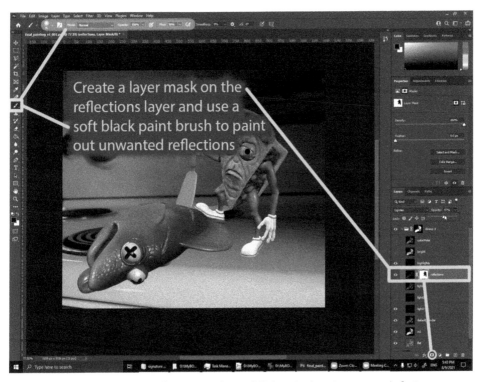

FIGURE 24.13 Create a layer mask on the reflections layer and use a soft black paintbrush to paint out unwanted reflections.

render pass as a new layer at the top of the layer stack, pick a blending mode, and then use a layer mask to control where the extreme effect occurs. Not all of the extra render passes will be useful. Still, these extra render passes will allow you to achieve a level of control over your final illustration that would be difficult to achieve using ZBrush alone.

Making shadows

There is one last thing that we need to add to our illustration: shadows under the fish and the character. First, collapse the layer group containing our ZBrush image layers, which will simplify your *Layers* panel. Then, add a new layer named "shadows." Next, select a large, soft, black paint brush and paint the shadows in.

Now duplicate the shadow layer, use the *Filter > Blur > Gaussian Blur* command, and adjust the *Radius* setting to blur this duplicate layer a lot. This blur will make the shadows softer and more natural looking. Press *OK* to accept the blur. Using a duplicate lets you keep the original layer around for later use.

Make another copy of the original shadows layer and add the *Gaussian Blur* filter to it again – but this time, reduce the *Radius* slider so the

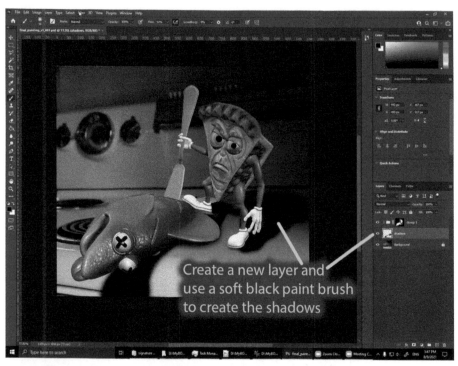

FIGURE 24.14 Create a new layer and use a soft black paintbrush to create the shadows.

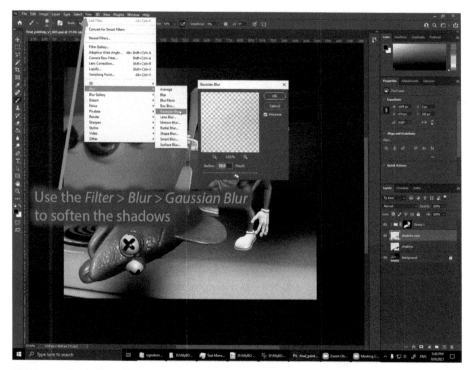

FIGURE 24.15 Use the *Filter > Blur > Gaussian Blur* to soften the shadows.

blur effect is not as strong. You can then set this layer's blend mode to *Multiply* and use it to strengthen the shadows to suit your taste.

Copyright

The last thing to do is to add your copyright data to the image. You can use the *Photoshop Text* tool, the *T* icon on the toolbox, to do so. A copyright notice should include either the "©" symbol, the word "Copyright," or "Copr." plus the year of publication and the name or alias that you go by. For example, "Copyright 2024 Greg Johnson," "© 2024 GregTheArtist," or "Copr. 2024 Gregory Johnson" would all work equally well. To examine copyright in further detail, you can pay a visit to the U.S. Copyright Office at their website (https://copyright.gov). It is important to place a copyright notice on any work that you intend to make publicly available. Otherwise, unscrupulous folks might reuse your work without attribution or, even worse, claim your work as their own. You may scoff a bit at the prospect, but it does happen quite frequently. I've had it happen to people I know and even experienced it myself. Another useful tidbit of advice is never to put the highest resolution version of your work online. Always save that version just for yourself. No one gets

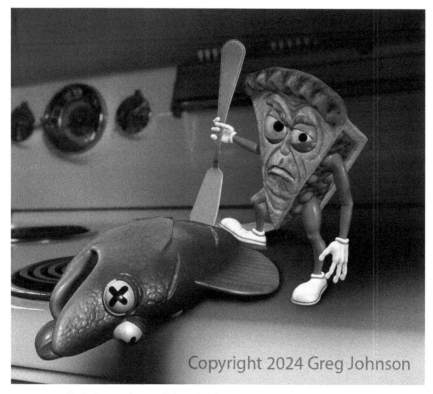

FIGURE 24.16 The final image with copyright data included.

that super high-resolution version except you. A client only receives a high-resolution copy after they have paid you, and no one gets the PSD file with all of the layers unless they pay for that privilege. Otherwise, you're going to get ripped off. I've seen it happen a lot of times. It is just the nature of doing business. You must always watch out for yourself a bit. A big part of this includes putting a copyright and watermark on your work, never uploading the highest resolution version to the Internet, and always being able to prove that you are the creator. With that little snippet of advice, we can finally wrap things up.

Conclusion

We have now finished this book! I hope that you have had a lot of fun learning about ZBrush and a few of the techniques associated with it. Remember to keep playing around with the program and exploring what it can do. You will find that your own artwork will evolve over time, and that is part of the joy of creating art. Remember that you can visit the publisher's website for the video recordings of each chapter of this book. Make sure that you visit my website at www.GregTheArtist.com for additional educational resources related to ZBrush and the many other subjects that I teach. If you have enjoyed this book, you can check out my other published works. Go to www.Toonzy.com and download a free PDF of "Toonzy! the Cartoon Role Playing Game" or purchase a copy of my game design book, "Developing Creative Content for Games." To continue your digital sculpting efforts, I can highly recommend the more advanced ZBrush books by Parrish Baker and Madeline Scott Spencer from this same publisher and look up the tutorial videos by Joseph Drust online. Good luck, happy learning, and just keep working. Hopefully, I will see some good work from you soon.

Take care and regards,

Gregory S. Johnson

Index

Note: *Italic* page numbers refer to figures.